RESEARCH IN THE HISTORY OF ECONOMIC THOUGHT AND METHODOLOGY

RESEARCH IN THE HISTORY OF ECONOMIC THOUGHT AND METHODOLOGY

Founding Editor: Warren J. Samuels (1933–2011)
Series Editors: Luca Fiorito, Scott Scheall, and Carlos Eduardo Suprinyak

Recent Volumes:

Volume 29A:	Research in the History of Economic Thought and Methodology: A Research Annual; Jeff E. Biddle and Ross B. Emmett; 2010
Volume 29B:	Research in the History of Economic Thought and Methodology: Frank H Knight in Iowa City; Ross B. Emmett; 2011
Volume 29C:	Wisconsin, Labor, Income, and Institutions: Contributions from Commons and Bronfenbrenner; Marianne Johnson and Warren J. Samuels; 2011
Volume 30A:	Research in the History of Economic Thought and Methodology: A Research Annual; Jeff E. Biddle, Ross B. Emmett; 2012
Volume 30B:	Research in the History of Economic Thought and Methodology: Documents on Government and the Economy; Ross B. Emmett, Marianne Johnson; 2012
Volume 31A:	Research in the History of Economic Thought and Methodology: A Research Annual; Jeff E. Biddle, Ross B. Emmett; 2013
Volume 31B:	Research in the History of Economic Thought and Methodology: Documents Related to John Maynard Keynes, Institutionalism at Chicago & Frank H. Knight; Ross B. Emmett; 2013
Volume 32:	Research in the History of Economic Thought and Methodology: A Research Annual; Luca Fiorito; 2014
Volume 33:	Research in the History of Economic Thought and Methodology: A Research Annual; Luca Fiorito, Scott Scheall, and Carlos Eduardo Suprinyak; 2015
Volume 34A:	Research in the History of Economic Thought and Methodology: Including a Symposium on Austrian Economics in the Wake of World War II; Luca Fiorito, Scott Scheall, and Carlos Eduardo Suprinyak; 2016

RESEARCH IN THE HISTORY OF ECONOMIC THOUGHT AND METHODOLOGY VOLUME 34B

RESEARCH IN THE HISTORY OF ECONOMIC THOUGHT AND METHODOLOGY

EDITED BY

LUCA FIORITO

University of Palermo, Palermo, Italy

SCOTT SCHEALL

Arizona State University Downtown Phoenix Campus, Phoenix, AZ, USA

CARLOS EDUARDO SUPRINYAK

Universidade Federal de Minas Gerais, Belo Horizonte, Brazil

Emerald

United Kingdom – North America – Japan
India – Malaysia – China

Emerald Group Publishing Limited
Howard House, Wagon Lane, Bingley BD16 1WA, UK

First edition 2016

British Library Cataloguing in Publication Data
A catalogue record for this book is available from the British Library

ISBN: 978-1-78560-962-6
ISSN: 0743-4154 (Series)

ISOQAR
REGISTERED
Certificate Number 1985
ISO 14001

ISOQAR certified
Management System,
awarded to Emerald
for adherence to
Environmental
standard
ISO 14001:2004.

INVESTOR IN PEOPLE

CONTENTS

LIST OF CONTRIBUTORS *ix*

EDITORIAL BOARD *xi*

VOLUME INTRODUCTION *xiii*

PART I
A SYMPOSIUM ON ALBERT O. HIRSCHMAN

INTRODUCTION
Marina Bianchi and Maurizio Franzini *3*

ALBERT O. HIRSCHMAN AND THE RISE AND DECLINE OF DEVELOPMENT ECONOMICS
Michele Alacevich *13*

IN PRAISE OF SMALL: ALBERT O. HIRSCHMAN AND THE QUESTION OF SCALE
Jeremy Adelman *41*

THE CONTEMPORARY SIGNIFICANCE OF A DISSENTER: ALBERT O. HIRSCHMAN'S IDEA OF DEVELOPMENT
Andrea Ginzburg *63*

MODELS AND MISPERCEPTIONS: CHENERY, HIRSCHMAN AND TINBERGEN ON DEVELOPMENT PLANNING
Neil De Marchi *91*

ALBERT O. HIRSCHMAN AND THE STRUCTURALIST–MONETARIST DEBATE IN LATIN AMERICA
Ana Maria Bianchi 101

HOMO POLITICUS: REFLECTIONS ON *THE PASSIONS AND THE INTERESTS*
Ruth W. Grant 123

SHIFTING VALUES: PRIVATE CONCERNS VERSUS PUBLIC ACTION
Marina Bianchi 139

"GOOD AND BAD" (NOT "GOOD OR BAD"): ALBERT O. HIRSCHMAN AS A BEHAVIORAL ECONOMIST
Shaun P. Hargreaves Heap 161

SPANNING EXIT AND VOICE: ALBERT HIRSCHMAN'S CONTRIBUTION TO POLITICAL SCIENCE
Peter John and Keith Dowding 175

EFFICIENT INSTITUTIONS: THE ROLE OF EXIT AND VOICE
Maurizio Franzini 197

PART II
ESSAYS

ROBERT FRANKLIN HOXIE: THE CONTRIBUTIONS OF A NEGLECTED CHICAGO ECONOMIST
Charles R. McCann, Jr. and Vibha Kapuria-Foreman 219

THE MISES-KNIGHT THEORY OF UNCERTAINTY AND ITS IMPLICATIONS FOR ENTREPRENEURSHIP, EQUILIBRIUM, AND THE THEORY OF THE FIRM
Per L. Bylund and G. P. Manish 305

THE ROAD LESS TRAVELED: MONETARY DISEQUILIBRIUM, AUSTRIAN CAPITAL THEORY, AND THE "KEYNESIAN DIVERSION"
Scott Burns *337*

PART III
FROM THE VAULT

J. M. KEYNES'S LECTURES ON FISHER IN 1909
Carlo Cristiano *367*

LIST OF CONTRIBUTORS

Jeremy Adelman	Princeton University, Princeton, NJ, USA
Michele Alacevich	Loyola University Maryland, Baltimore, MD, USA
Ana Maria Bianchi	Universidade de São Paulo, São Paulo, Brazil
Marina Bianchi	Università di Cassino e del Lazio Meridionale, Cassino, Italy
Scott Burns	George Mason University, Fairfax, VA, USA
Per L. Bylund	Oklahoma State University, Stillwater, OK, USA
Carlo Cristiano	University of Pisa, Pisa, Italy
Neil De Marchi	Duke University, Durham, NC, USA
Keith Dowding	Australian National University, Canberra, Australia
Luca Fiorito	University of Palermo, Palermo, Italy
Maurizio Franzini	Università di Roma, La Sapienza, Rome, Italy
Andrea Ginzburg	Università di Modena e Reggio Emilia, Modena and Reggio Emilia, Italy
Ruth W. Grant	Duke University, Durham, NC, USA
Shaun P. Hargreaves Heap	King's College London, London, UK
Peter John	University College London, London, UK

Vibha Kapuria-Foreman	Colorado College, Colorado Springs, CO, USA
G. P. Manish	Troy University, Troy, AL, USA
Charles R. McCann, Jr.	University of Pittsburgh, Pittsburgh, PA, USA
Scott Scheall	Arizona State University Downtown Phoenix Campus, Phoenix, AZ, USA
Carlos Eduardo Suprinyak	Universidade Federal de Minas Gerais, Belo Horizonte, Brazil

EDITORIAL BOARD

VOLUME INTRODUCTION

In this issue, our second of 2016, we are proud to present a symposium on the work of the famed political economist Albert O. Hirschman. Edited by Marina Bianchi and Maurizio Franzini, the symposium collects several papers first presented at a conference held in Hirschman's honor in Rome in the fall of 2014. Contributors to the symposium include Hirschman biographer Jeremy Adelman, the political scientist and philosopher Ruth W. Grant, historian of development economics (and *RHETM* editorial-board member) Michele Alacevich, eminent political scientists Peter John and Keith Dowding, and the distinguished historian of economic thought Neil De Marchi. We expect the symposium to make a prominent mark on the expanding field of Hirschman scholarship.

The present issue also features several excellent general research contributions. Charles R. McCann, Jr. and Vibha Kapuria-Foreman investigate the unduly forgotten work of the American Institutionalist and early labor economist Robert Franklin Hoxie. Per L. Bylund and G. P. Manish compare Frank H. Knight and Ludwig von Mises on the subject of uncertainty, and consider the implications of Knight and Mises for the theories of entrepreneurship, equilibrium, and the firm. In another essay that, like Bylund and Manish's contribution, we were, with disappointment, unable to accommodate in our recent symposium on *The Postwar Austrian Diaspora* (see *RHETM* Volume 34A), Scott Burns argues for a synthesis of the Austrian and monetary-disequilibrium theories of the business cycle.

Our "From the Vault" section features archival material from the pen of John Maynard Keynes. Carlo Cristiano discusses and, for the first time, makes available Keynes' 1909 lecture notes on Irving Fisher's *Appreciation and Interest* (1896) and *The Rate of Interest* (1907).

To close, as always, we thank the members of the staff at Emerald Publishing Group, who work unendingly and without hesitation to lighten our editorial burdens.

Luca Fiorito
Scott Scheall
Carlos Eduardo Suprinyak
Editors

PART I
A SYMPOSIUM ON ALBERT O. HIRSCHMAN

INTRODUCTION

Marina Bianchi and Maurizio Franzini

ABSTRACT

Albert Hirschman always distinguished himself by his unique approach in tackling economic problems, an approach that moved easily from literature and philosophy to political economy and social psychology, without ever losing sight of the real workings of social and political life.

The papers collected here stemmed from a desire to know more closely this rare economist who used the tools and features of one discipline to throw light upon those of another.

The methodological stance is the first element that emerges either explicitly or implicitly from this collection of papers: Hirschman's suspicion of all-encompassing theories and their issue in encompassing plans – development plans in particular. His was a piecemeal approach targeting the scarcest of all factors, such as the ability to mobilize resources and to solve problems. This matched Hirschman's own view that "petites idées," *to look at problems in the small, form the material for further observations and insights.*

The second element that emerges from these papers is the richness of themes explored – from how to voice *reasons for one's disappointment and distrust to the role of countervailing passions in institutional development, from the "bias for hope" to the problem of inequality – but also*

Research in the History of Economic Thought and Methodology, Volume 34B, 3–11

ISSN: 0743 4154/doi:10.1108/S0743-41542016000034B016

the strong connections that exist among them. These connections revolve around the problem of economic change and its dynamics: how to explain it, how to promote it.

Yet, no matter which of Hirschman's works we pick up for the first time or rediscover, we cannot avoid seeing that besides the scientist with his microscopic lenses, there is also the artist who looks at problems not for the final truth they might hide or the definite solution, but to make us aware of them, to open our eyes to curiosity and wonder. This is a difficult lesson, but not one Hirschman will let us forget.

Keywords: Albert Hirschman; development; public policy; institutional change

JEL Classifications: B31; B52; D40; O2

One need only look at some of the titles of Hirschman's many books – *A Bias for Hope*; *Political Economics and Possibilism*; *Essays in Trespassing*; *Shifting Involvements*; *A Propensity to Self-Subversion*; *Crossing Boundaries*, for example – to have one's interest raised, along with a desire to know more closely this rare economist who used the tools and features of one discipline to throw light upon those of another.

It was with this desire to explore Hirschman's unique approach in his tackling of economic problems, that we organized a Conference in Hirschman's honor, in Rome, on September 12–13, 2014.[1]

The conference brought together scholars of various disciplines, in particular, political scientists, economic historians, and economists. Most of the papers collected here were first delivered at this conference.

The titles of Hirschman's works that we have just referred to already tell us a lot about his inquisitive mind, a mind that moved easily from literature and philosophy to political economy and social psychology, without ever losing sight of the real workings of social and political life. They reveal an eye for enlarged possibilities, for unintended consequences, and also successes in the face of unpredictable difficulties.

As Jeremy Adelman shows in his engaging and insightful biography (2013), Hirschman's mark was his propensity to "prove Hamlet wrong," to make doubts the sources not of paralysis but of freedom and creativity.

This methodological stance is the first element that emerges either explicitly or implicitly from this collection of papers: Hirschman's suspicion of all-encompassing theories and their issue in encompassing plans – development plans in particular. His strong preference was for small ideas, ideas that emerge and develop out of unexplored connections, from the crossing of disciplinary boundaries. Hirschman also had an ability never to put a problem to rest but always to find value in possible alternative solutions. These proclivities showed themselves in his insistence on the importance of historical perspective, his love of paradoxes, and the unexpected turns ideas can take. He took joy in playing with words and inventing new expressions. He had a propensity to dissent, even from himself. And he invited others to join him in taking risks with analytical complexity, even at the expense of parsimony.

The second element that emerges from these papers is the richness of themes explored by Hirschman but also the strong connections that exist among them.

Though he is known principally for his small but dense book entitled *Exit, Voice, and Loyalty* (1970), Hirschman started as a development economist. Five papers in this collection are directly devoted to this crucial period of Hirschman's intellectual and working life. Michele Alacevich reconstructs the biographical and intellectual path that brought Hirschman to form his ideas, starting in the early 1950s when he was invited by the government of Colombia to assist with the implementation of a development plan for that country. This period and the years that followed formed the views expressed in what is known as Hirschman's "development trilogy": *The Strategy of Economic Development*, published in 1958, *Journeys toward Progress* and *New Development Projects Observed*, published respectively in 1963 and 1967.

As all the contributions devoted to the problem of development stress, Hirschman was systematically critical of over-all, integrated development programs. For him the problem in underdeveloped countries was not a shortage of domestic savings, or of foreign exchange, which inclined proponents of the "shortage" origins of "backwardness" to insist that escape therefrom can only come with encompassing or "Big Push" attacks that remove the shortages. This view typically was embodied in the form of models of balanced growth, whereas Hirschman stressed instead the ability to make development decisions, an ability that translated into a social desire for change, and a willingness to tackle difficulties encountered along that path. The resources for success were not so much physical blocks, but attitudinal commitments that could mobilize and use for development purposes resources and abilities that were hidden, dispersed, or badly utilized. To this end, Alacevich stresses, Hirschman's main focus was on finding the "inducement mechanisms" and the "hidden rationalities" that make growth possible, exploiting the "linkages" that connect industries or firms. It was through these mechanisms that the apparent shortcomings of a state of underdevelopment would become points of strength.

This ability to look for the small, micro-foundational elements of the development process and his skepticism about big schemata, a combination that characterizes Hirschman's work, was forged, as Jeremy Adelman tells us in his paper, not in the 1950s but in the 1930s. It made its first appearance when, as a militant Socialist in the waning days of the Weimar Republic, he stepped back both from Communist certainties and some of the rigidities of the Social Democratic party's leadership. Yet it was in his relationship with the Italian philosopher Eugenio Colorni, his close friend and eventually brother-in-law, that his questioning of given certainties took a new turn. Conversations about Montaigne and Machiavelli – whose books accompanied Hirschman in all his peregrinations and changes of domicile – led to what Colorni called "*piccole idee*." These evolved into Hirschmann's own view that "*petites idées*" are the real materials for any useful worldly reflections deposited in his memory bank of observations and insights. As he writes in a letter to his sister Ursula: "it is the trivial circumstances, the surface images, which strike us – the useless skins which objects slough off" (Adelman, 2016, p. 21).

The result was a piecemeal approach targeting the scarcest of all factors, such as the ability to mobilize resources and to solve problems. This was the premise of "unbalanced growth," a term, says Adelman, that Hirschman eventually abandoned because he did not want his work positioned only as an alternative to the mainstream of development thinking among economists, but that well expressed his view to look at the dynamics of the development process in the small.

Andrea Ginzburg's paper addresses Hirschman's ideas on development from the point of view of Hirschman as a dissenter. His dissent was threefold. First, dissent from orthodoxy, as exemplified by the distance, which Ginzburg analyzes, between Solow's and Hirschman's conceptions on growth and development. Second, dissent from heterodoxy, from scholars like Nurkse, Rosenstein-Rodan and other advocates of the balanced growth theory. Third, a dissent from Hirschman himself, his practice of "self-subversion" that Ginzburg discusses in the context of Hirschman's critical reappraisal of the dependency theory, to which he contributed indirectly as a young man. The paper's main thrust is that Hirschman's "possibilism," his openness to what might possibly happen and his interest in drawing people's attention in that direction, is not a generic psychological propensity to optimism, but stems directly from a critical attitude toward accepted ideas of other authors or of Hirschman himself.

Neil De Marchi sets Hirschman's position on development in the context of the then current debates and focuses on a specific episode: Hollis Chenery's review of Jan Tinbergen's *Design of Development* and Hirschman's *The Strategy of Economic Development*, a review that appeared in the *American Economic Review* in 1959, soon after the publication of both books.

Chenery praised Tinbergen's *Design*, seeing strong affinities between his own and Tinbergen's convictions on the importance of detailed planning. By contrast, he found Hirschman's book a wholly baffling one for an economist. Chenery was uncertain what (if anything) he should make of Hirschman, and not just of his unusual psychological borrowings. For, whereas he, Chenery, attributed backwardness to concrete obstacles, in his case primarily shortages of domestic savings and of foreign currency, Hirschman emphasized the need for a government to create a positive "image" of and desire for change.

De Marchi argues that Chenery misread Tinbergen and this may have also prevented him from understanding Hirschman. Tinbergen, in this respect not very different from Hirschman, stressed the key role of the human in everything, from applying expert experience to guess the necessary numerical values relevant in drafts of a plan when statistics were lacking or poor, to deciding whether to use shadow prices or market prices in assessment. Hirschman, however, went farther when he said that his interest was more "in widening the area of the possible, of what may happen, than it was in prediction, on the basis of statistical reasoning, of what will actually happen" (Hirschman, 1998, p. 96).

Ana Maria Bianchi in her paper addresses the standpoint of Albert Hirschman in a little known debate that took place in Latin America during the 1950s and 1960s: between structuralists and monetarists over the problem of price stability and growth. Though Latin American structuralists accepted the monetarists' view that inflation was the result of distortions in the economy, they nevertheless claimed that monetary control was not a workable solution to the problem of development. Hirschman, Ana Maria Bianchi tells us, had more affinities with Latin American structuralists, because of their common attention to the specificity of different historical contexts, but Hirschman did not take a clear-cut side in the debate, choosing, instead, to act as a go-between and avoiding the most extreme ideas of both contending groups.

With regard to the debate itself, Ana Maria Bianchi intriguingly remarks that Hirschman emphasized its rhetorical nature. Latin American structuralists, by drawing public attention to the problem of inflation and its underlying causes, had been successful in persuading public opinion and policy makers toward other, perhaps more fundamental, but less "loud" problems of development faced by their societies.

In 1970, Hirschman's *Exit, Voice and Loyalty* appeared. This book (dedicated to Eugenio Colorni) seems a rather sharp departure from his interest in the endogenous sources of development. Instead this book was the result of many of the small ideas that he had forged in earlier years and that now took on a new and more coherent form. If, before, the ability to look for imbalances and disequilibria was viewed as opening the way to creative solutions for growth, now the problem was the types of actions that would induce organizations and institutions to change and correct mistakes or misconduct. One such action was for individuals or social groups to *voice* reasons for their disappointment and distrust, the other was simply to *exit*. Hirschman's claim was that voice, a concept more familiar to political scientists than to economists, can do better than exit at counteracting the decline of an organization and promoting reform from within.

Two papers, one by Maurizio Franzini and the other by Peter John and Keith Dowding, analyze and discuss Hirschman's totally new approach to institutional design. Yet Hirschman's categories, both papers argue, despite their tremendous and well-deserved impact upon different social disciplines, need some refinement: Exit and (especially) Voice can encompass very different types of actions depending on the nature, whether public or private, of the organization. Their relationship too can take different forms under different circumstances. Hirschman's third category, Loyalty, is also in need of clarification.

John and Dowding, both political scientists, distinguish and review the several applications of Hirschman's categories to various types of political behavior. This helps us understand how profound the impact of book has been, and remains, on political theorists, more particularly on those whose concern is the design and evaluation of institutions.

Franzini analyzes in depth the relationship between Exit and Voice – also recognizing the role of Loyalty – and its implications for the design of institutions that can sustain a better mix of the two. Both papers testify to how Hirschman's categories are still able to inject new insights in the sometimes paralyzed institutional body of modern capitalism.

If *Exit, Voice and Loyalty* made Hirschman famous, *The Passions and the Interests* (1977) was his favorite. "It really was the fruit of free creation," he tells us. "That book gave me prolonged pleasure: to write, feeling free to discover things without having to prove someone wrong" (Hirschman, 1998, p. 110).

The *Passions and the Interests* had its origin in an attempt to shed light on the political consequences of economic growth, but its by-product was an intriguing new approach to the interpretation of capitalism and how it emerged. Going back to the philosophical and political economic thought of the seventeenth and eighteenth centuries, Hirschman introduces us to the principle of countervailing passions and shows us how the emergence of the language of interest replaced that of injurious physical force. But the book, says Ruth Grant, was meant also to warn against the impoverished and "simplistic" view of "*homo oeconomicus*," as a satisfactory basis for optimistic expectations about economic and political progress. If Hirschman rejected the idea that economic interests are always benign or positive in their political effects, he seems nonetheless to have accepted the idea that political passions are largely destructive. This leads Ruth Grant to the question: Who is *homo politicus* today? And to explore what an enriched and complex psychology, one that brings the political passions back into the picture, might look like.

Hirschman's attention to a richer psychology and the reflective moves that are behind changes in behavior is also at the basis of Marina Bianchi's discussion of Hirschman's plea for making economic theory more complex. Again the problem here is the process of economic change and the role that disappointment can have in this process.

In his *Shifting Involvements* (1982), Hirschman introduces two basic human endowments: the ability to communicate and persuade and the capability for self-evaluation and reflection. The first is an ability that is behind the possibility of pursuing voice and engaging in social action; the second is a capability that is behind the formation of meta-preferences and values. Disappointment, arising either from the practices of private life or from those of public engagement, measures the distance between preferences and meta-preferences and prompts their changes. This process gives rise, for Hirschman, to pendulum-like swings from private to public involvements and vice versa. Marina Bianchi stresses in addition, however, that disappointment, a negative motivation, is charged with too heavy a task, that of providing the *only* incentive to changes in values and behavior. There is also still missing in Hirschman's explanation an analysis of the specific attractiveness of alternative courses of actions, whether they involve a shift from private pursuits to public action or the reverse.

The fact that, at the basis of the formation of preferences, there is, as Hirschman stresses, a human capability for self-evaluation and reflection is also the starting point of Shaun P. Hargreaves Heap's paper. Hargreaves Heap argues that behavioral economics has in many respects provided empirical, mainly experimental, support for a richer view of the complexities of choices. In particular, Hargreaves Heap shows that, not only is there evidence of preference change following reflection, but also that both "good and bad" preference change may occur in a market society. He argues too, however, that Hirschman would not have been comfortable with the welfare implications that some behavioral economists have been recently espousing: that of nudging. Hargreaves Heap's reason is that behavioral economics interprets the behavioral evidence on anomalies in decision making (relative to the standard utility-maximizing models) as evidence of a form of malfunctioning, and "nudge" as a form of compensation. On the contrary, he says, so-called behavioral anomalies are best understood as evidence that we are unsure of our preferences and to some degree we are always engaging in creative decisions with respect to Mill's, and Hirschman's, "experiments in living."

There are other problems and topics in Hirschman's innovative work than the ones analyzed in the papers collected here and that are utterly relevant today. There is his "bias for hope," the idea that the most important premise for change is people's perception that they are already doing something right and that not everything is hopelessly wrong. There is the problem of inequality that he discusses through the innovative parable of the "tunnel effect." When in a traffic jam there are the first signs of moving, a general feeling of relief arises; it is only when *your* lane alone is not moving that your initial relief is replaced by disappointment and anger. There is his important *Rhetoric of Reaction* (1991) with its still illuminating discussion of the reactionary's defeatist objections to any proposal for reform. Here Hirschman classifies these objections with terms that many thought had always existed, but that were instead introduced by him for the first time. These are the rhetoric of "perversity," claiming that reform will only worsen the problem, the rhetoric of "futility," maintaining instead that reform will simply be ineffective and the rhetoric of "jeopardy," which holds that reform will jeopardize some existing social gain.

Yet, no matter which of Hirschman's works we pick up for the first time or rediscover, we cannot avoid seeing that besides the scientist with his microscopic lenses, there is also the artist who looks at problems not for the final truth and the definite solution, but to make us aware of them, to open our eyes to curiosity and wonder. This is a difficult lesson, but not one Hirschman will let us forget.

NOTE

1. The event was sponsored by the Dipartimento di Economia e Diritto, Università di Roma La Sapienza, the Dipartimento di Economia e Diritto, Università di Cassino, the Association "Etica e Economia" and Cream – Creativity and Motivations – research centre.

REFERENCES

Adelman, J. (2013). *Worldly philosopher: The odyssey of Albert O. Hirschman*. Princeton, NJ: Princeton University Press.

Adelman, J. (2016). In praise of small: Albert O. Hirschman and the question of scale. In L. Fiorito, S. Scheall, C. E. Suprinyak, M. Bianchi, & M. Franzini (Eds.), *Including a Symposium on Albert O. Hirschman*, Research in the History of Economic Thought and Methodology, Bingley, UK: Emerald Group Publishing Limited.

Hirschman, A. O. (1982). *Shifting involvements. Private interests and public action*. Princeton, NJ: Princeton University Press.

Hirschman, A. O. (1991). *The rhetoric of reaction: Perversity, futility, jeopardy*. Cambridge, MA: The Belknap Press of Harvard University Press.

Hirschman, A. O. (1998). Trespassing: Places and ideas in the course of a life. In A. O. Hirschman (Ed.), *Crossing boundaries. Selected writings* (pp. 45–110). New York, NY: Zone Books.

ALBERT O. HIRSCHMAN AND THE RISE AND DECLINE OF DEVELOPMENT ECONOMICS

Michele Alacevich

ABSTRACT

This paper discusses the role of Albert O. Hirschman as a founder of development economics in the postwar years. Although Hirschman maintained a strong interest in development matters throughout his entire professional career, his major contributions to development economics took place between the mid-1950s and the late 1960s. The paper examines Hirschman's innovative contributions to the new discipline. When, in the 1950s, development economics gravitated around the concept of "balanced growth," Hirschman opened new vistas with a theory of "unbalanced growth." In the early 1960s, Hirschman focused on reformist political approaches to development, against the opposed extremisms of reaction and revolution. Finally, in the late 1960s, Hirschman opened new perspectives on the importance of detailed analysis of development projects, against the theoretical drift of early development economics.

The discussion of Hirschman's development career is also an opportunity to observe the gap between theoretical debates and development policies.

Research in the History of Economic Thought and Methodology, Volume 34B, 13–39

ISSN: 0743-4154/doi:10.1108/S0743-41542016000034B001

Whereas development economists often clashed on theoretical issues, their views were remarkably closer on practical questions.

As a pioneer of development economics, Hirschman sought to establish it as a discipline theoretically distinct from mainstream economics. By the 1980s, this project had collapsed, and the development question was reabsorbed by the economic mainstream. This article, however, argues that current development debates remain deeply indebted to Hirschman's contribution. His reformist vision, rejection of one-size-fits-all solutions, his insistence on the ineluctable role of uncertainty, and his search for country-specific, incremental, and evolutionary policies make his approach central to current development discourse.

Keywords: Albert O. Hirschman; development economics; balanced growth and unbalanced growth; project appraisal; development policies

Reformers [...] behave like the country or the chessplayer who exasperatingly fights on when "objectively" he has already lost – and occasionally goes on to win!

Hirschman (1963, p. 271)

THE BIRTH OF DEVELOPMENT ECONOMICS AND HIRSCHMAN'S STRATEGY

As with many things in Albert O. Hirschman's life, his career as a development economist was not the outcome of any planning. Born Otto Albert Hirschmann, The son of a Berlin upper middle class family of assimilated Jews, he left Germany for good in 1933, when Hitler seized power and the 17-year-old Hirschmann, a Social Democrat activist, risked immediate arrest. He moved to Paris, where he frequented the circles of German and Italian anti-Fascists exiles; then, in 1936, to London for a one-year fellowship at the London School of Economics. In late 1936 he joined the international brigades that supported the Spanish Republic against the coup by Francisco Franco, fighting in the Asturias and Catalonia, but left when the communists radicalized their takeover of the Republican armies. He joined his older sister Ursula in Trieste, Italy, who had married there the anti-Fascist philosopher Eugenio Colorni (Colorni would be killed by the Fascists in Rome; after his death, Ursula would marry Altiero Spinelli, a friend of Colorni and one of the authors of the Ventotene Manifesto). In Trieste, Hirschmann continued his studies in economics, published his first articles on demographic and monetary issues in Italy and France, and continued as well his anti-Fascist militancy, until he was forced to leave Italy because of the increasingly difficult situation for Jews and anti-Fascist intellectuals. The war found him in Paris, where he once again collaborated with anti-Nazi and anti-Fascist movements: this time Hirschmann assisted the American journalist Varian Fry, who had established and managed an undercover organization that helped thousands of Jewish and Leftist refugees flee Europe for the United States.[1] Ultimately, Hirschmann also fled to the United States. At the immigration window, Otto Albert Hirschmann changed his name in Albert O., while his last name lost the second "n."[2]

At Berkeley, where he studied and wrote his first book, *National Power and the Structure of Foreign Trade* (1945), Hirschman married Sarah Chapiro, the daughter of a Lithuanian Jewish merchant family. He then enlisted in the US Army, worked for the Office of Strategic Services in Italy and Germany, and had the first of two daughters, Katia (born in 1944; Lisa would follow in 1946). Hirschman got his first proper job in the United States, after the end of the war, as an economic analyst for the Federal Reserve Board, where he focused on Western Europe, reconstruction, and Marshall Plan policies. Development issues were not prominent in his work, nor could one predict that they would soon become so. As Hirschman remembered this professional turn 40 years later:

> In 1952, the possibility of either going to Europe [...] in connection with the European Monetary Union, or of going to Colombia as an economic adviser arose. I opted to take the second road, because it was new. At that point my wife thought I had gone mad: she wanted to return to Paris, where, after all, she had lived most of her youth. But after a short time she was quite satisfied with my choice. [...]
>
> In Colombia it was not easy. [...] There was a new planning council that had been established on the recommendation of the World Bank, which had sent a mission to the country. But the Colombians said, "If you want us to set up a new planning council, send us an economist who is capable of advising us." The Bank looked around, my name was mentioned, and I was ready to come – and in fact did come. (Hirschman, 1998, pp. 80–81)

To the eye of a twenty-first century observer, Colombia in the early 1950s may seem a rather peripheral destination, not as important as other developing countries, such as India or Indonesia, which in the postwar years were committed to the goal of economic development and modernization. But in fact, in the early postwar years, Colombia appeared as a country rich in natural resources and full of potential: its government was committed to modernize the country, so much so that in 1949 it hosted the first "general survey mission" ever sent by the World Bank to a developing country. The goal of that mission was ambitious: to formulate "a development program designed to raise the standard of living of the Colombian people" (International Bank for Reconstruction and Development [IBRD], 1950a, p. xv), and to establish the model for future World Bank missions to less developed countries.[3] Colombia, in sum, was seen as a "laboratory" for the definition of development policies.

The 1949 mission to Colombia was headed by Lauchlin Currie, a prominent former New Dealer, top Fed officer under Governor Marriner Eccles and later personal economic advisor to Franklin D. Roosevelt and Roosevelt's envoy to China. Under his leadership, the mission prepared a thorough study of the social and economic conditions of the country and published a voluminous report envisioning a major comprehensive investments plan (IBRD, 1950a, 1950b).[4] As Currie remarked at a conference in Washington while he was drafting the report, "Economic, political and social phenomena are so inter-related and interwoven that it is difficult to effect any significant and lasting improvement in one sector of the economy while leaving the other sector unaffected [...]. Poverty, ill health, ignorance, lack of ambition, low productivity are not only concomitants – they actually reinforce and perpetuate one another" (Currie, 1950, p. 5).

Despite the widespread political and social violence that vexed Colombia before, during and after the mission as a consequence of the assassination of the opposition leader Manuel Gaitán in April 1949, the collaboration between the Colombian government and the World Bank remained strong. In 1950 a Committee for Economic Development – the Comité de Desarrollo Económico – was established to turn the mission's recommendations into actual policies. Lauchlin Currie, former head of the mission, was appointed as economic consultant to the Committee, in fact acting as its technical secretary and marking the continuity between the study phase of the mission and the implementation phase of the Comité.

Albert O. Hirschman moved to Colombia in 1952 as World Bank appointee to the body that meanwhile had replaced the Comité, the Consejo Nacional de Planificación (National Planning Council). It did not take long before Hirschman and Currie discovered that they were taking opposite positions on basically all the deliberations of the Consejo. More specifically, Hirschman had little patience for the rhetoric of the comprehensive plan that characterized Currie's approach to development planning. Hirschman's first published criticism appeared in a 1954 article where he described integrated development planning as a "myth," a futile exercise because the figures included in an investment budget could not be other than heterogeneous, tentative and imprecise. Actually, in Hirschman's words, "the pretense of total, integrated economic planning could and often does coexist quite amicably with, and may serve to cover up, unregenerated total improvisation in the actual undertaking and carrying out of investment projects" (Hirschman, 1954/1971, p. 47).

Over time, Hirschman began to recognize that his many disparate observations and disagreements with the comprehensive, integrated approach of the Consejo headed by Currie actually resulted in a larger, coherent critique of what Hirschman described as a "new orthodoxy" in development economics. In Hirschman's view, the comprehensive approach envisioned by Currie bore the same flaws as the theories that were quickly shaping development economics in those years. In a seminal 1943 article on the "Problems of industrialisation of Eastern and South-Eastern countries," for example, Paul Rosenstein-Rodan had made the establishment of an industrial sector and the massive transfer of manpower from agriculture to industry the central point of his development strategy. The new industrial sector, Rosenstein-Rodan claimed, was to be considered "like one huge firm or trust" (Rosenstein-Rodan, 1943, p. 204). The underlying assumption was that only the concerted establishment of many industries, as though they were different departments of one single huge firm as opposed to isolated factories, would create the external economies and the demand necessary for the new industrial sector to thrive. As Rosenstein-Rodan put it, if unemployed agrarian workers "were taken from the land and put, not into one industry, but into a whole series of industries which produce the bulk of the goods on which the workers would spend their wages, what was not true in the case of one [isolated] shoe factory would become true in the case of a whole system of industries: it would create its own additional market" (Rosenstein-Rodan, 1943, p. 206). Another prominent development economist, Ragnar Nurkse, thus concluded that "a frontal attack of this sort – a wave of capital investments in a number of different industries – can economically succeed while any substantial application of capital by an individual entrepreneur in any particular industry may be blocked or discouraged by the limitations of the pre-existing market" (Nurkse, 1953/1962, p. 13). These theories were soon described as a "balanced-growth" approach to development, because they envisioned a growth on many fronts, based on a fundamental complementarity between different sectors. A sector that would grow alone or too fast with respect to others was, in this perspective, not only useless for the purpose of development but also doomed to fail.

Hirschman's critique of these theories took full shape in his book *The Strategy of Economic Development*, published in 1958, two years after he and his family had returned to the United States from Colombia. In that book, Hirschman waged an attack against the balanced-growth approach:

> My principal point is that the theory fails as a theory of *development*. Development presumably means the process of change of one type of economy into some other more advanced type. But such a process is given up as hopeless by the balanced growth theory which finds it difficult to visualize how the "underdevelopment equilibrium" can be broken into at any point. [...] The balanced growth theory reaches the conclusion that an entirely new, self-contained modern industrial economy must be superimposed on the stagnant and equally self-contained traditional sector. (Hirschman, 1958/1963, pp. 51–52; emphasis in the original)

Since the key to development was the process of change starting from a condition of economic and social backwardness, then the elements considered by balanced-growth proponents as obstacles – scarce capitals, imperfect markets, the inability to coordinate entrepreneurial decisions – became the basic elements of Hirschman's analysis. The question, in other words, was not how to best invest scarce capital, how to create new and efficient markets, or how to substitute centralized decision-making for imperfect entrepreneurial business decisions. On the contrary, Hirschman claimed, the question was how to foster investment decisions in an imperfect situation. Hence, Hirschman's focus turned to the process of resource mobilization, or, as he put it, on finding the "inducement mechanisms" and the "hidden rationalities" that made growth possible, and the "linkages" that connected sectors or industries or firms – in a nutshell, the mechanisms that would facilitate additional investment in spite of the apparent shortcomings of an underdeveloped economic and institutional landscape. "Development depends not so much on finding optimal combinations for given resources and factors of production," Hirschman wrote, "as on calling forth and listing for development purposes resources and abilities that are hidden, scattered, or badly utilized" (Hirschman, 1958/1963, p. 5).

Hirschman's radical critique of the balanced-growth approach was widely discussed and reviewed. *Strategy* quickly became a standard reference in development studies, earning his author fame and tenure at Columbia University. Perhaps most important, from a disciplinary perspective, is that the book addressed so directly the core of the early postwar development debate that it immediately became an essential and defining element of it. The balanced- versus unbalanced-growth dichotomy is a central theme of early development theories. As Paul Krugman once put it, the "glory days of high development theory" span about 15 years, from the 1943 article by Rosenstein-Rodan to the publication of Hirschman's *Strategy* in 1958 (Krugman, 1994).

DEVELOPMENT ECONOMICS IN THEORY AND PRACTICE

Whereas the balanced- versus unbalanced-growth debate, which Hirschman so insightfully contributed to shape, was central to the *theory* of development economics, its influence on the *practice* of development policies is less obvious. This apparent contradiction can be explained with the help of an episode from the years in Colombia: how the Currie mission, the following national planning committees and Hirschman discussed the opportunity of building an integrated steel plant.

At the end of the Second World War, domestic steel production in Colombia was regarded as an overriding strategic national interest, and the project for an integrated steel plant near the city of Paz del Río, in an internal, mountainous region was in an advanced stage of implementation. The 1949 World Bank mission advised against the plant, both in terms of merit as a capital-intensive production requiring extremely high output, and in terms of location – the plant was isolated from the main lines of communication of the country, thus making it arduous and expensive to transport the output to the final destinations. Furthermore, this isolation would prevent the establishment of nearby plants that in principle could have harnessed the by-products of steel production (IBRD, 1950a, pp. 423–425).

A document prepared by the Comité de Desarrollo Economico added that "the maximum progress achievable" for the years 1951–1955 "is only possible if the amount devoted to each sector, for example transportation, agriculture, or industry, is proportional to its contribution to the overall Colombian economy during this period."[5] The alternative uses of the funds needed for the integrated steel mill were also listed: the construction of a hydroelectric plant covering half of the production of electric power in Colombia in 1950; or thermoelectric plants; or 30,000 private houses; or the purchase of 266 diesel locomotives and the increase of roads and railways by about 500 km; or the construction of 23,000 rooms for hospitals, or new schools accommodating 900,000 students.[6] Hirschman's critique addressed precisely this kind of reasoning, namely the idea that the development of a sector was to be proportional to the development of other sectors, and that an investment plan was a zero-sum exercise. As noted above, Hirschman underscored the dynamic character of industrialization, and thus the "backward" and "forward linkages" that a specific investment would have encouraged upstream or downstream that initial investment. A steel industry, according to Hirschman, was not only a "national symbol," as the Currie mission thought, but a veritable engine of regional and national industrialization: "Perhaps the underdeveloped countries are not so foolish and so exclusively prestige-motivated in attributing prime importance to this industry!" (Hirschman, 1958/1963, p. 108).

In this polemic, both sides overlooked many important points of contact between their apparently opposed perspectives. The considerations of technical and geographic nature in the report of the World Bank mission underscored the weak impact of the prospective steel plant on the development of other industrial sectors. The steel plant was unlikely to leverage a "growing point," which was considered the most desirable result for both the Currie mission and Hirschman, who dedicated an entire chapter of *Strategy* to growing points (Hirschman, 1958/1963, chapter 10). When it became clear that the Colombian government was determined to build the steel plant despite the mission's opposition, Lauchlin Currie recommended developing it in stages. This would have limited the costs of the unfortunate location and allowed the business to gain strength despite this initial handicap. There would have been gradual growth as staff and workers acquired competencies and the plant itself gained a bigger market share. This reasoning was not too different from Hirschman's attempt to find "hidden rationalities" in the process of growth. Thanks to these hidden rationalities, initial obstacles may play a positive role in the process of growth, as they help forge decisions and find new solutions. The mission and later the Comité tried to mediate between industrial and political motives, placing themselves at the center of a decision-making and problem-solving process. This is what Hirschman highlighted as the indispensable element (but also the rarest) for development: the ability to take entrepreneurial decisions.

A few perceptive commentators had noticed that despite the strong polemical tone of that early diatribe and its spillovers in the theoretical debate, the two seemingly irreconcilable approaches had many points of contact. As Amartya Sen put it, Hirschman seemed to be "overstating" his case: "Controversies on 'balanced' versus 'unbalanced' growth tend to leave the readers [...] a little puzzled. Put in their native forms, both the doctrines look right; examined from the other's point of view, each looks totally inadequate [...]. The 'balanced' and the 'unbalanced' growth doctrines have a considerable amount of common ground" (Sen, 1960, pp. 591–592). For example, when Rosenstein-Rodan and Nurkse discussed how to mobilize "disguised unemployment" in agriculture, they were in fact trying to bring up what Hirschman would have called "hidden or badly utilized resources."

It should be noted, however, that the years of "high development theory," as Krugman labeled it, were pioneering years for development economics. The focus of this new and thriving discipline – how backward societies are to develop – was quickly becoming one of the top priorities of the international agenda. With the onset of the Cold War, international development and foreign aid became fundamental strategic questions. Within a nascent discipline quickly gaining global relevance, the debate soon became overheated. Opposing theories are natural elements of any field of human inquiry, and admittedly the "balanced" and "unbalanced" approaches highlighted different aspects of the development process. But in addition to intellectual disagreements, another key conflict was about what should be the overarching goal of the discipline, and which approach should best incarnate this goal. As sociologist Robert K. Merton once noticed, "These controversies follow the classically identified course of social conflict [...]. Since the conflict is public, it becomes a status battle more nearly than a search for truth [...]. The consequent polarization leads each group [...] to respond largely to stereotyped versions of what is being done by the other [...]. Not that these stereotypes have no basis in reality at all, but in the course of social conflict, they become self-confirming stereotypes" (Merton, 1961/1973, pp. 55–56).[7]

NEW QUESTIONS AND THE SEARCH FOR A NOVEL PERSPECTIVE

As it happens, once the pioneering phase of a disciplinary field is over, the theoretical heat also diminishes. After the publication of *Strategy*, Hirschman himself quickly became less interested in high theoretical debates, shifting instead his focus to in-depth analysis of specific, highly contextualized processes of change. Hirschman's second and third book of what he would later describe as his "development trilogy" (Hirschman, 1994, p. vii) strongly rested on deep historical and context-specific analysis. How can we explain this shift?

After almost 20 years of expansion, the development field and development economics with it – was undergoing a major transformation.

In the pioneering days of the early postwar period, development policies were based on nothing more than trial and error, theories were only then starting to take shape, and observations and data were scant. As Lauchlin Currie, Hirschman's archenemy during the Colombian days, later pointed out, "there were no precedents for a mission of this sort [the 1949 mission to Colombia] and indeed nothing called development economics. I just assumed that it was a case of applying various branches of economics to the problems of a specific country, and accordingly I recruited a group of specialists in public finance, foreign exchange, transport, agriculture and so on" (Currie, 1967, pp. 30–31). By the early 1960s, however, the broad generalizations and big concepts that had shaped development economics during its initial years were considered increasingly inadequate to explain the causes of, and remedies to, the economic and social underdevelopment of the so-called Third World countries, which were quickly growing in number due to the demise of the colonial empires. It was increasingly apparent that these countries presented different, specific traits and challenges. But the sense of inadequacy of development theories was also due to the confusing record, to say the least, of development policies implemented until then. The outcomes of foreign development assistance were not easily interpretable, and in many cases they offered evidence of failure: "high development economics" apparently had not delivered what it had promised. A 1964 report by the Brookings Institution on foreign aid summarized this feeling of disorientation:

> Aid is being extended, bilaterally and multilaterally, to 100 countries, democratic and authoritarian, allied and neutral, progressing and retrogressing, without satisfactory standards for evaluating competing claims, promoting particular strategies, harmonizing aid with other available instruments of policy, or appraising the results achieved. There is need for a better political, moral and economic framework within which to review our foreign aid programs and to prepare recommendations regarding their future.[8]

Building on the methodological lesson of his former colleague, the economic historian Alexander Gerschenkron, Hirschman was among the first development scholars to recognize the need for a different approach. Gerschenkron had shown that the process of economic development of continental European countries (the so-called "second comers" and "late comers"), far from replicating the English model, had followed idiosyncratic paths of modernization depending on their institutional, political, financial, and social resources, their relative backwardness, and the timing and extent of their industrialization effort (Gerschenkron, 1962, which collects articles dating back to the early 1950s). The lesson was clear also for the "very late comers" of the mid-twentieth century: no "one size fits all" recipe or theory of development could provide all answers to the problems of underdeveloped countries.

Hirschman was also critical of the increasing appeal that revolution seemed to have on Latin American intellectuals and policy-makers in search of a way to overcome social and economic underdevelopment and inequality. Hirschman thought that comprehensive plans on one side of the spectrum and revolutionary solutions on the other side were inadequate: by attempting to overcome underdevelopment in one big leap, they left out the complexities of the process of change from a backward or pre-revolutionary society to a modern or post-revolutionary one. Hirschman would later summarize his criticism to both approaches in his foreword to the first book by Judith Tendler, a Ph.D. student whom he was mentoring in the early 1960s (now Professor Emeritus of political economy at MIT):

> Underdevelopment having been diagnosed as something so multifaceted, tangled, and deep-rooted, it was often concluded that the situation called for revolution, massive redistribution of wealth and power from the rich to the poor countries, or at least coordinated attack on pervasive backwardness through highly competent central planning.
>
> But what if none of these *dei ex machina* are available to take matters properly in hand? What if the fortress of underdevelopment, just because it is so formidable, can not be conquered by frontal assault? In that unfortunately quite common case, we need to know much more about ways in which the fortress can be surrounded, weakened by infiltration or subversion, and eventually taken by similar indirect tactics and processes. And I suggest that the major contribution to our knowledge of economic development must now come from detailed studies of such processes. (Hirschman, 1968, pp. vii–viii)

Judith Tendler's book was a fine example of this new approach.[9] In it, Tendler discussed how hydro and thermal power had affected the Brazilian economic development of the 1950s and the 1960s in different ways. From this specific case, Tendler was able to build a solid and broader analysis of certain development dynamics of postwar Brazil. In Tendler's words: "should the work therefore be properly identified as a narrow case study, with no pretension of relevance to more general questions of economic development? The answer [...] is in the negative, for this study is meant to illustrate the general thesis that technologies vary as to their political vulnerability, their ability to draw out and train competent talent, and their capacity to brook the coexistence of politically antagonistic institutions. The lesson of this particular case is not that hydro should be favored in developing countries, but that the technological configuration of a project, program, or economic activity is a valuable source of information in the study of opportunities for economic development" (Tendler, 1968, p. 6; see also Tendler, 1965).

THE POLITICAL ECONOMY OF DEVELOPMENT: JOURNEYS TOWARD PROGRESS

Of course this shift in perspective was also apparent in Hirschman's work. Historical narratives of specific economic problems in three Latin American countries make two-thirds of his 1963 book, *Journeys toward Progress*. As he put it, "the essence of this volume is in the flow of the three stories" about problems that had plagued Latin American countries for a long time, namely, drought in North-East Brazil, land reform in Colombia, and inflation in Chile (Hirschman, 1963, p. 1). Hirschman's interest lay in how governments in Latin America would solve these problems and the related policy-making processes. "The best method of looking for answers," claimed Hirschman, "was to scrutinize the record of a few specific, documented, protracted, significant policy problems" (Hirschman, 1963, p. 2).

However idiosyncratic the record of specific problems was, Hirschman was interested in finding elements that would improve the effectiveness of policy reform in the future. While he did not believe that any iron law governed social, economic, and political dynamics, his research aimed at understanding the features underlying the policy-making processes that he had examined in his country studies. His focus on historical analysis, thus, was not a goal per se, but a way to achieve a broader understanding of political processes in Latin America. Hirschman's terminological choices reveal his awareness of the difficulties to generalize from specific cases: he predicted that his analysis would produce only "tentative" and "dispersed" findings, and stated that his goal was not to produce a theory of policy-making, but to sketch "a Latin American 'style' in handling, learning about, and moving toward the solution of large-scale policy problems" (Hirschman, 1963, p. 227).

Underdeveloped societies, Hirschman noted, are characterized by inadequate and ineffectual communication between citizens and the government. In such a situation, violence and mass protest are often the only way for long neglected problems to get the attention of the government. Problems that are felt as "pressing" will often produce some reaction and attempt at solving them, but this is not necessarily based on a real understanding of the roots of the problem. "Motivation," in other words, would have priority over "understanding." The effects of this dynamic are often visible in underdeveloped countries: certain grandiose attempts to attack big problems frontally, disregarding narrower but perhaps more manageable targets; the launch of comprehensive plans to solve all problems at once; the frequent establishment of new institutions dedicated to solve once and for all a certain problem; the excessive reliance on imported solutions that appear to be lifesavers only because they are "foreign"; and finally, major policy shifts and ideological clashes.

Ideology, in particular, was a fundamental lens to understand the development debate in Latin America and the Latin American style of problem-solving and policy-making. Hirschman had specifically touched on the role of ideology in Latin America in the introductory chapter to his 1961 edited book *Latin American Issues* (Hirschman, 1961). In this collection of essays on the problem of inflation in Latin America, Hirschman's attempt was to discuss the role of ideology in shaping the surrounding debate. As Jeremy Adelman put it, "if economists were accustomed to thinking of themselves as outside societies looking in, like a doctor examining a patient, Hirschman turned them into the subject" (Adelman, 2013, p. 369).

When Hirschman examined ideology and the other elements of policy-making in *Journeys*, he discovered that they presented several interesting and promising features. Those seemingly dysfunctional features of Latin American policy-making, far from being hopelessly negative, actually functioned as by-ways through which countries lacking a political system capable of ensuring a dialogue between the public and policy-makers became aware of certain problems and committed, perhaps unevenly, to their resolution. For example, comprehensive plans proved to be particularly useful to link neglected problems to a pressing problem already under the spotlight. Thus the "Comprehensive Plan," the idea that no solution can come to any specific problem unless a whole set of issues is addressed in a coordinated way, became in Hirschman's perspective "a generalized device for indirectly achieving recognition for the stepchild problems" (Hirschman, 1963, p. 232). As mentioned above, Hirschman's aversion to comprehensive development plans had prompted his harsh critique of the balanced growth approach and his outline of an alternative, unbalanced approach in *The Strategy of Economic Growth*. But while in that case Hirschman was engaged in a theoretical debate on the mechanisms of industrial development in less developed countries, in *Journeys* he was discussing a very different set of questions. The comprehensive plan, economically inefficient and useless, was – from the perspective of policy-making – an important strategic device. As pointless and rigid a comprehensive plan might seem when the question was how to encourage economic entrepreneurship, it turned out to be rich and flexible when the question became how to bring about political decisions.

In the same vein, other characteristics of this "Latin American style" may have positive if unexpected sides. Excessive reform promises, for example, are usually followed by meager results. Yet, a "utopian phase of policy-making" often has the merit of generating legislation which, even though initially unenforced, nonetheless exists "on the books." In a subsequent round of reform efforts, this dormant legislation will probably be enforced, thus securing the legal basis for policy initiatives that would have otherwise been inapplicable. Likewise, the mix of outright criticism of previous policies and blind faith in new approaches that characterizes the policy swings studied by Hirschman in his case studies had a number of positive spinoffs. First of all, the habit of considering all government attempts at reform as eventually doomed made opposition to them weaker than it might have been. In other words, the rhetoric of failure opened up spaces for actual reform. At the same time, the bombastic announcements of new policies – while likely destined, like previous efforts, to less than successful epilogues – had an energizing effect on policy-makers: a selective amnesia on previous failures made new attempts possible. Hirschman's optimism seems excessive here, for the two effects of the rhetoric of failure and the rhetoric of success might as well produce outright reactionary results.

However, there was a method in this optimism. Hirschman's (1963) book, after all, is an attempt at explaining the mechanisms of economic and social reform short of revolutionary events. It should be noted that revolution, in early 1960s Latin America, was a rather fashionable concept, its most successful example being the recent Cuban revolution. Hirschman did not deny the existence of situations, in Latin America and elsewhere, in which opposition to reform and concentration of power were so rigid that the only hope to bring about some change was through a revolution. However, his main interest lay in those cases where reform was feasible. In such cases, calls for revolution were unnecessary, and revolutionary intellectuals were analytically weak: instead of explaining social change, they contented themselves by invoking a "cataclysmic interlude between two static societies," the pre-revolutionary one, rotten and unjust and unresponsive to reform, and the post-revolutionary one, just and harmonious and no longer in need of further improvement. Similar to what Hirschman had already observed in his criticism of the balanced-growth approach, which he thought superimposed a developed society to a backward reality, he found this time that calls for revolution impeded the analysis on the truly interesting question, that is, how change happens. There was a lot to be explored in the space between effortless reforms at one extreme and revolutions at the other. Hirschman's study was a way to unravel material for a "reformmonger's manual." As he put it, "perhaps it is time that such a text be written and offer some competition to the many handbooks on the techniques of revolutions, coups d'état, and guerrilla warfare" (Hirschman, 1963, p. 256).

Indeed, Hirschman's goal was "to show how elements of both reform and revolution are present in the sequences of policy-making which we have studied" (Hirschman, 1963, p. 256), and from this perspective, violence itself could become an ingredient of reform. Colombian peasants, for instance, had often seized uncultivated land illegally and violently. But those eruptions of violence, far from leading to revolution, made it possible for reformist governments to legislate about land redistribution in ways that would have been unthinkable without the peasants' violent land seizures. Hirschman was amused by the "highly disorderly sequence" the Colombians had invented: instead of the predictable two-step sequence from revolution to land redistribution within the framework of the new revolutionary legal order, Colombian peasants had first enacted decentralized and illegal redistribution, which was later legalized thanks to a reformist government (Hirschman, 1963, p. 260). More generally, Hirschman highlighted the enormous complexity of reformist action in Latin American countries and the mixed character of reform policies, for they appeared to be made of both non-antagonistic and antagonistic dynamics.

The whole book and the research on which it was based, which Hirschman had conducted during multiple trips to Latin America with his wife, Sarah, and his colleague and friend, political scientist Charles E. Lindblom, was an uncompromising attempt at introducing public policy analysis in the realm of development economics. Dissatisfied with the relegation of public decision-making to the mere role of "pre-conditions" to economic growth, in *Journeys* Hirschman was determined to show how processes of decision-making and problem-solving play a decisive role at all stages of development. He explicitly connected this goal to his previous book, *Strategy*, in which he had investigated a variety of mechanisms able to generate entrepreneurial resources to advance economic development.

Hirschman's attempt at connecting economic and political analysis, perhaps not unexpectedly, was appreciated mostly by political scientists, whereas fellow economists advanced more than one criticism. Mancur Olson considered *Journeys* probably the best book published until then on the two-way relationship between economic development and policy-making (Olson, 1965). Several economists, however, noted that the economic analysis of the three case studies was insufficient and at times unconvincing. As Dudley Seers put it in an otherwise positive review, "it is one thing to say that economic theory needs to take account of political factors, another to leave economics very largely out of the picture" (Seers, 1964, p. 158).

THE POLITICAL ECONOMY OF PROJECT APPRAISAL: DEVELOPMENT PROJECTS OBSERVED

The research that resulted in Hirschman's (1967) book, *Development Projects Observed*, rested on the same methodological approach of *Journeys*. Although the book does not contain the stories of the individual projects studied by Hirschman, the research had an "intensive concern with 'cases'" and all the projects considered had "an extended history." "Immersion in the particular," Hirschman claimed, "proved [...] essential for the catching of anything general" (Hirschman, 1967, p. 3). The book was the result of Hirschman's collaboration with the World Bank, Brookings Institution, the Ford Foundation and the Carnegie Corporation to study some general elements of project appraisal, or, as he put it, "to explore in detail the direct effects as well as the broad repercussions of a project on economy and society" and to reach "some improvements in the process of project evaluation and selection."[10] An additional purpose, after two books exclusively based on Latin American cases, was for Hirschman to broaden his expertise to Asia and Africa.

Hirschman selected 13 World Bank projects and travelled to Latin America, Asia, Southern Europe, and Africa between July 1964 and August 1965 to study them in detail. Bank officers were enthusiastic: "Probably for the first time," remarked a senior economist, "the contemporary theory and practice of project appraisal in infra-structure will be subjected to a systematic *ex-post* methodological scrutiny on a wide basis."[11] This was all the more important, since the World Bank had not yet established an internal and independent evaluation function.

Back from his travels, Hirschman circulated a memo with some preliminary observations. These focused on what he called "Behavioral characteristics of development projects in different sectors." As he put it: "having learnt in fairly rapid succession about a wide variety of projects, I became alerted to the characteristic advantages or handicaps under which power projects, say, proceed as compared to irrigation projects."[12] The principal aim of Hirschman's interim observations was clearly methodological. Far from addressing questions such as the economic return of World Bank loans, or the traditional distinctions of, say, infrastructure versus agricultural and industrial projects, or human versus physical capital, Hirschman focused on questions such as the degree of uncertainty in a project: "the element of the unknown, the uncertain and the unexpected which deflects projects from the originally chartered course is considerable in all projects. But it is far more important in some projects than in others and it may be of interest to the Bank to gain an approximate idea about the principal determinants of this uncertainty."[13] Among these determinants, Hirschman listed the existence of visible linkages between the project's new supply and local demand, and the influence of social and political variables. In addition, Hirschman discussed the difficulty of calculating benefits and measuring results in several types of projects. This change in perspective called for a corresponding change in the Bank's behavior. The Bank, Hirschman wrote, should avoid the "air of pat certainty" that emanated from the prospects of new projects and expose instead the uncertainties underlying them. Moreover, the Bank should take into account the distributional and the social and political effects of its lending. Focusing only on the technical merits of a project, Hirschman concluded, was not enough.[14]

It is no wonder that Bank staff, initially delighted when Hirschman started his study, was instead upset when those first observations were circulated. The final outcome of Hirschman's research, his 1967 book *Development Projects Observed*, did not help defuse tensions. In it, Hirschman focused on the side effects of projects, and described project appraisal as the art of visualizing them. In his definition, side effects were not just "secondary effects": they were "inputs essential to the realization of the project's principal effect and purpose." They were equally essential for the project to mature into a long-lived endeavor (Hirschman, 1967, p. 161). What was the difference, for instance, between a highway project and a railway one? A side-effect of investment in highways is that it develops the heavy motor vehicle industry and thus enhances entrepreneurship. But "entrepreneurship means political power, which in turn means the ability to change the rules of the transportation game decisively in favor of the highways" (Hirschman, 1967, p. 162). A secondary effect, in other words, may become a decisive element for the future of transportation policies in a given country.

With this methodological approach to project appraisal, it is not surprising that Hirschman believed that cost-benefit analysis was an excessively rigid process, hampered by too many arbitrary assumptions. The search for a yardstick to rank potential projects was, according to Hirschman, a futile exercise. "How could it be expected," he wondered, "that it is possible to rank development projects along a single scale by amalgamating all their varied dimensions into a single index when far simpler, everyday choices require the use of individual or collective judgment in the weighing of alternative objectives and in the trade-off between them"? (Hirschman, 1967, p. 179). Hirschman was suspicious of cost-benefit analysis because he thought its allegedly "scientific" index offered no useful tools for better policy-making. "Each project," Hirschman remarked, "turns out to represent a *unique constellation* of experiences and consequences, of direct and indirect effects. This uniqueness in turn results from the varied interplay between the structural characteristics of projects, on the one hand, and the social and political environment, on the other" (Hirschman, 1967, p. 186, emphasis in the original). Uncertainties and latitude (if and how a project can be turned in one direction or another regardless of outside occurrences) condition a project's functioning and outcome and they must be at the center of the appraising exercise.

As interesting and stimulating as Hirschman's approach was, it offered few elements for World Bank officers to make project appraisal operational. How could Hirschman's analysis be embedded in an organizational routine for internal evaluation? As a World Bank senior manager put it, the book "is well written and contains a number of interesting observations. But by and large it does not contain any operationally useful analysis of the merits and priority of the particular projects observed by Professor Hirschman or of the kind of reshaping or rethinking of the projects which might have made them better. In short, I for one gained no significant new insights into the process of project preparation and evaluation."[15]

Hirschman's attempt to establish a qualitative approach to project appraisal was based on detailed historical reconstruction of the "personal profiles" of projects as well as their larger political and social context. It aimed at underscoring "the element of the unknown, the uncertain and the unexpected," as Hirschman put it, in order to understand what caused projects to change direction from their originally charted course. Finally, the goal was to assess the broader political, social and economic impact of a project. Hirschman's approach to project appraisal was a natural evolution of his previous work, which had underscored his increasing distance from the early debates in development theories. The "failure of several of the earlier ideas as *practical* policy solutions," as Tony Killick put it (Killick, 1978, p. 27, italics in the original), prompted Hirschman's detailed examination of the mechanisms of economic policy-making in *Journeys* and project appraisal in *Development Projects Observed*. But while Hirschman and the World Bank had agreed on what was needed, they ultimately disagreed on how to meet this need. Hirschman tried to transform the Bank's approach to project design, management, and appraisal. The Bank, instead, expected Hirschman to make project design and management somehow more measurable, predictable, and scalable. World Bank officers asked Hirschman to collaborate on an operational version of his book, but this ultimately did not see the light, primarily because of Hirschman's lack of interest in the project.[16]

When, a few years later, the World Bank established an Operations Evaluations function, Hirschman's work was virtually forgotten. Project appraisal and evaluation was solidly based on the cost-benefit analysis approach pioneered in the 1920s and 1930s for water-resources development and public investment activities and further developed in the 1960s and 1970s by a new wave of studies, such as those by Little and Mirrlees (1968, 1974) and Dasgupta, Marglin, and Sen (1972). Although these studies were not ignoring the role of uncertainty in project design and appraisal, in practical matters they tended to conflate this term with what is usually meant by "risk," that is, something subject to measurement. Hirschman, instead, following the dichotomy between "risk" and "uncertainty" put forth by Frank Knight, considered uncertainty impossible to measure. As he wrote in the early 1960s, "it is clearly impossible to specify in advance the optimal doses of [...] various policies under different circumstances. The art of promoting economic development [...] consists, then, in acquiring a feeling for these doses" (Hirschman & Lindblom, 1962/1971, pp. 83–84).

Hirschman, in sum, recognized that the uncertainty intrinsic in the nature of development projects constituted an unavoidable question, to be addressed on a case-by-case basis. Accordingly, he refrained from recommending all-encompassing appraisal criteria. Rather, as he put it, his attempt was "to provide project planners and operators with a large set of glasses with which to discern probable lines of project behavior, in the expectation that the analysis of each individual project would require different and rather limited subsets of the full set of glasses which has been exhibited" (Hirschman, 1967, p. 186).

THE CRISIS OF DEVELOPMENT ECONOMICS

Development Projects Observed was the last major work in Hirschman's opus on development. Although he would remain interested in development issues for his entire life and would publish further important essays on development questions, his subsequent book, *Exit, Voice and Loyalty* (1970), belonged to the broader social sciences. For its part, development economics was by then entering a process of decline. While the promise of rapid economic expansion had motivated an entire generation of economists between the 1940s and the 1950s, the failures of the subsequent development strategies shattered the foundations of the field. Hirschman's tone was particularly mournful in acknowledging the crisis of development economics:

> Some twenty-five years later, that early optimism has largely evaporated, for a number of reasons. Growth, while substantial, has by no means overcome the division of the world into the rich "north" and the underdeveloped "south." In the south itself, moreover, the fruits of growth have been divided more unevenly than had been anticipated. And there is another, often unacknowledged reason for the disenchantment: it looks increasingly as though the effort to achieve growth, whether or not successful, brings with it calamitous side effects in the political realm, from the loss of democratic liberties at the hand of authoritarian, repressive regimes to the wholesale violation of elementary human rights. (Hirschman, 1979/1981, pp. 98–99)

Especially for a scholar like Albert O. Hirschman, whose work was guided by a reformist perspective and was equally distant from the opposing options of revolution and acceptance of the status quo, the blow was strong. Hirschman wrote that "little light had been shed on the connections between economic growth and political disasters by my contemporaries" (Hirschman, 1979/1981, p. 99), but his own work was similarly exposed to this kind of critique, especially that celebration of reformmongering that was *Journeys toward Progress*. When Hirschman, in the early 1960s, was circulating the drafts of his country studies, and later when the book was published, several scholars noticed his excessive optimism. David Felix, reviewing the book, joked that while *The Strategy of Economic Development* might well be subtitled, paraphrasing a seminal article by W. Arthur Lewis, "Economic Development with Unlimited Supplies of Labour, Foreign Exchange and Everything Else except the Will to Invest," *Journeys toward Progress* could be similarly be subtitled "Social and Economic Reform with Unlimited Amounts of Time," for Hirschman's optimism rested on the judgment that after many false starts, the Brazilian, Chilean and Colombian governments would eventually focus on solving their long-lasting problems. As Felix concluded, "this may, however, only reflect a failure of imagination on Hirschman's part" (Felix, 1964, p. 202). The U.S. Ambassador to Brazil, who read a draft of Hirschman's analysis of the drought problem in the Nordeste, commented that things "may well go worse before they go better."[17]

CONCLUSIONS: HIRSCHMAN'S DEVELOPMENT LEGACY

The analysis above seems to suggest that, after all, Hirschman's legacy in development economics has been rather limited. Nothing comparable to the pervasiveness of a Harrod-Domar model – rigid and mistaken though the foreign aid policies based on that model were – could be mentioned in the case of Hirschman's legacy to development thinking. The balanced- versus unbalanced-growth approach diatribe defined the borders of early development economics, but had only limited influence on the actual policies of development institutions. Even champions of one or the other approach, when confronted with the implementation of development projects, picked eclectically from seemingly incompatible theories. Thus, alleged balanced-growth supporters and comprehensive planners in Colombia thought in terms of linkages and inducement mechanisms à la Hirschman, while Hirschman praised the comprehensive approach of the regional development agency of Northern Brazil. Furthermore, Hirschman's *Journeys*, although highly stimulating, complex and interesting, was weak in terms of predicting future paths of reform in Latin America. Finally, the analytical recommendations in *Development Projects Observed* were quickly left behind by its major prospective client, the World Bank, and the whole field of project appraisal and operations evaluation all but forgot Hirschman's pioneering studies, focusing instead on cost-benefit analysis.

Yet, Hirschman has been a pioneer in many aspects of postwar development studies, and he has remained an influential thinker for development matters, if not in any particularly structured way – certainly not in a "school" – surely from a methodological point of view. The crisis of development economics, paradoxically, may have helped.

Development economics as an autonomous disciplinary subfield no longer exists. Hirschman had given a very interesting, if biased, contribution to defining this discipline's specific identity. Development economics, he wrote, was defined by two connected claims. The first was the rejection of monoeconomics. According to Hirschman, underdeveloped countries "are set apart, through a number of specific economic characteristics common to them, from the advanced industrial countries" and thus traditional economic analysis, which has historically focused on economically advanced countries, must be significantly recast to deal with underdeveloped countries. The second was the mutual-benefits claim, that is, the view that both developed and developing countries can yield economic gains from mutual economic relations (Hirschman, 1981, p. 3).[18] In recent years, a prominent development scholar, Dani Rodrik, argued instead that what matters is not the different theoretical constructs for different realities such as developed and less developed countries, but rather to apply different recipes based on the same economics. Ironically, for his 2007 book, unequivocally titled *One Economics, Many Recipes* (2007a), Rodrik was awarded the Albert O. Hirschman Prize, the highest award of the Social Science Research Council. But even though Rodrik may be at variance with Hirschman's old definition of development economics, his methodological approach is instead very much in line with Hirschman's thought. For example, Rodrik has consistently underscored the need for pragmatism, policy experimentation, and deep knowledge about local contexts, against general "best practices" or rules of thumb. Similarly, he has privileged selective approaches to policy reform or – in his words – "hitting the right targets and not doing everything at once" (Rodrik, 2007b, p. 5).[19]

If development economics has disappeared as a discipline, the problem of development is still very much alive in public and scholarly debate. Liberated from identity questions, the development field is thriving again, and its approach is much more eclectic than before. Among the major features of the so-called new development economics, Rodrik (2008, pp. 27–28) has emphasized its being experimental (in the broad sense of "a predisposition to find out what works through policy innovation"), based on monitoring and evaluation, aimed at selective and targeted reforms, focused on policy reforms, and diagnostic rather than presumptive – all features that have a distinctive "Hirschmanesque" flavor. In addition, it should be noticed that Hirschman's approach has always had a strong influence on the Latin American development discourse (Adelman, 2008; Ocampo, 2008).

A central element of Hirschman's approach, of which current development scholarship is only partially aware, is the importance of historical perspective. We have noticed the importance of detailed historical analysis in *Journeys* and *Development Projects Observed*, and Hirschman's interest in reconstructing the "personal profiles" of specific projects or questions. But Hirschman's historical sensitivity was evident even in his most theoretical works. Sequences, inducement mechanisms, linkages, are elements of processes that unfold through time and, like all historical processes, they are intrinsically uncertain and open to unexpected shifts and turns and do not fit in any pre-ordained framework. Hirschman highly valued historical analysis to discover perhaps hidden but nonetheless open possibilities for change and reform. As he put it in a 1980 talk:

> Following in detail the process of a revolution gives us a strong feeling, as the structuralist approach does not, for the many might-have-beens of history [...]. As a result, the event-minded historian is less likely than the sociologist to declare that, given such a structural condition, the outcome was preordained. [This] emphasis on the revolutionary process [...] in effect promises to restore a few degrees of freedom we were in danger of losing to the structuralists. (Hirschman, 1980/1986, pp. 171–172)[20]

NOTES

1. On this episode, see Fry (1945/2013), and the 2001 TV movie *Varian's War*, directed by Lionel Chetwynd, with William Hurt and Julia Ormond.

2. Jeremy Adelman's biography of Hirschman (Adelman, 2013) is a fundamental reading. Interesting information can be also found in Hirschman (1998) and in the memories of his older sister, Hirschmann (1993).

3. "Outgoing wire," John McCloy to Lionel Robbins, March 1, 1949, quoted in Alacevich (2009). For a detailed analysis of the World Bank 1949 mission to Colombia, see Alacevich (2009). For an analysis of the whole group of early World Bank "general survey missions," see Alacevich (2011a). For earlier assessment of those early missions, see Spengler (1954) and Moore (1960).

4. On Lauchlin Currie, see Sandilands (1990).

5. Comité de Desarrollo Economico (1950).

6. Comité de Desarrollo Economico (1950).

7. For a thorough discussion of the early debates in development economics, see Alacevich (2011b).

8. The Brookings Institution, Division of Foreign Policy Studies, "Proposal for a Program of Studies Dealing with American Foreign Assistance," April 1964 (Revised), p. 5, Projects and Studies – Projects Evaluation – Professor Albert O. Hirschman – Volume 1, Operations policy files – Projects and studies – General Files – General 1946–1968, World Bank Group Archives (henceforth World Bank Hirschman Folders, WBGA).

9. For other examples, see Weaver (1968) and Echeverría (1969).

10. Albert O. Hirschman, "A study of completed investment projects which have received financial support from the World Bank," June 1963, World Bank Hirschman Folders, Vol. 1, WBGA. This and the following documents are discussed more in detail in Alacevich (2014). See also Alacevich (2015).

11. Dragoslav Avramovic to Department Heads, IBRD and IFC, "Investment in Developing Countries – Effects, Expectations and Reality," February 18, 1964, World Bank Hirschman Folders, Vol. 1, WBGA, italics in the original.

12. Hirschman, A. O. (1965, August). A Study of Selected World Bank Projects Some Interim Observations, World Bank Hirschman Folders, Vol. 1, WBGA.

13. Hirschman (*Ibid.*).

14. Hirschman (*Ibid.*).

15. Richard H. Demuth to Mr. Robert E. Asher, September 13, 1966, World Bank Hirschman Folders, Vol. 2, WBGA.

16. Herman G. van der Tak to Professor Albert O. Hirschman, December 20, 1966, World Bank Hirschman Folders, Vol. 2, WBGA; Herman G. van der Tak to Professor Albert O. Hirschman, January 18, 1967, World Bank Hirschman Folders, Vol. 2, WBGA; Albert O. Hirschman to Mr. Alexander Stevenson, May 1, 1967, World Bank Hirschman Folders, Vol. 2, WBGA; Alexander Stevenson to Professor Albert O. Hirschman, May 18, 1967, World Bank Hirschman Folders, Vol. 2, WBGA.

17. Lincoln Gordon to Albert O. Hirschman, September 3, 1963, quoted in Adelman (2013, p. 380).

18. This was a particularly restrictive definition, as it excluded from the territory of development economics structuralist and dependency theorists who argued that trade relations between developed and underdeveloped countries were disadvantageous for less developed countries.

19. For Hirschman's affinity to other scholars in the development field, see Ellerman (2001a, 2001b).

20. For one more testimony to Hirschman's sensitivity to the role of historical reconstruction, see his opinion of Marx's work: "*The Eighteenth Brumaire of Louis Bonaparte* was a particularly fine work. His historical books were much less orthodox than his economic ones. [...] I like to understand how things happen, how change actually takes place" (Hirschman, 1998, p. 67).

ACKNOWLEDGMENTS

I am grateful to Marina Bianchi, Maurizio Franzini, and my co-panelists in the memorial roundtable on "Albert Hirschman and the Social Sciences," Columbia University, New York, December 10, 2013: Jeremy Adelman, Victoria de Grazia, Ira Katznelson, and Nadia Urbinati, for their valuable comments and insights on a previous version of this paper. A slightly modified version of this paper will appear in the *Elgar Handbook of Alternative Theories of Economic Development*, edited by Jayati Ghosh, Rainer Kattel & Erik Reinert, Cheltenham, UK: Edward Elgar, forthcoming in 2016

REFERENCES

Adelman, J. (2008). Observando a Colombia: Albert O. Hirschman y la Economía del Desarrollo. *Desarrollo y Sociedad*, *62*(June), 1–37.

Adelman, J. (2013). *Worldly philosopher. The Odyssey of Albert O. Hirschman*. Princeton, NJ: Princeton University Press.

Alacevich, M. (2009). *The political economy of the world bank. The early years*. Stanford, CA: Stanford University Press.

Alacevich, M. (2011a). The World Bank and the politics of productivity: The debate on economic growth, poverty, and living standards in the 1950s. *Journal of Global History*, *6*(1), 53–74.

Alacevich, M. (2011b). Early development economics debates revisited. *Journal of the History of Economic Thought*, *33*(2), 145–171.

Alacevich, M. (2014). Visualizing uncertainties, or how Albert Hirschman and the World Bank disagreed on project appraisal and development approaches. *Journal of the History of Economic Thought*, *36*(02), 137–168.

Alacevich, M. (2015). Albert Hirschman observed. In A. O. Hirschman, *Development projects observed* (pp. 175–190). With a new Foreword by Cass R. Sunstein and a new Afterword by Michele Alacevich. Washington, DC: Brookings Press.

Comité de Desarrollo Economico. (December 15, 1950). *Informe de la mision para el Comité. Fomento de una industria colombiana de acero*, draft, p. 15, Lauchlin B. Currie Papers, Duke University.

Currie, L. (1950). *Some prerequisites for success of the point four program*. Address before the American Academy of Political and Social Sciences, Bellevue Stratford Hotel, Philadelphia, PA., April 15, 1950, mimeo, published in *Annals of the American Academy of Political and Social Sciences*, *270* (July 1950), pp. 102–109.

Currie, L. (1967). *Obstacles to development*. East Lansing, MI: Michigan State University Press.

Dasgupta, P., Marglin, S. A., & Sen, A. K. (1972). *Guidelines for project evaluation*. New York, NY: United Nations.

Echeverría, R. P. (1969). *The effect of agricultural price policies on intersectoral income transfers*. Dissertation. Ithaca, NY: Cornell University.

Ellerman, D. (2001a). *Hirschmanian themes of social learning and change*. World Bank Policy Research Working Paper No. 2591.The World Bank, Washington, DC.

Ellerman, D. (2001b). *Helping people help themselves. Toward a theory of autonomy-compatible help*. World Bank Policy Research Working Paper No. 2693.The World Bank, Washington, DC.

Felix, D. (1964). Review of *Journeys Toward Progress: Studies of Economic Policy-Making in Latin America* by Albert O. Hirschman. *Economica*, *31*(122), 201–203.

Fry, V. (1945/2013). *Assignment: Rescue*. With and Introduction by Dr. Albert O. Hirschman. New York, NY: Argo Navis.

Gerschenkron, A. (1962). *Economic backwardness in historical perspective*. Cambridge, MA: The Belknap Press of Harvard University Press.

Hirschman, A. O. (1945). *National power and the structure of foreign trade*. Berkeley, CA: University of California Press.

Hirschman, A. O. (1954/1971). Economics and investment planning: Reflections based on experience in Colombia. In A. O. Hirschman (Ed.), *A bias for hope. Essays on development and Latin America* (pp. 41–62). New Haven, CT: Yale University Press.

Hirschman, A. O. (1958/1963). *The strategy of economic development*. New Haven, CT: Yale University Press.

Hirschman, A. O. (1961). Ideologies of economic development in Latin America. In A. O. Hirschman (Ed.), *Latin American issues: Essays and comments* (pp. 3–42). New York, NY: Twentieth Century Fund.

Hirschman, A. O. (1963). *Journeys toward Progress*. New York, NY: Twentieth Century Fund.

Hirschman, A. O. (1967). *Development projects observed.* Washington, DC: The Brookings Institution Press.

Hirschman, A. O. (1968). Foreword. In J. Tendler (Ed.), *Electric power in Brazil: Entrepreneurship in the public sector.* Cambridge, MA: Harvard University Press.

Hirschman, A. O. (1970). *Exit, voice, and loyalty: Responses to decline in firms, organizations, and states.* Cambridge, MA: Harvard University Press.

Hirschman, A. O. (1979/1981). The turn to authoritarianism in Latin America and the search for its economic determinants. In A. O. Hirschman (Ed.), *Essays in trespassing: Economics to politics and beyond* (pp. 98–135). Cambridge: Cambridge University Press.

Hirschman, A. O. (1980/1986). In defence of possibilism. In A. O. Hirschman (Ed.), *Rival views of market society and other recent essays* (pp. 171–175). New York, NY: Viking.

Hirschman, A. O. (1981). The rise and decline of development economics. In A. O. Hirschman (Ed.), *Essays in trespassing: Economics to politics and beyond* (pp. 1–24). Cambridge: Cambridge University Press.

Hirschman, A. O. (1994). Author's preface: A hidden ambition. In A. O. Hirschman, Development *Projects Observed.* Washington, DC: The Brookings Institution, 1967, second edition 1995, pp. vii–xii.

Hirschman, A. O. (1998). Trespassing: Places and ideas in the course of a life. An Interview by Carmine Donzelli, Marta Petrusewicz, and Claudia Rusconi. In A. O. Hirschman (Ed.), *Crossing boundaries. Selected writings.* New York, NY: Zone Books.

Hirschman, A. O., & Lindblom, C. E. (1962/1971). Economic development, research and development, policy making: Some converging views. *Behavioral Science*, *7*(2), 211–222. reprinted in Albert O. Hirschman, A Bias for Hope. Essays on Development and Latin America, New Haven, Conn.: Yale University Press, 1971.

Hirschmann, U. (1993). *Noi Senzapatria.* Bologna: Il Mulino.

International Bank for Reconstruction and Development [IBRD]. (1950a). *The basis of a development program for colombia: Report of a mission headed by Lauchlin Currie, and sponsored by the international bank for reconstruction and development in collaboration with the government of Colombia.* Washington, DC: International Bank for Reconstruction and Development.

International Bank for Reconstruction and Development [IBRD]. (1950b). *The basis of a development program for Colombia: Report of a mission. The summary.* Washington, DC: International Bank for Reconstruction and Development.

Killick, T. (1978). *Development economics in action. A study of economic policies in Ghana.* New York, NY: St. Martin's Press.

Krugman, P. (1994). The fall and rise of development economics. In L. Rodwin & D. A. Schön (Eds.), *Rethinking the development experience* (pp. 39–58). *Essays Provoked by the Work of Albert O. Hirschman.* Washington, DC: The Brookings Institution. Cambridge, MA: The Lincoln Institute of Land Policy.

Little, I. M. D., & Mirrlees, J. A. (1968). *Manual of industrial project analysis in developing countries, Vol. II, Social cost benefit analysis.* Paris: Development Centre of the Organisation for Economic Co-operation and Development.

Little, I. M. D., & Mirrlees, J. A. (1974). *Project appraisal and planning for developing countries.* New York, NY: Basic Books.

Merton, R. K. (1961/1973). Social conflict over styles of sociological work. In R. K. Merton (Ed.), *The sociology of science* (pp. 47–69). *Theoretical and Empirical Investigations.* Chicago, IL: The University of Chicago Press.

Moore, F. T. (1960). The World Bank and its economic missions. *Review of Economics and Statistics*, *42*(February), 81–93.

Nurkse, R. (1953/1962). *Problems of capital formation in underdeveloped countries*. Oxford: Basil Blackwell and Mott Ltd.

Ocampo, J. A. (2008). Hirschman, la industrialización y la teoría del desarrollo. *Desarrollo y Sociedad*, *62*(June), 41–61.

Olson, M., Jr. (1965). Some social and political implications of economic development. *World Politics*, *17*(3), 525–554.

Rodrik, D. (2007a). *One economics, many recipes*. Princeton, NJ: Princeton University Press.

Rodrik, D. (2007b). One economics, many recipes: What we have learned since Albert Hirschman. *Items and Issues*, *6*(1–2), 1–7.

Rodrik, D. (2008). *The new development economics: We shall experiment, but how shall we learn?* Mimeo, prepared for the Brookings Development Conference, May 29–30, 2008.

Rosenstein-Rodan, P. N. (1943). Problems of industrialisation of Eastern and South-Eastern Europe. *Economic Journal*, *53*(209), 202–211.

Sandilands, R. J. (1990). *The life and political economy of Lauchlin Currie: New dealer, presidential adviser, and development economist*. Durham, NC: Duke University Press.

Seers, D. (1964). Review of *Journeys toward Progress: Studies of Economic Policy-Making in Latin America* by Albert O. Hirschman. *American Economic Review*, Part 1, *54*(2), 157–160.

Sen, A. K. (1960). Review of *The Strategy of Economic Development*, by A. O. Hirschman; *The Struggle for a Higher Standard of Living: The Problems of the Underdeveloped Countries*, by W. Brand; and *Public Enterprise and Economic Development*, by A.H. Hanson. *The Economic Journal*, *70*(279), 590–594.

Spengler, J. J. (1954). IBRD mission economic growth theory. *American Economic Review*, Vol. 44, no. 2, Papers and proceedings of the sixty-sixth annual meeting of the American Economic Association, pp. 583–599.

Tendler, J. (1965). Technology and economic development: The case of Hydro vs. thermal power. *Political Science Quarterly*, *80*(2), 236–253.

Tendler, J. (1968). *Electric power in Brazil: Entrepreneurship in the public sector*. Cambridge, MA: Harvard University Press.

Weaver, F. S. (1968). *Regional patterns of economic change in Chile (1950–1964)*. Dissertation. Ithaca, NY: Cornell University.

IN PRAISE OF SMALL: ALBERT O. HIRSCHMAN AND THE QUESTION OF SCALE

Jeremy Adelman

ABSTRACT

This paper looks at the origins of Albert O. Hirschman's distinctive approach to economic development. It argues that Hirschman's style was the result of several, sequenced, influences. One was the impact of his brother-in-law, the Italian philosopher, Eugenio Colorni, who raised the curtain on a Renaissance approach to knowledge that privileged the importance of close observation. The second was an aversion to abstract theorizing, based in part on Hirschman's distaste for what "theory" produced in the 1930s and 1940s. Finally, the paper suggests that the experience of looking at development experiences from the ground up while living and working on Colombia in the 1950s was pivotal. Thus, it was set of conceptual, political, and empirical influences that molded the classic work, The Strategy of Economic Development *(1958).*

Keywords: Colombia; development; foreign expert; literature; planning; unbalanced growth

Research in the History of Economic Thought and Methodology, Volume 34B, 41–61

ISSN: 0743-4154/doi:10.1108/S0743-415420160000034B011

INTRODUCTION

Social scientists are obsessed with method. Compared to their cousins in the humanities, economists, political scientists, and sociologists spill a lot of ink worrying about sample sizes, units, independent variables, and rationality. The use and misuse of the case study is one of the fixations. What can an example reveal? In our age of big data and big history, there has been a significant tilt to large scales and wide angles. "Big is back," notes one observer. The bounded case study, especially if it is small, is a relic of a bygone age.[1]

Big brings baggage. The accent on large scales and long terms often presumes a standpoint on the subject; in scaling up, we have to pull back. Getting a view of the granular detail meant closing in, narrowing the field of vision, following a tradition of micro-history or the ethnographic turn to emphasize pointillist features and contingent processes; not surprisingly, this kind of research required immersive field work and archival sleuthing. Both are taking a hit. Even among disciplines that once burnished the ethnographic style, like anthropology, "immersion" is increasingly contested. What's more, nowadays, we can get a view of the whole world just from our laptops; from this vantage point we derive theories of boundless significance. Certainly, more and more graduate students in the social sciences rely on, their screens in this way, culling the web for data about the world beyond. They don't even need to know what time it is "out there" in the places where they harvest their information.

This has led to some dramatizing. Some bemoan the end of immersive fieldwork and the eclipse of country studies. The old ethnographic field report written by the solitary, heroic, social scientist has given way to the image of a dissertation fueled by "large N" results from a graduate student who spent more time hunched over a screen than sweating in an archive. There is also euphoria. The cyberview and portable methods mean less and less worry about context or noise. Finally, the social sciences have been liberated from that age-old constraint: the subjective categories that framed the creation of information in the first place. This emancipation has even captivated some historians, a sub-tribe of social scientists more anxious than others about the limits of their sources. Recently, Armitage and Guldi (2014), two British imperial historians, have happily gone on the assault against "short-term thinking" and the study of minor scales. Instead, they celebrate the triumph of the "long-term" and the pursuit of public histories about large questions unfettered from constraints of source, place, or viewpoint. Guldi's website, in an especially eyebrow-raising flourish, has gone on to argue that History should be the master social discipline for the twenty-first century that Economics was for the twentieth. This could be read as a warning that the state of the world could get even worse if she's correct.[2]

This lack of humility is a bit of a surprise. After all, bigness once had a bad reputation. It came under assault in the 1970s. World Bank mega projects made the headlines for the disasters they caused in India and Brazil. Big theories – from modernization to Marxism – lost their charms as they could not explain events around them; when applied, big theories and big projects seemed to make things worse. Smaller claims, mid-range theories, and partial perspectives climbed back onto the social science stage in the 1970s, when times were tougher and doubt was easier to admit. One of the best-selling books in economic thinking was in fact E. F. Schumacher's *Small is Beautiful: A Study of Economics as if People Mattered* (1973), which aimed to restore some balance and modesty to the equation. Aided by feminist theory, cultural studies, Edward Said's *Orientalism* (1978), and other prompts, there was a strong push to be "perspectival," to challenge the authority of big, universalizing claims and the confidence of the outsider's concept-filled gaze on the Other.

The moment of humility was perhaps destined to pass; one is almost tempted to say that the coincidence of the fall of the Berlin Wall and the discovery of globalization (and the popularization of the term itself) ushered in a new era. Certainly, Francis Fukuyama's (1989) essay and 1992 book, *The End of History and the Last Man* had a self-consciously prophetic purpose. The ensuing attack came in waves. Ethnographers came in for criticism for their impressionism – or shameless exploitation. Economics-envy drove many to the comforts of impersonal numbers. Many historians took flight from social science method-anxiety altogether, turned to cultural analysis (which was about to shatter against a different set of shoals). Nowadays, with the advent of easier computing, aggregated data collection, and the urgency of the planet's baking, smallness and perspective are back on their heels. When Bill Gates discovered "big history" we saw the alliance of big philanthropy, big money, and big scales. Oddly enough, the sense of social sciences adrift and anxiety about slow growth, inequality, and the resurgent social divides have not checked the swagger.[3]

Given the pendular swings of recent decades, it's hard to remember a time in which methodological questions did not yield such polarizing positions, an era in which big questions did not require outsized units, scales, and durations. This paper is about a big thinker who worked on small scales, Albert O. Hirschman, and how he discovered and refined a craft of drawing general insights from particular places and examples. His was a style, which would eventually get formalized, and stylized as "the case method." With the case method, it came under increasing assault; even as Hirschman's emerged as one of the world's most distinguished social scientists, his style was increasingly at odds with his maternal discipline: economics. It also steered him away from any quest for general and generalizable theories, the tickets to academic success. But viewing the small, being aware of perspective, and relying on experience did give Hirschman the freedom to take a more skeptical stance when faced with social scientific orthodoxies that relied on large-scale, abstract schema.

Hirschman studiously avoided methodological issues and debates. This has vexed many of his readers, who often mine his books and articles looking for operational clues for how to replicate a research project or to apply a theory of his. Hirschman was never smitten by the positivist turn for testing hypotheses against carefully collected data; so he seldom proffered any hypotheses. At best, he was a fount for something different: the pithy aphorism or memorable metaphor. Partly, this was because he was himself notoriously eclectic; so eclectic that some of his critics felt this was cover for being elusive or obscure. When Hirschman authored a report for the World Bank in 1966 on how to assess development projects, the economists inside the organization fumed that the prose was elegant and even lyrical – but utterly bereft of clear, quantifiable, testable, *useful*, guidelines, or criteria (Adelman, 2013). When pressed, Hirschman insisted that he did not want to be pinned down to any school. And when asked why he didn't want to create a Hirschman School himself, he'd laugh at the idea; the supply of schools had long since eclipsed demand.

Where did this disposition come from? It was not the result of being schooled in a mold. Educated in various places – the University of Berlin, the École des Hautes Études Comerciales in Paris, the London School of Economics, and the University of Trieste – Hirschman was never truly trained, but more self-taught. Indeed, one is tempted to see Hirschman more as a figure who floated above schools of thought; whenever he was invited in to become a member of a club, he'd quickly move on, as if phobic about intellectual crowds. When Marxism was all the rage as a Socialist activist and studying at the University of Berlin, Hirschman read Adam Smith. Later, when at the London School of Economics, he did not flock to Lionel Robbins; nor did he become a Keynes devotee – though he did line up with other students to get an early copy of *The General Theory*. When Hirschman did venture up to Cambridge, it was not to visit the master of macroeconomics; it was to visit a relative of his closest friend,

Eugenio Colorni. The relative was Piero Sraffa, and they appeared to have spent a day discussing not economic theory but the political economy of the struggle against fascism in Italy. Then, when he went to Berkeley in 1941, urged by the Rockefeller Foundation to get proper training in economics, Hirschman did not take the advice. Instead, he wrote his first book, *National Power and the Structure of Foreign Trade* (1945). The book was a flop; it was out of synch with prevailing fashions. Hirschman's career as an intellectual – to the extent that he yearned for one – was over.

So, if one of our questions is where the disposition comes from, a second question might be, how did it serve a career that would then become famous precisely because of its doubt about orthodoxies about development and modernization. This doubt, inscribed in his second book, *The Strategy of Economic Development* (1958), happened to catch the emerging distemper about what rich countries were doing to poor ones in the name of development, fueled by the crises in Cuba, Algeria, and Vietnam. But there was a hidden subtext to the book, one that got lost in the furor over development in the 1960s – one which I want to bring to the fore here: the status placed on lessons from experience in a particular place and specific problems.

SKETCHING ADVICE

In the preface to Hirschman's *The Strategy of Economic Development*, a book which turned Hirschman's career, he made one of his rare passes at the question of method and the problem of scale and perspective. He began with a quote from Alfred North Whitehead's *Process and Reality* (1929): "The elucidation of immediate experience is the sole justification of any thought; and the starting point for thought is the analytical observation of components of this experience." In a world and at a time that embraced scientism, distance, and objective observation on a reality separate from the observer, this was an odd departure. But, Hirschman went on to explain, this was not a methodological dogma as much as an "encouragement" that the experience of living in the tropics in the 1950s and the ground-level observation of development offered insights into the wider process of economic change, one which – he would go on to explain – could perforate many of the presumptions and misguided precepts of economic orthodoxy. "I had long felt dissatisfaction with the present state of our knowledge," he admitted. "Existing theories had seemed to me to be particularly unhelpful to the decision-maker in underdeveloped countries." But there was a problem, he admitted, to how he was going about creating a more helpful alternative: his experience and vantage point was from one place, anecdotal, and limited. In his self-defense, Hirschman proclaimed, "intimate acquaintance with an individual country has in fact produced many of our most useful generalizations about the social process" (Hirschman, 1958, p. v).

Where was this place from which he would draw generalizable concepts? It comes up when turning the page to his acknowledgments: Colombia. For someone who took location and vantage point seriously, it's a curiously cursory mention. Indeed, Colombia is only five more times over the course of the whole book – which is rich in general arguments but threadbare on empirical insights. When Colombia appears, it's never more than a casual mention; there is no plunge into any in-depth examples, no "thick description." In the bulk of the 200-some page book, the prose is deliberately abstract and de-linked from specific places and experiences of development, despite the professed commitment to "intimate acquaintance with an individual country" as the empirical foundation for the book. The case itself was absent.

Strategy was short on details and more deductive and conceptual. This did not mean that he diminished the significance of empirical fieldwork. It may have been that Hirschman worried that a single "case study" would pigeonhole the book. But it was not absent from his experience; nor was Colombia just a convenient setting. His Colombian years from 1952 to 1956 were formative, and the lessons he drew would buoy him through a checkered history of encounters and debates in the career of development thinking.

Hirschman wound up in Colombia by accident; the case study appeared not by design but by default. This would have lasting implications because Hirschman arrived in the tropics with few priors. He was certainly no expert in development economics in its early days. If anything, his writings until the mid-1950s were focused largely on European reconstruction, balance of payments issues, and foreign trade. But the rising tide of political intolerance in the United States during the McCarthy years drove him from employment at the Federal Reserve offices in Washington. Under the aegis of a World Bank approved initiative in the Colombian Banco de la República, Hirschman relocated to Bogotá in 1952. There, Hirschman reinvented himself as an expert in development though he was bereft of expertise. As we shall see, this would also color his understanding of "expert advice."

From the start, Hirschman had several tasks; all of them involved, in different ways, dispensing advice to policymakers. One was as part of a brain trust – the Planning Council – in the Central Bank guiding policy.

This, as it turns out, was an increasing source of friction. There were two reasons. First, Colombia was in the midst of historic turmoil and a spiral into fratricidal violence. While Hirschman was never directly exposed to or threatened by the carnage, it did affect the mood – and gave the "outside expert" a sense of a basic disconnect between policymaking expertise and the legitimacy of the regime. When, finally, the military, led by General Gustavo Rojas Pinilla, seized power, about a year after Hirschman's arrival, the teamwork began to dissolve. Hirschman disliked the General and his entourage. He also increasingly disliked some of his fellow "expert advisers," whose confidence was the antithesis of Hirschman's curiosity. For a while, he tried to muddle through until finally, a year later, when his contract expired, he struck out on his own and became a private consultant. This was his last foray into advising governments and being involved in top-down planning of development.

TO THE FIELD

But there were other ways of dispensing advice. Even as he was working as part of the brain trust in Bogotá, Hirschman began to skip out of the capital. Some of his teammates' confidence in master plans and pseudo-data-informed models seemed, under the political circumstances, so abstract. And besides, though Hirschman was interested in policy, he grew increasingly fascinated, as he came to learn more about Colombia, with what was happening on the ground and in the private sector. This took him, without necessarily planning it this way, to the field, scouring the countryside and smaller cities for investment opportunities to present to the bosses in the capital. A trademark of his later research style, conversing with as many people about as many topics as possible to spot possibilities drawn from everyday practices of problem-solving, took shape in Colombian fields and factories. Getting to know the country meant getting near its people, lots of travel to talk to farmers, local bankers, industrialists, and artisans who labored to improve their lot in small, ordinary and, to the lofty-minded social scientist, often imperceptible ways. Rather than concern himself with rumblings in the capital and courtly intrigue, Hirschman preferred the micro-foundations of economic development and became especially intrigued by the role, neglected in so much official development thinking at the time, of the private sector. He focused on evaluating of firms, industries, and sectors as prospects for major investments, presenting their cases to the brain trust in the capital as it sifted the worthy from the unworthy.

Then, as a private consultant, he took the work to a new level – hired by firms, construction, insurance, and others, to evaluate specific irrigation, housing, and infrastructure projects for their management and prospects. To date, Hirschman had only worked on one side of the economy, evaluating macro-economic data from the heights. While his day-to-day work involved assessing projects for investment, The *Consultor's* first contracts were with private businesses and banks who asked Hirschman to evaluate investment proposals, like the Caja de Crédito Agrario. Some firms, like Ebasco Inc., a New York-based paper and box maker interested in expanding to South America to set up a pulp and paper mill, hired Hirschman to evaluate the market. Hirschman and his partner, George Kalmanoff, pored over the data for Ebasco to profile a strong and expanding local demand, and also noted the opportunity to converge with several local partners, like the Institute for Industrial Promotion, as well as several firms like Cartón de Colombia. "The creation in Colombia of such an enterprise," he wrote of Ebasco's venture, "is no doubt one of the most important next steps in the country's rapidly advancing industrial development, and we hope our report will contribute to this end." While the consultants had no doubt that they serviced their clients, they were not above smuggling in some ulterior, broader goals of promoting Colombian development through private sector mobilization.[4]

Hirschman criss-crossed Colombia, pen in hand and paper handy, examining irrigation projects, talking to local bankers about their farm loans, and scribbling calculations about the costs of road-building. He leaned toward what his future colleague, Clifford Geertz, would call "experience-near" knowledge, the insights of an actor, keeping the "experience-distant" concepts of the detached observer at bay, at least for the time being (Geertz, 1985).

Observing and advising in a different key yielded to a very different outlook on development than the master planners who focused on overturning pathologies. By 1954, Hirschman was fixating less on what was wrong than on what it was going right. In early March he put the final touches to a research project that he had been mulling for some time. His "Case Studies of Instances of Successful Economic Development in Colombia" never saw the light of day. Almost everything about it was at odds with the expectations of development and practices in the precincts of the Banco de la República. The country and its people were moving forward, according to Hirschman, not wallowing in the lethargy of tradition. Indeed, the proposed research method ran against the grain. Instead of compiling general national statistics, he proposed a study of successful businesses, starting with an analysis of the "personality and background of founders and managers" – their training, decision-making styles, methods of financing, the elements of a different analytical approach. The cases, drawn from the projects he knew from direct observation, included Manuelita, the sugar plantation and refinery in the Cauca Valley, Coltejer, Medellín's big cotton textile plant, Bavaria, the beer-maker, and Banco Popular de Bogotá, which specialized in small loans to individuals, artisans, and small firms "which has experienced remarkable expansion recently due to novel methods and political support." The idea of building a different model of research on development went nowhere.[5]

OUT OF COLOMBIA

From the blue came an invitation to participate in a conference at the Massachusetts Institute of Technology sponsored by the Social Science Research Council about scientific solutions to problems of economic planning in the tropics. Five economists with first-hand "experience" in the field were asked to share their thoughts with "scholars." It was an occasion noteworthy mainly for its emblematic separation of field experience from scholarship, with the former as agents for deep conceptualizing by the latter. At the time, MIT was the hub of a lot of thinking about development, especially by Max Millikan and Walt W. Rostow. Hirschman had come to Millikan's attention when he sent the draft of his research proposal on Colombian successes in early 1954. Hoping his research ideas could be parlayed into a grant from MIT, he accepted the invitation to deliver a paper as a consolation; it spurred him to formulate more general thoughts. Hirschman plunged into it with a verve he had not mustered since his Marshall Plan days. He read as widely as he could given his miniscule library in Bogotá. He got his hands on some recent theories on growth and pored over David Lilienthal's ("Mr. TVA") history of the Tennessee Valley Authority. "In my free time," he told his friend George Jaszi, "I am now reading mostly background material for the paper I am supposed to write for the MIT-SSRC conference," for which he was pinning more and more hopes of switching careers and cycling his influence through different channels.[6]

Millikan's conference in October 1954 was decisive because it brought Hirschman face-to-face with a scholarly field for the first time, only to discover how "off" he was. At the time, though development was on the lips of so many social scientists, few still had the kind of direct experience that Hirschman had. More often, ideas about development conformed to what was soon called "modernization" theory and its foreign policy implications, which suffused the pores of MIT's Center for International Studies. An outgrowth of an effort to design counter-Communist models of social change for poor societies – Rostow was committed to promoting ways to roll back the appeal of "the Communist disease" in underdeveloped countries – the CIS had close ties to the State Department and the Central Intelligence Agency. Eradicating poverty was supposed to diminish the appeals of radicalism. When Rosenstein-Rodan joined MIT in 1952, he brought more economic rigor to the group. His famous 1943 essay about backwardness and industrialization in eastern and southern Europe led Rosenstein-Rodan to urge a "Big Push" to overcome the entrapments of poverty. A liberal anti-Communist, he believed that a comprehensive and concerted assault was the only way to prevent specific advances from being swallowed up by the inertia of tradition. His thinking was to mark Rostow's later writings and recommendations to various White House occupants (Gilman, 2003, pp. 161–165).

Hirschman had only a partial grasp of these early shifts in the field. What he did get he found tedious. Besides, there was precious little empirical work of the sort he valorized. Too much of it smacked of more "theoretical" takes on what he was observing in the Council. In retrospect, it was perhaps inevitable that his MIT paper was going to run into trouble. But we can see how it would anticipate a broader debate and controversy about how best to tackle poverty and growth in the Third World, a debate that had precursors in the 1950s. But for now, Hirschman's was a solitary, not fully developed, cry for a different spirit of development thinking. On hand were some of the gurus of the field like Rosenstein-Rodan, Hollis Chenery, and Robert Solow. It is not clear whether Rostow was present. None were impressed. What they heard were doubts about investment planning and the economics of development, doubts that did not shy away from uneasy questions about aggregated analysis and unflattering words about the role of foreign "experts." As career-defining papers go, this one was a flop (Hirschman, 1971).

"Economics and Investment Planning: Reflections Based on Experience in Colombia" is the work of an author in a transition of which he was only just becoming aware. He was coming from obscurity in the field and had not yet been stamped by what passed as academic orthodoxy. But these were part of the reason why his thinking was so orthogonal; instead of referring to large schemata and big ideas, he did the opposite. His opening words must have burned the ears of his listeners, as he warned that too little was known before drawing big conclusions of the sort the MIT organizers sought. "Our abilities will sooner or later invite reactions of the type 'But the Emperor has nothing on!'" Economists, he noted, suffer from the universal "desire for power" and often fail to "admit that there are limits to his prowess." The result was "an optical illusion that economics as a science can yield detailed blueprints for the development of underdeveloped societies." Hirschman did not disavow the economist; he simply cautioned against the allure of over-aggregated analysis and the siren calls of "over-all, integrated development programs" of the type that brought him to Colombia in the first place. They might do better with a commitment to reality and content based on observation from the ground up, precise understandings and models instead of a blind faith in general statistics (Hirschman, 1971, p. 41). Doing so might reverse the insidious relationship between foreign experts and their hosts, one which was doomed to compound problems. Like any marriage, the misunderstandings came to light when ideas ran into the messy nuisance of practice. The expert blamed the government for sloth, corruption, or more. The host, in turn, binged on self-incrimination for being unable to live up to the "rigid rules of conduct" and lofty expectations of the planners. It was all doomed because both sides bought into romantic dreams spun of a Platonic plan that could not help but fall short of expectations. Not surprisingly, planning orthodoxies ended in mutual stereotypes about foreign expertise and local futility. Hirschman threw down a verbal gauntlet. Instead of a "propensity to plan," Hirschman advocated a "propensity to experiment and to improvise" – a spirit missing from the Council, and which deprived all sides from actually learning from experience precisely because the planners were so convinced that it was not them that had to be converted. After all, they were "experts" (Hirschman, 1957).

With words like these, whose Hayekian harmonics flew over the heads of those present, it is not surprising that Hirschman's foray into the academic world was greeted with icy politeness. It looked like Hirschman's affection for small, modest claims and incremental theorizing based on everyday efforts and the practices of improvability was going nowhere professionally.

ADVISING OTHERWISE

Hirschman was not exactly an ingénue when he arrived in Colombia. Though he later professed to have no knowledge of development when his plane touched down in Bogotá, his was not a blank slate waiting to be filled with experiences that landed, willy-nilly, on his lap. There is a great deal of *fortuna* in the story that Hirschman told of his own life, and he would make of *fortuna* an important force in the development process. But there was a variant of *virtù* at work too, his version of a worldview which shaped his dispositions to field work, small scales, and a different style of advising. To grasp this, we need to reckon with his encounters with the Renaissance.

Hirschman's skepticism about big schemata had been forged not in the 1950s but in the 1930s. It made its first appearance when, as a militant Socialist in the waning days of the Weimar Republic, the young Hirschman read Marx for his insights but recoiled from Communist certainties. He even complained about some of the rigid thinking in the leadership of the Social Democratic party. Questioning certainty took a new turn, and one might say real force, in a relationship with the Italian philosopher Eugenio Colorni, his close friend and eventually brother-in-law. This relationship was more important to the making of Hirschman's concept of *economie élargie* than we have hitherto appreciated, in large part because Hirschman was tight-lipped about earlier, darker, chapters of his life; it also points to some non-economic influences in his style of conceptualizing. Colorni would marry Hirschman's sister, Ursula, and their fitful union eventually dissolved when Colorni was in prison in Ventotene; he was then gunned down by fascist thugs in Rome in 1944. But in the meantime, Colorni would share many hours of conversation in Paris and Trieste with Hirschman. More than anyone, in fleeting moments forged of a shared anti-fascist struggle and affection for books, Colorni influenced Hirschman (Adelman, 2013, chapter 3).

It was above all in Trieste, from the winter of 1936 after Hirschman got injured in battle in the early days of the Spanish Civil War, to September 1938, that the two formed their bond. What Colorni had was books – many books. His personal library was supplemented by the shelves at the famous antiquarian bookstore on via San Nicolò operated by the Jewish poet Umberto Saba. Saba's was the unofficial center of unofficial cultural life. Flaubert, Saint Simon, Laclos, Constant, all of these turned Hirschman away from German idealism and Marxism; henceforth, he would always treat economics as a branch of literature. For instance, he became fascinated by Flaubert's attention to the particularity of each word in his prose and correspondences; the search for the right word, *le mot juste*, was as worthy as a political cause.[7]

Two authors loomed especially large in Hirschman's style of economic thinking. One was Michel de Montaigne. The highly personal vignettes, meditations, and moral reflections of Montaigne's *Essais* (1987) shook him to his core. Hirschman immediately grasped the power of his essays – Montaigne questioned absolute forms of knowledge by submitting everything to the interrogating eye of the observer, starting by looking at himself, turning himself over and over to capture the multiple points of perspective or the multiple forms of the self. "We are never 'at home': we are always outside ourselves," Montaigne wrote. "Whoever would do what he has to do would see that the first thing he must learn to know is what he is ...." The roof beams over his library were painted with Pliny the Elder's words,

> Only one thing is certain: that nothing is certain
>
> And nothing is more wretched or arrogant than man.

Montaigne's affection for the aphorism, for accumulating quotes, rubbed off on Hirschman instantly, and he began to stockpile his own, starting with a mantra from Montaigne; "observe, observe perpetually." The tales of personal experience, which filled the *Essais*, recounted a fascinatingly complex and playful challenge to, the absolute distinctions between subjective and objective worlds. As Hirschman procured his own copy of the *Essais*, either from Umberto Saba or during one of his trips back to Paris, Montaigne's ironic detachment corroded the obsession with outer truths and realities. "Except you alone, O Man, said that god, each creature first studies its own self, and according to its needs, has limits to his labors and desires. Not one is as empty as you, who embrace the universe: you are the seeker with no knowledge, the judge with no jurisdiction and, when all is said and done, the jester of the farce" (Montaigne, 1987, pp. 1132–1133). According to Montaigne, nothing was too trivial for consideration, for what we lose when we give up certainty we gain with clarity.

The other great influence was Machiavelli. Reading Machiavelli began when he was 20 years old ("a good time to read 'M'," he once told an audience), living in Paris and making his first steps into exiled Italian antifascist circles "reading Machiavelli and Leopardi." He read "M" again in Trieste, with Eugenio. When he got to Berkeley (with Montaigne's *Essais* under his arm), he went to the library and signed out a copy of "M"s' correspondences. This was how he started his first book, with Machiavelli's confession to Francesco Vettori that he knew little about the "art" of the economy, which resigned him "to reason about the state." *The Prince* traveled with him as a member of the Office of Strategic Services during the Italian campaign of the Second World War. Hirschman always kept Machiavelli close to hand, not just for *what* he thought about the mysteries of power, but for *how* he thought, how a writer portrayed man – including himself – as a stage upon which competing drives played out their drama.[8]

This is one of the reasons why Machiavelli's epistles to Vettori became a refrain. Seven months after confiding his feeble command over trades to the Tuscan diplomat, friend, and hoped-for patron, Machiavelli shared an embellished account of his exile from Florence as a wanderer, hunting for thrushes and gathering firewood, playing cards and backgammon with the local "lice [to] ease my brain from its rot," he would return home in the evenings, cast off his dirty clothes and boots and "put on the garments of court and palace." Properly attired, he went to his study to dine in "the courts of the ancients." There, "I am unashamed to converse with them and to question them about the motives for their actions, and they, out of their human kindness, answer me. And for hours at a time I feel no boredom, I forget all my troubles, I do not dread poverty, and I am not terrified by death." From these conversations with the ancients, Machiavelli explained, he wrote what he learned, a "short study, *De principatibus*, in which I delve as deeply as I can into the ideas concerning this topic, debating what a princedom is, of what kinds they are, how they are gained, how they are kept, and why they are lost" (Najemy, 1994).

Machiavelli wrote *The Prince* between 1513 and 1514. It was a "little work" (*opusculo*), he claimed. Short, dense, full of advice and rules for the exercise of princely power, the book also staked out some methodological claims about the significance of perspective. What he argued was that it helped to look at things askance, from the outside, but to look closely at them nonetheless. Machiavelli's reasoning was partly self-justificatory – after all, here was a banished man writing for a ruler from outside the kingdom. But part of the reasoning may have reflected some lessons he drew from Leonardo da Vinci's style of drawing. Machiavelli may have met Leonardo, hired as a military engineer for the Court of Cesare Borgia, while Machiavelli was the official ambassador of the Republic of Florence. Ever since, there has been a debate about their overlap (Boucheron, 2008). Leonardo's landscape map of Imola, depicted from above, was an example of the point: that one gains a deeper view depending on one's angle. For the man who wanted to share helpful advice for the prince about political "realities," and who professed an aversion to authors who relied on ideals and imaginary republics, it was important to be aware of the vantage point. As he explained in a letter to Lorenzo de Medici (Machiavelli, 1975, p. 30):

> Nor I hope will it be considered presumptuous for a man of low and humble status to dare discuss and lay down the law about how princes should rule; because, just as men

> who are sketching the landscape put themselves down in the plain to study the nature of the mountains and the highlands, and to study the low lying land they put themselves high on the mountains, so, to comprehend fully the nature of the people, one must be a prince, and to comprehend fully the nature of princes one must be an ordinary citizen.

Like Machiavelli, Hirschman wanted to author a work of advice, not for the prince but for the planner, based upon the real world observations in the planning process, and not premised on abstract schemes.

ON DEVELOPMENT

Conversations about Montaigne and Machiavelli led to what Colorni called "*piccole idee*" of jottings, and aphorisms inscribed in what Montaigne would have called "commonplace books." These evolved into Hirschmann's own "*petites idées*" as the materials for worldly reflections deposited in his memory bank of observations and insights; he opened a file for his "favorite quotes." He would later describe the practice thus: "We can be distracted and diverted and divested by small things, since small things are capable of holding us. We hardly ever look at great objects in isolation; it is the trivial circumstances, the surface images, which strike us – the useless skins which objects slough off."[9]

This predisposition to think about what advice might help the development policymaker or the investor turned Hirschman away from the obsession in the 1950s to find the big *primum mobile* – the key to economic success. Was it to industrialize? To export? Borrow capital? For Hirschman, advising was not premised so much on what was absent in the Third World as much as what was present, even if it was small, modest, and hard to spot, and to build on that. Noting what was presently required, however, getting rid of some predetermining styles of thinking, and searching at lesser, often local, scales to observe what was happening on the ground, and *then* beginning to conceptualize.

Who appreciated this turn, and helped nurture it in Hirschman's thinking as he labored on *Strategy* was an old friend, Thomas Schelling. What is an "insight," Hirschman mused? Here, the influence of Schelling, his most influential manuscript reader, was subtle but important. It was also Schelling who had arranged to bring Hirschman on a one-year fellowship from Colombia to Yale University for the academic year 1956–1957, when Hirschman would start to pen the elements of *Strategy*. Schelling, without knowing how weighty he would be, pushed Hirschman from the start to translate the lessons from his Colombian immersion into more general insights, to connect the observations of small, local changes to shape the broad view. Hirschman told his sister, after one of his chats with Schelling, that he found his friend "one of the most intelligent people that I know (almost scary) – he turned away from economics and is now more interested in questions of foreign policy and peace strategy." What helped was a distinction between human *strategies*, a keyword for both thinkers, and not *theories*, as motors of social processes. Moreover, they shared an affinity in dealing with the relationship between case studies and general insights. Neither bothered too much that a single case of multiple strategies would constrain conceptual innovation, handled the right way; Hirschman noted that Karl Marx wrote *Capital* based on observations of industrialization in one country without having to add "Capital – a Case Study of England."[10]

There was one last matter to consider. There were also immovable practicalities to the thorny relationship between the case study and the theory. Even if Hirschman had wanted to compose a classical case study, rich in detail and narrative, there were certain rules of evidence to follow – rules he could not obey. In the rush, Hirschman had left Colombia to take advantage of the Yale fellowship in early fall, 1957. He had only learned of the fellowship a few months earlier. There was no time to organize his data or to collect any systematically. Besides, if he wanted a career-maker in the United States (which he was eager to pursue), it would be better to be as universal as possible, and he wasted little time striking in that direction. Colombia, as a result, receded from the treatment in the book that would indeed put Hirschman's academic career on a fast track to stardom, even though Colombia and the *petites idées* culled from years of field work there was the book's foundation.

Strategy immediately singled itself out as an important dissenting tract to large-scale thinking about development, promulgated by the master planners and advocated under the mantle of "balanced growth" models. Hirschman's original working title was in fact *Unbalanced Growth*. This is not the place to sideline into a discussion about that debate, except to note that Hirschman fully intended to provoke some discussion with his dissenting voice. His was not the only one, as he acknowledged in the preface to the 1961 paperback edition of the book. Banfield (1958) had made the case for hidden advantages of backwardness, and most importantly Paul Streeten had published "Unbalanced Growth," in *Oxford Economic Papers* in 1959. But what the debate revealed to Hirschman was not that economic activities were so inter-related (that was clear enough in his analysis of "linkages" – from chapter six of *Strategy* – that became a major keyword in development economic thereafter). Balanced growth advocates had used inter-relatedness as a cudgel to argue for all-encompassing, grand plans; partial measures were doomed to fail because their beneficial effects would be choked off by obstacles and rigidities lurking everywhere else in the traditional, backward, economy. Inter-relationships was not so much the problem as much as scale was. "As in the atom," wrote Hirschman in the new preface in 1961, "there is much energy here that can be and is in fact being utilized in building up economic development nuclei." As the nuclei drew attention, the original, micro, and unbalanced sequence that set off economic change – planned or unplanned – faded from view. "To look at unbalanced growth," he told readers, "means, in other words, to look at the dynamics of the development process *in the small* (emphasis original)" (Hirschman, 1958, p. ix).

The figure in his sights was Paul Rosenstein-Rodan, the man behind the "big push," which required an assault on all of an economy's weaknesses at the same time. In chapter 3, Hirschman went for his quarry directly, observing that big pushers reminded him of the paradox of the string that is equally strong everywhere. It therefore would either never break or break everywhere at once. Montaigne made his appearance to make the case for smallness. Here are Hirschman's words: "However, as Montaigne pointed out in considering this paradox, its premise 'is contrary to nature' for 'nothing is ever encountered by us that does not hold some difference however small it may be'." The trick, for Hirschman, was to find those differences, even if they were miniscule, and focus on them; it was not the grand scheme that would reveal the opportunities – or strategies, a word he preferred to *theory* (Hirschman, 1958, p. 52).

Looking for the small, the micro-foundational elements of the development process had Hirschman thinking hard about development not as something that could be imposed or introduced from without. Nor could it be unlocked with some special secret force like a *deus ex machina*. Instead, he fingered social agents overcoming difficulties as the central pieces of his conceptual rebuilding. But how to think about this as a process? Overcoming a difficulty meant not just removing an obstacle, but seeing that it began as a perception – that is, that the impediments to moving forward lay as much within human agents' heads; the inner fetters were the hardest to overcome. If this could be applied to how people dealt with the emotive world, why not the economic one too, just as a therapist might urge a patient to confront an obstacle by apprehending it? Many times, this exercise might end in failure, and frustration. But over time it would yield a change. "The repeated coming up to it (the obstacle) – you get to know it," he noted. This centerpiece of analytic practice now transposed to thinking about society, was not altogether new. Characteristically, Hirschman found the classics already mulling these kinds of dilemmas. He found special significance in Burke's line from *Reflections on the Revolution in France*, that "our antagonist is our helper. He that wrestles with us strengthens our nerves and sharpens our skill"; to this Hirschman added his own line about "our evasion of and intimate acquaintance with difficulty."[11]

Zeroing in on the small shifted attention from big, missing pieces or preconditions of development, to focus on more prosaic, everyday practices, many of them lodged in the way people thought about their agency and the scales at which they make decisions and judgments. To say this was a very different way to think about social change would be an understatement; but the way in which Hirschman stated it, it often got underappreciated. By the end of *Strategy* the core of Hirschman's thinking about what is scarce in traditional societies becomes clear. It was not capital. It was not a middle class. It was not "entrepreneurship" or the right kind of cultural bedrock of striving individualism. It was altogether more original: the capacity to problem-solve in a capitalist world, the "ability to make development decisions." Balanced growth presumed that core of the vicious cycle of poverty was a shortage of capital. To Hirschman, capital was simply underutilized for lack of perceived opportunities. In fact what was in short supply was "the ability to carry out cooperatively decisions and activities for development," now compounded by development gurus who insisted on an *idea* of progress as an uphill struggle whose success depended on a concerted, expensive, overall push on indivisible economic fronts. With this as the only way out of the trap, no wonder people in the Third World felt – or were made to feel – incapable of making effective decisions on their own!

CONCLUSION

The result was an optimistic charter that took aim at the prevailing view that there were so many constraints on development, so many scarce factors, that the enterprise required a totalizing approach to tackle them all in one swoop – or be condemned to fail. Given the proliferation of scarcities and shortages, Hirschman wondered whether such "objective scarcities of specific factors" were quite so central at all. Why not consider "manmade difficulties" in mobilizing resources, like the ability to solve problems? The more Hirschman thought about it, the more he realized that a closer examination "permitted a more sanguine view." The result, in contrast to expensive, expansive, intellectually seductive general plans and combined assaults, was a piecemeal approach targeting the scarcest of all variables. This was the premise of "unbalanced growth," a term he eventually abandoned because he did not want his work positioned only as an alternative to a mainstream. There was also a matter of scale, and of what was knowable. Once more in contrast to the all-encompassing big-push-or-nothing standpoint, Hirschman featured modesty. In a phrase he liked to share with readers and listeners, he summarized his view of unbalanced growth thus: "To look at unbalanced growth means, in other words, to look at the dynamics of the development process *in the small* [emphasis original]. But perhaps it is high time that we do just that."[12]

He did not even try to contain the surge of pride as he wrapped up his manuscript and sent it to the press. What had grown out of an assortment of field insights, *petites idées*, and readings, was, he felt, a framework for an intellectual agenda. As the book was about to appear in the fall of 1958, he shared his sense of triumph with his sister, Ursula in Italy. "The reason why I would like to force it on you is that for the first time I have the feeling that I have produced or captured more than just a *petite idée*."[13]

Years later, he reflected on the man he was when he arrived in Colombia. "I looked at 'reality' without theoretical preconceptions of any kind." When Hirschman returned to the United States almost five years later, he discovered that "I had acquired a point of view" – one that was at odds with orthodoxies forged in American universities. While playful, this claim to self-enlightenment can be misleading. Hirschman was hardly an ingenue when it came to markets and hidden springs of change. The frustrations as a Marshall Planner hardened his skepticism of ideological formulae in the drag of abstract theories. What made the Colombian experience so distinctive was proximity: observing so closely, and for enough time, the process and effects of the decisions of which he was a part. The art of learning from doing and then watching closely, a sensibility already encoded from Colorni, Machiavelli, and Montaigne's personal tutorials, accented his fascination with small things and routine behavior; it would become a cornerstone of a disposition that Colombia brought to fruition though it seldom got the credit.

NOTES

1. http://www.historytoday.com/blog/2014/03/big-back-return-public-history
2. http://www.joguldi.com/. For a quick sample of the problem, Guldi now claims to be working on global land reform movements, from 19th century Ireland

to modern-day Chennai. It's a fascinating project. But of course, the spear-carriers in Brazil are not the Movimiento sin Tierra (which is Spanish) but the Movimento Sem Serra. Portuguese. But I guess in the big scheme of things, language doesn't matter much anymore either.

3. https://school.bighistoryproject.com/bhplive; at the bottom of the landing page, you can watch Bill Gates gush with excitement about his discovery.

4. Albert O. Hirschman Papers, Princeton University Library, Seeley Mudd Manuscript Library (hereafter AOHP), "The Market for Pulp and Paper in Colombia," June 15, 1956, Box 37, f. 2.

5. AOHP, Research Project, Case Studies of Instances of Successful Economic Development in Colombia, March 8, 1954, Box 36, f. 4.

6. Hirschman Personal Papers in possession of Katia Salomon (hereafter PP), Albert O. Hirschman-George Jaszi, undated letter 1954.

7. Interview Sarah Hirschman, August 23, 2007.

8. PP, Albert O. Hirschman-Katia Solomon, October 13, 1975.

9. PP, Albert O. Hirschman-Ursula Hirschmann, March 23, 1966.

10. PP, Albert O. Hirschman-Ursula Hirschmann, January 27, 1958.

11. AOHP, Strategy Notes, File 2, Box 80, f. 16.

12. AOHP, "The Economics of Development Planning," Institute on ICA Development Programming, 5/15/59, Strategy Notes, File 2, Box 80, f. 16. This would later appear as the preface of the 1961 paperback edition.

13. PP, Albert O. Hirschman-Ursula Hirschmann, August 23, 1958.

REFERENCES

Adelman, J. (2013). *Worldly philosopher: The Odyssey of Albert O. Hirschman*. Princeton, NJ: Princeton University Press.

Armitage, D., & Guldi, J. (2014). *The history manifesto*. New York, NY: Cambridge University Press.

Banfield, E. C. (1958). *Moral basis of a backward society*. New York, NY: Free Press.

Boucheron, P. (2008). *Léonard et Machiavel*. Paris: Éditions Verdier.

de Montaigne, M. (1987). *Essays*. London: Penguin.

Fukuyama, F. (Summer, 1989). The End of History? The National Interest.

Fukuyama, F. (1992). *The end of history and the last man*. New York, NY: Free Press.

Geertz, G. (1985). From the native's point of view: On the nature of anthropological understanding. In Geertz (Ed.), *Local knowledge: Further essays in interpretive anthropology* (pp. 55–71). New York, NY: Basic Books.

Gilman, G. (2003). *Mandarins of the future: Modernization theory in cold war America*. Baltimore, MD: Johns Hopkins University Press.

Hirschman, A. O. (1945). *National power and the structure of foreign trade*. Los Angeles, CA: University of California Press.

Hirschman, A. O. (1957). Economic policy in underdeveloped countries. *Economic Development and Cultural Change*, *4*, 362–370.

Hirschman, A. O. (1958). Economics and investment planning: Reflections based on experience in Colombia. In Hirschman (Ed.), *The strategy of economic development* (pp. 41–61). New Haven, CT: Yale University Press.

Hirschman, A. O. (1971). *A bias for hope: Essays on development and Latin America* (pp. 41–62). New Haven, CT: Yale University Press.

Machiavelli, N. (1975). *The prince*. London: Penguin Books.

Montaigne, M. d. (1987). *The complete essays* New York, NY: Penguin.

Najemy, J. M. (1994). *Between friends: Discourses of power and desire in the Machiavelli-Vettori letters of 1513–1515*. Princeton, NJ: Princeton University Press.

Said, E. (1978). *Orientalism*. New York, NY: Vintage.

Schumacher, E. F. (1973). *Small is beautiful: A study of economics as if people mattered*. New York, NY: Blond and Briggs.

Whitehead, A. N. (1929). *Process and reality*. New York, NY: Macmillan.

THE CONTEMPORARY SIGNIFICANCE OF A DISSENTER: ALBERT O. HIRSCHMAN'S IDEA OF DEVELOPMENT

Andrea Ginzburg

ABSTRACT

As Hirschman wrote of himself in an essay of 1984, he was a dissenter. The paper focuses on three dimensions of this dissent. Dissent from orthodoxy, in the first place, even if his stance rarely assumed the feature of a frontal opposition. His distance from mainstream economics clearly emerges in the contrast between growth and development, here exemplified through a comparison of Solow's and Hirschman's conceptions. Second, dissent from heterodoxy: from Nurkse, Rosenstein Rodan and the balanced growth theory, but also a distance from the kind of economic theorizing recently exemplified by Krugman's critical appraisal of Hirschman's contribution. Third, a dissent from Hirschman himself. He developed a practice defined as "self-subversion" to convey the meaning of a self-critical dialogue with his own positions. In this context, two examples will be discussed, namely his critical reappraisal of the dependency theory, to which Hirschman as a young man contributed indirectly,

Research in the History of Economic Thought and Methodology, Volume 34B, 63–90

ISSN: 0743-4154/doi:10.1108/S0743-41542016000034B005

and his after-thoughts on the choice between sequential or simultaneous strategies. Hirschman's reflections on the last theme appear relevant to address the problems of current Eurozone crisis: its roots may be traced back to the faulty construction of the Monetary Union, which in turn largely stemmed from the misplaced confidence in the "automatism" of the sequence Monetary Union-Fiscal Union-Political Union.

The paper's contention is that Hirschman's "possibilism," often mentioned, is not the result of a generic psychological propensity to optimism but stems from analytical observations and penetrating critical analysis of received ideas or categories, of other authors or of Hirschman himself.

Keywords: Growth; development; unbalanced growth; linkages; dependency theory; Eurozone crisis

INTRODUCTION

Hirschman's writings are intended to provide a grammar for the perception of change. They are intended to free us from "mental cages" that constitute obstacles to the comprehension of reality. These obstacles are also impediments to taking action aimed at eliminating unacceptable situations of distress. Their removal allows us to seize opportunities previously neglected, to construct non-rhetorical confrontations, to start constructive dialogues. There is a relation between his idea of development, the possibility to modify social agents' attitudes through social practices and experiences, and democracy: the removal of "conceptual cages" opens up new possibilities of intervention on reality and of establishing new bases for a democratic dialogue. Hirschman offers some devices to escape from these "constructs-cages" that propose absolute obstacles, inescapable sequences, imaginary dilemmas. Hirschman's "possibilism," often mentioned, sometimes described in a banalized and cloying way, is not the result of a generic psychological propensity to optimism but stems from analytical observations and penetrating critical analysis of received ideas or categories, of other authors or of Hirschman himself.

As he wrote in an essay of 1984,[1] Hirschman was a dissenter. In fact, his dissent was threefold. Dissent from orthodoxy, in the first place, even if his stance rarely assumed the features of a frontal opposition. Here, I will outline the contrast between growth and development as exemplified by the distance between Solow's and Hirschman's conceptions. Second, dissent from heterodoxy (from Nurkse, Rosenstein Rodan and the balanced growth theory but also, to quote a more recent contrast, a distance from the kind of economic theorizing exemplified by Krugman's critical appraisal of Hirschman's contribution). Third, a dissent from Hirschman himself. He developed a practice defined as "self-subversion" to convey the meaning of a self-critical dialogue with his own positions. In this context, two examples will be discussed, namely his critical reappraisal of the dependency theory, to which Hirschman as a young man contributed indirectly, and his after-thoughts on the choice between sequential or simultaneous strategies. Hirschman's reflections on the last theme appear, in my opinion, relevant to address the problems of current Eurozone crisis: its roots may be traced back to the faulty construction of the Monetary Union, which in turn largely stemmed from the misplaced confidence in the "automatism" of the sequence Monetary Union-Fiscal Union-Political Union.

Can these three dissents help us to understand our current development problems?

DISSENT FROM ORTHODOXY

In addition to several essays, Hirschman's contributions to the theme of development are contained in three books, which, as he wrote in 1995,[2] with hindsight have gone on to compose "a unified trilogy." The three books (*The Strategy of Economic Development*, *Journeys towards Progress*, and *Development Projects Observed*), written respectively in 1958, 1963, and 1967,[3] reflect *all* his field observations (the first in Colombia, the second in Latin America, and the third in Asia, Africa and Southern Europe, including the Italian Mezzogiorno). Recalling that these reflections on development start out from observation, I wish to mention the sentence from Whitehead chosen as an epigraph to *Strategy*, a sentence that sounds pretty provocative vis-à-vis the deductivist approach often adopted by economic science: "the elucidation of immediate experience is the only justification for any thought, and the starting point of thought is the analytic observation of this experience" (cf., Hirschman, 1958/1961, p. vii).

One year before the publication of *Strategy*, Solow had published a famous article on "Technical progress and aggregate growth."[4] With the benefit of hindsight, we can say that this article has come to exert a pervasive influence on how to interpret growth in both developed and underdeveloped (or emerging) economies and on the design of policy interventions.

The triumphant twin concepts of "Growth accounting" and "Total Factor Productivity" (a quick measure of efficiency) offer a ready-made toolkit to be applied to both groups of countries, a neat example of "armchair economics" (the differences, if any, are traced back to institutional differences, considered more or less pro-market). In the mid-1950s, however, attempts were made to build a sub-discipline of economics, the theory of development, to address the specific problems of developing countries (DCs). But 25 years later the hopes of renewal had vanished: in 1981 Hirschman published an article entitled "The rise and decline of development economics,"[5] where the decline of the sub-discipline was attributed both to changes in the historical setting and to ideological conflicts. Among the former, the diversification within the developing countries' group, in contrast with the stereotype of a single ideal type of underdeveloped country. Among the second, concentric attacks from right and left (from orthodox economics and from economists of the *dependencia* school, i.e., Latin American Marxists, including Gunder Frank).

The reabsorption of the sub-discipline within mainstream economic theory was favored also by the attempt to interpret the problems of the developing countries as a special case of a more general pattern. How did developed countries differ from developing countries according to orthodox theory? Productivity is in both cases the key variable for growth. And growth consists in producing *more of the same thing* per unit of labor (or, in general, of factor of production). But, according to orthodox economics, developing countries had problems defined as "structural," which instead were absent in the "developed" countries: that is, they had a relatively larger share of employment in agriculture, where, by hypothesis, labor productivity was lower than that of industry. Growth in developing countries was then due to a reallocation of labor between the two sectors. In the transfer of workers from one sector to another, the average productivity rose, owing to the simple fact that a higher share of relatively more productive workers showed up in the relatively more productive sector.

Defining changes in the sectoral composition of employment as "structural," the conclusion was that "developed" countries did not have structural problems, since the share of labor in industry had stopped increasing. The growth could be then analyzed in terms of an aggregated single composite good, the GDP. "Thus there has been history, but there is no longer any," Marx wrote[6] about the way economists looked at the capitalist economy with respect to previous socio-economic formations. According to Solow (1957), technical progress (not explained, exogenous) falls like manna from heaven and leads to an increase of the aggregate output per worker (or, in more recent models, technical progress is the endogenous outcome of the application of a stock of knowledge, which is supposed to enjoy the properties of cardinality, i.e., to be measurable and additive[7]). In the given circumstances, there is only one viable economic policy: to remove the obstacles to price competitiveness. Competition will take care of coordinating individual decisions, of achieving "fair" prices (equal to marginal costs), and of obtaining full employment and growth. In the assumed one-commodity world with the same production function and exogenous technical progress, the possibility that a developing country could choose its own development path based on product competition instead of price competition is eliminated at the outset.

The orthodox view of growth proposes a fixed pattern, a preordained sequence of stages presented as the best way to growth. This is a special case of modernization theory, in which the most advanced country indicates to the less advanced one the way to reach its higher level of income. This conception of growth can be assimilated to the pre-formist biological theory of the XVII century[8]: the adult animal (i.e., the most advanced country) has already in the embryo, in miniature, the characteristics that it will manifest as an adult, just as a balloon containing scant air appears as a copy in scale of a totally inflated balloon.

The non-orthodox conception of *development* (as opposed to *growth*) is completely different. Rather, it approaches, in some respects, the epigenetic biological theory, in which the adult emerges from the undifferentiated embryo through a series of transformations and differentiations.

In *Strategy*, development is in fact seen as a *transformation* of the space of products obtained through the dynamics of two forces that can operate in a cumulative way: product complementarity and diversification. In the coordination mechanisms, relative prices (except movements in the exchange rate, in some given situations) tend to have a limited role or no role. Hirschman writes: "Development depends not so much on finding optimal combinations for given resources and factors of production, as on calling forth and enlisting for development purposes resources and abilities that are hidden, scattered or badly utilized."[9]

This statement may have been perceived as particularly heterodox in relation to the conceptions of the time because the developing countries' economies, owing to their lack of spare productive capacity, were considered *as if* they were full-employment economies. The main obstacle to development, Hirschman maintains, is not the lack of prerequisites (such as the abundance of savings or, in general, of factors of production, or the absence of rational, maximizing agents), but the inability to take development decisions, whether they relate to investments or to institutional reforms by public and private agents, in the dimensions and timing needed to exploit the existing potentialities in the given situation. In this perspective, economic *and* political forces play the role of endogenous variables (therefore, the idea of an omniscient and apolitical State is rejected).

The decision-making processes are considered as dominated not by the scarcity of factors but by confusion, influenced by ambiguous and contradictory signals and especially by the uncertainty of how to solve, *sequentially*, the many technological, administrative, financial and demand problems associated with the expansion of productive activities. "Development theory and policy therefore face the task of examining under what conditions development decisions can be called forth in spite of these imperfections ... [in the decision-making process] ... through pacing devices or inducement mechanisms." To illustrate the idea of "induced decision making," Hirschman makes use of two analogies. The first concerns the effects on investment and consumption respectively by the accelerator and multiplier (the latter in a situation of cyclical unemployment) (see *Strategy*, pp. 26–27). The second analogy concerns the function of magic observed by Malinowski in a non-industrialized economy like the Trobriand Islands: "The magician, in carrying out the rites, sets the pace, compels people to apply themselves to certain tasks, and to accomplish them properly and in time. There is no doubt that by its influence in ordering and regulating work, magic is economically invaluable" (Malinowski, 1922/1961), *Argonauts of the Western Pacific*, quoted in *Strategy*, p. 149.) Therefore, decisions (particularly investment decisions) can be divided into two groups. On the one hand, the "genuine," autonomous ones subject to uncertain elements, on the other hand, "routinized" decisions that "we feel confident will be taken *because there is some extra pressure behind them* as a result of pacing, routines responses, threatened penalties, certain and high profitability, or other forces" (*Strategy*, p. 27, italics in the original). Since the fundamental bottleneck in developing countries is the "decision making ability," Hirschman is searching for "reasonably effective inducement mechanisms" aimed at maximizing "induced or routinized decision making" in both the private and public realm (i.e., relative to market and non-market forces).

In conclusion, both in highlighting the conditions of "bounded rationality" within which decision-making processes take place and in giving a central role to the activation mechanisms of induction of investment decisions, Hirschman distanced himself in two important points from the marginalist scheme, the postulate of "homo economicus" in possession of a complete knowledge of its environment, and the idea that the level of investment is determined, at the equilibrium interest rate, by the full employment savings rate.

It is no coincidence that the 1958 book bears the title *Strategy* of economic development: it alludes to a sequence of decisions, not to a static equilibrium. Society is not considered as a mechanism, nor as an organism, but as a process.[10] In contrast to functionalism, in which it is believed that the origin can be derived from the function, and the structure thus explained, here structure, process and function interact according to not preordained and non-linear modalities (important here is the lesson of Gerschenkron[11] in criticizing the concept of "prerequisites" to development, and in proposing functional equivalences, inverted sequences, unexpected ways "to turn the corner of history"[12]).

For Hirschman, therefore, development poses a problem of coordination of sequential decisions in a situation of deep uncertainty. In this situation, the "binding agents" that coordinate scattered and missing elements cannot be relative prices (the solution given by Hayek to the lack of centralized information) nor the abstract administrative capacity of an omniscient, centralized State. The "binding agents" considered by Hirschman are the linkages. The production linkages are forces that at the same time generate investments *and* the diversification of products. By a frequent misunderstanding, the linkages are interpreted as registrations ex post of inter-sectoral productive relations. As recognized by Hirschman himself, if on the one hand his reference to the Leontief matrix facilitated the absorption of the concept of linkages in the culture of economists, on the other hand, through this hint, the diachronic dimension was completely lost: in fact this reference proved to be misleading since linkages are forces that generate investment decisions that develop *in time*, driven by bottlenecks and other imbalances. The socio-political and economic pressures induce to perform those upstream and downstream investments that the presence of bottlenecks signals as necessary.

The backward linkages generate investment in the stages preceding the final market (they are investments that fill the need for equipment or inputs in stages located downstream in the supply chain). The forward linkages (connections downstream) generate downstream investment and fill the need for equipment (or, more generally structures such as commercial distribution) that uses downstream products produced upstream in the supply chain.

It may be recalled that even Adam Smith finds a relation between the development of the division of labor in society and the diversity of products. He writes: "It is the great multiplication of the productions of all the different arts, which occasions, in a well-governed society, that universal opulence which extends itself in the lowest ranks of people."[13]

In an important 1977 article, Hirschman proposed a generalization of the idea of linkages in order to consider, in addition to production linkages, consumption linkages (induced consumption such as in the Keynesian multiplier) and fiscal linkages (extraction of revenue from exports of a key product in the economy). In addition, he stressed that linkages could be positive or negative: from this point of view, the development of underdevelopment proposed by Gunder Frank can be reinterpreted as a special case in which negative linkages tend to prevail (they can be considered analogous to expenditures and income leakages in the Keynesian framework). What, then, is development?

"Development is essentially the story of how one thing leads [or fails to lead[14]] to another, and the linkages are that record, from a specific point of view. They focus on certain characteristics inherent in the productive activities already in process at a certain time. These ongoing activities, *because of their characteristics*, push or, more modestly, invite some operators to take up new activities. Whenever that is the case, a linkage exists between the ongoing and the new activity."[15] The linkage pattern may account for the formation of new markets (and not only for the enlargement of existing ones): we may recall that the creation of new markets is one of the most obscure and problematic areas of mainstream theory.

Compared to the forces that in orthodox theory promote growth (productivity and resources' supply), here we are dealing with "weaker" forces that, in a disaggregated perspective, are acting both on the demand and on the supply side. In addition – Hirschman clarifies – the linkages are special "push factors" of private and public investment decisions, which *add* to "the pull of incomes and demand."[16]

As we said, the linkages are associated with a boost to diversification, the process of expanding the range of goods produced. This may involve a higher value-added version of the same goods: firms may sell a product at a higher price for example incorporating different designs, exploring new ways of marketing, enhancing performances. Diversification may also involve producing a wider range of products.[17] The relevance of the distinction between these two dimensions of diversification – vertical, measured by the number of products of different price per category of product, and horizontal, measured by the different number of categories of products – can be highlighted by an empirical observation contained in a recent study by the Economic and Social Commission for Asia and the Pacific (ESCAP).[18] As *per capita* incomes of countries rise, the vertical and horizontal diversifications of exports of various countries occur simultaneously but show an asymmetric behavior. For countries with low *per capita* income, horizontal diversification tends to grow more rapidly than vertical diversification. The limited range of varieties within each category of product implies that in each market competition is predominantly based on price. In the richest countries in terms of *per capita* income, instead, vertical diversification tends to grow while horizontal diversification remains almost constant, suggesting the prevalence of competition based on quality rather than on price.

On this issue, we can remember the famous sentence of Schumpeter:

> As soon as quality competition and sales effort are admitted into the sacred precincts of theory, the price variable is ousted from its dominant position ... This kind of competition is as much more effective than the other as a bombardment is in comparison to the forcing of a door, and so much more important that it becomes a matter of comparative indifference whether competition in the ordinary sense functions more or less promptly; the powerful lever that in the long run expands output and brings down prices is in any case made of other stuff.[19]

A research strategy carried out by two Harvard economists, Hidalgo and Hausmann,[20] referred openly to Hirschman's ideas in proposing a "Network View of Development." Starting from a measure of connection or proximity between the goods exported by each country, these authors have replaced scalar aggregate metrics – such as GDP per capita, physical capital per worker, human capital measured in school years – with the search for *patterns of complementarity* between products, countries and capabilities, all described in great detail. Here, as in Hirschman, development does not consist in the accumulation of some form of capital stock (physical, social, human), but in the coordination and organization around heterogeneous products of a plurality of skills that also are heterogeneous.[21]

The return to the concept of "linkages" has enabled important evidence of some Hirschman's insights to be found: the description of development as a history of different linkage constellations, or the idea of the greater difficulty in developing production linkages in the presence of "strangeness" or "alienness" of new activities, and this opens up a space for State intervention to reduce the "distance" between products, the characterization of underdevelopment as absence of product diversification, and thus also as lack of product complexity, and so on.

DISSENT FROM HETERODOXY

Given his biography, Hirschman can be inserted in the cohort of Italian anti-fascist economists who drew from observation of the fascist economy's mode of functioning a strong aversion to the despotic use of bureaucratic power and privilege, and more generally to excessively invasive State intervention in the economy. As Paolo Baffi clarified,[22] these economists also developed a deep mistrust of Keynes's conceptions, which they identified with protectionist policies closely associated, in turn, with Nationalism.[23] Hirschman accepted Keynes's hypothesis on the existence of slack, defined as "hidden, scattered or badly utilised resources," and generalized it to the long period development processes, but he also took seriously[24] some aspects of Hayek's premises on the limits of centralized state planning as stated in the *Road to Serfdom*. These premises, inserted in a quite different analytical framework, generated in turn very different policy solutions from those advocated by Hayek: an example of Hegelian sublation (*Aufhebung*) by a dialectical thinker as Hirschman.[25]

The kind of heterodoxy that emerged in the 1950s among development economists was anyway far from Keynesian. In the mid-1950s, Rosenstein Rodan and Nurkse proposed a substantially similar strategy to address the issue of imparting a "big push" to development in an economy considered immobile and "indifferent": the strategy of balanced[26] growth. The proposal was simultaneously to actuate numerous production activities in order to obtain two advantages: to achieve, through a "push" from above, significant economies of scale and to solve the problem of demand (the broadening of supply would automatically also take care of demand through the formation of mutual market outlets: behind this formulation Say's principle can be detected). For Hirschman, the idea of balanced growth contains a paradox. On the one hand, the economy is assumed immobile and indifferent to change, on the other hand, these economists are willing to implement the ambitious plan to start development on a broad front, and this would require massive doses of entrepreneurial skills. It is necessary instead to economize the scarcest resource: the lack of decision-making ability. Hence the need to give course to disequilibriating "pressure mechanisms," starting from the identification of development bottlenecks. Initial autonomous decisions would in time trigger sequences of induced decisions, upstream and downstream along the supply chain, but also horizontally in the productive matrix (lateral linkages include the "general purposes" goods).

Among these sequences, we may expect some to be more stringent than others: for example, the backward linkages upstream tend to be relatively more binding than the forward ones, and the linkages related to productive investments more stringent than those related to infrastructures[27] (that may fail, by themselves, to promote industrialization, as for instance – I may add – the experience of public intervention in the Italian Mezzogiorno has shown).

The "pressure mechanisms" enacted by the unbalanced development strategy mainly focus on three areas: they turn on new resources and new decision-making capacity, they activate learning mechanisms stimulated by problem-solving activities, they contribute to reduce, at least in part, the areas of uncertainty and this, in turn, may trigger new initiatives. On the latter point, on which I shall return later, an important example is provided by the information signals emitted by the presence of imports, for instance the import of a consumer good: they reveal the presence of a market for that good and this may encourage entrepreneurs to start an activity with greater confidence. This import substitution activity may be oriented at a later time to activate new export flows.

It must be stressed that all the analytical devices and the intervention measures proposed by Hirschman (unbalanced development, backward and forward linkages, import induced development, latitude of performances, etc.) are at the same time inducement mechanisms *and* learn ing devices.

The pressure mechanisms activate learning through the activation of problem-solving abilities. For, in the gradual transformation of behaviors great importance is given to the inducement of actions, that is social practices directed toward change. A change in beliefs and attitudes follows the action, rather than precedes it. For this reason Schön (1994, p. 68) has linked the name of the Great Russian social psychologist Vigotsky to that of Hirschman. For the latter, the theory of development is also a theory of decentralized social learning. Rather than a real learning theory, argues Schön, we are faced with a "generative metaphor," given Hirschman's reluctance to put his ideas in rigid frames, preferring revisable and open formulations in order to take into account variable historical circumstances. For Schön, Hirschman's idea is to use "naturally occurring or artificially induced disequilibria to trigger social learning" (*ibid.*, p. 71), often exploiting in a constructive way apparent obstacles or hidden rationalities.[28] The same principle of social learning underpins the criteria that Hirschman proposes for granting international aid to developing countries: instead of imposing abstract and universal, externally conceived conditionality criteria, the combination of shared programs and social learning can "help people to help themselves" (Ellerman, 2005, pp. 210–213), achieving longer lasting and more sustainable results (according to the well-known formula, "it is more effective to teach to fish, than provide fish").

In the conceptions of orthodox economists, competition is "the all-powerful social institution bringing pressures for efficiency. Strangely and somewhat inconsistently, some of these economists seem intent on granting competition a monopoly in this field."[29] But competitive pressure is often very weak, and this explains the search for additional mechanisms that "would force" a society to be efficient. Hence the proposal (a provocative proposal with respect to the theory that prevails among economists) that developing countries apply higher capital intensity techniques leaving little room for poor performances. The recognition of the limits of competition goes hand in hand with the awareness of the limits of centralized planning. Hirschman's dissent with respect to the latter recalls some Hayekian themes: the existence of uncertainty precludes the formulation of large centralized plans, the importance of distributed knowledge redeems, against the abstract and illusory centralism, the concreteness of a priori unpredictable individual initiatives. But the activation of decentralized automatisms leading to save the scarce resource – the ability to make decisions – cannot be delegated to the competitive mechanism; it should be entrusted to the public initiative with a central plan "*point of view*," which means a responsibility toward detecting and managing the critical linkages that are blocking the development of the whole economy. In a paper written jointly with Lindblom, Hirschman clarifies his position versus his co-author (and also to balanced growth exponents and Hayek):

> Hirschman's cautions about centralism only secondarily refer to general difficulties of managing complex affairs that strain man's incentives and intellectual capacities. Instead he argues that a conventional, centrally planned attempt to define and achieve a balance *among varied lines of development* will be less helpful than a *similarly central attempt* to estimate and manage the critical linkages through which economic growth is forced or induced. Hirschman's explicitly declared view of decision making for economic development is almost entirely one of central planning, problem solving or at least by persons – such as planning board or managers officials of international agencies – *who assume some responsibility toward the general economy as a whole*, and therefore *whose point of view is that of a central planner*.[30]

One example of the difficulty of those economists whose culture is patterned on the natural sciences to understand Hirschman's conceptions comes from Paul Krugman's intervention in a conference organized in 1992 by the Department of Architecture at MIT to discuss Hirschman's contribution to development theory and policy. Krugman (1994) argued that Hirschman has contributed to the decline of development economics by not having been able, at the time, to formalize in a mathematically rigorous model his insights on development strategy: these were formulated in qualitative terms by narratives and in "situation-specific" terms (this was considered a beyond-repair limit). According to Krugman, the "core insights" pioneered by Rosenstein Rodan and Hirschman were based on the recognition that "self-reinforcing growth in poor countries depends on the ability to create the size of the market necessary to make possible economies of scale" (Rodwin, 1994, p. 10). (According to Krugman, it was irrelevant to make a distinction between the above-mentioned authors, though we know that at the time their conceptions were fiercely opposed.) To demonstrate that the ideas of the pioneers could have been fully embodied in economic discipline and not relegated to the margins, if only they had received a formalized representation, Krugman presents a model (adapted from Murphy, Shleifer, & Vishny, 1989) that exhibits increasing returns to scale.[31] According to this model, an individual entrepreneur's decision to shift to modern production is rational when investments in the modern sector can afford the higher wage required to draw labor from traditional activities. The likelihood of meeting the thresholds required for establishing new markets and expanding activities is shown to be greater when all modern firms expand simultaneously than when an individual entrepreneur is the only one to modernize. According to Krugman, this formalization[32] shows "how a low-level trap can arise with rational entrepreneurs, full information – and a whiff of reference to cultural influences, or problems of information and learning" (p. 56). "The model is so simple – Krugman concludes – three pages, two equations and one diagram ... What would have happened to development economics, even to economics in general, if someone had *legitimized* the role of increasing returns and circular causation with a neat model thirty-five year ago?" (p. 57, emphasis added).

Krugman's essay should be read more as a contribution to understanding the "ego-oriented" way of thinking of the author than to demonstrate the easy translatability of Hirschman's ideas into a formalized language. It is also revealing of the circumstances that determine the legitimization of economists in the community,[33] and of the confusion between reality, theory, and model, three terms that must be kept carefully distinct. He places himself among those who "try to understand the world through the metaphors provided by models" (p. 58). But theory, that in some way arises from the attempt to understand reality, is always much richer than a model that formalizes and focuses only on some particular aspect of the theory. In not taking this difference between theory and model into account, Krugman provides a formalized representation that ignores the premises and the basic features of Hirschman's theoretical contribution: pervasive uncertainty and lack of capacity in taking investment decisions, criticism of "atomistic" dualism (where the "traditional" and the "modern" sector have no connection, whereby the second rises entirely from scratch), critique of the illusory and abstract models of Rosenstein Rodan and Nurkse, unbalanced development and positive and negative linkages, learning by problem solving, etc.

In an interesting contribution to the 1994 volume that collected the contributions at the MIT Conference (Rodwin & Schön, 1994), Donald Schön emphasized *inter alia* that also the model presented by Krugman implicitly calls learning problems into question: the time and ways concerning the decision to take the path of modernization involve processes that require learning, such as the preparation and implementation of the project, increased productivity and the ability to exploit the potential benefits of economies of scale. Instead, in the model the transition from tradition to modernity is instantaneous, and this is equivalent to considering economic variables as "revealed" proxies of the happy *result* of learning efforts, but this is equivalent to eliminating the learning problem at its root, as is customary among economists. The price paid for this elimination, says Schön, is the inability to explain the different development experiences of different countries and the difficulties involved in choosing among alternative investment projects – two themes that obviously occupied a central place in Hirschman's reflection.

On development issues, remarkable similarities with the ideas of Hirschman can be found in the "Flying Geese Model of Economic Development" originally developed in the 1930s by the Japanese economist economist Akamatsu, and enriched by him with new elaborations in English in the early 1960s (Akamatsu 1961, 1962). This model has played a significant role in interpreting and perhaps also promoting Japan's development, and has subsequently been extended by other authors to analyze the take-off of other Asian economies, including, after the Four Tigers, China. It may be interesting to recall here that Akamatsu refers to the possibility that imports signal the existence of a market, extant or potential, to the firms of a latecomer country. Imports activate a sequence of adaptive innovation through imitation and adaptation, upgrading and export. Export markets set the production standards and focalize the efforts of domestic producers. (For a similar idea, see Hirschman's observations in *Strategy*, p. 99.) The proximity of the Flying Geese model with some of Hirschman's ideas in the field of the analysis of development processes, in particular the idea of unbalanced development, is recalled in Akamatsu's (1961) article. The original version of the "Flying Geese Model" proposed by the Japanese economist differs fundamentally from the subsequent interpretations in the neoclassical framework and Raymond Vernon's product cycle theory. The differences include the role of linkages in economic development, the effects of supply and demand, the role of learning in the upgrading process, as well as the dynamic and dialectical character of Akamatsu's thinking.[34] Later reformulations of the "Flying Geese model" that attempted to combine aspects of Akamatsu's theory with neoclassical thinking introduced a number of unnecessary assumptions together with the removal of Akamatsu most original insights.[35]

DISSENT TOWARD HIMSELF

Hirschman's self-criticism toward his proto-*dependencia* theory is interesting per se, but it also sheds light on some more general methodological aspects of his thought. This self-criticism figures in the article "Beyond asymmetry: critical notes on myself as a young man and some other old friends." Originally published in 1978, it was published again in 1980 as a preface to the reprint of his important book of 1945, *National Power and the Structure of Foreign Trade*.[36] In this book, the expansion of Nazi influence on the Eastern and Southern European countries was attributed not to a diabolical but to a *normal* ability to exploit foreign trade opportunities, and in particular the threat of trade interruption[37] as a pressure instrument on poor and smaller countries (hence the asymmetry of the title).[38] The book had been considered in the 1970s as a forerunner of the theory of *dependencia*, which attributes the stagnation of developing countries exclusively to external causes, namely the asymmetrical power relationships between center and periphery. This asymmetry is shown in a series of circumstances: developed countries specialize in activities with greater value added, while developing countries are mono-specialized in raw materials, often under-paid, or in lower value-added activities, and are often hampered by unfavorable terms of trade, etc. But the analysis – Hirschman writes – stopped too early. While he was writing *Strategy*, Hirschman jotted down this sentence by Kafka that appears relevant in this context: "All human error is impatience, a premature breaking-off of methodical procedure, an apparent fencing in of what is apparently at issue." At the time of writing *National Power*, this further question was not raised[39]: "How solid or stable is the resulting relation of domination and dependency?" There is indeed "the possibility of a dialectical movement" that attenuates the original asymmetry (*ibid*., p. 31).

The "basic economic disparity [of the center towards the periphery] generates a disparity of *attention* [...] and this disparity now favours the *dependent* country; that country is likely to pursue its escape from domination more actively and energetically than the dominant country will work on preventing this escape" (*ibid*., p. 30). "Any theory" – Hirschman pointed out in another essay – "dismissing or ignoring one of the possible courses events may take, selects its own blindspot."[40] So *every theory* introduces a premature interruption of methodical procedures.

The analysis should instead continue: "The failure to discover the countertendencies [...] must be attributed to an intellectual orientation that is both undialectical and what I would call antipossibilist. For many of the countertendencies that can be discovered are possibilities rather than certainties, and social scientists often consider it beneath their scientific dignity to deal with possibility until *after* it has become actual and can at least be redefined as a probability."[41]

In regard to the mistakes that one can make when prey to "anxiety for change" Hirschman mentions, in another context, in a somewhat provocative way, a sentence written by Lenin in 1920, which states: "Revolutionaries sometimes try to prove that there is absolutely no way out of a crisis [for the ruling class].This is a mistake. There is no such thing as an absolutely hopeless situation."[42]

The instruments used by Hirschman in the fight against the blindspots of the analysis are essentially threefold:

(1) the effort to silence ourselves and to let things and others speak by themselves, as different from us, fighting anthropomorphism, that is the unreflective projection of our needs and our illusions, often generous but deceitful. In this mental orientation, and in the anti-metaphysical fight against "closed" systems of thought, deep – I would say omnipresent – has been the influence of Eugenio Colorni,[43] Hirschman's brother-in-law, a philosopher with interests in epistemology and the history of science, engaged in the anti-fascist struggle, killed by the fascists a few days before the liberation of Italy;

(2) the dialectical orientation in an open conceptual system. This orientation was influenced by the reading as a young man of Hegel's *Phenomenology of Spirit*, and by the analysis of counter-tendencies in Marx. The dialectic here has no metaphysical implications[44]: it implies the adoption of a processual perspective, the revaluation of the negative as the spring of change, attention to the bi-directional nature of relationships, the importance of the transformation of quantity into quality, the interaction between economic and political forces, the recognition of the difficulty of prediction given the large number of forces and counter-tendencies (the affinity of the theoretical perspective of Hirschman with that adopted by some recent strands of complexity theory should not be considered as accidental);

(3) the reduction of the scale of the analysis (this practice, too, is a way to escape from the grand, inevitably teleological philosophy of history). Important here is the influence of Simmel's conceptions. To look at unbalanced growth means "to look at the dynamics of the development process *in the small*."[45] The intent to bring out from the minute and specific characteristics of products and of their technology forms of political and social relations[46] may suggest a translation on a small scale of the relationship between productive forces and relations of production. It can thus be considered a form of Marxism on a small scale (in fact Hirschman defines micro-marxism the analysis of the constellation of linkages that describe development, or explain underdevelopment).[47] To avoid deterministic interpretations, Hirschman hastens to point out that from the characteristics of products and processes (to which economists pay but scant attention) only *provisional* indications of political and social characteristics can be drawn, since the problem of the scale considered is relevant, and very many economic and political forces and counter-forces become involved in the plot, thus disproving the idea of a simple and univocal relationship between economic structure and political form.

A "self-subversive" theme on which Hirschman's reflection concentrated in his later writings[48] is the risk that a sequence activated to solve a specific problem at a certain point could get stuck, vanishing the positive outcome. The sequence of import substitution in Latin America is a case in point: the transition from the "easy" stage of import substitution of consumer goods may encounter several difficulties when it comes to the more arduous substitution of intermediate goods, and especially of capital goods.[49] Another example is the military dictatorship in Argentina established in 1968. To Hirschman's dismay,[50] a supporter of the military junta had boasted about having applied the unbalanced growth theory, arguing that the junta would enact initially measures for growth, then for greater social equity, and finally for a restoration of civil liberties. Here the concept of unbalanced growth is transferred from the differential growth of different sectors of the economy to the differential advancement between different areas of social life, namely between economic and political progress. But in this domain – Hirschman observed, "a strengthening of democracy can go hand in hand with a weakening of the economy" and vice versa.

"There is no *general* reason – Hirschman points out[51] – why these various good things should necessarily go together except for the fact that we wish it were so," an example of an anthropomorphic projection of our desires on reality. In a different form, Hirschman writes, this risk can also occur in the progression of the social conquests sketched by the English sociologist T. H. Marshall: from individual liberties to universal suffrage and on to welfare state policies. A society that has distinguished itself in promoting individual liberties is likely to experience special difficulties in subsequently establishing comprehensive social welfare policies: the insistence on individual achievement and responsibility so favorable in the first phase may be a hindrance when a communitarian ethos and solidarity must be stressed.[52] Compared to the unbalanced growth theory, in which the sequence is induced by the interdependence of the elements of the economic matrix that is under construction, here there is a specific difficulty: in the progression of social conquests we often encounter the claim that "the proposed change, though perhaps desirable in itself, involves unacceptable costs or consequences"[53]: for instance the achievements in the field of welfare, being considered as an interference with the "market" – as Hayek (1944) argued in *The Road to Serfdom* and elsewhere – could undermine the achievements in the field of individual and democratic liberties. This argument, that Hirschman calls "rhetoric of jeopardy" – in addition to two other forms of "Reactionary Rhetoric," the futility and perversity thesis[54] – would pose important obstacles to the deployment of the sequence of the social conquests envisaged by T. H. Marshall. In this case, Hirschman notes, it is assumed that there is no *interdependence* among rights. These rights, functions, tasks are *even too much separable* from each other.[55] Given these obstacles, concludes Hirschman, the "all at once" solution rather than the sequential one would be preferable.

It is tempting to apply these Hirschman's considerations on the presence or absence of interdependence between the elements of a sequence to the problems encountered in the construction of a fully integrated Europe. We may recall that at the end of the 1980s countries belonging to the European Monetary System had to face the choice of whether to build the European Union through a simultaneous solution (removal of controls on capital movements, monetary and fiscal union, political union) or undertake a sequential way that would have started with the liberalization of capital movements, followed by monetary union and, lastly, the other stages. Several economists, including the authors of the MacDougall Report, had warned of the danger of getting stuck in the early stages.

It duly happened. The trust in automatism in the successive phases of the sequence was clearly misplaced. The phases are *separable* because the costs of the failure to complete the sequence are not uniformly allocated among the countries. The rhetoric of "jeopardy" of the creditor countries' achievements if the debtor countries were put in a condition to repay their debts through growth has, today, become more and more insistent, such as to dominate the press organs and public opinion, even in a period of synchronized austerity measures. This is, of course, the price that must be paid for the mistake of having designed the architecture of European institutions on monetarist bases. But it is also the price to be paid for having optimistically believed that the transfer of sovereignty over some areas would automatically trigger a sequence of successive enlargements of the supranational sphere, with the gradual extinction of sovereign states. As history itself and the studies by Stanley Hoffmann (1966/1995) and, above all, by Alan Milward (1992)[56] have shown, this neo-functionalist conception[57] (which could be called a modern version of the thesis of *doux commerce*[58]) rests on very fragile foundations. Contrary to the neo-functionalist thesis, there is no contradiction between well-delimited transfers of sovereignty over some areas, and asymmetric strengthening of national states, which can also be reached through supranational institutions. The resources freed up in a sector (monetary, agricultural, R&D, international trade negotiations, etc.) can be directed to an even *greater asymmetric recovery* of sovereignty and national power in other fields. At a certain point, during the recent European crisis, it became clear that there has been a substantial reshuffle in the distribution of intra-European sovereign powers (increased German leadership, weakening of France and crisis in Southern European countries).

In the "Beyond Asymmetry" essay mentioned above, in which Hirschman took a distance from his youthful position, he writes that in the 1945 book, having in various ways spoken of dependency, domination, and ability to influence countries through foreign trade, he abruptly concluded by invoking a *deus ex machina*, that is the "in retrospect infinitely naïve proposals" (Hirschman 1978/1981, p. 28) to arrive at "an internationalization of the power arising from foreign trade."[59] But in the preceding pages of the 1945 book he had developed arguments well away from any neo-functionalist sentimentality. He had recalled that the first supporters of international trade liberalization had speculated that the political and power aspects of trade would be efficiently *neutralized* by a universal free trade system (an anticipation of the themes later developed in *The Passions and the Interests*). But he added[60]: "... the conditions which were supposed to lead to a neutralization of the power aspects of international economic relations are not merely "unrealistic," but entirely fantastic. They presuppose, indeed, a multitude of states of approximately equal importance each with approximately the same volume of foreign trade, the trade of each country being spread equally over all other countries and no country possessing a monopoly with respect to any peculiar skill or natural endowment. In such a world there would be no special need to guard against the offensive weapons of national economic sovereignties. If universal free trade could give reality to this world, it would undoubtedly be the solution to the problem. Actually, the division of the world into big and small, rich and poor political units combined with the fact that the poor and small countries trade but little among themselves renders this solution completely impracticable."

Hirschman's conclusion was that: "Approximation to the free trade principle, which is by no means tied up necessarily with the institutions of private enterprise,[61] remains a goal for which, despite all the difficulties of realization, it is important to strive for on the grounds of economic welfare. But if the case for free trade, on economic or welfare grounds, has remained unanswerable since Adam Smith and Ricardo, our analysis shows that it does not have the additional merit of doing away with the political aspect of international economic relations."

Both the current global economic crisis in the West and the crisis of the "single thought" urge us to rethink in-depth previous tools of analysis, in the direction of giving adequate account of the complexity of social processes and of their changes (not necessarily in a positive direction). In this endeavor, Hirschman's approach, with his strongly anti-determinist stance, seems particularly timely. Taking advantage of his deeply critical rethinking of the standard relation between economics and politics that, with its trust in economic automatisms, historically brought about political disasters, it is possible to conceive and construct intervention policies more respectful of democratic processes and of the historical specificity of individual countries. Paraphrasing his strategy of unbalanced development, we can say that Hirschman's contribution to the theory and policies of development is not only important for the results already achieved but also for the additional "unexpected and open ended" researches and experiments that his perspective may generate.

NOTES

1. See Hirschman (1984).
2. See Hirschman (1995, p. 126). The occasion for this work was provided by the addition of a new preface (1994) to the reprint of Hirschman (1967).
3. See Hirschman (1958, 1963, 1967).
4. See Solow (1957).
5. See Hirschman (1981).
6. Cf., Marx (1847/1963, p. 121) and Marx (1867/1967, p. 81), note 1.

7. Cf., Steedman (2001).

8. Cf., Ellerman (2004). The author emphasizes the similarities between the conceptions of Hirschman on economic development and the ideas proposed by Jane Jacobs on the development of cities. What interests us here is only to note that while Jacobs never mentions Hirschman, some famous phrases of Hirschman (such as the idea that development is "how one thing leads to another") are present almost *verbatim* in Jacobs (1969, pp. 51–63). As recalled by Ellerman, in his well-known article on endogenous growth, Lucas (1988) wrote: "I will be following very closely the lead of Jane Jacobs, whose remarkable book *The Economies of Cities* seems to me mainly and convincingly concerned (although she does not use this terminology) with the external effects of human capital" (p. 37). As in the game of Chinese whispers in which a word is murmured from one child to another, and the final result appears wholly deformed from the initial input, so from Hirschman to Jacobs to Lucas the notion of "linkage" associated with technological and product diversification is downgraded to a more generic "spillover," up to undergo a further transformation in "human capital external effects" so that, in the end, it appears wholly unrecognizable.

9. Cf., Hirschman (1958/1961, p. 5). In the above-mentioned essay written in 1984/1986, after referring to the convergence of the point of view mentioned in the text with researches carried out on advanced countries by Cyert and March, Simon, Rosenberg and Leibenstein, Hirschman writes. "It appears, therefore, that the very characteristics on which I had sought to build an economics specially attuned to the development countries have a far wider, perhaps even a universal, range and that they define, not a special strategy of development for a well-defined group of countries, but a much more generally valid approach to the understanding of change and growth" (Hirschman, 1984/1986, p. 14). Accepting this point of view, it seems that it is not mainstream economics that declared the death of development economics, but, if anything, quite the opposite.

10. See Stark (1962).

11. See Gerschenkron (1957/1962).

12. See Hirschman (1971, p. 27).

13. Cf., Smith (1776/1910, p. 10).

14. Cf., Hirschman (1986, p. 74).

15. Cf., Hirschman (1977a/1981, p. 75), italics added.

16. *Ibid.*, p. 63.

17. Diversification, the strategy to enter into a new market or industry while also creating a new product for that market, usually requires a company to acquire new skills, new techniques, and new facilities. See Ansoff (1957).

18. ESCAP (2012, pp. 156–158).

19. Cf., Schumpeter (1942/1992, p. 84).

20. See Hidalgo and Hausmann (2008, 2009, 2010).

21. See Hidalgo and Hausmann (2010, p. 131). "Our line of research – Hidalgo and Hausmann (2009, p. 10575) write – would justify and provide guidance to development strategies that look to promote products (or capabilities) as a way to create incentives to accumulate capabilities (or develop new products) that could themselves encourage the further coevolution of new products and capabilities, echoing ideas put forward by Albert O. Hirschman [in *Strategy of Economic*

Development] more than 50 years ago, but adding the capacity to analyze them in practice."

22. Cf., Baffi (1985, p. 13), Hirschman (1984), now in Hirschman (1986, p.6), and Hirschman (1989/1995, p. 145).

23. In Italy, the extension of the Keynesian scheme to foreign trade has made very slow headway, as well as the crucial distinction between Keynesian analysis, namely the principle of effective demand (independence, in a market economy, of investments and full employment savings) and specific policies, not necessarily focused on the expansion of *aggregate* demand. On this distinction, see Ackley (1957) and Garegnani (1962).

24. Adelman (2013, pp. 237–239 and pp. 338–339) recalls that in two important periods of Hirschman' intellectual biography, in 1945 and in the mid-1950s during the writing of *Strategy*, he found in *The Road to Serfdom* arguments against what Adelman describes as "the rage to plan": his dissent "gave way to a broader cautionary position about the role of governments as mechanisms to rationalize the world" (*ibid.*, p. 339).

25. Hirschman (1995, p. 59), quotes Niels Bohr as arguing that "there are two kinds of truth: the truth of 'simple and clear' statements whose opposite is obviously wrong, and the 'deep truths' whose opposite also contains some truth." In a similar vein, Sen (2004), in occasion of the 60th anniversary of the *The Road to Serfdom*, wrote: "Dialectics is critically important for the pursuit of understanding, and Hayek made outstanding contributions to the dialectics of contemporary economics."

26. According to Hayek (1944/2007, p. 209), "characteristic catchwords, such as the 'balanced economy' which professor Laski now demands for Great Britain, or the 'community consumption' toward which production is to be centrally directed, are bodily taken from the German ideology."

27. On the scepticism towards development strategies based on "purely permissive sequences" like that based on the expansion of "Social Overhead Capital" instead of "Directly Productive Activities," see Hirschman (1958/1961, pp. 83–97).

28. For examples of hidden rationalities, see Hirschman (1984/1986, pp. 9–12).

29. See Hirschman (1984/1986, p. 20).

30. Cf., Hirschman and Lindblom (1962/1971, p. 80), italics added. See also, on the first Monnet plan, Hirschman (1958/1961, p. 205) and Hirschman (1947), quoted in Meldolesi (2014, p. 70).

31. Also for Hirschman, as for Allyn Young, "increasing returns result from economies of specialisation rather than economies of scale as conventionally understood" (due to large-scale production). In Allyn Young's LSE lectures as recorded by his student Nicholas Kaldor, "most of the advantages of increasing returns can be had in an industry *not consolidated* … Rather they are those of increased specialization, those of reorganization, not mere increase in size of the operating units." All quotations from Chandra and Sandilands (2005, pp. 465–466), italics added.

32. It is a supply side model that accepts Rosenstein Rodan's and Nurkse's idea about the automatic satisfaction of Say's principle when the size of the market enables large economies of scale.

33. Ross (1991), in a compelling reconstruction of the intricate interweaving of American exceptionalism and professionalization of economics in the United States,

writes that in the 1920s scientism ultimately prevailed. "Neoclassical economists … found a paradigm, modelled on physical science and presumably rooted in the necessities of nature and human nature, that exempted American experience from history, at least any history other than the track of perpetual liberal progress that could be extrapolated from the paradigm itself" (p. 467).

34. As Hirschman (1971, p. 26), also Akamatsu focuses on sequences based on oscillation and alternation, as opposed to optimal combination. It is worth noting that Akamatsu spent the years 1924–1925 in Germany, attending courses in philosophy at the University of Heidelberg. For Hegel's influence on Akamatsu, among also his "deterministic optimism" see Korhonen (1994, pp. 98–99), Schroeppel and Mariko (2002) and Ginzburg and Simonazzi (2005, p. 1055).

35. According to Schroeppel and Mariko (2002), this reformulation that has become popular in Japan might be explained by the change in Japan's perspective from that of a developing country to that of an advanced country.

36. See Hirschman (1978/1981, 1945/1980).

37. There is no need to stress here the importance, for current international policy issues, of the threat of trade interruption in the context of the geopolitics of energy supply.

38. Quoted in Adelman (2013, pp. 325, 340). See Kafka, *The Blue Octavo Notebooks* in Kafka (1917–1919/2004). Another sentence often quoted by Hirschman is by Flaubert: "La rage de vouloir conclure" (The rage of wanting to conclude), which is equivalent to "The compulsion to theorize" prematurely (see Hirschman, 1970/1971, p. 349, note). But one could also cite an aphorism of Paul Valéry: "metaphysical is the man who talks too early."

39. See Hirschman (1978/1981, p. 29).

40. Cf., Hirschman (1976/1981, p. 175).

41. Cf., Hirschman (1976/1981, pp. 32–33).

42. Cf., Hirschman (1976/1981, p. 176).

43. See the writings collected in Colorni (2009). See also the pages dedicated to Colorni in Hirschman (1987/1995).

44. For example, in an essay in which Hirschman notes the "reversals" that the opposition exit-voice may suffer in concrete situations like the processes that led to the extinction of the German Democratic Republic in 1989, he adds (1995/1997, p. 43, third italics added): "The German language has a peculiar gift for compact verbs, such as *umschlage* and the famous Hegelian *aufheben*, which endow these turnabouts with seeming reality. I deliberately avoided these terms, as they evoke the famous dialectic, the 'negation of negation' and similar mysterious, *if preordained*, processes that dissolve all conflicts and reconcile all opposites." On the one hand, the "dialectical approach" discussed in the text leads to investigating processes not mysterious and, above all, far from preordained. On the other hand, the term "dialectic," in my opinion, must be considered in a historical perspective, in the first 20 years of the twentieth century a group extremely heterogeneous by cultural orientation and political views (such as Antonio Labriola, Gramsci, Lukács, Max Adler, John Dewey) have turned to the dialectic, in the meaning briefly mentioned in the text, *to distance* themselves from the passivity-inducing evolutionism and from the positivist mechanicism of orthodox Marxism. If this historical perspective – and the necessary distinction from the very different use of dialectic

accomplished by Marxism-Leninism – is neglected, the texts of the authors mentioned would be incomprehensible.

45. See Hirschman (1958/1961, p. ix), italics in the original. As Stark wrote about Simmel, "the organicists, with their tendency to play up the social factor, had always seen more than the mechanicists, but even they had been half blind, for they had only investigated those phenomena of human interaction which had become solidified, and not those which were, so to speak, still in solution." Hirschman uses a similar metaphor when he writes (preface to the paperback edition of *Strategy*, (1958/1961, pp. viii–ix): "I propose that we take advantage [of interrelatedness of various economic activities], that we probe into the structure that is holding together these interrelated activities. As in the atom, there is much energy here that can be and *is* in fact being utilized in building up economic development nuclei. *Later on* these nuclei look as though they could never have been separated even for a single instant when in actual fact they might never been assembled had not a sequential solution, i.e. an unbalanced growth sequence been found, by accident, instinct, or reasoned design. To look at unbalanced growth means, in other words, to look at the dynamics of the development process *in the small*" (italics in the text).

46. See Hirschman (1977a/1981, pp. 90–91). Among the researches conducted along these lines, Hirschman quotes, for the period of industrialization in the periphery, works by F. H. Cardoso, G. O'Donnell and J. R. Kurth, while for the period of the staple-based development in the periphery, in addition to the writings of Harold Innis, essays by F. Ortiz Fernandez and R. Guerra y Sànchez are mentioned.

47. It also belongs to the reduction of scale, the choice of the ongoing experience as the starting point of the analysis: a safe anchoring in contrast with abstract prerequisites, predetermined paths, closed systems, and cathartic teleologisms.

48. Cf., Hirschman (1995), introduction, and chapters 2, 3, 17.

49. Cf., Hirschman (1968/1971, p. 85 and ff).

50. Cf., Hirschman (1990/1995, p. 70).

51. The title of the essay is "The case against 'One thing at a time'" (Hirschman, 1990/1995, p. 74).

52. In the 1990 essay, the author was trying to explain the lesser capacity to accept welfare and solidarity values in the United States and England than in the Germany of Bismarck, which did not have a strong liberal tradition. Michael Walzer has recently argued that, in the era of globalization, the rights of citizens are often *opposed* to those of humanity to refuse hospitality to refugees and displaced persons. All the more then the recent U-turn in the German immigration policy, in August 2015, with Chancellor Angela Merkel's resolution to accept refugee immigrants must be considered favorably. Since in Germany the European social model does not appear as an important legacy to be defended, this important but delimited policy change may be considered another instance of the lack of interdependence among *rights*.

53. See Hirschman (1991, p. 81, 110 and ff).

54. According to the futility thesis "the attempt to change is abortive … any alleged change is illusory as the deep structures of society remain wholly untouched" (*ibid.*, p. 43), while the perversity thesis maintains that any "attempt to push society in a certain direction will result in its moving … in the opposite direction" (*ibid.*, p. 10).

55. See, in addition to Hirschman (1990/1995, 1991), also Hirschman (1993/1995).

56. For a discussion of Milward's contribution, cf., Guirao et al. (2012).

57. The neo-functionalist theory, associated with the name of E. B. Haas, suggested that the increasing economic interdependence would gradually lead, through a succession of functional spin-offs, also to a growing institutional and political integration.

58. For the relationship between trade expansion and spread of gentleness (*douceur*) and peace in Montesquieu, see Hirschman (1977b, pp. 60–63). Hirschman identifies in the absence of analysis of the counter-forces at play the error implicit in the vision proposed by Montesquieu and Steuart (*ibid.*, p. 117 and ff.). See also Hirschman (1982/1986) where, after a presentation of four theses on capitalist development, he concludes (p. 135): "it is conceivable that, even at one and the same point in space and time, a simple thesis holds only a portion of the full truth and needs to be complemented by one or several of the others, however incompatible they may look at first sight." "A mature appraisal surely needs to be aware of ... [multiple] ... lines of influence, and the balance is likely to be different in each concrete historical situation" (*ibid.*, pp. 138–139). On the psychological difficulty of the social "scientist" to acknowledge that "contradictory processes may be at work in society" since this may imply the impossibility "to impress the general public by proclaiming some inevitable outcome of current processes," see *ibid.*, p. 139.

59. Cf., Hirschman (1945/1980, p. 80).

60. Cf., Hirschman (1945/1980, pp. 75–76).

61. Here Hirschman inserts a footnote quoting J. Meade, *The economic basis for a durable peace*, London (1940, p. 94). Meade argued that a planned economy could draw from foreign trade the same benefits of a free trade economy if it had chosen to obtain from the exchange with other countries a quantity of goods greater than that obtainable through domestic production. Unlike Hayek, Meade admitted that in a planned economy it would be possible to use a valuation system that would permit calculations of this type.

ACKNOWLEDGMENTS

I wish to thank the editors for helpful comments.

REFERENCES

Ackley, G. (1957). Analisi 'keynesiana' e problemi economici italiani. *Moneta e Credito, 10*(39), 271–292.

Adelman, J. (2013). *Worldly philosopher. The Odyssey of Albert O. Hirschman*. Princeton, NJ: Princeton University Press.

Akamatsu, K. (1961). A theory of unbalanced growth in the world economy. *Weltwirtschaftliches Archiv, 86*, 196–217.

Akamatsu, K. (1962). Historical pattern of economic growth in developing countries. *The Developing Economies*, *1*, 3–25.

Ansoff, I. (1957). Strategies for diversification. *Harvard Business Review*, *35*(5), 112–124.

Baffi, P. (1985). Via Nazionale e gli economisti stranieri. *Rivista di storia economica*, *2*(1), 1–45.

Chandra, R., & Sandilands, R. J. (2005). Does modern endogenous growth adequately represent Allyn Young? *Cambridge Journal of Economics*, *29*, 463–473.

Colorni, E. (2009). *La malattia della metafisica*. Torino: Einaudi.

Economic and Social Commission for Asia and the Pacific (ESCAP). (2012). *Economic and social survey of Asia and the Pacific 2011*. Bangkok: United Nations.

Ellerman, D. (2004). Jane Jacobs on development. *Oxford Development Studies*, *32*(4), 507–521.

Ellerman, D. (2005). *Helping people help themselves: From the world bank to an alternative philosophy of development assistance*. Ann Arbor, MI: University of Michigan Press.

Garegnani, P. (1962). *Il problema della domanda effettiva nello sviluppo economico italiano*. Roma: Svimez.

Gerschenkron, A. (1957). Reflections on the concept of 'Prerequisites' of modern industrialization. *L'industria*, *2*, 357–372; now in Gerschenkron, A. (1962).

Gerschenkron, A. (1962). *Economic backwardness in historical perspective and other essays*. Cambridge, MA: The Belknap Press of Harvard University Press.

Ginzburg, A., & Simonazzi, A. (2005). Patterns of industrialization and the flying geese model: The case of electronics in East Asia. *Journal of Asian Economics*, *15*, 1051–1078.

Guirao, F., Lyinch, F., & Ramirez Pérez, S. M. (Eds.). (2012). *Alan S. Milward and a century of European change*. London: Routledge.

Hayek, F. A. (1944/2007). *The road to serfdom*. London: Routledge.

Hidalgo, C. A., & Hausmann, R. (2008). A network view of economic development. *Developing Alternatives*, *12*(1), 5–10.

Hidalgo, C. A., & Hausmann, R. (2009). The building blocks of economic complexity. *Proceedings of the National Academy of Sciences*, *106*(26), 10570–10575.

Hidalgo, C. A., & Hausmann, R. (2010). Inferring macroeconomic complexity from country-product network data. *AAAI Spring Symposium Series*. Retrieved from http://www.aaai.org/ocs/index.php/SSS/sss10/paper/view/1183

Hirschman, A. O. (1945/1980). *National power and the structure of foreign trade*. Berkeley, CA: University of California Press.

Hirschman, A. O. (1947). France and Italy: Patterns of reconstruction. *Federal Reserve Bulletin*, n. 4.

Hirschman, A. O. (1958/1961). *The strategy of economic development*. New Haven, CT: Yale University Press. [Paperback edition with a new preface].

Hirschman, A. O. (1963). *Journeys toward progress*. New York, NY: Twentieth Century Fund.

Hirschman, A. O. (1967). *Development projects observed*. Washington, DC: The Brookings Institution.

Hirschman, A. O. (1968). The political economy of import-substituting industrialization in Latin America. *The Quarterly Journal of Economics*, *82*(1), 1–32; now in Hirschman, A. O. (1971).

Hirschman, A. O. (1970). The search for paradigms as a hindrance to understanding. *World Politics*, *22*(3), 329–343; now in Hirschman, A. O. (1971).

Hirschman, A. O. (1971). *A bias for hope*. New Haven, CT: Yale University Press.

Hirschman, A. O. (1976). On Hegel, imperialism, and structural stagnation. *Journal of Development Economics*, *3*(1), 1–8; now in Hirschman, A. O. (1981).

Hirschman, A. O. (1977a). A generalized linkage approach to development, with special reference to staples. *Economic Development and Cultural Change*, *25* (Suppl.), 67–98; now in Hirschman, A. O. (1981).

Hirschman, A. O. (1977b). *The passions and the interests: Political arguments for capitalism before its triumph*. Princeton, NJ: Princeton University Press.

Hirschman, A. O. (1978). Beyond asymmetry: Critical notes on myself as a young man and on some other old friends. *International Organization*, *32*(1), 45–50; now in Hirschman, A. O. (1981).

Hirschman, A. O. (1981). *Essays in trespassing. Economics to politics and beyond*. Cambridge: Cambridge University Press.

Hirschman, A. O. (1982). Rival views on market society. *Journal of Economic Literature*, *20*(4),1463–1485; now in Hirschman, A. O. (1986).

Hirschman, A. O. (1984). A dissenter's confession: Revisiting the strategy of economic development. In G. M. Meier & D. Seers (Eds.), *Pioneers in development*. Washington, DC: The World Bank. New York, NY: Oxford University Press; now in Hirschman, A. O. (1986).

Hirschman, A. O. (1986). *Rival views of market society and other recent essays*. New York, NY: Viking.

Hirschman, A. O. (1987). Doubt and Antifascist Action in Italy, 1936–39, Speech held at the Università degli studi di Torino, October; now in Hirschman, A. O. (1995).

Hirschman, A. O. (1989). How the Keynesian revolution was exported from the United States. In P. A. Hall (Ed.), *The political power of economic ideas: Keynesianism across nations*. Princeton, NJ: Princeton University Press; now in Hirschman, A. O. (1995).

Hirschman, A. O. (1990). The case against 'One Thing at a Time'. *World Development*, *18*(8), 1119–1122; now in Hirschman, A. O. (1995).

Hirschman, A. O. (1991). *The rhetoric of reaction. Perversity, futility, jeopardy*. Cambridge, MA: The Belknap Press of Harvard University Press.

Hirschman, A. O. (1993). The rhetoric of reaction – Two years later. *Government and Opposition*, *28*(3), 292–314; now in Hirschman, A. O. (1995).

Hirschman, A. O. (1994). "A Hidden Ambition", new preface to the reprint of id. (1967), also in id. (1995), pp. 127–131.

Hirschman, A. O. (1995). *A propensity to self-subversion*. Cambridge, MA: Harvard University Press.

Hirschman, A. O., & Lindblom, C. E. (1962). Economic development, research and development, and policy making: Some converging views; now in Hirschman, A. O. (1971).

Hoffmann, S. (1966). Obstinate or obsolete? The fate of the nation-state and the case of Western Europe. *Dædalus*, *95*(3), 862–915; now in Hoffmann, S. (1995), *The European Sisyphus: Essays on Europe 1964-1994*, Westview Press, Oxford, pp. 71–106.

Jacobs, J. (1969). *The economy of cities*. New York, NY: Vintage Books.

Kafka, F. (1917–1919/2004). *The blue octavo notebooks*. Boston, MA: Exact Change.

Korhonen, P. (1994). The theory of flying geese pattern of development and its interpretations. *Journal of Peace Research*, *31*(1), 93–108.

Krugman, P. (1994). The fall and rise of development economics. In L. Rodwin & D. Schön (Eds), 1994.

Lucas, R. E. (1988). On the mechanics of economic development. *Journal of Monetary Economics*, *22*, 3–42.
Malinowski, B. (1922/1961). *Argonauts of the Western Pacific*. New York, NY: Dutton.
Marx, K. (1847/1963). *The poverty of philosophy*. New York, NY: International Publishers.
Marx, K. (1867/1967). *Capital. A critique of political economy*. New York, NY: International Publishers.
Meade, J. (1940). *The economic basis for a durable peace*. London: Allen & Unwin.
Meldolesi, L. (2014). *L'ultimo Hirschman e l'Europa*. Soveria Mannelli: Rubbettino.
Milward, A. S. (1992). *The European rescue of the nation-state*. London: Routledge.
Murphy, K. M., Shleifer, A., & Vishny, R. W. (1989). Industrialization and the big push. *Journal of Political Economy*, *5*, 1003–1026.
Rodwin, L. (1994). In L. Rodwin & D. Schön (Eds.). *Rethinking the development experience. Aims, themes and theses*.
Rodwin, L., & Schön, D. (Eds.). (1994). *Rethinking the development experience. Essays provoked by the work of Albert O. Hirschman*. Washington, DC: The Brookings Institution and The Lincoln Institute of Land Policy.
Ross, D. (1991). *The origin of American social science*. Cambridge: Cambridge University Press.
Schön, D. A. (1994). Hirschman's elusive theory of social learning. In L. Rodwin & D. Schön (Eds), 1994.
Schroeppel, C., & Mariko, N. (2002). The changing interpretation of the Flying Geese model of development. *Japan Studien. German Institute for Japanese Studies*, *14*, 203–236.
Schumpeter, J. (1942/1992). *Capitalism, socialism and democracy*. London: Routledge.
Sen, A. K. (2004). An insight into the purpose of prosperity. *Financial Times*, September 20.
Smith, A. (1776/1910). *An inquiry in the nature and causes of the wealth of nations*. London: Everyman's Library.
Solow, R. M. (1957). Technical change and the aggregate production function. *The Review of Economics and Statistics*, *39*(3), 312–320.
Stark, W. (1962). *The fundamental forms of social thought*. London: Routledge.
Steedman, I. (2001). On 'Measuring' knowledge in new (endogenous) growth theory. In N. Salvadori (Ed.), *Old and new growth theories: An assessment* (pp. 127–133). Cheltenham: Edward Elgar.

MODELS AND MISPERCEPTIONS: CHENERY, HIRSCHMAN AND TINBERGEN ON DEVELOPMENT PLANNING

Neil De Marchi

ABSTRACT

In the 1950s, when development as a subject for study was as yet poorly defined, misunderstandings were not uncommon. The grounds were often methodological, but substantive analytical differences were also involved. I focus on an unusual context, the invitation given to one economist, Hollis B. Chenery, who promoted the neo-classical approach to growth, to review two works stemming from very different perspectives. One of these was The Design of Development *by econometrician Jan Tinbergen; the other was* The Strategy of Economic Development *by the highly original thinker Albert O. Hirschman. Chenery found himself baffled by Hirschman's stress on the capacity to make quick and strong decisions in favor of development, if backwardness was to be overcome. But he was equally drawn to Tinbergen's advocacy of detailed development plans. I argue that Chenery was wrong on both counts. He failed to understand Hirschman's argument, which admittedly was novel,*

Research in the History of Economic Thought and Methodology, Volume 34B, 91–99

ISSN: 0743-4154/doi:10.1108/S0743-41542016000034B004

and misperceived Tinbergen's approach as of a piece with his own convictions. The episode is instructive chiefly in opening up to reconsideration the ideas and misperceptions of three pioneers of development economics.

Keywords: Development economics; planning; decision-making

A SETTING FOR HIGHLIGHTING DIFFERENCES

In the early years after World War II notions abounded as to the causes of economic "backwardness" and how best to address them. Differences marked everything, from the theoretical modeling of growth, to the design and implementation of development plans.

Some differences of course were real, but there were also misperceptions. I have chosen to examine one instance of the latter. I wish to argue that the misperceptions in this instance were rooted in diverging methodological approaches to the problem of backwardness, divergences that had a much larger and more persistent impact on development economics than my selected episode, which played out in the late 1950s. First the setting, then the participants and their differences will be addressed.

The setting was an invitation in 1958 to up-and-coming development economist Hollis B. Chenery, from the editors of the prestigious *American Economic Review*, to write an assessment of two recent texts on development. One of these was *The Design of Development* (hereafter *Design*) by Jan Tinbergen, the other, *The Strategy of Economic Development* (hereafter *Strategy*) by Albert O. Hirschman.

THE MATTER OF DISAGREEMENT: A FIRST PASS

Chenery, in the early 1970s, would be appointed the World Bank's Vice-President for development policy, but for a decade and a half prior to that he had collaborated with and led other academically based economists in attempts to adapt traditional microeconomic theory (optimization on the part of one producer/consumer agent) to development analysis. Of these efforts more in a moment.

First, however, a quick presentation of the two texts the editors of the *American Economic Review* asked Chenery to review.

Tinbergen's was a smallish (99 page) manual commissioned in 1955 by the then-Director of the Economic Development Institute of the International Bank for Reconstruction and Development (soon to be World Bank). The Institute, as explained by its Director, existed to enable administrators from member countries of the Bank engaged with or considering a development plan, to convene for discussion and instruction on drawing up and implementing such plans.

We may infer that Tinbergen's text served the Institute well. Not only was it in use from 1955 in manuscript form, before being published in 1958, but following its publication it was immediately re-published in the same year, and went through five printings in as many years.

Hirschman, following a period after the War working for the Marshall Plan, was tapped in the early 1950s by the Government of Colombia to assist with the implementation of a development plan for that country. At the time this was the most ambitious intervention by the Bank in Latin America. After roughly two and a half years Hirschman resigned his official position but remained in Colombia as a private researcher and adviser.

His biographer notes that Hirschman, while in Colombia, traveled about constantly, interviewing and discussing with persons of every rank and occupation their experience with the plan. Was it working, or not? In what respects? And in either case, why? (Adelman, 2013, esp. 303 ff.). Hirschman's first attempt at ordering what he had experienced and imbibed was his *Strategy*. It immediately stirred controversy because Hirschman challenged the efficacy of encompassing development plans applied out of the blue and in isolation. Not surprisingly, *Strategy* continued to raise the hackles of many development economists through successive editions, though the original text saw three printings within a year and a half of publication and a separate paperbound edition appeared in January 1961.

To return to Chenery, he accepted the *American Economic Review*'s invitation and his joint appraisal of the two texts appeared in December, 1959 (Chenery, 1959, pp. 1063–1065).

CONCEPTUAL DIFFERENCES

As to backgrounds, Tinbergen was a pioneer of Econometrics and shared the first-ever "Nobel" Prize in Economics in 1969. At the time of writing his *Design* he was a Professor of Economics at the Netherlands School of Economics in Rotterdam having been, in the mid-1940s, Director of the semi-autonomous Dutch *Central Plan Bureau* in The Hague. The Bureau was responsible for preparing official macroeconomic forecasts for the Dutch economy. This involvement undoubtedly shaped Tinbergen's convictions concerning planning in the development context. His early training was in physics and mathematics but he turned to economics, in the hope that the application of mathematics to that subject might help it toward being more useful.

As to Chenery, in the late 1950s he was at Stanford University and already busy, as part of a mixed group of prominent young scholars, with a project that for him would define his life's work, namely, "attempts to interpret empirical findings in terms of the neo-classical theory of production and distribution" (Harcourt & Laing, 1971, p. 131).

Aside from the so-called "Capital Controversies," which was the specific field of battle of Harcourt and Laing, macroeconomists more broadly, in the period from, roughly, 1955 through the mid-1980s, began to insist that not all models are equal; to be acceptable a macro model must satisfy certain constraints. In particular, so-called "real business cycle" models were held to the standard that, while they are in principle driven by the single optimizing producer/consumer of microeconomic theory, their parameters "are assigned values that are meant to be representative of facts about the economy." Quantitative inferences may then be drawn from models thus "calibrated" that compare favorably with "analogous variables in the world" (Hoover, 2001, p. 38).

Initially Chenery joined others in identifying a production function flexible enough to allow for the various degrees of substitution between labor and capital observed in different sectors of some economies, including trade sectors, which were important to many developing economies (Arrow, Chenery, Minhas, & Solow, 1961).

In the 1960s, however, Chenery joined the US Agency for International Development, where he headed a team of economists using United Nations historical data series for multiple industrial sectors (as many as 23 recognized 3-digit sectors, for up to 19 economies). Scrutinizing these series yielded what Chenery would later describe as the pattern of "normal industrialization," a term, for him, synonymous with development.

In Chenery (1969) he caste this thinking in the form of a model that permitted simulation experiments. Thus, taking growing income per head as the chief among a small number of plausible and observable exogenous factors potentially driving development, he noted that growth stimulates additional demands. Using the data that generated his "normal industrialization" prototype he could then, in principle, trace the ways in which these demands would be supplied, either domestically or through trade.

But this was all in the future. As Chenery read Tinbergen's *Design* in 1958, he felt himself in the presence of a kindred spirit, one who strongly advocated detailed development plans in order to secure coherence/consistency on the one hand, and to make good use of interconnectedness on the other, the latter thought of in terms of open-economy Leontief input-output tables.

Hirschman agreed with the need to identify and make use of interconnectedness, which he thought of in two complementary ways. When domestic production of a particular new product begins, there are, on the one side, "attempts to utilize its outputs as inputs in some new activities." This is "forward linkage." But there will also be attempts to supply the new product's needs domestically. This he dubbed "backward linkage" (*Strategy*, 1961, p. 100).

Chenery could identify with this Hirschman. However, there was much more to Hirschman that he did not appreciate. For Hirschman took issue with Chenery's commitment to the popular view that backwardness is due to one or more "obstacles." Remove these once and for all, was the belief, and, like racehorses at the starter's gate, whose pent-up energy is released with the raising of the gate, so too will development simply occur. Chenery focused on shortages of domestic savings and a persistently negative balance of payments, though those stressing shortages also identified many more. For an overview from Chenery's perspective see Chenery and Bruno (1962).

Hirschman, who did not at all share Chenery's view, noted, by way of undermining the plausibility of the obstacles argument, that naysayers might add all manner of things to the list of obstacles, easily arriving at so many, indeed, that the obstacle argument loses all definition. Thus Hirschman: an inadequate banking system might be counted an obstacle, so too a poor extension of good education, a lack of the proper banking expertise to attract and make available more capital, both domestic and foreign, or social institutions such as the extended family and an inappropriate land tenure system, plus socio-political obstacles such as administrative instability, and so on … and on.

Hirschman insisted that the analogy with racehorses does not hold, for, while there are many forms that obstacles might take, almost all are due to a lack of appropriate measures having been put in place. Where the infrastructure to make use of capital has been created, it has usually been both available and used creatively. The real problem, according to Hirschman, was thus a lack of the wish and will in a country "to take the steps necessary to create, direct, or procure capital for education, say, or to introduce the proper financial institutions," to relate his message to just two frequently blamed shortages (*Strategy*, 1961, p. 25).

But it follows that "If backwardness is indeed due to an insufficient number and speed of development *decisions* and to inadequate performance of developmental *tasks*" (*ibid.*, p. 25, italics added) then this is the problem. It is not the multiplicity of obstacles that defines and explains backwardness but rather the need to generate and energize human action in a certain direction (*ibid.*).

Hirschman's insistence that backwardness is due to the absence of a "growth perspective," meant that he placed the difficulties of development "where [according to him] all difficulties of human action begin and belong: in the mind" (*Strategy*, 1961, p. 11). He would add later (see *A Bias for Hope*, 1971) that it also helps if there is a willingness to see difficulties as opportunities to succeed through overcoming.

I should add that Hirschman rejected the possible remedy of changing factor proportions; for example, adding more of the less scarce factors to the truly scarce decision-taking capacity. This does not work because each development move requires its own specific kind of decision-taking (Hirschman, 1961, p. 27). One cannot simply add more decision-making capacity to other factors; for each time what is needed to secure appropriate decision-making is somewhat unique (*ibid.*, p. 27).

Chenery's response to Hirschman's *Strategy* in his review was in part a polite summing up of the latter's alternative perspective as "elusive." That could, though need not, mean: there is nothing measurable here. But in fact Chenery probably found the overall Hirschman message closer to mumbo-jumbo; for he also offered the tart summing up that there seemed nothing left for the economist to do beyond maximizing decision-taking capacity. This was risible, given that Hirschman had made it clear that no simple summation of such capacities is possible.

I am left feeling that Chenery simply could not place Hirschman's unusual ideas and emphases in the modeling traditions he felt comfortable with. This judgment applies both to theoretical analysis, as in Arrrow et al. (1961) joint exploration of a production function that allows for varying labor: capital ratios during development experiences, and to his (1969) data-based identification of "normal industrialization."

It can also be shown, I believe, that Chenery erred in the other direction when it came to his assessment of Tinbergen's *Design*. He perceived his own thinking to be much closer to Tinbergen's than was the case.

The textual support for Chenery's belief is thin; but even more glaring is its lack of methodological foundation.

MISPERCEPTION

To return to the other book Chenery was asked to review, Tinbergen's *Design of Development*, I have noted already that the reviewer in this case sensed in his author a kindred spirit. However, some of the similarities were quite elemental, both authors insisting that detailed plans are a safeguard against incoherence or inconsistency.

In terms, instead, of the implications that economics is not a laboratory science and must try to incorporate endogenous micro and dynamic choice behavior by "the" economic agent, Chenery and Tinbergen were far apart. Tinbergen sought, though without success, to effect any real incorporation – "an exact system of [behavioral] equations does not exist ... and if it did it would be very complicated" (Tinbergen, 1958, p. 81), but Chenery in the 1960s left such modeling problems aside, largely ignoring choice altogether and contenting himself with tracing in historical data the consequences of *exogenous* rather than endogenous change (Chenery, 1969).

There were other disparities too. Rather than pretend that the needed data for precise planning are both good and available, or some planning model complete and reliable, Tinbergen allowed that the estimates that go into plans are just guesses, and require frequently to be re-done, according to the best insights of experienced planners (Tinbergen, 1958, p. 6).

In line with this conviction, rooted as it is in the notion that there is usually some merit in a variety of judgments, it has become established practice within the Dutch Central Planning Bureau, for all forecasts, before publication, to be screened and debated by in-house experts. Consensus plays a large role. The approach has a good record, especially where short-term forecasts are concerned (paraphrasing Boumans, 2015, p. 169).

Lastly, and most damaging for Chenery's desire to see himself and Tinbergen as kindred spirits, we find Tinbergen quite frequently insisting on the importance to success in development of a willingness by the people to be part of the government's plans for change, and on the part of planners a sensitivity to the social fabric in general. Thus, when it comes to stimulating private investment one cannot ignore "the general attitude of the population with regard to government measures, and the quality of the administrative apparatus" (Tinbergen, 1958, p. 8). Indeed "The possibilities for development are dependent on certain factors such as the willingness of the government and the people to make special efforts ..." (*ibid.*, p. 11). This same insistence recurs in somewhat altered wording. Hence, "A fourth important influence on the character of programming is to be found in *the general attitude of the people* with regard to government measures: the degree of public spiritedness and the willingness to cooperate, and in the quality of administration" (*ibid.*, p. 27).

There is even a section of Tinbergen's *Design* headed "Lessons to be Learned from Failures," under which reading we read:

> Economic life is beset with uncertainty and challenges ... But failures are not completely negative ... statisticians engaged in programming tend to underestimate the changes that actually take place. Qualitatively this is connected with the continuous occurrence of new factors. These are mostly technical, but also political and psychological ... Whenever possible, attempts should be made to widen knowledge of the process of scientific development," [but] "the role to be played by scientific knowledge and insight in the field of development policy will for a long time to come be only a modest one. The relevant facts of life are too many and too varied to make it possible to reach decisions without "an intuitive feeling for human relations." (Tinbergen, 1958, p. 69)

CONCLUSION

On the basis of such assertions on Tinbergen's part, Chenery would seem to have been odd man out in the Tinbergen-Chenery-Hirschman triumvirate, despite his sense of affinity with Tinbergen's work and his dismissal of Hirschman's analysis. This episode of tangled perceptions is not merely curious; it has the merit of drawing attention to Hirschman's discernment and originality as attested to by Tinbergen's independent discovery and deployment of many of Hirschman's notions. Chenery too appreciated Tinbergen but he transposed onto his own approach to development planning almost nothing of Tinbergen's "intuitive feeling for human relations," nor of the Dutch econometrician's sensitivity to choice-based endogenous behavior, or of his openness to examining on their merits experts' attempts to predict plan outcomes. These losses perhaps made it quite impossible for him to see much if any merit in Hirschman.

I do not wish to claim that Hirschman and Tinbergen were closer than Tinbergen and Chenery, merely that the two first-named shared more of what the planner can expect to accomplish, and by what means.

REFERENCES

Adelman, J. (2013). *Worldly philosopher. The Odyssey of Albert O. Hirschman*. Princeton, NJ: Princeton University Press.

Arrow, K. J., Chenery, H. B., Minhas, B. S., & Solow, R. M. (1961). Capital-labor substitution and economic efficiency. *Review of Economics and Statistics*, *43*, 225–248.

Boumans, M. J. (2015). *Science outside the laboratory – Measurement in field science and economics*. Oxford: Oxford University Press.

Chenery, H. (1959). Review of Hirschman. The strategy of economic development, and Tinbergen. The design of development. *American Economic Review*, *49*(December), 1063–1065.

Chenery, H. B. (1969). The process of industrialization. Economic Development Report No. 146. Contract No. AID/csd-1543. Project for Quantitative Research in Economic Development, *Center for International Affairs*, Harvard University, Cambridge, MA. Retrieved from pdf.gov/_docs/PNAB%201355%20pdf

Chenery, H. B., & Bruno, M. (1962). Development alternatives in an open economy: The case of Israel. *The Economic Journal*, *72*(285), 79–103.

Harcourt, G. C., & Laing, N. F. (1971). *Capital and growth: Selected readings*. Harmondsworth: Penguin Books.

Hirschman, A. O. (1961). *The strategy of economic development*. Paperback edition 1958. New Haven, CT: Yale University Press.

Hirschman, A. O. (1971). *A bias for hope. Essays on development and Latin America*. New Haven, CT: Yale University Press.

Hoover, K. D. (2001). *The methodology of empirical macroeconomics*. Cambridge: Cambridge University Press.

Tinbergen, J. (1958). *The design of development*. Baltimore, MD: The Johns Hopkins Press.

ALBERT O. HIRSCHMAN AND THE STRUCTURALIST–MONETARIST DEBATE IN LATIN AMERICA

Ana Maria Bianchi

ABSTRACT

This paper analyzes the standpoint of Albert O. Hirschman in the structuralist–monetarist debate that took place in Latin America during the 1950s and 1960s. It claims that Hirschman had many affinities with the structuralist approach, in virtue of his methodological stance and of his view of the role to be performed by economic advisers in foreign countries. Similar to the structuralists, Hirschman did not make the control of inflation a central tenet of his development theory; also like them, he dissented from the orthodox approach. However, Hirschman did not take a clear-cut side on the debate, choosing, instead, to act as a go-between.

Keywords: Hirschman; Latin America; development economics; structuralism; inflation

Research in the History of Economic Thought and Methodology, Volume 34B, 101–122

ISSN: 0743-4154/doi:10.1108/S0743-41542016000034B014

Living in Latin America and closely interacting with its intellectual elite had a major impact on Albert O. Hirschman's approach to development economics (Adelman, 2013; Meldolesi, 1995). This proximity led Hirschman to diverge from pioneers such as Paul Rosenstein-Rodan, choosing to see development as an unbalanced process set in motion by backward and forward linkages (Ascher, 1996; Bianchi, 2012; Charusheela, 2005; Ellerman, 2004; Streeten, 1959).

Not enough has yet been said about how Hirschman viewed the inflation problem, which was an extremely severe and persistent trademark of Latin American economies throughout the twentieth century. Do Hirschman's writings show a thorough concern with the negative impact of high inflation rates on Latin America's growth potential? On the contrary, did Hirschman consider inflation as a minor problem, to be tackled alongside other negative facets of underdevelopment and poverty? Where exactly did he stand in the feud between monetarists and structuralists, which prevailed in the economic debate in Latin America in the mid-twentieth century?

Providing answers to the above questions is the main goal of this paper, which will look deeper into Hirschman's books, articles, and documents in order to describe his viewpoint of the inflation problem in the social development of Latin America. I shall start by saying that there are no simple either–or answers to the above questions. Hirschman did express some concern with the persistence of high inflation rates in the continent; conversely, he did not make the control of inflation a central tenet of his development theory. Specifically, in the debate between structuralists and monetarists, he did not take a clear-cut position.

The point that I will make in this paper is that Hirschman's standpoint in this debate should be understood in connection to his method of investigation, specifically, in his view of the role of economic advisers issuing policy recommendations for foreign countries. In his professional experience as a consultant to the World Bank, the government of the United States and different Latin American countries, as well as other international organizations and private business groups, Hirschman was deeply convinced that doing his job required a close examination of the social, political, and economic conditions prevailing in each country and geographical area (Hirschman, 1984, p. 91, 1998, p. 88).

The section following this introduction is devoted to describing Hirschman's view of inflation in Latin America based on a case study of Chile, where he describes the political dimension of this phenomenon. The subsequent two sections will present an overview of the debate between structuralists and monetarists, starting with the latter. This will be followed by a section where I analyze Hirschman's standpoint in the debate and try to connect it to his choice of methods. I will conclude with some general remarks.

THE POLITICAL DIMENSION OF INFLATION

Chronic inflation has afflicted a great number of countries in Latin America during most of the twentieth century (ECLA, 1961; Kaldor, 1959).[1] It is therefore natural that it would stand out as a major issue, worthy of theoretical and practical attention from development economists.

Nevertheless, in the first book of his trilogy on economic development, *The Strategy of Economic Development*, 1958, Hirschman says very little about inflation. He talks about different perspectives on development and describes many facets of the development process. His bibliographical references basically include the pioneers in the field, such as Alexander Gerschenkron, Gottfried Haberler, Simon Kuznets, Arthur Lewis, Paul Rosenstein-Rodan, W. W. Rostow, and Hans Singer. Only two Latin American authors are mentioned, in footnotes, namely, Roberto Campos and Raul Prebisch.

This pattern changes a bit in the second book of Hirschman's trilogy, *Journeys toward Progress*, first published in 1963,[2] where references to Latin American literature abound. The chapter on Chile, which basically deals with the inflation problem, composes the first part of *Journeys*, together with two other national case studies. Hirschman considers these case studies to be "the essence" of the volume, the empirical ground where his contribution to development economics was settled (Hirschman, 1963, p. 1). They were directly inspired by the author's conviction that historical reconstruction was an essential step in the understanding of development (Alacevich, 2012, p. 5).

The chapter on Chile immediately follows a study of the drought problem in Northeastern Brazil and of land reform in Colombia. Hirschman sees in Chile's recurrently high inflation rates, the origin of which he traces to the late nineteenth century, an ideal setup for understanding the political dimension of development, and its immediate and long-term implications for public policy. The length and virulence of inflation in Chile made it the locus classicus of the problem of inflation – high inflation prevailing for more than 80 years, with short intervals of comparative price stability. However, despite the fact that Hirschman chooses Chile as the focus of his enquiry, he notices the widespread presence of inflation in Latin America, thus widening the potential scope of his conclusions (Hirschman, 1963, p. 161).

A permanent disposition to cross-disciplinary frontiers is an important feature of Hirschman's approach to economic matters (Cot, 2010, p. 61). In *Journeys*, his main goal is to investigate the problem-solving capabilities of public authorities in Latin America. Far from looking at inflation as a purely monetary phenomenon, he sees it as a problem of public policy, which requires moving beyond the strict realm of economic analysis. His review of the Chilean history as a sequence of political measures conceived to fight inflation results in a detailed account of when and how successive governments built anti-inflationary plans, quite often relying on the advice of missions of foreign specialists.

At this point, I must take notice of another distinguishing feature of Hirschman's research methodology. At the outset of *Journeys*, the author declines his intention of assisting the United States, his country of residence, at the time involved with the Alliance for Progress,[3] in the promotion of social reforms in Latin America. This implied learning about the usual policy-making strategies, on which depended the success of different types of social reforms. Unlike many of his predecessors in the field, Hirschman refuses to list "prerequisites" to development, be it physical capital formation, a dexterous elite, a collective psychological mindset, an ideology, or anything similar. He does not point out a single set of universal pre-conditions, which, once overcome, would bring about the desired social changes. Rather, he decides to examine the circumstances surrounding each historical manifestation of chronic inflation in Chile in order to "show how a society can begin to move forward *as it is, in spite of what it is and because of what it is*" (Hirschman, 1963, p. 6, emphasis in original).

One of Hirschman's initial remarks comes from a comparison between the drought problem in Brazil, the subject matter of his previous chapter, and inflation in Chile. He states that, unlike drought, inflation is a man-made calamity, to be traced to the defective functioning of the monetary system, which is one of the most relevant social institutions (Hirschman, 1963, p. 162). Public consciousness is particularly acute, in this regard, because price fluctuations are subject to month-to-month or even day-to-day measurement, thus allowing for a permanent scrutiny by public opinion. Besides, the repeated failure of anti-inflationary programs in Chile had generated animosity among different social groups, and led to policies conceived along partisan or antagonistic lines.

In *Journeys*, Hirschman adopts a procedure that from that point in time on is typical of his style, by making a thorough research of the Latin

American literature. Hirschman cites more than 100 Latin American names, including social scientists, novelists, journalists, and politicians. He refers extensively to a Chilean historian, Frank W. Fetter (Hirschman, 1963, p. 168). In 1931 Fetter had published a monograph that was still considered to be the last word on the subject of inflation in Chile, where he attributed the source of inflation to the struggle between social classes. According to Fetter, a conservative land aristocracy (the *hacendados*) was the real profiteer of lengthy periods of high inflation. Given their political ascendancy, this aristocracy managed to be in permanent debt with the Chilean government. While their products were sold to England, against gold, their own currency was depressed by frequent paper-money emissions. This observation leads Fetter to argue that not only did inflation benefit this social class, it was planned and organized by it.

Hirschman is critical of this "sociological" view of inflation, and questions its support by historical evidence. More importantly for my later argument, he does not tend to see inflation as a major problem for the economy, remarking that it may attract a "disproportionate amount of public attention" (Hirschman, 1963, p. 221). He nevertheless admits that inflation somehow echoes the struggle of different groups of the society, who, moved by a widespread aspiration toward higher standards of living, try to amplify their share in the national income (Hirschman, 1963, p. 195).

Hirschman's criticism stems from the kind of bond that he sees between inflationary pressures and social conflict. In his view, the unequal share of income by different social groups is not at the root of inflation, as preached by Chilean analysts, but it is certainly a consequence of it. This implies that inflation can be counterbalanced by political measures framed to reduce the sources of conflict. *Journeys* provides a concrete example: by means of the "shared sacrifices" doctrine, the Ibañez administration (1953–1955) in Chile was able to establish, for a certain period of time, a social pact. This toned down the pretenses of the various social groups, and thus succeeded both in controlling inflation and avoiding violent conflicts.

In his historically grounded analysis, Hirschman introduces a character that would turn out to be central to his theses: the foreign economic adviser, or, as he often says, the visiting-economist. Long periods of severe inflation would nurture among Chilean politicians a recurring hope that somewhere outside the country there was an "expert" who could prescribe just the right therapy for their problem.[4] Based on their technical competence and presumed impartiality, successive missions of foreign specialists were invited to assist the government in the design of anti-inflationary policies; with a disappointingly small practical success, however.

Hirschman notes that these foreign missions provided the government with scapegoats, who could (and would) be blamed for the unpopular measures that were taken in order to control inflation. With the repeated failure of anti-inflationary policies, the visiting specialists were bound to face a high risk of demonization. Their therapeutic power was quickly contested and the initial reverence with which they were greeted at their arrival in the country would give way to a critical attitude.

One of the major flaws in these missions and their specialists, as pointed by Hirschman, was the propensity to take imported doctrines more seriously, and to try to apply them in a more dogmatic manner, in the country they were visiting than in their country of origin (Hirschman, 1963, p. 180). Here, again, Hirschman shows his understanding of the complex nature of inflation, when criticizing the foreign adviser for his inability to supplement a purely monetary analysis with an examination of the underlying political and sociological factors (Hirschman, 1963, p. 195). Inflation is a highly technical problem, but it is, at the same time, a political problem. More specifically, it is a political and distributional problem, requiring an accommodation among social groups (Hirschman, 1963, p. 196). Foreign specialists can do little to promote this accommodation, and, in the best-case scenario, it will last for only short periods of time.

Hirschman concludes his chapter on Chile with a few comments about the structuralist thesis on inflation, so named in contrast to the "monetarist" position, which he identifies with the ideas of the International Monetary Fund. I shall postpone this discussion, however, in order to introduce an overview of the debate between the two opposing approaches to inflation.

THE MONETARIST APPROACH

Before defining the side Hirschman took on the strife between structuralists and monetarists, let me give a general idea of what was at stake. Boianovsky (2012) points out that after going on for almost a decade, the controversy gained its momentum in 1963, when an international conference reuniting prestigious economists from several parts of the world was held in Rio de Janeiro, Brazil. In the proceedings of this conference, there are a few reports on inflationary experiences in Asia and Eastern Europe, but the spotlight is undoubtedly on the Latin American experience (Baer & Kerstenezky, 1964).

The Rio conference was one of the first and few opportunities for Latin Americans to discuss inflation among themselves and with specialists of high international reputation, such as John M. Adler, Werner Baer, Hollis Chenery, David Felix, Joseph Grunwald, Gottfried Haberler, A. C. Harberger, Albert O. Hirschman, Nicholas Kaldor, W. Arthur Lewis, Friedrich and Vera Lutz, G. W. Mitchell, Dudley Seers, and Gordon Smith. The Latin American participants included Roberto Campos, Carlos Diaz-Alejandro, Eugenio Gudin, Isaac Kerstenetzky, Anibal Pinto, Osvaldo Sunkel, Mario Henrique Simonsen, Victor Urquidi, and Guido diTella.[5]

The heart of the controversy lay on the orthodox anti-inflationary programs supported by the International Monetary Fund (Felix, 1961) and, in the case of Chile, by the Klein-Saks mission (Hirschman, 1963, pp. 199–210). This highlights the normative side of the conflict, since, far from being engaged in a mere intellectual debate, economists from both tendencies had opposite recommendations for policy making.

I shall start by defining the monetarist approach, which was the target of the structuralist's bullets. Monetarism is usually associated with the work of Milton Friedman who, together with Anna Schwartz, published a book on the monetary history of the United States (Friedman & Schwartz, 1963). Friedman links monetarism to the quantity theory of money, in turn founded on an accounting identity: the money supply multiplied by the velocity of circulation (which is supposed to be constant) equals the nominal expenditures in the economy, expressed by the number of goods and services sold multiplied by their average price. The monetarist prescription can be summarized in a simple proposition, namely, in order to stabilize the economy, governments must control the amount of money in circulation by means of monetary instruments such as interest rates. Policy implications are straightforward: given that monetary disequilibrium is put into motion by public expenditure financed through deficits, monetary policy is the main tool to which governments must resort in order to improve the overall performance of the economy.

For monetarists, the elimination of occasional supply rigidities can be achieved by stopping inflation and abolishing a number of direct controls and subsidies (Felix, 1961, p. 88). Albeit unpleasant, this contractionary mechanism is a necessary and a virtually sufficient condition to reactivate the economy, because it is capable of removing distortions and obstacles to growth. The latter include occasional supply inelasticities and bottlenecks, which are generated by the inflationary process itself (Campos, 1961, pp. 69–70; Little, 1982, p. 80).

Regarding Latin America, monetarists believed in a dynamic private sector, with plenty of possibilities for attracting foreign investment, from which capital would flow to finance development (Felix, 1961, p. 88).

However, to purge themselves of distortions and obstacles to growth induced by inflation, Latin American economies should undergo a painful anti-inflationary therapy. It follows that the control of monetary expansion and the elimination of direct controls (such as price controls) were considered to be virtually sufficient to reset economic growth into motion. In this scenario, foreign investment is the key independent variable, whereas public investment plays a definitely minor role. Monetarists did not postulate an increase of taxes to compensate for public deficits, either as part of the stabilization effort or during the subsequent development process.

THE STRUCTURALIST APPROACH

The structuralist–monetarist debate is in its essence a Latin American debate (Little, 1982). In Latin America, the controversy took place during the 1950s and 1960s, preceding the monetarist debate that would dominate macroeconomics in the United States and Europe some time later (Boianovsky, 2012, p. 284).[6]

In a broad sense, however, the origins of Latin American structuralism have been traced to the doctrine of market failures, which emerged in England during the 1930s and 1940s (Arndt, 1985, p. 151). The proponents of this doctrine question the effectiveness of price mechanisms, claiming that, due to monopoly and other causes, prices may be unable to provide the correct signals, and production factors may respond inadequately, or with a considerable time lag, to changes in prices.

This skepticism about the adequate operation of the price system is shared by the pioneers in development economics, for whom government must be ready to deal with the possibility of market failures, resorting to planning and political controls to cope with them (Arndt, 1985, p. 153).

Juan Noyola-Vasquez and Osvaldo Sunkel are considered to be the first Latin American economists to formally expose a structural theory of inflation (Arndt, 1985; Danby, 2005). The Mexican Noyola-Vasquez had worked in the Economic Commission for Latin America (ECLA) with Raul Prebisch and Celso Furtado. In his study of inflation in Mexico and Chile, he holds that, rather than being a strictly monetary phenomenon, sustained upward price movements reflect processes of structural disequilibrium, especially in underdeveloped countries (Noyola-Vásquez, 1956).

In Noyola's terminology, "structural" can be taken as synonym for "fundamental" or "basic" (Danby, 2005, p. 165). Inflation primarily results from pressures caused by economic rigidities, which include the inability of the agricultural sector to fulfill the demands of the domestic sector. It is further nourished by "propagation mechanisms," which stem from the need to accommodate competing income claims from different social groups, by means of a continuous monetary expansion, thus contributing to aggravate the inflationary problem.

The same distinction between structural rigidities and propagation mechanisms, emphasizing the later labeled *inertial* component of inflation, is made by the Chilean Sunkel (1958, p. 571). Sunkel claims that the structural characteristics of productive systems are at the root of inflation in underdeveloped countries. The underlying thesis is similar to Noyola's: propagation mechanisms are the natural outcome of inflationary conditions, because of the government's incapacity to deal with pressures stemming from different social groups, who compete for their share of the national income. This is another instance where Latin American thinkers make room for social factors, pointedly for social conflict, in their account of the inflationary problem.

Two years after Sunkel, the Chilean Aníbal Pinto, who was also a member of the ECLA staff, published a short book challenging the policy prescriptions of the International Monetary Fund and of the Klein-Saks mission in Chile. In his view, the correct solution to the problem of recurrent inflation was not orthodox monetarist policies, but, instead, the elimination of bottlenecks that were the true cause of inflation (Pinto, 1960).

One of these bottlenecks was the low productivity of the agricultural sector, where a very concentrated pattern of land tenure prevailed, and which was therefore unable to attend the increasing demand for food resulting from urbanization. A low import capacity was another significant bottleneck, since, as the terms of trade deteriorated, the price of imported goods, essential for the industrialization process, tended to rise.

As pointed out by Boianovsky (2012), the list of early exponents of the structuralist theory of inflation would not be complete without the Brazilian economist Celso Furtado. In a paper Furtado published in 1961, but which was disclosed to a smaller audience two years before, he questions the applicability of monetarist policies to the developing countries. Another reason for mentioning his name is the fact that he had a concrete participation in building politics along structuralist lines: his *Three Year Plan*, implemented in 1963, was the first structuralist stabilization program in Latin America (Boianovsky, 2012, p. 278).[7]

Notwithstanding some internal differences in the group of structuralist authors, there are many points of convergence. Campos (1961), who, according to Boianovsky (2012, p. 284), was the first person to adopt the terminology "structuralist" and "monetarist," summarizes the structuralist approach in three propositions: (i) inflation naturally accompanies economic growth; (ii) due to supply rigidities such efforts to curb inflation through monetary and fiscal mechanisms will lead to unemployment and stagnation; and (iii) low import capacity and supply inelasticities in the growth process render it impossible to control inflation in the short run; a gradual confrontation is thus desirable (in pace with the availability of foreign capital), creating the necessary conditions to overcome the import capacity bottleneck (Campos, 1961, p. 70).

To put it in simple terms, structuralists diverged from monetarists by assuming that growth was more important for economic development than price stability (Simonsen, 1964, p. 108). Latin American structuralists conceded to monetarists that inflation was the manifestation of a deformed economy, but claimed that controlling the emission of money was not, in itself, a workable solution to the development problem (Felix, 1961, p. 91). They strongly disagreed with the proposition of "putting the monetary house in order *first*" (Grunwald, 1961, p. 96; emphasis in the original). In their view, this kind of therapy could produce quick results, but it tended to hide the symptoms without attacking the causes. Structuralists were skeptical about the efficacy of credit constraints, cuts in public expenditures, and the elimination of direct controls, arguing that these measures do not attack the true cause of inflation to be found in the "structure" of the productive system. They denied the existence of an automatic bond between economic development and stabilization, and believed that the positive effects of a stabilization policy would only last for short periods of time. Actually, the underlying inflationary pressures would persist, and the perverse side effects of the stabilization policy would further exacerbate social conflicts.

Therefore, instead of swallowing a bitter medication, why not tolerate mild inflation as the price to be paid for economic progress? With different emphases, Latin American structuralists tended to believe that a high rate of economic growth could reconcile the income demands of various interest groups. Better still, instead of being a sine qua non condition, monetary stability could turn out to be a by-product of economic development (Grunwald, 1961, p. 96).

There is a clear normative component in the structuralist–monetarist debate, with each side prescribing radically different ways of conducting the economy (Baer, 1967, p. 11). However, although policy recommendations are an important matter of contention, they are not the only source of antagonism, and not even the most important one. In its essence, the structuralist–monetarist dispute is about causation – which variables should be treated as endogenous and which as exogenous? (Boianovsky, 2012, p. 287; Little, 1982, p. 81; Thorp & Whitehead, 1973, p. 14; Watcher, 1979). The importance of this distinction is the fact that it can point out which factors are potentially responsive to public policy. Monetarists assume that the supply of money is exogenously determined, and should therefore be the target of a stabilization policy. Structuralists criticized monetarists for focusing on the visible side of inflation, emphasizing propagation mechanisms that lead to a persistent rise in the general price level. For structuralists, instead, emphasis should be laid on structural factors, such as agricultural bottlenecks or changes in the terms of trade, which are the actual source of inflationary pressures. If this is the case, a stabilization policy requires structural reforms in the economy.

After this brief portrayal of the structuralist–monetarist debate, the next section will analyze Hirschman's participation in the debate.

HIRSCHMAN'S STANDPOINT

Hirschman's approach to the structuralist–monetarist debate is scattered throughout a number of his writings. Despite the attention that inflation was getting from professional and academic economists during the 1950s and 1960s, it does not seem to be a major concern for Hirschman. His early writings include a paper about inflation in Italy (Hirschman, 1948), but not much of it shows up in his subsequent research. A simple count illustrates this claim: out of the 1,447 pages in the books and chapters that Hirschman published in the 1958–1971 period, only 89 (six percent) were devoted to inflation.

Not only does Hirschman not write much about inflation, but also when he does so, he tends to question the monetarist thesis that inflation was the most crucial problem for Latin America. As mentioned before, he refers to the "disproportionate amount" of public attention that inflation was gathering, comparatively to other less eye-catching, "but perhaps more fundamental," problems (Hirschman, 1963, p. 221).

This allusion to the public visibility of inflation does not seem to be an accidental feature of Hirschman's standpoint. In the 1963 Rio conference, he draws attention to the impact of inflation on public opinion. He argues that by bringing up the subject of inflation, Latin American structuralists, who had direct communication channels with public opinion and policy makers, succeeded to mobilize their attention toward other, more demanding, problems of development Hirschman even suggests that structuralists got some "external economies" out of the problem of inflation, using it to create social pressure for the purpose of solving the other, "perhaps more fundamental but less 'loud'," problems faced by their societies (Hirschman, 1964, p. 455).

In the same document, Hirschman questions the causal relationship between inflation and distortions in investment patterns. He holds that there is no conclusive empirical evidence about the existence of this causality, adding that more empirical evidence was necessary to verify whether the changes in relative prices that come along with inflation are growth-promoting or are an obstacle to growth.

In this setting, Hirschman conjectures that the long coexistence of inflation and growth in Brazil could not be just a happy coincidence, since "once inflation has proven itself as an ally of growth ... it, in turn, picks a variety of allies" (Hirschman, 1964, p. 457). Brazil would be an example of an inflation that was "not bad at all" in the context of an unbalanced growth process. This was a country where public acquiescence to inflation was compatible with the simultaneous occurrence of two movements, a generalized increase in prices and a rise in national income.

Hirschman further argues that disagreements between structuralists and monetarists could be attributed to the type of society from which each group of scholars came. Monetarists came largely from societies where public opinion tended to bring each social problem to the attention of the policy makers independently, on its own. In these societies, interest groups were able to organize themselves (and were allowed to), and thus pressure public authorities toward any desirable social reform. In contrast, specifically in the case of Latin America, the "submerged" classes had no direct access to policy makers, and were therefore incapable of acting as pressure groups, or perhaps not allowed to do so. Inflation was an exception to this rule, by virtue of its great public visibility. By establishing a causal link between inflation and other social evils, structuralists would influence public opinion and thus generate social pressure toward reforms that were deemed necessary to promote development (Hirschman, 1964, pp. 454–455).

In defense of this very original and definitely controversial point, Hirschman adopts strong language, defining structuralism as "... an attempt to utilize inflation, as long as it exists, anyway, for something worthwhile" (Hirschman, 1964, p. 455). His reasoning is straightforward: since we cannot avoid some degree of inflation, let's make the best out of it. For the policy maker, moderate inflation could provide the argument that he needed to resist political pressures toward more spending. On the other hand, in a critical situation, when expenditures systematically outweigh revenue, inflation could persuade public opinion of the need to raise taxes for financing public investments.

In his subsequent writings, Hirschman does not go back to his thesis about specialized or totalizing pleas coming from pressure groups typifying two types of society. However, he insists on the persuasion role to be carried out by the supporters of the structuralist school. In *Journeys*, he states that, thanks to their ability to influence politicians and public opinion about the need to fight inflation's underlying causes, structuralists had contributed to promoting periods of social progress in Chile. They had helped to create social pressure toward a set of desirable reforms, which were endorsed because of their supposed usefulness to curb inflation, the privileged focus of their concern, and not only or mainly in virtue of their own merits (Hirschman, 1963, p. 215).

At this point, I must remark that Hirschman never stands up for the thesis that inflation can lead to economic growth. Rather, he supports the structuralist claim that the search for inflation's underlying causes may induce action on more fundamental problems. More precisely, he claims that an inflationary milieu provides the atmosphere where structuralists can exert a positive impact on public opinion, which, in turn, stimulates social reforms (Hirschman, 1963, p. 215).[8]

Hirschman further speaks in favor of a gradualist approach, arguing that moderate levels of inflation can serve as an antidote to violence and social revolution. By means of mechanisms such as automatic wage readjustments, the Chilean society was given some extra time to deal with social tensions before they assumed unbearable proportions (Hirschman, 1963, p. 222). The emphasis here is on the possible impact of a moderate inflation in contrast with a chronic and accelerating process.

In a later text, Hirschman goes back to this reasoning, holding that structuralists used the evidence of inflation to induce action "on a country's more hidden, but perhaps also more fundamental ills" (Hirschman, 1981, p. 205). He states that structuralists were quite successful in persuading policy makers and public opinion in general of the necessity of social reforms:

> Those who feel that inflation is due to certain fundamental flaws of the social and political structure are likely to be convinced at the outset that there are such flaws; once so convinced they will be strongly tempted to link the abolition of a widely acknowledged evil, such as inflation, to the achievement of a program for sociopolitical change that has normally a much narrower appeal. (Hirschman, 1981, p. 182)

Whenever the supporters of the structuralist school succeeded in persuading public opinion that social reforms were necessary to curb inflation, they created a favorable environment for these reforms to take place.[9] However, Hirschman warns the reader that this is a mere possibility. Inflation might have had this desirable outcome "here and there in the real world," but nothing guarantees that this will always be a successful crusade (Hirschman, 1981, p. 205).

To sum up, Hirschman's basic claims in the three above-mentioned texts can be expressed in four propositions: (1) public opinion and policy makers are sensible to the problematic aspects of inflation; (2) structuralists are able to persuade public opinion that inflation is caused by structural bottlenecks that can only be overcome through social reforms; (3) public opinion presses political authorities to perform these reforms; (4) political authorities agree to launch these reforms, even at the expense of tolerating a small level of inflation.

Werner Baer, who was also a participant in the 1963 Rio conference, criticized Hirschman's bold and rather unusual thesis (Baer, 1967, p. 19). He states that it was difficult to build a sound judgment about the inflation problem before conducting a "hard empirical-analytical work," which was necessary to improve knowledge about the causes and consequences of inflation.

There is no doubt about that, especially when one considers the lack of empirical data at the time when Hirschman and the participants in the structuralist–monetarist debate were writing. However, the fact is that Hirschman was not justifying inflation on the account of its power to attract public attention – he was simply observing that there was such a fortunate association. However controversial, Hirschman's claim about the use of inflation as a rhetorical device can be related to what he writes in a later article about the persuasion and recruitment impact of new ideas. Defining himself as a "dissenter," Hirschman claims that, together with many others, his ideas had contributed to make the field of development economics more interesting and thrilling, turning it into "the arena where lively debates took place" (Hirschman, 1984, p. 111). In addition to their power of persuasion, new ideas had the indirect recruitment effect of eliciting discussion and controversy. This turned out to be very positive for the advancement of development economics.

Hirschman writes about other more technical aspects of inflation and the ways to control it. He discusses how demonstration effects and mass consumption may exert upward pressures on prices; he analyses the impact of an unequal land tenure system on the agricultural output, and, consequently, on the domestic prices of food. He writes about the relationship between inflation and balance of payments; inflation, investments and savings; inflation and foreign-exchange rates; the impact of population pressures on inflation; inflation and fiscal policy; inflation and the intersectoral income distribution (Hirschman, 1958, 1963, 1968, 1971). From the viewpoint of his participation in the structuralist–monetarist debate, however, these discussions do not alter the above conclusions.

WHICH SIDE?

It is now time to go back to the initial question: which side did Hirschman take in the structuralist–monetarist debate? He was certainly not a monetarist, and, after acquiring a certain familiarity with Latin America, he never went back to what he had said in an earlier paper about inflation in Italy: "Once more it has been proven that it is possible to stop an inflation when there is a will to do so" (Hirschman, 1948, p. 605). This type of voluntarism collapsed when he realized the many constraints faced by Latin American economies in their fight against inflation.

Was Hirschman, then, a supporter of structuralism? The answer is again no, but this time with some qualifications. He certainly sympathizes with structuralist ideas, and he shows clear points of contact with its authors; but this interpretation, although somewhat plausible, is definitely wrong.

Hirschman praises structuralism for being the first well-built, native doctrine conceived by Latin American economists as an alternative to imported doctrines.[10] Like the structuralist authors, he denies the adequacy of looking at the non-developed world with the same theoretical lenses that were used to see development in the early industrialized countries (Hirschman, 1984, p. 110). In this important aspect, Hirschman and Latin American structuralists can be classified as "dissenters," in the sense of being critical of orthodoxy.

The second point of contact between Hirschman and the structuralists is that they all hold that inflation is not the basic problem of underdevelopment. Rather, they define inflation as part of a complex mixture of perverse circumstances that typify underdevelopment, and which should be the target of social and political reforms.

A third common element between structuralists' and Hirschman's approach is that they all acknowledge that there is a social conflict dimension in inflation, or, to put it in other words, a distributional conflict. Hirschman and the structuralists looked beyond a purely monetary interpretation of inflation to understand it and to propose therapies. Nevertheless, Hirschman does not see this conflict as a classical class struggle, as did Fetter, the above-mentioned Chilean historian. He most often refers to the struggle between different interest groups. As a matter of fact, neither did structuralists think in these terms, and Hirschman admits this; besides emphasizing economic variables, they usually referred to the interests of wage-earners as opposed to those of price-makers (Hirschman, 1963, p. 215).

These points of contact explain the plausible, albeit wrong, interpretation of Hirschman supporting the structuralists. As said before, Hirschman believed that a careful investigation of the concrete historical reality of a country was necessary before an economic adviser like he was ready to make policy recommendations. Instead of relying on general principles and abstract prescriptions, the adviser should actually visit the "patient," carrying "an empirical lantern" (Hirschman, 1998, p. 88).

This attitude can be related to the general characteristics of Hirschman's methodological standpoint. Hirschman's approach to inflation was clearly influenced by his stay in Colombia and his many subsequent visits to Latin America. In the continent he was able to testify a set of "elements of disorder," such as abject living conditions in the cities and in the countryside, uneven distribution of land, high levels of illiteracy and violence (Hirschman, 1961, p. 39). In comparative terms, price instability did not look as bad, although the structuralists were unable to persuade Hirschman that inflation was not a problem, especially when it reached persistently high levels.

Visiting the patient also implied reading the relevant locally produced literature and getting in touch with the country's intellectual and political leaders. The foreign adviser should be ready to answer a number of questions: what had been written about inflation? What do scholars in this particular country think about it? What constraints do policy makers face in their decision process, and how do they perceive them? What is the public opinion?

Hirschman was sympathetic to the locals' perspective, and this was a direct implication of his method. However, what seems to move him most was the search for a common terrain for both structuralists and monetarists to exchange their thoughts about the possible causes of inflation and therapeutic measures to cope with it. By temper, Hirschman was not exactly a peacemaker, but, in this particular case, he tried to act as a diplomat between the two antagonistic approaches, blaming what he called "a dialogue of the deaf" (Hirschman, 1964, p. 454). It was necessary to stimulate the flow of ideas between the contending parties. After all, monetarists did have some interesting ideas about how to stabilize the economy, while structuralists had a strong point about the underlying causes of inflation, and definitely should be heard.

In a nutshell, Hirschman cannot be considered a structuralist, in spite of showing a permanent disposition to listen to their claims. Like the structuralists, he was a dissenter, he did not see inflation as an isolated evil, and he acknowledged the social conflict dimension of inflation. These points of contact are not sufficient to turn him into a structuralist, however.

In order to better define Hirschman's standpoint, still another argument should be added to this analysis. Latin American scholars were not unanimous in their support of the structuralist approach, at the same time that structuralists were not a well-defined, cohesive, group of writers, who had entire control of the intellectual scene. Monetarist ideas also had some appeal in the continent, and prestigious economists spoke in favor of the related policies. One of them was Roberto Campos, who was held by Hirschman in high intellectual esteem. Hirschman invited Campos, "probably the most outspoken of ECLA's critics" (Hirschman, 1961, p. 27), to write a chapter for the book on Latin America that he was organizing.

Campos played a strategic part in the book, since he took responsibility for presenting both sides of the structuralist–monetarist debate. He criticized many precepts of the structuralist view of inflation, arguing that its proponents might have been unduly influenced by the peculiarities of the Chilean inflation. The so-called "structural bottlenecks" seemed much less relevant in countries such as Mexico, Venezuela, and Argentina. Besides, even if these bottlenecks were originally caused by inflation, at a later stage, they became inflation-feeding. Campos further accused structuralists of not being able to grasp the full significance of a monetary and fiscal policy (Campos, 1961, p. 78).

In his role as mediator, Hirschman did not explicitly subscribe to Campos's criticism. However, the fact that he included his chapter in his book of readings is telling.

After this overview of Hirschman's standpoint in the structuralist–monetarist debate, I will now proceed to my final considerations.

FINAL CONSIDERATIONS

A noisy intellectual debate took place in Latin America in the mid-twentieth century, opposing structuralists to monetarists. The two groups diverged about the causes of inflation and the proper ways to deal with it. For monetarists, a development-promoting policy essentially involved monetary stabilization, whereas structuralists stood up for economic and social reforms settled to eliminate structural bottlenecks.

Hirschman had plenty of affinities with Latin American structuralists, first of all, because he resented the automatic transposition of economic doctrines to different historical contexts, and, as such, was also a dissenter. His methodological stance and his view of the role to be played by foreign advisers put him under the influence of structuralist authors. He made himself available to listen to their claims and understand their perspective.

However, Hirschman did not take a clear-cut side in the debate, choosing, instead, to act as a go-between. He did not want to close doors to either structuralists or monetarists, as the latter had good arguments to counteract the most extreme ideas of their contenders.

With regard to the debate itself, Hirschman curiously emphasized its rhetorical nature, claiming that structuralists had been successful in persuading public opinion and policy makers of the need to fight the underlying causes of inflation. The spread of their ideas aroused demands for basic social and economic reforms, which were more likely to occur because of their public support.

The participants in the structuralist–monetarist debate, now with the inclusion of Hirschman as a third party, had many matters of contention. They shared a conviction, however, which was particularly strong in development economics: that economics had an important normative content, and should always have something to say about policy making. Like his peers in the field, Hirschman was policy-oriented. His theoretical research, empirical research, and his professional role as an economic adviser were strongly intertwined.

Although inflation remained (and is still) a problem for many Latin American countries, the structuralist–monetarist debate eventually lost its visibility, structuralism making room for another typically Latin American current of thought, which was the dependency theory.

Hirschman, however, did not write much about the dependency theory. By the late 1960s his research agenda changed, as he decided to cross the threshold of development economics. With the publication of his most famous book, *Exit, Voice and Loyalty*, in 1970, he progressively stepped outside the strict field of economics, to face new intellectual challenges in the neighboring territories of political science, philosophy, and the history of ideas.

NOTES

1. This is a rather impressionistic statement, especially for the first decades of the century, when the debate between structuralists and monetarists took place. There are few statistical series, one exception being a six volumes report by the Economic Commission for Latin America – ECLA, and Kaldor (1959), who wrote about Chile. Baer (1967, pp. 3–4, 19) complains about this lack of systematic investigation, claiming that the scarce available evidence could be used to support either side of the controversy.

2. This change can be interpreted as a reaction to Celso Furtado's review of *The Strategy* in a Brazilian periodical (Furtado, 1959). Furtado praises the book, which he considers to be "very useful," and refers approvingly to the fact that a Yale professor had acknowledged the structural causes of inflation. However, he criticizes Hirschman for not mentioning the Latin American literature, in particular the work of the ECLA (Economic Commission for Latin America) economists (Furtado, 1959, p. 65). A few months later Hirschman circulated a manuscript version of his article "Ideologies of economic development in Latin America," which turned out to be the first chapter of his book of readings on Latin America (Hirschman, 1961).

3. The Alliance for Progress was an aid program established by U.S. President Kennedy in 1961, designed to improve the U.S. relations with Latin America, hence avoiding the threat of the Soviet influence in the area.

4. Actually, these foreign specialists were responsible for providing market signals (Eichengreen, 1994). Their role was to evaluate whether a given country was able to handle capital loans, therefore endorsing financial, fiscal, and monetary policies consistent with the priorities of the lenders (Bianchi, 2011, p. 221).

5. This conference was preceded by a meeting in Bellagio, Italy, in July 1960, that gathered economists from Europe, North America, and Latin America. Out of this meeting came the recommendation to organize a conference on inflation and growth to be held in Latin America, and to be sponsored by private research institutions.

6. There was another significant debate going on during the 1960s, opposing a cost-push approach to inflation to a demand pull approach. Although the issues at stake were not the same, there are some points of contact between both debates, as discussed by Olivera (1964).

7. The four above-mentioned economists worked for ECLA with Raul Prebisch, its founder. However, they diverged from Prebisch on their approach to the inflation problem (Boianovsky, 2012, p. 282).

8. In his field notes during his visit to El Salvador, Hirschman writes: "Inflation may be better than stagnation; Inflation may be better than revolution; Inflation may be better than civil war." Albert O. Hirschman Papers, Mudd Manuscript Library, Princeton University, Box 5, Latin America.

9. The importance that Hirschman attributes to social pressures coming from various sources, including popular movements, in promoting social changes, is a visible facet of his general perspective, and shows up in his subsequent writings (Maluf, 2015, p. 61).

10. To which Campos (1961, p. 71) ironically reacted: "... this effort at theorizing would seem an exercise in 'unnecessary' originality." I will go back to Campos later.

ACKNOWLEDGMENTS

I am indebted to Ariel Akerman for useful hints, and to Marina Bianchi, Mauro Boianovsky, and Maurizio Franzini for helpful comments and suggestions on an earlier version of this work.

REFERENCES

Adelman, J. (2013). *Worldly philosopher. The odyssey of Albert O. Hirschman*. Princeton and Oxford: Princeton University Press.

Alacevich, M. (2012). *Visualizing uncertainties, or how Albert Hirschman and the World Bank disagreed on project appraisal and development approaches*. World Bank, Policy Research Papers 6260, November.

Arndt, H. W. (1985). The origins of structuralism. *World Development*, *13*, 151–159.

Ascher, W. (1996). The evolution of postwar doctrines in development economics. *History of Political Economy*, *28*(Suppl.), 312–336.

Baer, W. (1967). The inflation controversy in Latin America: A survey. *Latin American Research Review*, *2*(2), 3–25.

Baer, W., & Kerstenezky, I. (Eds.). (1964). *Inflation and growth in Latin America*. Homewood, IL: Richard D. Erwin.

Bianchi, A. M. (2011). A. M. Bianchi, visiting-economists through Hirschman's eyes. *The European Journal of the History of Economic Thought*, *18*(2), 217–242.

Bianchi, A. M. (2012). Albert Hirschman in Latin America: Notes on Hirschman's trilogy on economic development. *Nueva Economia*, *19*(36), 103–123.

Boianovsky, M. (2012). Celso Furtado and the structuralist-monetarist debate on economic stabilization. *History of Political Economy*, *44*(2), 277–330.

Campos, R. (1961). Two views of inflation in Latin America. In A. O. Hirschman (Ed.), *Latin American issues. Essays and comments* (pp. 69–79). New York, NY: The Twentieth Century Fund.

Charusheela, S. (2005). *Structuralism and individualism in economic analysis: The contractionary devaluation debate in development economics*. New York, NY: Routledge.

Cot, A. L. (2010). Albert O. Hirschman: An intellectual maverick. *The Tocqueville Review*, *31*(2), 61–79.

Danby, C. (2005). Noyola's institutional approach to inflation. *Journal of the History of Economic Thought*, *27*(2), 161–178.

Economic Commission for Latin America (ECLA). (1961). *Inflation and growth*. 6 volumes. Unpublished typescript. E/CN.12/563.

Eichengreen, B. (1994). House calls of the money doctor: The Kemmerer missions to Latin America, 1917–1931. In P. W. Drake (Ed.), *Money doctors, foreign debts, and economic reforms in Latin America from the 1890s to the present* (pp. 110–132). Wilmington, DE: Jaguar Books on Latin America.

Ellerman, D. (2004). Revisiting Hirschman on assistance and unbalanced growth. *Eastern Economic Journal*, *30*(2), 311–331.

Felix, D. (1961). An alternative view of the 'monetarist'-'Structuralist' controversy. In A. O. Hirschman (Ed.), *Latin American issues. Essays and comments* (pp. 81–93). New York, NY: The Twentieth Century Fund.

Friedman, M., & Schwartz, A. (1963). *A monetary history of the United States* (pp. 1867–1960). Princeton, NJ: Princeton University Press.

Furtado, C. (1959). Bibliográficas – The strategy of economic development. *Economica Brasileira*, *5*(1–2), 64–65.

Grunwald, J. (1961). The 'structuralist' school on price instability and development: The Chilean case. In A. O. Hirschman (Ed.), *Latin American issues. Essays and comments* (pp. 95–123). New York, NY: The Twentieth Century Fund.

Hirschman, A. O. (1948). Inflation and deflation in Italy. *American Economic Review*, *38*(4), 598–606.

Hirschman, A. O. (1958). *The strategy of economic development*. New Haven and London: Yale University Press.

Hirschman, A. O. (1961). Ideologies of economic development in Latin America. In A. O. Hirschman (Ed.), *Latin American issues. Essays and comments*. New York, NY: The Twentieth Century Fund.

Hirschman, A. O. (1963). *Journeys toward progress. Studies of economic policy-making in Latin America*. New York, NY: Greenwood Press.

Hirschman, A. O. (1964). Panel: Investment policy. In W. Baer & I. Kerstenezky (Eds.), *Inflation and growth in Latin America* (pp. 454–457). Homewood, IL: Richard D. Irwin, Inc.

Hirschman, A. O. (1968). The political economy of import-substitution industrialization in Latin America. *Quarterly Journal of Economics*, *82*(1), 1–32.

Hirschman, A. O. (1971). *A bias for hope. Essays on development and Latin America*. New Haven and London: Yale University Press.

Hirschman, A. O. (1981). *Essays in trespassing. Economics to politics and beyond*. Cambridge, London, New York, New Rochelle, Melbourne, Sidney: Cambridge University Press.

Hirschman, A. O. (1984). A dissenter's confession: "The strategy of economic development" revisited. In G. M. Meier & D. Seers (Eds.), *Pioneers in development* (pp. 87–111). London: Oxford University Press.

Hirschman, A. O. (1998). *Crossing boundaries. Selected writings*. Cambridge and London: Zone Books. Retrieved from http://www.jstor.org/stable/23394800

Kaldor, N. (1959). Problemas económicos de Chile. *El Trimestre Económico*, *26*(2), 170–221. Retrieved from http://www.jstor.org/stable/23394785

Little, I. M. (1982). *Economic development. Theory, policy, and international relations*. New York, NY: Basic Books, Inc..

Maluf, R. (2015). Hirschman e a dessacralização da epopeia do desenvolvimento por um desenvolvimentista. *Revista de Economia Política*, *35*(1), 43–63.

Meldolesi, L. (1995). *Discovering the possible. The surprising world of Albert O. Hirschman*. Notre Dame: University of Notre Dame Press.

Noyola-Vásquez, J. (1956). El desarrollo económico y la inflación en México y otros países latinoamericanos. *Investigación Económica*, *16*(4), 603–648. Retrieved from http://www.jstor.org/stable/42782949

Olivera, J. H. G. (1964). On structural inflation and Latin American 'structuralism'. *Oxford Economic Papers*, *16*(3), 321–332.

Pinto, A. (1960). Estabilidad y desarrollo. ?metas incompatibles o complementárias? *El Trimestre Económico*, *27*(106), 258–273.

Simonsen, M. (1964). Comment. In W. Baer & I. Kerstenezky (Eds.), *Inflation and growth in Latin America* (pp. 160–176). Homewood, IL: Richard D. Irwin, Inc.

Streeten, P. (1959). Unbalanced growth. *Oxford Economic Papers*, *11*(2), 167–190.

Sunkel, O. (1958). La inflación chilena: Un enfoque heterodoxo. *El Trimestre Económico*, *25*(4), 570–599.

Thorp, R., & Whitehead, L. (1973). Introduction. In R. Thorp & L. Whitehead (Eds.), *Inflation and stabilisation in Latin America* (pp. 1–22). London: The Macmillan Press Ltd.

Watcher, S. M. (1979). Structuralism versus monetarism: Inflation in Chile. In J. R. Behrman & J. Hanson (Eds.), *Short-term macroeconomic policy in Latin America* (pp. 227–256). Cambridge, MA: National Bureau of Economic Research.

HOMO POLITICUS: REFLECTIONS ON *THE PASSIONS AND THE INTERESTS*

Ruth W. Grant

ABSTRACT

In The Passions and the Interests, *Hirschman explored a movement in 18th century thought whose aim was to shape human motivations by establishing the prominence of interests, particularly material interests, in order to diminish the negative effects of the passions in political life. If the pursuit of gain could replace the pursuit of glory, for example, commercial transactions might replace bloody wars as a means of resolving conflict. Hirschman finds this claim overly optimistic. And, in his view, in making their case, these thinkers oversimplified and impoverished our understanding of human psychology by reducing all motivation to interest – a problem that persists in contemporary social science. After exploring Hirschman's account of 18th century thinkers, this paper attempts a discussion of a richer psychology identifying the variety of passions that motivate action toward different political goals; viz. status, justice, solidarity, and security. These political*

Research in the History of Economic Thought and Methodology, Volume 34B, 123–137

ISSN: 0743-4154/doi:10.1108/S0743-41542016000034B009

passions – including ambition, compassion, righteous indignation, loyalty, and fear – can have positive as well as negative political consequences.

Keywords: Hirschman; interests; 18th century thought; political psychology

INTRODUCTION

In the preface to the twentieth anniversary edition of *The Passions and the Interests*, Hirschman indicated the special status of this book for him. He wrote that his usual tendency to self-subversion, rethinking, and critiquing his own work did not apply to this book. He wrote: "I had hit on 'my' truth, so I never gave any thought to revising it" (Hirschman, 1977/1997, pp. xxii–xxiii). It might be surprising that Hirschman gave so much importance to this work. After all, 18th century intellectual history appears to be a digression from his main concerns as a development economist. But he tells us that the *question* that motivated his historical investigations in *The Passions and the Interests* was a pressing contemporary question for a development economist in Latin America: what are the political consequences of economic development? Or more particularly, why was economic growth so often coupled with political authoritarianism in Latin America, contrary to expectations? (Hirschman, 1981, p. 99). And moreover, where did those overly optimistic expectations for political improvements come from? The *answer*, described in *The Passions and the Interests*, involved, according to Hirschman "a story of the progressive impoverishment of the prevailing concept of human nature over a period of some three centuries" (Hirschman, 1981, p. 288). This impoverished and "simplistic" view – a view that came to be called "*homo oeconomicus*" – became the basis for the optimistic expectations that economic development would bring political progress as well. And this same concept of human nature grounded the assumptions built into contemporary social science models (Hirschman, 1981, pp. 287–288, 303). Hirschman's assessment of the social science enterprise throughout his work relies heavily on this analysis. Thus both the *question* that drives *The Passions and the Interests* and the *answer* it provides tie this study of 18th century thinkers to the central concerns of a contemporary social scientist in the field of development economics.

What did Hirschman find when he turned to the 18th century? He found an intellectual movement whose aim was to shape human motivations by establishing the prominence of interests, particularly material interests, in order to diminish the negative effects of the passions in political life. If the pursuit of gain could replace the pursuit of glory, commercial transactions might replace bloody wars as a means of resolving conflict. If the bourgeois, with his limited ambitions and preference for stability, could replace the aristocrat, with his drive for distinction and dominance, politics would become much more manageable. In considering the question of the effects of economic development on politics, these thinkers turned to psychological explanations – the mechanism of change would involve a profound change in human nature and the creation of a new human type, the bourgeois. Interests, especially material interests, would displace the passions as the primary motivators of human action.

This could have profound political effects. "The passions that most need bridling belong to the powerful, who are in a position to do harm on a huge scale and were believed to be particularly well endowed with passions in comparison to the lower orders" (Hirschman, 1977/1997, pp. 69–70, 111–112). Common people are too absorbed in daily subsistence to pose much of a problem. With the rise of a commercial class, a social power appears which can contest aristocratic power and whose members are driven by interest and not by wild and violent passions, such as ambition, associated with the aristocracy. Over time, of course, aristocratic orders disappeared. But the idea that economic interest was a less threatening motivation than political passion remained.[1]

Hirschman found in the 18th century authors he explored a complex argument with several related claims. First, there is the implicit claim that, ultimately, what drives both economics and politics is the psychology of motivation. Then there are two explicit claims: (1) that political passions are responsible for a great deal of destruction in our common political life and (2) that, in contrast, the pursuit of economic interests is at least a relatively benign motivator and at best a positive one, supporting stable and calm politics.

Hirschman was critical of what he found in his historical investigations, but not on every point. I believe that he completely accepted the implicit claim that psychology is foundational for understanding politics and economics. His article, "Changing Tolerance for Income Inequality," is an excellent example of how important he believed psychological dynamics are for economics and politics (see below). The problem with the 18th century thinkers was that they got the psychology wrong. As we have already noted, he thought their view was "simplistic" and "impoverished." As for the explicit claims, he seems to have accepted, in this work, the idea that political passions are largely destructive. However, he rejected the idea that economic interests are always benign or positive in their political effects. He devoted a chapter of *The Passions and the Interests* to a discussion of Adam Ferguson's and Alexis de Tocqueville's doubts on this score. The single-minded pursuit of material well-being can produce people who have little interest in public affairs and an excessive concern for stability that can jeopardize freedom. For this reason, he criticized the 18th century turn to interests as overly optimistic.

Thus, Hirschman leaves us with two bits of unfinished business. The first is to explore what an enriched and complex psychology, one that brings the political passions back into the picture, might look like. Who is *homo politicus* today? The second is to question the claim that was left unquestioned by both Hirschman and the thinkers he examined – that is, to question whether the political effects of the passions are necessarily as negative as they assumed. Before turning to these two tasks, we will begin with an exposition of Hirschman's argument in *The Passions and the Interests* and then provide some critical commentary on it.

THE PASSIONS AND THE INTERESTS

The lines of argument that Hirschman traces arose in response to the perception that "moralizing philosophy and religious precept could no longer be trusted with restraining the destructive passions of men" (Hirschman, 1977/1997, pp. 14, 15). "...[T]he search was on for a behavioral equivalent to religious precept, for new rules of conduct and devices that would impose much needed discipline and constraints on both rulers and ruled ..." (Hirschman, 1977/1997, p. 129). There were three primary alternatives for addressing this problem: coercion, harnessing the passions, and what Hirschman calls "the principle of countervailing passions." The second of these, harnessing the passions, appears in the work of Bernard de Mandeville, who famously suggests that institutions and policies can be structured so that the effects of the passions, or "private vices," will be "public benefits" (Hirschman, 1977/1997, pp. 18–19). There is no need to suppress the passions if their effects can be prudently managed. In contrast, "the principle of countervailing passions" operates on the passions themselves. The idea is that relatively innocuous passions could be used as a counterweight to more dangerous passions. David Hume is a prominent exponent of this view, in Hirschman's account. Hirschman shows the reader how this idea develops: interest in particular, considered as one of the passions, serves to counteract the wilder passions; interest becomes increasingly identified with material interest; whereas reason is ineffectual and most other passions are violent, interest leads men to behave predictably and calmly (Hirschman, 1977/1997, pp. 43–44). Thus, the development of commerce, because it fosters the pursuit of material interest, will have salutary effects. Hirschman calls this the "doux commerce thesis" and sees the Baron de Montesquieu as its strongest advocate.

In 1982, in an article called "Rival Interpretations of Market Society," Hirschman returned to a consideration of this thesis as one alternative account of the effects of capitalist development on society and morality broadly speaking. In this context he stressed the ways in which the "doux commerce thesis" predicted that commercial development would shape human character. It would create

> ... a more polished human type – more honest, reliable, orderly, and disciplined, as well as more friendly and helpful, ever ready to find solutions to conflicts and a middle ground for opposed opinions. Such a type will in turn greatly facilitate the smooth functioning of the market. (Hirschman, 1982, pp. 1465–1466)

In *The Passions and the Interests*, Hirschman stressed the political effects of commercial development. He explored the claims of Montesquieu, Sir James Steuart, and John Millar that the spread of domestic, as well as international, commerce would improve political life both by constraining rulers and diminishing warfare.

According to Hirschman, others disagreed. Neither the Physiocrats nor Adam Smith believed that politics would automatically improve as a result of commercial development. In Hirschman's view, Smith's justification for elevating the pursuit of self-interest was economic, not political. And here Smith's role in Hirschman's narrative becomes crucial. According to Hirschman, Smith sees interest as the only source of human motivation. Though he acknowledges the importance of status in *Theory of Moral Sentiments*, status has no independent motivating power, since it is achieved by economic advancement. All of the passions collapse into the concept of interest, and no argument regarding the need for countervailing forces remains. "*The Wealth of Nations* marks the end to the speculations about the effects of interest-motivated on passionate behavior that had exercised the minds of some of Smith's more illustrious predecessors" (Hirschman, 1977/1997, p. 112).

Hirschman's narrative traces the gradual triumph of the view that interest is *the* source of human motivation. He goes so far as to characterize

17th and 18th century thinkers as discovering in "'interest' a principle that could replace 'love' and 'charity' as the basis for a well-ordered society" (Hirschman, 1982, p. 1467). This characterization is difficult to square with Hume's extensive discussions, in *An Enquiry Concerning the Principles of Morals*, of benevolence and justice as social virtues grounded in natural moral sentiments. It contrasts starkly as well with the well-known opening line of Smith's *The Theory of Moral Sentiments*.

> How selfish soever man may be supposed, there are evidently some principles in his nature, which interest him in the fortune of others, and render their happiness necessary to him, though he receives nothing from it except the pleasure of seeing it.

Hirschman did not pay sufficient attention to the moral sentiments and their complex relations with passions and interests, particularly in his discussion of Smith, but also in his discussion of Hume. I turn now to a brief consideration of this issue. I believe that there are good reasons to doubt that these thinkers endorsed the view that interest could be "the foundation of a well ordered society" or that interest could be successfully enlisted to constrain human behavior by overpowering dangerous passions.

THE PASSIONS AND THE INTERESTS – AND THE MORAL SENTIMENTS

Recall that Hirschman begins by identifying the problem facing 17th and 18th century thinkers as the problem of finding an alternative foundation for morality given the weakness of both reason and religious precepts. That interest might be enlisted to restrain the passions in the service of morality is the solution that he explores. But for Hume and for Smith, interest is at least as much a part of the problem as of the solution.

Hume has some very harsh things to say about interest:

> All the other passions, beside this of interest, are either easily restrained or are not of such pernicious consequence when indulged ... This avidity alone of acquiring goods and possessions for ourselves and our nearest friends is insatiable, perpetual, universal, and directly destructive of society ... no affection of the human mind has both a sufficient force and a proper direction to counterbalance the love of gain .... (Hume, 1948b, p. 61)

According to Hume, interest must be directed against itself through the establishment of social conventions and institutions of government (Hume, 1948b, pp. 61–62, 97–101). Interest is satisfied better in the long run when restrained by social conventions that establish property and justice.

But Hume also insists that, entirely independent of self-interest, the interests of society as a whole "are not indifferent to us." "Everything which contributes to the happiness of society recommends itself *directly* to our approbation and good will (emphasis added)" whether or not we ourselves benefit. Social utility is a source of moral sentiment (Hume, 1948a, pp. 211–212). For Smith too, self-interest is part of the moral problem. Even in a competitive race, one can run hard, but cannot throw down one's opponent (Smith, 1984, p. 83). There must be some restraints on interest. Moreover, the idea of the impartial spectator, so central to Smith's discussion, is that we must judge our own behavior as an objective, *disinterested* observer would judge. That is what impartiality means. The voice of conscience, the impartial spectator, curbs self-interested behavior by teaching us to view ourselves as others would view us; that is, to view ourselves as if we were not a party to the case.

These observations are merely suggestive of the intricacies of the moral and political psychology of these authors. The "impoverished" and "simplistic" psychology that reduces everything to interest is, I believe, a later development. Perhaps an indication of this is that the term, *Homo Oeconomicus*, was first used by late 19th century critics of John Stuart Mill. The 18th century authors Hirschman considers had a more complex psychology than he allows, as well as a richer understanding both of the problem of encouraging moral behavior and of the relation between the passions and political society.

HOMO POLITICUS[2]

In order to recapture some of that complexity and richness, I offer here a brief catalog of passions that motivate political action, meant to be suggestive, rather than exhaustive. In doing so, I return to the question raised at the outset: who is *homo politicus* today? The categories of this analysis derive from human purposes that become political aims when pursued through collective action in the public arena: (1) status, (2) justice, (3) solidarity or community, and (4) security. Status passions include ambition, pride, vanity, envy and so forth. Pity and anger drive action in the name of justice. Loyalty and attachment ground the sense of communal solidarity. And finally, fear is the passion most closely associated with the desire for security. It is worth noting, first, that these passions are related to interest in a variety of ways and, second, that they are each capable of producing positive, as well as negative, political effects.

The political motivations sketched here are broader than and cannot be reduced to the self-interested desire to better one's condition. If politics were indeed reducible to interests and the political passions could effectively be suppressed, there would be no such thing as symbolic politics. "Symbolic politics" means politics where material interests or tangible advantages are not at stake. Symbolic politics engages passions associated with status, justice, and solidarity. For example, in the United States, controversies over flying the flag of the Southern Confederacy on public buildings have this character. Or consider the many political demands for respect. Some groups are not satisfied with tolerance, even when tolerance allows for the satisfaction of every group interest. They want something more; they want forms of recognition that imply respect. This is why civil union for gay couples is not equivalent to gay marriage. The concern for status is at work here. To take another recent example, consider the sense of insult produced by the publication of cartoons of Mohammed and the rage it produced. Those passions were surely manipulated by interested parties; but the conflict itself was triggered by symbolic issues.

To understand political events such as these, we need to take into account the operation of the passions. This is why explanations of politics based on economic models which assume the rational actor psychology of *homo oeconomicus* are particularly weak in explaining social movements (Goodwin, 2001; Gould, 2004; Jasper, 1997; Wood, 2003). Passions associated with status, with justice, and with solidarity usually combine together to produce political conflict and political mobilization. To put it somewhat differently, these passions overcome collective action problems.[3] There is little temptation to "free ride" if what I really want is to assert my dignity or express my outrage, my sympathy, my hatred, my sense of solidarity, or all of these simultaneously – nobody else can do these things for me. I must do them for myself.

With this in mind, let us begin by considering the "status passions," those that aim at distinction or recognition relative to others. Some of these passions are inherently competitive; we cannot all be winners when it comes to honor or ambition. Others are not necessarily "zero sum"; the passions which aim at esteem, recognition, or respect, for example (Brennan & Pettit, 2004, pp. 18–21). In principle, the desire for esteem can be satisfied by equal respect. Similarly, while envy or jealousy is inherently destructive – its satisfaction comes in harming a rival and bringing him or her down – emulation can be positive because it aims at raising oneself up. When brought into the political arena, we should thus expect different status passions to have different effects. Moreover, in politics, we need to be concerned, not only with extraordinarily ambitious people who thirst for distinction and hunger for glory, but also with much more ordinary demands for recognition.

What I am calling "status passions," Rousseau (1755/1964) calls *amour-propre*. He makes a fundamental distinction between *amour-propre*; the sort of self-love that produces a desire to be preferred, and *amour-de-soi*, a very different sort of self-love that is concerned exclusively with self-interest. In his account, the two sorts of self-love, one status-oriented and the other interest-oriented, arise independently of one another. Of course, the two are often confused, particularly in societies where riches are a sign of status. But even in this case, status is an independent motivation.[4] This is evident where their aims compete. People will satisfy their vanity, for example, at the expense of their interests. People will react at least as much to insult as to injury. As a result of *amour-propre* or "status passions," people will choose to hurt a rival, rather than to attain the original object of their desire. Rousseau identifies these passions as the true source of evil and conflict in human societies.

A second set of political passions revolves around a concern for justice. Here I have in mind primarily anger and pity. The political form of anger – call it outrage or righteous indignation – depends on the conviction that suffering is unnecessary, willfully imposed, and, most importantly, undeserved. Righteous indignation implies a claim that injustice has been done. For example, to be treated with contempt or slighted – that is, to be treated with less respect than you believe you deserve – always provokes anger. There is thus a connection between this "justice passion" and the status passions.[5] But anger can also be provoked by all kinds of injustice, many of them completely unrelated to status issues and not at all personal. A person who "has a sense of justice" will react with anger upon hearing about injustices suffered by people at a considerable distance from himself.

And he will pity them. Like anger, pity can be provoked by the conviction that people are not getting what they deserve. In the case of pity, however, the feeling is aroused whether the undeserved suffering is accidental or deliberately caused. If it is deliberately caused, pity for the victims will be joined with anger directed at the victimizers. Pity and anger are two sides of the same coin where a judgment has been made that injustice has been done. On the other hand, if we believe that suffering is deserved, we are less likely to feel pity, more likely to harden our hearts, and we call it punishment or revenge. Aristotle (1932/1960, 1386b) tells us that good men feel both pity and indignation. What he means by "indignation" is a particular form of righteous anger. It is the opposite of pity; it is pain at undeserved good fortune. It is to be distinguished from envy, which can be aroused by the good fortune of another, whether deserved or not, and may even be exacerbated by the thought that the envied one is deserving because he possesses meritorious qualities that the envier lacks. Ambitious and worthy people are most apt to feel indignation, rather than envy, because they are most concerned with recognition of "just deserts."

Anger and pity involve a judgment with respect to justice, and they both can arise independently of self-interest. In fact, they often occur as reactions to things that befall other people besides ourselves, people with whom we empathize or identify. Pity, for example, is aroused when we can imagine ourselves in the position of the suffering one. But, if we believe that we are in danger of suffering the same fate imminently, our reaction is more likely to be fear than pity (Aristotle, 1932/1960; II.8). Pity requires both distance and identification. Finally, both pity and anger, as reactions to perceived injustice, can motivate people to act politically on behalf of others in an attempt to restore justice.

This brings me to the third category of passions that motivate political action. These are tied to the psychological processes of identification that produce a sense of solidarity or community. Events that happen to other members of a group with whom a person identifies can trigger immediate and passionate responses in that person even when he or she is not directly affected and is unlikely *ever* to be directly affected by similar events. Identifications can ground political behaviors that have little, if anything, to do with interests. The passions associated with these identifications include loyalty and attachment. Identification can produce very close personal ties but also the more attenuated sense of shared fate within a group. Aristotle (1932/1960; II.4) captures a core component of the phenomena in his discussion of *philia*, usually translated as "friendship" or "love." It is the passion that describes the condition of sharing another's pleasures and pains. If I identify with you, I am happy at your good fortune, and vice versa.

The opposite of this passion is hatred or enmity. We are unhappy when our enemies prosper and pleased when they suffer. Though some think of hatred as something like sustained anger, hatred is unlike anger in very important respects (Allport, 1954, pp. 363–366; Gaylin, 2003, p. 21). Most importantly, unlike anger, hatred does not require an argument about justice. And, in politics, it is joined with group identifications, which is not necessarily the case with anger. A positive identification with "us" can involve demonizing, and hating, "them." It is important to remember hatred, along with anger and pity, in the list of political passions lest we give the false impression that political mobilization is generally righteously motivated by concern for victims of oppression. As Aristotle said, pity and indignation move good men. The same cannot be said for hatred. Moreover, recognizing the distinction between hatred and anger can clarify political possibilities. To confuse the two will surely lead to an underestimation of the tenacity of ethnic conflicts, for example. Hatred is an obstacle to the negotiation of conflicts of interest. A solution that gives both parties half a loaf robs those who hate of the pleasure of seeing their enemies get nothing. Anger, aroused by perceived injustice, is easier to address through the redress of grievances. Anger can be mollified by forgiveness; hatred is more difficult to appease.

There is another set of political motivators that deserve mention. These include commitment and a sense of duty or responsibility. Along with a sense of efficacy, these are crucial for motivating the step from feelings of loyalty, pity, anger, or hatred to action (Wood, 2003, pp. 231–237). It is tempting to include commitment, duty and responsibility among the passions associated with community and solidarity. Where there is loyalty or a sense of solidarity, there is usually commitment and responsibility also. But the reverse is not the case. To classify commitment and a sense of responsibility with the passions associated with solidarity as an aim is a mistake.[6] First, they can operate independently of group identification. I may take very seriously my obligations toward people with whom I do not identify or consider as part of my community. And second, the passion that enforces such obligations is guilt; it is not clear that commitment and the sense of duty are themselves passions. (We might refer to them instead as moral sentiments!).

Lastly, we must consider fear – the passion that motivates us to seek security. This is surely a political passion. Like the status passions, but unlike justice and solidarity, the concern for security is necessarily self-regarding. And to the extent that security can be understood as identical to self-preservation or as the necessary condition for the pursuit of self-interest, fear and its aim do not have the same independence from interest as the passions associated with any other political aim.

I have said nothing about acquisition – the desire for gain. That is because, in a discussion that sets economic interests against political passions, the desire for gain is identified with economic interests. It should be obvious, however, that the desire for gain becomes a political passion to the extent that it is an avenue to status and power and a condition of security.

A good deal could be said about the ways in which the various political passions interact with one another, despite my assigning them to different categories. Anger is aroused by injuries to pride, for example. Personal ambition can become responsible leadership through processes of identification with the group. A complex political psychology could be elaborated here. Such a psychology would not only explore the interactions among the various political passions, but also identify both their positive and negative political potentialities. We need a complex psychology, one that takes the full range of the passions and the interests into account in seeking to explain such phenomena as the political consequences of economic development. One reviewer, commenting on *The Passions and the Interests*, wrote that Hirschman's core message was this: "Those who neglect the passions are either fools or economists" (Lekachman, 1977, p. 34).[7]

CONCLUSION

The 18th century notion that political passions might be suppressed by the dominance of economic interests, leading to diminished and softened political conflicts, failed to take the political passions seriously enough. The idea that gain could replace glory, and commerce replace warfare, now appears to be a pipe dream. *Homo politicus* cannot be reduced to *homo oeconomicus*. Political passions are embedded in human nature and tied to legitimate political aims. Politics must allow somehow for the satisfaction of desires for distinction, for respect, and for community. It must contend with anger and ambition, hatred, envy and contempt. Conflicts involving these "zero sum" passions are not so amenable to negotiated solutions, and they can be extremely threatening. There is no doubt that these political passions can be the source of terrible conflict and destruction.

But this is not to say that politics must always end in tragedy. Political passions can have positive effects. This is the possibility that is not given full consideration in *The Passions and the Interests*. The political passions can be shaped and channeled, and many of them clearly have positive as well as negative possibilities – righteous indignation and loyalty, for example. Hirschman himself provided a subtle account of the positive impact of loyalty on political processes. Loyalty encourages the use of "voice" and increases the possibilities for change from within (Hirschman, 1970). There are countless possibilities. Pride can be satisfied with independence, rather than domination. Symbolic politics can be used to reinforce solidarity. Promoting equal respect can diminish the more corrosive forms of the desire for recognition. By making opportunities available, envy might be transformed into emulation. Even by believing that opportunities are available, that transformation can be fostered. That is how the myth of the American dream functions. Hirschman, in his article, "Changing Tolerance for Inequality," provided an account of how understanding the dynamics of envy could help identify positive political possibilities. In the early phases of development, people react to the economic advancement of some with the hopeful expectation that they will be next, and they remain loyal and supportive of the state. There is a moment of opportunity here for positive political development. But if too much time passes and their turn does not come, people become disaffected, envious, and angry at perceived injustice. The possibility for positive political development diminishes as a result (Hirschman & Michael, 1973).

As I said at the outset, Hirschman wrote that the question that motivated him to write *The Passions and the Interests* was the question of the impact of economic development on politics. It turns out that this relationship is mediated by psychological processes. The implicit claim that psychology is fundamental for economics and politics – a claim that Hirschman and his 18th century interlocutors share – is the crucial claim. We need a much better answer to the question, "Who is *homo politicus*?" Both for the sake of understanding politics and for the sake of improving politics, the full array of passions needs to be acknowledged and their potential for good or harm understood.

NOTES

1. In a democratic context, Abraham Lincoln warned of the political dangers of ambition (1838). De Tocqueville argued that revolutions would become rare in democratic societies where people are tied to their material well-being and have the moderate temperament of traders (1969, Volume II, part 3, chapter 21). The authors of *The Federalist Papers* worried about checking political ambition (2003, p. 51).
2. The material in this section is drawn from my article, "Passions and Interests Revisited: the Psychological Foundations of Economics and Politics" (2008).
3. I am grateful to David Soskice for this suggestion. Donald Horowitz argues that the satisfaction of discharging aggression, "killing and degrading," overcomes collective action problems for participants in ethnic riots (2001, pp. 534–535).
4. Hirschman collapses interest and status in his discussion of Smith. See section The Passions and The Interests, p.127 above.
5. Hobbes (1658/1972, pp. 56–57) stresses the connection between anger and status insults, but not the connection to justice found in Aristotle (1932/1960; II.2).
6. Compare Sen (1985).

7. Note that what I am calling the political passions can also motivate economic behavior. For example, conspicuous consumption is driven by status passions; loyalty applies to corporations as well as political communities, and so forth (see Grant, 2008).

REFERENCES

Allport, G. W. (1954). *The nature of prejudice*. Cambridge, MA: Addison-Wesley.

Aristotle (1932/1960). *The rhetoric of Aristotle*. New York, NY: Appleton Century Crofts.

Brennan, G., & Pettit, P. (2004). *The economy of esteem: An essay on civil and political society*. Oxford: Oxford University Press.

de Tocqueville, A. (1969). Democracy in America *(G. Lawrence, Trans.)*. Garden City, NY: Anchor Books.

Gaylin, W. (2003). *Hatred: The psychological descent into violence*. New York, NY: Public Affairs.

Goodwin, J. (2001). *Passionate politics: Emotions and social movements*. Chicago, IL: University of Chicago Press.

Gould, D. B. (2004). Passionate political processes: Bringing emotions back into the study of social movements. In J. Goodwin & J. M. Jasper (Eds.), *Rethinking social movements: Structure, meaning and emotion*. Lanham, MD: Rowman and Littlefield.

Grant, R. (2008). Passions and interests revisited: The psychological foundations of economics and politics. *Public Choice*, *137*, 451–461.

Hamilton, A., Madison, J., & Jay, J. (2003). *The federalist papers*. New York, NY: Signet Classics.

Hirschman, A. O. (1970). *Exit, voice and loyalty: Responses to decline in firms, organizations and states*. Cambridge, MA: Harvard University Press.

Hirschman, A. O. (1977/1997). *The passions and the interests: Political arguments for capitalism before its triumph*. University Park, PA: Pennsylvania State University Press.

Hirschman, A. O. (1981). *Essays in trespassing: Economics to politics and beyond*. Cambridge: Cambridge University Press.

Hirschman, A. O. (1982). Rival interpretations of market society: Civilizing, destructive, or feeble? *Journal of Economic Literature*, *20*, 1463–1484.

Hirschman, A. O., & Michael, R. (1973). The changing tolerance for income inequality in the course of economic development. *The Quarterly Journal of Economics*, *87*(4), 544–566.

Hobbes, T. (1658/1972). *Man and citizen*. Garden City, NY: Doubleday and Co.

Horowitz, D. (2001). *The deadly ethnic riot*. Berkley, CA: University of California Press.

Hume, D. (1948a). An enquiry concerning the principles of morals. In *Hume's moral and political philosophy*. New York, NY: Hafner Press.

Hume, D. (1948b). A treatise of human nature. In *Hume's moral and political philosophy*. New York, NY: Hafner Press.

Jasper, J. M. (1997). *The art of moral protest*. Chicago: University of Chicago Press.

Lekachman, R. (1977). Book review of the passions and the interests. *The New Republic*, September 24, pp. 33–34.

Lincoln, A. (1838). The perpetuation of our political institutions: Address before the young men's lyceum of Springfield, Illinois. Retrieved from www.abrahamlincolnonline.org/lincoln/speeches/lyceum.htm

Rousseau, J. J. (1755/1964). Discourse on the origin and foundations of inequality. In R. D. Masters (Ed.), *First and second discourses* (pp. 77–182). New York, NY: St. Martin's Press.

Sen, A. (1985). Goals, commitment, and identity. *Journal of Law, Economics, and Organization*, *1*, 341–355.

Smith, A. (1984). *The theory of moral sentiments*. Indianapolis, IN: Liberty Fund Press.

Wood, E. J. (2003). *Insurgent collective action and civil war in El Salvador*. Cambridge: Cambridge University Press.

SHIFTING VALUES: PRIVATE CONCERNS VERSUS PUBLIC ACTION☆

Marina Bianchi

ABSTRACT

In his essay Against Parsimony *(1985), Hirschman argued in favor of "complicating" economic theory. This paper focuses on two of the economic phenomena that, according to Hirschman, are in need of greater complexity.*

The first refers to the process of preference formation: a change in tastes that is preceded by the formation of meta-preferences is in fact, for Hirschman, a change in values. These autonomous, reflective kinds of changes, as opposed to non-reflective kinds, do not take place simply in response to price changes. Contrary to the standard economic assumption, de valoribus est disputandum.

The second phenomenon refers to the existence of non-instrumental actions. Striving for truth, love, beauty, justice, and liberty has

☆Paper presented at the Conference in honor of Albert O. Hirschman, *The gift of (self)subversion*. Universita' di Roma La Sapienza, September 12–13, 2014.

Research in the History of Economic Thought and Methodology, Volume 34B, 139–160

ISSN: 0743-4154/doi:10.1108/S0743-41542016000034B010

non-calculable outcomes. According to instrumental reasoning such actions are "a mystery." Moreover they are often painful to achieve. Why then are they pursued?

According to Hirschman, changes in choice behavior implying changes in values are the expression of a conflict between meta-preferences and preferences, and this, in its turn, is the result of disappointment. If disappointment is with private consumption, social and public commitments can provide alternative values; if, vice versa, disappointment is with public action, private concerns might provide the prevailing values. In discussing these points, I shall show that there are other sources of conflict, besides disappointment, that have both a cognitive and affective dimension and whose effects on preferences might result in altered choices.

Keywords: Preferences; meta-preferences; economic change; public action

JEL Classifications: D11; D12; D61; H4

INTRODUCTION

In his essay *Against Parsimony. Three Easy Ways of Complicating some Categories of Economic Discourse* (1985) Albert O. Hirschman starts by recognizing that, in the construction of a theory, parsimony is an undoubted virtue. Economizing the conceptual tools that allow for simplifying and ordering complex phenomena is a goal that any theorist should pursue. Yet, like any virtue, Hirschman adds (paraphrasing Sen, 1977), parsimony can be overdone and prevent the gains that could be reached by making a theory more refined. This is particularly true of economics. This is a problem, says Hirschman, that he himself discovered when he started to introduce "voice," as a force that might keep firms and organizations alert to customer discontent, alongside the more traditional "exit" option. It took a whole book, he declares, his *Exit, Voice and Loyalty* (1970), to cope with the resulting complications (Hirschman, 1985, p. 8).

Hirschman identifies three ways in which economics needs to be made more complex and far reaching. The first involves the distinction between first-order and second-order preferences, or between preferences and meta-preferences. The existence of meta-preferences reveals for Hirschman that humans can step back from choice and ask themselves whether this or that choice is what they really want. In economics however the study of the complex psychological and cultural processes that are behind observed market choices has been left to the work of psychologists, sociologists and anthropologists. Yet, he continues, by failing to address these processes, economists prevent themselves from addressing an important phenomenon: the problem of economic change. It is through the interconnections between meta-preferences and preferences, between values and choices, that one might hope, according to Hirschman, to better disentangle some of the features at work in the changes of the economy.

The second possible way of increasing complexity is to be found in the realm of non-instrumental actions. These, for Hirschman, are a mystery for instrumental reason (Hirschman, 1985, p.13). Striving for truth, love, beauty, common good, justice, liberty, friendship, and salvation has non-calculable, non-measurable outcomes. For these activities then the usual economic distinction between effort and result, means and ends, between costs and revenues cannot be applied. Moreover they are often painful and costly to pursue. Why do we strive for them nevertheless? To attempt an answer involves tapping into human motivations and feelings, such as the feelings of self-development, belonging, and personhood.

The third context in which added complexity seems necessary, to Hirschman, refers to such attitudes and actions as public morality, trust, and civic spirit. Economists equate these attitudes to other economic factors that are scarce and in need to be economized. But these abilities may well increase through use and experience, and be depleted if economized and not used. At the same time, they differ from those skills and abilities that can be endlessly improved through learning. One can learn to be more benevolent and trustworthy, but there are limits to the benevolence and trust one can exercise. Indeed, says Hirschman, if the demands that are put on people to perform their civic duty and to trust are excessive, re-entering institutional arrangements that rely more on self-interest can achieve better results. Conversely, were demands on benevolence and community values very low, it would be more effective to reduce incentives based on self-interest.

These arguments in favor of greater complexity in economics were not new in Hirschman's analysis. The whole parable of his life, vividly and richly narrated by Adelman's (2013) biography of Hirschman, shows Hirschman's propensity to break established disciplinary boundaries, trespassing, doubting and subverting acquired certainties, including his own.

Against parsimony then iterates and further clarifies Hirschman's long-standing plea for an economic discipline more sensitive to the richness and multifaceted nature of human experiences.

In this paper I shall concentrate on the first two of Hirschman's suggestions for a less parsimonious economic theory, highlighting the strong connections that exist between them. For Hirschman it is from the conflict between preferences and meta-preferences that new values emerge, in particular those that are connected with public involvement and actions. These actions and concerns, being self-rewarding and autonomous, can provide a way out of that which is disappointing about following one's existing preferences and behavior. Hirschman in this way provides a glimpse into the human motivations that might explain behavioral and institutional changes. What I shall show however is that more is needed for a fuller understanding of these changes. In the second part of the paper I shall discuss Hirschman's response to Tibor Scitovsky's theory of motivation, which addressed similar themes around the same time and relied on a body of psychological research that opened a new way of looking at the determinants of individual behavior and choices.

PREFERENCE FORMATION: THE IMPORTANCE OF VALUES

According to Hirschman, there is a specifically human ability that allows men and women to step back from their existing wants, volitions, and preferences, and to ask themselves whether these volitions are really what they want and prefer. This process of exercising one's own preferences over preferences is a fact worth stressing, says Hirschman, first, because these "meta" preferences may differ from preferences, and second because this difference, as it manifests itself in changes in behavior, can reveal something of the status of meta-preferences and how they too may possibly change (Hirschman, 1985, p. 9).

Not all changes in behavior, however, are the result of a conscious and often tortuous process of deliberation: "there are also preference changes that take place without any elaborate antecedent development of meta-preferences" (*ibid.*, p. 9). These are a type of preferences that, Hirschman recalls, the philosopher Harry Frankfurt had called "wanton" preferences.

For Frankfurt, wantonness in agents reflects an absence of concern about the desirability of their desires, despite their being perfectly rational and able to defend their course of actions. Such persons have first-order desires but not second-order volitions (Frankfurt, 1971, p. 11). Yet the capacity for self-evaluation that manifests itself in the formation of volitions of the second order – of wanting to be or not to be the way one is – is exactly what distinguishes human from non-human behavior, and conduces to the freedom of the will.

Changes in preferences that are unreflective, impulsive, uncomplicated are then, for Hirschman, following Frankfurt, wanton. In contrast, a change in tastes that is preceded by the formation of meta-preferences, a non-wanton change of preference, is not really a change in tastes at all. A taste, says Hirschman, is almost defined as a preference about which you do not argue – *de gustibus non est disputandum*. A taste about which you argue, with others or yourself, ceases ipso facto to be a taste – it turns into a value. Hence the further conclusion that, when a change in preferences has been preceded by the formation of a meta-preference, when, that is, much argument has gone on within the self, then the change typically represents a change in values rather than a change in tastes.

The consequence of this active process of deliberation is that the economic incentives, such as price changes, are not enough to induce changes in behavior of the reflective type. On this point Hirschman distances himself sharply from, say, Gary Becker who, having reduced values to wanton tastes, can dismiss both as ineffective and elicit changes in behavior simply through changes in relative prices (*ibid.*, p. 11; Stigler & Becker, 1977; see also Becker, 1996).[1] The same can be said for those policy measures that try to combat unethical behavior by simply raising the cost of this behavior rather than by promoting public standards and imposing regulations. They simply neglect the value-molding function of the law. Instead, changes in meta-preferences stem from deeper, more complex, and less readily knowable shifts that involve values and ideals. Hence Hirschman's conclusion: *De valoribus est disputandum*.

In this first call for complicating economic theory Hirschman makes several relevant points that can be summarized as follows.

In order to understand the forces that might shape economic change, it is important for economists to distinguish between Preference, P, and Meta-preference, M. Only when P has been preceded by M are we indeed dealing not with haphazard changes in tastes but with more complex changes in values. It is from changes in behavior, those changes that in fact reveal that $M \neq P$, that we can start to have a glimpse of the deeper status of M and, correspondingly, of the possible directions that economic change can take.

In raising these valid points Hirschman nonetheless leaves several questions unanswered. The first, and most pressing of these, is: what is the type of conflict or discrepancy that might occur between P and M? From this question there arises a second: how might a situation of conflict that causes $P \neq M$ lead to a deeper and more tortuous resolution such as one that involves changing current P into new values?

Indeed, Hirschman, here following Frankfurt, seems to create too strong a dichotomy between the unreflective/wanton P and the reflective/higher volition, M. In (correctly) attempting to stress the importance of values and their role in choices, Hirschman makes too much of the difference between M and P, leaving P in the realm of matters indisputable – simple tastes that are not worth discussing. This renders it more difficult not only to understand how to go from P to M and vice versa, but also to discriminate between changes in behavior that are simply wonton from those that are not.

We shall see that Hirschman himself found it not easy to answer these questions and the answers he provided still leave some queries unaddressed. I shall start with the first of the questions above: what causes M to diverge from P?

SOURCES OF DISAPPOINTMENT

"As is well known from works of fiction, a persuasive account of important decisions by individuals to move in a new direction is often produced through the conjunction of preexisting doubts and unease – second order volitions of sorts – with some catalytic event or experience" (Hirschman, 1982, p. 72).

It is from Hirschman's essay *Shifting Involvements* (1982) that we can begin to articulate his answer to the types of conflicts that may arise between P and M and that are at the basis of M-formation.[2] The basic point of Hirschman's argument is straightforward.

Individual activities, such as acts of consumption but also participation in social and public life, are undertaken in the expectation of the satisfaction they may yield (Hirschman, 1982, p. 10). Yet, besides being a source of satisfaction, these activities may also be disappointing and fall below what one expected from them. When this happens and expectations do not adjust downward, disappointment and discontent will tend to persist. As a result, these patterns of consumption and activities are destined to change and move toward activities that promise to be more rewarding. Preferences change and, as we shall see, meta-preferences change too.

> *The world I am trying to understand in this essay is one in which men think they want one thing and then upon getting it, find out, to their dismay, that they do not want it nearly as much as they thought or don't want it at all and that something else, of which they were hardly aware, is what they really want.* (Hirschman, 1982, p. 21, author's italics)

The possible sources of disappointment are, obviously, many, but Hirschman's chosen focus is on that category of disappointment that comes from the private consumption of goods and services. As Simmel had pointed out in his *Philosophy of money* (1978 [1900]), says Hirschman, goods are richer than money because they "harbor either surprises or disappointments,"[3] while money, which is abstract in nature and devoid of any quality, can bring neither (Hirschman, 1982, p. 26).

Yet not all goods are equal as possible sources of disappointment. Within their universe, there are some whose disappointment potential is higher. This is the case, contrary to what one might expect, with goods that are durable. Indeed, says Hirschman, some of the most durable pleasures come from truly *non*-durable goods, those that are entirely consumed and vanish. Just because they perish in the act of consumption, these goods are a source of renewed pleasure when they are consumed again, and again (*ibid.*, p. 28). Contrary to these "disappointment-resistant" goods, durable goods are much more likely to bring discontent. This is true particularly of those that are in continuous or even intermittent use (the apartment, the refrigerator, the washing machine, the car). In this case the pleasure that their acquisition might have provided at the beginning is supplanted, in time, by simple comfort – a feeling that is inimical to pleasure.[4] They start to be taken for granted (*ibid.*, p. 32). It is at this point, when they fail to bring the hoped-for private happiness, that their durable existence becomes a source of self-reproach and dissatisfaction.[5] When then present experience does not match anymore what was expected or experienced in the past, current practices of consumption become a source of disappointment, a disappointment that transfers into a conflict between preference and meta-preferences.

But it is from the historical reconstruction of these practices and from the way they were echoed by the writers of the time that the instability of the private happiness of consumption is made clear.

If one looks, Hirschman argues, at how new affluence and greater availability of goods have been received in Western countries in the course of time, one cannot but notice that along with appreciation and praise there came strong feelings of resentment and distrust. From Adam Smith who, besides celebrating the advantages of more affordable goods, also often remarked that true happiness does not lie in accumulating goods, to Flaubert's cry against the ugliness of new, cheap, mass-produced articles (*ibid.*, p. 53), affluence seemed to produce, along with its benefits, also strong feelings of frustration and hostility.

One obvious reason for this hostility was that new goods represented a threat to the established hierarchies of social order. But another, opposed, reason was that new articles of wealth were also seen to increase the gaps between the rich and the poor, not only in relative terms but absolutely.[6]

Once so viewed, these opposite sources of discontent seem to provide no room for a resolution. If the new riches diffuse and filter down to the have-nots, the conservatives will denounce the threat to social order that this process causes. On the other hand, if they remain confined to the rich and do not filter down, progressives will denounce the widening disparity between social classes. The result of this *double bind*, Hirschman tells us, is that, regardless of the reason, the new consumption practices become the target of hostility and resentment.

But there is also a second, even more important, kind of double bind, deriving, according to Hirschman, from two additional sources of discontent. These give rise, in writers who have explored growing riches, to two different forms of criticism. One is directed at exposing the disproportion between the effort and trouble that are needed in order to acquire the new riches and the trifling and evanescent pleasure they give. This criticism, which started with 18th century debates over luxury, aims at *deflating* the high claims that are put on novelties and is a reminder that there is no escape from the human condition of anxiety and sorrows.[7]

Correspondingly, however, there is a second form of criticism that is the most common and is directed at *inflating* the impact of the new riches. In this version they become the repository of all sorts of evils. All the myths that, from the Biblical story of The Fall to Pandora's box, list the dire consequences of acquiring forbidden knowledge, but also contemporary denunciations of the pollution and health impairments that follow the acquisition of mass-produced goods, are an instance of this second form of criticism (*ibid.*, pp. 57–58).

Growing riches then are rejected on a double account that seems to allow no escape: because they are the source either of vain and transitory pleasures or of corruption and doom.

Does this mean that the products of technological advances come always wrapped in a prospect of hostility and discontent? Not necessarily, answers

Hirschman. The real negative effects that often accompany their initial introduction might perhaps, in time and through use, be corrected and yield a net social benefit.

However, if all these initial inconveniences and problems were revealed at the beginning and all at once, it might have happened that both consumers and public intervention would never have suffered them to appear on the market in the first place.[8] That this did not happen is another instance of what Hirschman calls the *principle of the hidden hand*, a mechanism that provides a way of inducing action through error, the error being that at the beginning all the costs and difficulties that an action or project may require are underestimated (Hirschman, 1967, p. 21).

According to Hirschman, then, both the analysis of current practices of consumption and their historical reconstruction suggest that private consumption can be the source of a disappointment that measures the distance between the expected and the realized benefits. The mis-alignment and consequent conflict between preference and meta-preferences that Hirschman stresses in his 1985 paper originates in this form of disappointment.

Yet, if these are for Hirschman the possible causes of $M \neq P$, the next question becomes: how can we go from this situation of conflict to a resolution, and one, moreover, that appears to be such a radical shift as to induce a change in values?

The changes in values that are here at stake are those that might provide a valid counterpoint to the disappointments of private involvement. These, for Hirschman, are those that involve engagement in public life and social concerns. The question, then, that he tries to answer is: Can we conceive a major shift from consumption experiences that were presumed to be dispensers of happiness but have disappointed, to a pursuit of happiness that relies on corrective public action? (Hirschman, 1982, p. 62).

PRIVATE CONCERNS VERSUS PUBLIC ACTIONS

Hirschman's own answer to the possibility of a shift toward an active involvement in public life is that we may indeed envisage such a shift, provided that some specific conditions are met.

The first of these is that consumers are aware and recognize that both the private and the public sphere are available options. This condition would offer them the possibility, if disappointed, to *exit* from private concerns and to embrace public life.[9] Disappointment in this case would work like a ladder that consumers could use to climb gradually out of private life and into the public sphere. But they may also exercise the *voice* option. If they do, however, and contrary to what happens under competition, voice is not an alternative to the exit response, but would reinforce it (1982, p. 65).

The second condition is that consumers have a self-reflective ability – Frankfurt's second order volitions – that may equip them for deeper changes such as changes in life styles. In this case too disappointment is an essential element in a series of reflective moves that leads up to more radical decisions (*ibid.*, p. 74).

Though these conditions are undoubtedly relevant, one might not fail to notice nevertheless that they rest only on the negative, not the positive reason for shifting to a new involvement. Disappointment may well be the motivational incentive to abandon private consumption, but it does not necessarily follow from this condition that one would find public engagement and social action worth pursuing. In fact, as Hirschman himself recalls, several obstacles to reaching this outcome exist and have been often matter of discussion. One has to do with the well-known voters' paradox, according to which the social effectiveness of the single voter's action appears to be much lower than the costs of the action. Yet, says Hirschman, despite this paradox, people continue to vote, showing a public concern that goes beyond the cost-benefit calculus.[10]

There is however another more critical obstacle, the problem of free riding (1982, p. 77). This problem was formulated by Mancur Olson who, in his *The Logic of Collective Action* (1965), showed that participation in collective action can be prevented even when the benefits of participation exceed the costs. The reason is that, since the outcome of collective action is a public good, enjoyable by all independently of their contribution, the individual has an incentive to skip the costs of participation, and free ride. Such responses, when generalized, would eventually undermine the collective outcome and render public engagement useless.

Hirschman found Olson's argument particularly troubling and continued at length to search for a convincing answer. This was also the reason that pressed him to come back to the topic in his 1985 paper.

Hirschman's first objection is that people in Olson's *Logic* are represented as ingenious and strategic, yet without a background history. There are instances instead in which bygones are not bygones and have a sort of "rebound" effect on the present. When previous experiences ended unhappily, for example, this unsavory end can bias people to underestimate the costs of an alternative action and to exaggerate its positive potential. In the case of disappointment with consumerism, then, an opposite bias in favor of public concerns may render public involvement attractive. It is as if this rebound effect made the transaction costs of the alternative action negative. Still, this counter-argument, Hirschman concedes, even if it might have weight, does not solve the problem of free riding (*ibid.*, p. 78). Not only, but to derive the motivation for public engagement from something like biased expectations and errors might appear as a difficult-to-accept solution (*ibid.*, p. 81).[11]

It was at this point that Hirschman introduced a new twist into his argument. Partly following Scitovsky's line of reasoning (though, as we shall soon see, also critical of it), Hirschman started to stress what, according to him, is one of the main attractions of public action over private pleasures. In the case of private pleasures, striving for them, either through direct production or through the production of income, carries a cost. This, however, is not the case with public-oriented choices (*ibid.*, p. 84). For these belong to that set of human actions for which there is no clear distinction between striving and attaining. Like the search for community, beauty, truth, knowledge and salvation, these human actions all share the characteristic of being self-rewarding and valuable in themselves. For them the benefits are not the result of a *difference* between the hoped-for outcome and the effort of attaining it, but of the *sum* of these two magnitudes. In this new light then free riding is no more a maximizing strategy (*ibid.*, p. 86).

This additional twist is really significant and one that Hirschman had already addressed in his *Essays in Trespassing* (1981). It provides us with a positive, and not simply a negative, reason for embracing public actions. However, despite its relevance, we continue to sense that even this argument is inconclusive as long as we pose the question *why* public actions can be self-rewarding. Hirschman offers some initial possible answers remarking that participation in public life often involves a positive and fulfilling cognitive shift. On one side there is the realization (even if illusory) that social change is possible, and on the other the awareness that participation in public life becomes the condition for self-development (*ibid.*, pp. 89–90). These positive reasons however are not developed further.

NON-INSTRUMENTAL ACTIONS VERSUS INSTRUMENTAL REASON

Hirschman's account of preference changes, especially those involving values and commitments, has implicated a whole new set of complex phenomena: missed expectations and disappointment, double binds, exit with voice, rebound effects, self-rewarding actions, as well as his principle of the hiding hand. These new complexities are all steps that Hirschman deemed necessary for more realistic and operational understanding of social change, and many of which he had already applied innovatively to the analysis of economic development. Yet these steps do not sum up into a comprehensive explanation.

In fact what Hirschman seems to lack is a more articulated and richer view of human motivations, a condition that forces him to make discontent, a negative feeling, the only motivational underpinning of all the shifts in preference and meta-preferences.

Hirschman recognizes that disappointment might have also a positive side since the human condition of dissatisfaction and disquiet is the inevitable counterpart of human ability to entertain high aspirations and ideals (1982, p. 23).

Yet, since his main concern and attempts at an explanation are limited to the negative sides of disappointment, we are left in doubt as to how, from such a negative motivation, there could come a positive – and felt to be positive – sustained engagement in public involvement and vice versa. Disappointment tells us what we do not want, but not what we do want. It tells us what to abandon but not what to embrace. In fact the lack of guidance as to what to choose next may be the source of further discontent. A condition Hirschman was well aware of since he describes symmetrically also the disappointments that the involvement in public action has in store. Here too, as in the case on consumer durables, inflated expectations as to the real impact and effectiveness of political action may become an easy source of disillusion.

What Hirschman seems to describe is a human condition of endless private-public-private cycles.

In his biography of Albert O. Hirschman, Jeremy Adelman (2013) tells us about the gestation of the set of ideas that came to form Hirschman's *Shifting Involvements* and that, as we have seen, were taken up again in his *Against Parsimony*. These issues were first tried out in two lectures delivered in December 1978 at Princeton University, entitled "Private and Public Happiness: Pursuit and Disappointment." Here he attempted to address the problem of the shift from private pursuits to public engagements and back again. If *Exit, Voice and Loyalty* had been a book on how people made choices, what Hirschman wanted to discover now was *why* they made those choices (Adelman, 2013, p. 551). In all his analyses and contributions Hirschman favored a methodology of doubt, of devotion to small ideas, rather than to big, all-encompassing theories. Yet *Shifting Involvements* was meant to be a theoretical book, and it caused him, says Adelman, much anguish and many doubts (*ibid.*, p. 557).

It was also a book that attracted strong reactions, many of which were critical. What was mostly regarded as a weakness was a lack of empirical analysis and too strong a dichotomy between private and public involvements.

This was probably the reason why Hirschman felt the need to address the topic two years later in his essay against parsimony in economics.[12] It is here that, as a second instance of complicating economic theory he discusses again the role of non-instrumental actions, of those actions that are a mystery for instrumental reason. They are a mystery because, as he had argued in 1982, for these activities, pursued for their own sake, the usual metric that compares efforts and results, means and ends, or costs and revenues does not apply. So what makes them worth pursuing?

Some progress can be achieved, adds Hirschman in 1985, if one looks at the varied degrees to which the intended outcomes of an activity can be predicted. Certain activities, mostly those that are of a routine character, have wholly predictable outcomes that allow for the separation of the process into means and ends and correspondingly into costs and benefits. "But there are many kinds of activities, from that of a research and development scientist to that of a composer or an advocate of some public policy, whose intended outcome cannot be relied upon to materialize with certainty" (1985, p. 12). For this kind of non-routine activities there is instead a combination of short-term uncertainty with long-term certainty of achievement, a peculiar combination that makes these activities especially attractive, "stimulating," "exciting" (*ibid.*, pp. 12, 13). Yet because of the quasi certainty of the achievement we can still rely on an instrumental distinction between costs and benefits. This is no more the case for those non-routine undertakings for which such certainty of result is missing. From love to truth, from friendship to liberty, the uncertainty of outcome breaks any reliable comparison between costs and benefits and generates that (con)fusion of striving and attaining that for Hirschman is so characteristic of these activities. Yet, as if in compensation for the uncertainty of result and the strenuousness of effort, striving is colored by the savoring of the goal, a feeling that can be intoxicating (1982, p. 90, 1985, p. 14). It remains, concludes Hirschman, the difficulty to think instrumentally about non-instrumental reasons.

In stressing the existence and importance of non-instrumental actions Hirschman came very close to the type of arguments that Tibor Scitovsky had advanced some years earlier in his *Joyless Economy* (1976) for explaining the existence of those stimulating activities that have no antecedent in pain. I shall address this point in the next section.

What should be noted, however, is that it was in connection with Scitovsky that Hirschman returned to the themes that he had discussed in his 1982 book and taken up again in his 1985 essay. He does it in a paper written in 1996 for a special issue of the *Critical Review* dedicated to Tibor Scitovsky's *The Joyless Economy* after Twenty Years. Here Hirschman not only declares his indebtedness to Scitovsky's work but also introduces, in accordance with his view that self-subversion may be the means to self-renewal (Hirschman, 1995), some amendments to the arguments he had maintained in *Shifting involvements*. He had hoped, in so doing, to subvert what appeared too strong a dichotomy between private and public engagement. What he had earlier failed to realize was that private and public engagements were not mutually exclusive categories. There are in fact several instances in which they meld and merge (Hirschman, 1996, p. 536). Hirschman identified one such instance in the practice of the common meal, where, as a result of the pleasure of commensality, important social and public links form. These bondages can be as rich in consequences as, for instance, the formation of the political union of Athenian democracy, an example he discusses at length.

As we can see, then, Hirschman continued to struggle to find the positive reasons that might overcome the objections to the possibility of collective action. A struggle that had opened the way to the recognition of the importance of self-rewarding actions and of the (con)fusion between striving and attaining. Relevant also is the "self-subverting" view that consumption too is an activity that has a strong social dimension, one that mitigates the separation between the private and social spheres of life.

Yet the struggle is not completely won, since we are still left without an analysis of positive motivations for embracing public involvement rather than private-sphere activity and vice versa. A complexity, then, still to be explored and disentangled.

SOURCES OF POSITIVE ENGAGEMENT

The influence of Scitovsky's approach had been present already in Hirschman's earlier discussion of the sources of discontent, as several references to the first edition of *The Joyless Economy* make clear.

Like Hirschman, Scitovsky too had criticized the traditional identification in economic theory of preferences with choice and had argued that preferences can be inferred from choices only if any tension or conflict between them is erased (1976, p. 4). In fact Scitovsky had devoted his entire book, *The Joyless Economy* (1976), to inquiring into the likely sources of conflict that might lead to a divorce between choice and preferences.[13] Yet, as he himself tells us, once he started to question these traditional assumptions and to inquire into what might make life enjoyable, he also discovered that, as an economist, he had no knowledge that would enable him to address his own question (*Memoirs*: 105a, 106). Some lesser-known writings of leading Cambridge economists such as Marshall, Keynes, Harrod and in particular Hawtrey (1926) provided some early suggestions (Scitovsky, 1985). But a real breakthrough came only when Scitovsky discovered the findings of a new line of experimental research in psychology and early neurobiology that was emerging in the 1960s and early 1970s. The most important and decisive of these findings were those of Daniel Berlyne, whose studies of the motivations of human action deeply influenced the direction of Scitovsky's own future research (see Berlyne, 1965, 1971; Berlyne & Madsen, 1973).[14]

What Scitovsky took away from these studies was that pleasure, satisfaction, and well-being – the goodness of life – came not only from the reduction of negative feelings and sensations – ranging from hunger to anger, as economists had commonly assumed. They came also from the search for purely stimulating activities that had no necessary link to need or to pain reduction.

Scitovsky called those activities that were pursued for pure positive pleasure and lacked any antecedent of pain, creative. These ranged from conversation to art, from playing sports to novel ways of cooking food, from music to science. They were creative because, thanks to their complexity and combinatory potential, they lent themselves to being constantly renewed and changed, thus becoming a sustained source of positive engagement and interest.[15]

Berlyne's experimental studies had suggested that the sources of positive pleasure were linked to experiences characterized by variables such as novelty, change, surprisingness, complexity, and uncertainty (Berlyne, 1965, p. 245). These variables are all expressions of a condition of conflict, of a mismatch between the known and the experienced, or the expected and the realized. And they are all knowledge-related, expressing at different levels a gap in our knowledge (*ibid.*, p. 246). This gap may be experienced as being too high, a condition that brings uneasiness, disappointment and anxiety, or too low, a condition associated with a lack of stimulation, and boredom. Pleasurable feelings arise in the process of relieving situations characterized by levels of conflict that are perceived either too low, as when one exposes oneself voluntarily to novelty and uncertainty just for the desire of experiencing and discovering something new, or too high, as when one deliberately increases familiarity to reduce novelty and complexity.[16]

For Scitovsky, creative activities, with their capacity to be self-renewing and engaging in ever-new ways, matched well Berlyne's model of the sources of pleasure and interest. Scitovsky contrasted them with those activities that he called defensive or comfort-related whose instrumental role was instead to reduce pain and discomfort, a role that ended as soon as the discomfort was relieved.

Hirschman admired Scitovsky's work, even if he raised several points of criticism, of "intimate disagreements" (1982, p. 82). The first of these was that Scitovsky's insistence on pleasure as opposed to comfort led him to undervalue and almost to neglect the pleasures that come from non-durables, from catering to our physiological needs, and which are a source of renewable pleasures (*ibid.*, p. 27). Moreover, Scitovsky, for Hirschman, in praising novelty, was at risk of forgetting that novel goods and their diffusion are also a cause of discontent, as was indeed shown by the hostility with which the introduction of new wealth had been received across the centuries (*ibid.*, p. 54).[17]

But there was a third cause of disagreement, one that is the most relevant for Hirschman. This relates to the types of activities that Scitovsky found stimulating, and that were related, for Hirschman, only to forms of private consumption, with no regard being paid to those that involve public concerns. Even if, as we have seen in his paper discussing the pleasures of commensality (1996), Hirschman had partly withdrawn this criticism and recognized that private forms of consumption may have as well a social and public dimension, he continued to think that Scitovsky had undervalued the importance of public involvement among an individual's choices.

Hirschman's last criticism is telling, as Scitovsky himself readily acknowledged (1996). Yet this intimate disagreement probably prevented Hirschman from discovering that in Scitovsky there were to be found the bases of a new theory of motivations that could well complement his analysis of how and *why* we make choices.

What this new approach to motivation showed, and recent research has confirmed, is that for activities to be compelling and engaging they have to match ever-new knowledge with ever-new challenges (what Csikszentmihalyi, 2008, called a condition of "flow").

In this process of sustained positive engagement both conflict and cognition play a role. Conflict – between the expected and the realized, the known and the experienced – in fact plays a double role, being the source of a negative feeling in the form of disappointment and frustration, but also providing, when not too high, a positive source of stimulation and interest. Cognition is involved because what is novel, surprising and engaging for some can be threatening and disappointing for others, and this relativity reflects the accumulated knowledge and experience of each actor. We may conjecture, too, in answer to Hirschman, that probably it is this very relativity that, throughout history, has caused reactions to novel goods and riches to oscillate between praise and rejection, between their being experienced as engaging and challenging or disruptive and threatening.

Within this different framework of motivations we find hope for a more unified theory of choice, one that breaks the separation between preferences and meta-preferences and correspondingly between private consumption goals and action in the public interest. The contrast is not between indisputable wanton preferences and reflective, autonomous values, or between private or public concerns. It is not even between Scitovsky's comfort and pleasure. The contrast that matters is between activities that are self-renewing and engaging, that stimulate exploration, curiosity, and interest, and that for this reason are self-rewarding, and those that are not. Furthermore, these are the same creative activities that, even when more apparently individual, such as reading a novel, have a social dimension and an interconnectedness with others that cannot be overlooked.

CONCLUSIONS

For Hirschman the various complications of traditional economic concepts that he has proposed have a common source: "the incredible complexity of human nature which was disregarded by traditional theory for very good reasons, but which must be spoon-fed back into the traditional findings for the sake of greater realism" (1985, p. 19).

He began to do this reverse spoon-feeding by introducing two basic human endowments: the ability of communication and persuasion, an ability that is behind the possibility of pursuing voice, and the capability of self-evaluation and reflection, a capability that is behind the formation of meta-preferences and values. These two human endowments are at the origin of two basic tensions that are also part of the human condition: those between preferences and meta preferences and those between self-interest and Smithian "benevolence."

I have focused on the discussion of the first of these two forms of tension, one that is also the cause of possible shifts in values and consequent changes in behaviors.

Hirschman's analysis brought him to take disappointment seriously and to study what individual and social responses to disappointment might be.

I have stressed in addition, however, that disappointment, a negative motivation, is charged with too heavy a task, that of providing the *only* incentive to changes in values and behavior. There is also still missing from Hirschman's explanation an analysis of the specific attractiveness of alternative courses of actions, whether they involve a shift from private pursuits to public action or the reverse. Hirschman came very close to an answer in his discussion of the positive feelings of attainment and self-development that accompany self-rewarding activities. These seem to break the traditional distinction between costs and benefits, striving and attaining, and call instead upon the human capabilities of self-evaluation and reflection.

Yet an inquiry over the reasons of why these activities have the force of eliciting active engagement and interest and become self-rewarding is still missing in Hirschman. It was probably one of the main contributions of Scitovsky's analysis to have brought to the attention of the economists the existence of a new psychological approach to motivation that might indicate the direction of an answer. What this new approach had showed, and more recent psychological research has confirmed, is that for activities to be compelling and constantly engaging they have to match the new knowledge that comes from experiencing them with ever-new challenges. In this process not only disappointment but also positive stimulation and interest play a role. Decisive too, of course, is the role of knowledge, and correspondingly of education and acquired skills, in identifying and creating the attractiveness of alternative courses of action.

It is within this different framework of motivations that we seem likely to develop the unified theory of choice toward which Hirschman took such important initial strides.

NOTES

1. The economists' concentration on wanton preference changes, says Hirschman, has tended to downgrade changes of the reflective kind to the wanton kind by assimilating them to changes in tastes: thus, for example Becker (1957) ascribed patterns of discriminatory hiring to a "taste for discrimination" (Hirschman, 1985, p. 10).

2. Though Hirschman had often criticized attempts to construct paradigms that proved to be too rigid for multifaceted reality (Hirschman, 1971), his own aim

in this essay was to attempt a theoretical analysis of endogenously changing preferences.

3. Though in footnote 4 of the same page, Hirschman stresses that here Simmel was thinking more of disappointment than surprise (Hirschman, 1982, p. 26). The reason why not much attention will be paid in his inquiry to the opposite of disappointment is that this seems to happen so infrequently and that "it is more common for expectations to exceed reality than for reality to exceed expectations." This bias, he adds, also has a counterpart in language where there seems to be no word for the antonym of disappointment (*ibid.*, pp. 12–13).

4. To make this point, Hirschman refers to Scitovsky's distinction between comfort and pleasure (Scitovsky, 1976). I shall come back to this point later.

5. A new and increasing category of consumer expenditures, notes Hirschman, is devoted to services, especially education, health, and recreation. Here too the likelihood of disappointment is high because their quality is uneven and uncertain and there is a higher tolerance of their deterioration (Hirschman, 1982, p. 40).

6. It was Rousseau, Hirschman recalls, who had even remarked: "If there were no luxury, there would not be any poverty" (*ibid.*, p. 56). Though the opposite argument was made by Mandeville: that from frugality one obtains more frugality (1924 [1732]).

7. On page 45, paragraph 7 of *The Theory of Moral Sentiments* (1982 [1759], Smith asks: "What can be added to the happiness of the man who is in health, who is out of debt, and has a clear conscience? To one in this situation, all accessions of fortune may properly be said to be superfluous; and if he is much elevated upon account of them, it must be the effect of the most frivolous levity. This situation, however, may very well be called the natural and ordinary state of mankind."

8. Another source of discontent is that stressed by Hirsch (1976) and related to positional consumption: the problem that none of us competing for higher position is able to realize his or her hopes, namely the reward of status that certain types of goods are thought to confer, since one's gain is at another's expense and no net increase in status is realized. For Hirschman this sort of discontentment is of less relevance than that which derives solely from having acquired what one was striving for.

9. The discovery that a product is unsafe could induce consumers to question political arrangements in general. Additionally, disappointment might contribute to deflating an ideology which claimed that private interest is good and one should not feel guilty about it (Hirschman, 1982, p. 65).

10. Some recent literature analyzing the individual motivations for donating to politics addresses the problem of how to explain the "irrationality" of any such action, if private interest is of concern. For a review, see Ansolabehere, De Figueiredo, and Snyder (2003) Hirschman, however, further on in his 1982 essay mentions the fact that a voter's paradox might arise for different reasons. People might refrain from voting not because of its ineffectiveness but because the option of *only* voting is not enough to express the intensity of their preferences (1982, p. 108).

11. Hirschman, who does not share this conviction, goes on to argue that mistake-making is one of the most characteristic of human actions and the social world would be un-understandable if it were assumed away (1982, p. 81).

12. A shortened version of this paper appeared in the *American Economic Review, Papers and Proceedings*, vol. 74, 2, 1984: pp. 89–96.

13. These are: the possible conflict between comfort and pleasure; conflict too between standardized goods and individual needs and desires; and the gap between specialized knowledge and generalist skills (see Bianchi, 2003).

14. The suggestion to look at this literature came from a psychologist colleague and friend at the Medical School at Stanford, to whose Economics Department Scitovsky had returned in 1970 after a two-year stay in Europe. This friend drew his attention to some fresh studies in motivation made by a group of physiological psychologists (Scitovsky's Memoirs: 105a). See Bianchi (2012).

15. As for Hirschman, so too for Scitovsky, the existence of these activities shows that many individual motivations are not primarily economic, and by consequence do not respond exclusively to economic incentives. They direct attention to the importance of outside influences and to the view that the market economy is an open system (Scitovsky, 1985, p. 194).

16. See Bianchi (2008, 2014).

17. These two objections do not really apply to Scitovsky's theory of motivation. Novelty is clearly a relative concept that depends first on time: when time elapses, the repetition of an experience regains some novelty and so does the pleasure and this is true for non-durables but also for durables. It depends also on previous experience and knowledge, which explains why novelty is two-edged: threatening for the inexperienced, pleasurable for the experienced; and why also it may cause opposite reactions.

ACKNOWLEDGMENT

Paper presented at the Conference in honor of Albert O. Hirschman, *The gift of (self)subversion*. Universita' di Roma La Sapienza, September 12–13, 2014. I wish to thank an anonymous referee and all the participants at the Conference for their helpful comments and suggestions.

REFERENCES

Adelman, J. (2013). *Worldly philosopher: The odyssey of Albert O. Hirschman*. Princeton, NJ: Princeton University Press.

Ansolabehere, S., De Figueiredo, J. M., & Snyder, J. M. (2003). Why is there so little money in U.S. politics? *Journal of Economic Perspectives*, *17*(1), 105–130.

Becker, G. S. (1957). *The economies of discrimination*. Chicago, IL: Chicago University Press.

Becker, G. S. (1996). *Accounting for tastes*. Cambridge, MA: Harvard University Press.

Berlyne, D. E. (1965). *Structure and direction in thinking*. New York, NY: Wiley.

Berlyne, D. E. (1971). *Aesthetics and psychobiology*. New York, NY: Appleton Century Crofts.

Berlyne, D. E., & Madsen, K. B. (Eds.). (1973). *Pleasure, reward, preference*. New York, NY: Academic Press.
Bianchi, M. (2003). A questioning economist: Tibor Scitovsky's attempt to bring joy into economics. *Journal of Economic Psychology*, *24*, 391–407.
Bianchi, M. (2008). Time and preferences in cultural consumption. In M. Hutter & D. Throsby (Eds.), *Value and valuation in art and culture* (pp. 236–260). Cambridge: Cambridge University Press.
Bianchi, M. (2012). A joyful economist. Scitovsky's memoirs. *History of Economic Thought and Policy*, (2), 57–73.
Bianchi, M. (2014). The magic of storytelling: How curiosity and aesthetic preferences work. *Economics, Open Access Journal*, (Published in Special Issue *Economics, Psychology and Choice Theory*), *8*, 1–31. Retrieved from http://www.economics-ejournal.org/economics/journalarticles/2014-44
Csikszentmihalyi, M. (2008). *Flow: The psychology of optimal experience*. New York, NY: Harper Perennial.
Frankfurt, H. G. (1971). Freedom of the will and the concept of a person. *The Journal of Philosophy*, *68*(1), 5–20.
Hawtrey, R. G. (1926). *The economic problem*. London: Longmans, Green and Co.
Hirsch, F. (1976). *Social limits of growth*. Cambridge, MA: Harvard University Press.
Hirschman, A. O. (1967). *The principle of the hiding hand*. Retrieved from http://www.nationalaffairs.com/public_interest/detail/the-principle of-the-hiding-hand
Hirschman, A. O. (1970). *Exit, voice, and loyalty: Responses to decline in firms, organizations, and states*. Cambridge, MA: Harvard University Press.
Hirschman, A. O. (1971). *A bias for hope. Essays on development and Latin America*. New Haven, CT: Yale University Press.
Hirschman, A. O. (1981). *Essays in trespassing: Economics to politics and beyond*. Cambridge: Cambridge University Press.
Hirschman, A. O. (1982). *Shifting involvements. Private interests and public action*. Princeton, NJ: Princeton University Press.
Hirschman, A. O. (1985). Against parsimony. Three easy ways of complicating some categories of economic discourse. *Economics and Philosophy*, *1*, 7–21.
Hirschman, A. O. (1995). *A propensity to self-subversion*. Cambridge, MA: Harvard University Press.
Hirschman, A. O. (1996). Melding the public and private spheres: Taking commensality seriously. *Critical Review: A Journal of Politics and Society*, Special Issue: Tibor Scitovsky's The Joyless Economy after Twenty Years, *10*(4), 533–550.
Mandeville, B. (1924 [1732]). *The fable of the bees: Or, private vices, public benefits*. Oxford: The Clarendon Press.
Olson, M. (1965). *The logic of collective action*. Cambridge, MA: Harvard University Press.
Scitovsky, T. (1976). *Memoirs*. Undated typescript, In *Scitovsky papers*. Special Collections Library/Economists' Papers, Duke University, Durham, NC.
Scitovsky, T. (1985). How to bring joy into economics. In T. Scitovsky (Ed.), (1986) *Human desires and economic satisfaction. Essays on the frontiers of economics* (pp. 183–203). New York, NY: New York University Press.
Scitovsky, T. (1992 [1976]). *The Joyless Economy: The psychology of human satisfaction* (Rev. ed.). Oxford: Oxford University Press.

Scitovsky, T. (1996). My own criticism of *The Joyless Economy*. *Critical Review: A Journal of Politics and Society*, Special Issue: Tibor Scitovsky's The Joyless Economy after Twenty Years, *10*(4), 595–606.
Sen, A. K. (1977). Rational fools: A critique of the behavioral foundations of economic theory. *Philosophy & Public Affairs*, *6*(4), 317–344.
Simmel, G. (1978[1900]). *The philosophy of money*. London: Routledge and Keegan Paul.
Smith, A. (1982 [1759]). *The theory of moral sentiments*. Indianapolis, IN: Liberty Fund.
Stigler, G. J., & Becker, G. S. (1977). De Gustibus non est disputandum. *American Economic Review*, *67*(2), 76–90.

"GOOD AND BAD" (NOT "GOOD OR BAD"): ALBERT O. HIRSCHMAN AS A BEHAVIORAL ECONOMIST

Shaun P. Hargreaves Heap

ABSTRACT

Albert O. Hirschman famously wrote against parsimony. He wanted to complicate economics. The locus of these complications was often individual behavior. This paper makes three arguments about such complications. The first is that the growing experimental evidence on individual behavior broadly supports many of Hirschman's proposed complications. In particular, there is evidence of preference change under "reflection." Second, I argue that there is experimental evidence of both "good and bad" preference change in market society. The third is that the policy of "nudging" would not sit well with Hirschman. "Nudging" is a return to the "parsimonious" instinct in economics; and it misses the real implications for policy of the insights from behavioral economics, which, of course, are more complex.

Keywords: Learning-by-doing; pro-sociality; autonomy; nudging

Research in the History of Economic Thought and Methodology, Volume 34B, 161–174

ISSN: 0743 4154/doi:10.1108/S0743-41542016000034B006

INTRODUCTION

Albert O. Hirschman wanted to complicate economics. His 1984 AER essay, "Against Parsimony ....," makes this explicit. His first complication in that essay was that individual preferences are not fixed. We reflect on our preferences and, through such reflection, they change. The second complication came from the uncertainty present in non-routine activities. Routine activities admit the cost benefit calculations of instrumental reason because the range of actions and outcomes are well understood. But there are some activities, non-routine ones, where outcomes are uncertain. The pursuit of something, for example, like love, justice, beauty, is perhaps best thought of as an end in itself rather than a means to that end. The distinction in such cases between means and ends, that instrumental reason needs to get a purchase, slips away. Finally, there are some skills like loving and being public-spirited that are learnt-by-doing. They are not a resource that is depleted through use. Scarcity ceases, therefore, to be the key to understanding their economics.

In the same essay, he also ventures an interpretation of his earlier famous work on "voice" that is in the same vein. He was objecting to the rational choice model as the exclusive model of individual agency in economics. "Exit" makes perfect sense for the rational choice agent: he or she surveys the benefits and costs of staying and leaving and when the one outweighs the other, they leave. "Voice" is a more subtle response to organizational failure. It is a move in a conversation. It is more open-ended and more indeterminate in conclusion that will permit the instrumental reason of weighing benefits against costs. It is akin to a commitment and so may be nurtured by feelings of loyalty.

Although, he did not extend this reflection in the AER essay to another of his earlier books, *The Passions and the Interests ...*, he could have. That book involves on the face of it a different kind of complication: a complication with respect to our understanding of the market. But it turns on complicating the model of individual agency too. When he was writing that book, the engagement between the "left" and the "right" over the market was in part a dispute over whether preferences could be taken as given. For instance, someone like Friedman could parade the virtues of the market on the assumption that people had exogenously given preferences, but critics on the left could out-flank this argument by suggesting that such an insight is nugatory when markets mold the kind of preferences that we have. It was the genius of Hirschman, in recovering the debates at the dawn of the rise of the market, to see that issue was more complicated than this. It is not whether preferences change in market society. Of course, they do. The complexity is that they plausibly change for both the good and bad: the "doux-commerce" thesis suggests that markets are civilizing force while the "self-destruction" thesis suggests that markets undermine the moral values which are its own underpinning (see Hirschman, 1982). There is the rub: weighing this good of the market with its bad is much more difficult than choosing between say Friedman or the left critics simply on the basis of whether you take preferences to be exogenous or endogenous.

In this paper, I want to argue that behavioral economics has in many respects provided empirical, mainly experimental, support for these complications. I do so in the next two sections. In the section "Preferences Do Change," I focus on the evidence of preference change. In the section "Markets and Preferences," I consider the experimental evidence ("good and bad") on the influence of the market on our preferences. In this sense, Hirschman was always a behavioral economist as we now understand the term. I argue, however, in the section "Behavioral Welfare Economics" that Hirschman would not have been comfortable with the development most closely associated with behavioral insights when applied to welfare economics: nudging. In the course of making these arguments, one of Hirschman's great contributions emerges: the elevation of "learning-by-doing" to one of the central concepts in social science.

PREFERENCES DO CHANGE

There is much experimental evidence that preferences change, at least under the revealed preference interpretation of behavior. It takes many forms.[1]

There is evidence, for example, that preferences change when apparently simple choices are modified in what seem from a standard perspective to be irrelevant. One example of this comes from the [$, P] preference reversal experiments. In these, there is a choice between a P-bet (offering a modest prize with high probability) and a $-bet (offering a relatively large prize with a small probability). Subjects typically prefer the P to the $ one in a straight choice. But, when asked to place a monetary value on the two, they reveal the contrary preference by valuing the $ one more highly.

It is important for my argument, linking such evidence to Hirschman's suggestion that people's preferences change through some kind of reflection, that the variation in choice is not random. People might simply not have preferences over such bets and so decide randomly. This would produce reversals but there would be no pattern to these reversals in the aggregate. The fact that people tend to reverse systematically suggests that there is some cognitive process governing choice in these circumstances. People may not have well-formed preferences but they are "thinking" about how to make a choice and this "thinking" is what produces the particular pattern. Indeed, a natural inference is that while they cannot integrate in their mind the probability and monetary aspects of each bet, they focus on one or other aspect when making their choices and it is this aspect that varies with how the choice is framed. Frame the choice in terms of money, and some people focus on the money differences and so choose the $-bet. When the choice is not framed in terms of money, the probability element weighs more heavily and so there is more of a tendency to go for the P-bet in this setting. The quotation marks around "thinking" are used advisedly here, however. My point is not that these decisions are made through some process of deep reflection on what preferences to have. What matters is that they seem to be guided by some cognitive process. We have ways of "thinking" about our choices when we do not have clear preferences to guide our action. Otherwise they would be random; and they are not. The mechanisms in this instance may be no more than heuristics that we have found useful when tackling such decision problems, but these heuristics are the resources that we use when "thinking" about what to do quickly in a relatively trivial decision problem.

Another example comes from evidence of "anchoring" in decision making with the result that choices change when the anchor does. For instance, suppose there are three options: (a) a weekend in Rome, all-expenses paid; (b) weekend in Paris, all-expenses paid; and (c) weekend in Paris, with all-expenses *except* breakfast paid. Whether (c) is in the choice set or not should not affect decisions because it is dominated by (b). However, when (c) is included, people tend to go for (b) with much greater frequency than when the choice is only between (a) and (b). Again it is the patterning of the changes that is important. One can well imagine that people do not have well-formed preferences over the all-expenses paid weekends in Paris and Rome. Each has its own merits. The romance of Paris versus the classical heritage of Rome, for example; and these are difficult to integrate into a single ordering. But if people chose randomly as a result, there would be some reversals between them when the set of options is expanded to include (c), but there should be no pattern to these reversals. That the reversals are non-random suggests that people are reflecting on the choice and these reflections generate the pattern of shifting to Paris when the inferior (c) Paris option is also offered. Indeed, it is natural to infer that (b) gains weight because it is better than (c) when (c) is in the choice set.

Of course, these examples suggest only that we do not have settled preferences and that we do not decide randomly. Hirschman's first complication involves, however, something more than the heuristic-like cognitive interventions that seem to be in play in these cases. He imagines a Mill-type sense of progress to these reflections. One develops a sense of autonomy through such reflection and change in preferences. These experiments do not capture this aspect of Hirschman's argument because the patterning merely points to some cognitive process and not its content. Indeed, since the typical decision problem in the laboratory deals in rather simple, and scarcely existential choices, it would seem an unlikely source of evidence on this aspect of Hirschman's argument. Nevertheless, there is some suggestive evidence that a concern for autonomy might motivate reflection and behavior outside the laboratory in the burgeoning "happiness" literature within behavioral economics. There are two findings with respect to reported subjective well-being that seem both robust across different studies and to point in this direction. The first is that subjective well-being is associated with a sense of control over life. (There are also experiments that in a complementary fashion reveal "control aversion": see Falk & Kosfeld, 2006.) The second is that people's subjective wellbeing typically increases with age from about the age of 30 onwards (e.g., see Cheng, Oswlad, & Powdthavee, 2016; Oswald, 1997). This last result has not attracted as much attention in this literature as the influence of, say, unemployment and a rich social life on wellbeing but it is in many respects very difficult to reconcile with the standard model.

The standard model pictures individuals maximizing "utility" that is a function of current "utility" and future discounted "utility" (and possibly remembered past "utility"). With the passage of age, the shadow of death seems likely to erode the value of this utility function, making the relationship between age and reported wellbeing puzzling. It is not puzzling if, however, wellbeing is closely connected to the sense of autonomy that comes from the process of reflection on and change in preferences that Hirschman (and Mill) refer to. This is a version of "learning-by-doing" and the passage of time means that one has done more learning as one gets older resulting in a greater sense of wellbeing.

Stigler and Becker (1977), in fact, *analytically* tweak the standard model in the same way in their famous essay "*De gustibus est non disputandum*" paper in order to account for apparent preference changes. Their model retains the utility function framework but allows for some activities to be both consumption and investment goods. That is, they generate current wellbeing and, *ceteris paribus*, increase the wellbeing associated with that activity in the future (i.e., through "learning-by-doing" there is an investment aspect to the activity). This makes the activity relatively more attractive when facing the same decision in the future rather than now, with the result that more is done: "preferences" appear to have changed and people feel better. The explanatory gloss is slightly different but the analytic mechanism for explaining preference change and heightened senses of wellbeing is the same. It is "learning-by-doing."

The point is also broader both in terms of Hirschman's own work and for economics in general. Much of Hirschman's arguments, for instance, about development could also be thought to turn on learning-by-doing. He also makes the point in the AER essay with which I started that many pursuits like love, beauty, and justice are governed by learning-by-doing. Adam Smith, one of Hirschman's great influences, also makes much of learning-by-doing in explaining differences in skill and personal incomes. There is Arrow, a colleague of Hirschman's, one of whose famous papers is on "learning-by-doing" and growth; "learning-by-doing" is important for hysteresis in unemployment and growth (see Hargreaves Heap, 1980). The list quickly grows and I want on this basis to broaden the argument. It is not just that there is behavioral evidence to support Hirschman's first complication: that our preferences change through reflection. The Hirschman's attention to how this is based on "learning-by-doing" helps elevate this principle to a position that it deserves, along with such ideas as opportunity costs and comparative advantage, as one of the central insights from economics.[2]

MARKETS AND PREFERENCES

There is another kind of apparent preference change that has been documented through experiments. These "changes" arise because social preferences seem to be sensitive to what can be broadly understood as institutional context. In particular, there is accumulating experimental evidence that people behave differently when making what is otherwise an identical decision in a market context as compared with a non-market one. The famous example of such an influence at the time Hirschman was thinking and writing on this topic came from Titmuss's (1971) comparison of the UK and US systems for collecting blood. It spawned an interesting debate over whether the market really had this corrosive effect on what we now call social preferences. Hirschman's intervention in this was typically nuanced. It complicates the picture.

His (1977) *The Passions and the Interests* book and the 1982 JEL paper offer both a good and a bad side to market (at least in the history of economic thought). Markets are, on the one hand, a civilizing force. He uses Montesquieu's words on how "commerce polishes and softens manners" and traces this piece of conventional 18th century wisdom through the work of Condorcet and others. On the other hand, there is both Marxist and conservative argument that worries about the way that capitalism and markets corrode all non-industrial values: "All that is solid melts into air ...."

Experimental economics supplies a similarly mixed vision of what markets do. There have been many experiments that find a similar kind of "crowding-out" of social preferences by the monetary incentives of the market to that of Titmuss. Bowles and Polania-Reyes (2012) provide a recent survey. Interestingly, however, they also document experiments where the reverse has occurred. That is, where monetary incentives appear to have "crowded-in" pro-social behavior. The weight of the experimental evidence is heavily in favor of "crowding-out" but the point is that markets seem sometimes to have beneficial effects on pro-sociality.[3]

Pro-social behavior in these experiments is typically gauged by the extent to which people seem to take account of the welfare of others. In this sense, the contrasting evidence in Bowles and Polyania-Reyes survey belongs within a debate over whether the market is "good" or "bad." It is just that the evidence is mixed. Sometimes markets are good sometimes bad, but the balance is that they are bad (echoing Titmuss's original finding for blood donation). There is experimental evidence, however, that is closer to Hirschman's shift in the debate toward "good and bad" because markets seem to have a further effect along a different dimensions. I will sketch two of my experiments where this is the case. Specifically, it seems in these experiments that markets encourage the equal treatment of individuals. (Or to echo those earlier 18th century insights on this side of the argument, one might say that markets appear to encourage manners.) Thus, the issue of the market is not just whether it promotes or undermines pro-sociality, where the balance of the evidence is that it is bad. It involves weighing this bad with what is a difficult to compare other kind of good: the equal treatment of individuals. The market is not "good or bad"; it is tricky combination of both.

In one of these experiments, people make three decisions: they play a trust game, a public goods game and they must decide whether to enter a competition with others over the payment rate for a real effort task (or accept a simple piece rate). The last of these decision problems has an explicit market frame. In some treatments, they make these decisions in the knowledge that they are affiliated with minimal groups (they are identified by a blue or red marker on their screen and they know the affiliation of their co-player). In the baseline treatment there are no such group affiliations. We found in common with many studies that there was a robust in-group bias in the Trust and Public Goods game: that is, when subjects are affiliated to these minimal groups, subjects trusted or cooperated more when playing with someone who was affiliated to the same group as themselves. This bias did not exist in the Competition decision. Subjects were just as likely to choose to compete with fellow group members as with those who belonged to the other group.[4]

In the second experiment (see Hargreaves Heap, Tan, & Zizzo, 2013), subjects were differentiated by their endowments. Some had more than others. There were, in this sense, "poor" and "rich" participants. They played a trust game and a gift exchange market game. Both games involve the first mover deciding whether to trust the second. The major difference is that one (the gift exchange game) puts the trusting decision in a market context and the other (the trust game) does not. The "giving" in the trust game becomes "price/wage setting" in the gift exchange; and "returning" in the trust game becomes a "quality/effort" decision in the gift exchange

Table 1. Average Giving and Return Rates across Pairings.

Giving Rate			
	To 10	To 50	To 90
From 10	0.504	0.565	0.573
From 50	0.454	0.55	0.496
From 90	0.45	0.506	0.525

Return Rate			
	To 10	To 50	To 90
From 10	0.284	0.225	0.206
From 50	0.286	0.275	0.21
From 90	0.297	0.236	0.183

Table 2. Average Approved Wages and Work Efforts across Pairings.

Wage Approved			
	To 10	To 50	To 90
From 10	13.55	14.1	13.991
From 50	16.817	16.357	15.729
From 90	16.092	15.508	15.93
Effort			
	To 10	To 50	To 90
From 10	0.319	0.331	0.286
From 50	0.299	0.287	0.261
From 90	0.232	0.276	0.315

version.[5] Table 1 reproduces the average "giving" and "return" rates for the trust (non-market) game. Table 2 does the same for the analogous decisions in the market version of the game (gift exchange): that is, what are traditionally known as the "wage" and "effort" decisions (although in our experiment as others they were more neutrally described in terms of price and quality).

In Table 1 with the simple trust game, there is a clear suggestion that the status (in terms of endowment) of the two players affects subject behavior. Low endowment first movers trust Higher endowment players more than Low endowment ones. This can be seen most easily by tracing the proportion "given" horizontally in the table for any given endowment level for the acting agent. It typically rises. For example, a "poor" player with an endowment of 10 typically "gives" 50% of his or her endowment to someone who is also poor (i.e., endowed with 10) and this rises to 57% when the other person is "rich" (i.e., with an endowment of 90). This influence of status has also been found in experiments with natural groups (see Fershtman & Gneezy, 2001). Status effects also operate for the "return" decision of second movers, but in the reverse direction. "Poor" return less to the "rich." Again this can be seen most easily by tracing the return rates horizontally for an endowment level of the acting agent. It typically now falls. For example, the poor person with an endowment of 10 "returns" 28% to a fellow "poor" person but only 20% to a "rich" person. When we test for these status-based differences in behavior in regressions on individual behavior, they are statistically significant. It is "as if" feudal attitudes of "seignorage" and "noblesse oblige" respectively still infected the 1st and 2nd mover decisions in this Trust Game.

In Table 2, however, this pattern is much less clear. For example, the rich wage setter typically now offers a lower wage to a fellow rich subject than a poor one, even though the poor still offer a higher wage to a rich person than a poor one. Indeed, in the individual regressions there is no evidence that status affects wage decisions and only weak evidence of status effects in the second mover "effort" decision (i.e., it is borderline 5% significant).

In short, the institutional context of the market seems to weaken the influence of status, which otherwise leads people to treat people differently (i.e., according to their status) in simple trust games.

I want to conclude this section by considering how Hirschman's insights in these respects produce a bias toward incremental change. Such a bias naturally arises from what has already been said about the importance of "learning-by-doing." It is reinforced by Hirschman's keen attention to the importance of groups. Loosely defined, groups encourage "voice" and Hirschman was adamant that "voice" was in many circumstances a more useful response to organizational or institutional difficulties than "exit." But he was equally clear, as I have suggested earlier, that individuals needed to be able to develop and become themselves through experimentation, mistake, and adaptation. The puzzle is that membership of a group often seems to make such individual experimentation difficult because the group supplies pressures toward conformism. A natural resolution of this tension is to constrain experiments to small deviations from the group's norms. In this way, individuals can develop distinct identities without threatening the integrity of the group, but the individual experiments have to be small.[6]

BEHAVIORAL WELFARE ECONOMICS

Grant the argument so far that Hirschman would seem to sit comfortably among behavioral economists, I want to suggest now that he would, nevertheless, be unhappy with the now famous use of behavioral insights in welfare economics: "nudging."

Sunstein and Thaler (2008) have argued that governments can usefully intervene over the "choice architecture" where there is evidence that some people (those given to behavioral biases/anomalies in decision making, like the ones I have described in the section "Preferences Do Change") can be manipulated through such architecture but where agents, if fully rational, would not be affected. Their point is that if such manipulations or "nudges" are effective, the government should perform them (in support of the interests of those who are affected) rather than allow private agents to do so to further their own private interests. In this way, it is paternalistic for those who are influenced by the "choice architecture" but it is also "libertarian" for the fully rational agents because the "nudges" do not affect their behavior.

One of their examples is changing the default on pension provision (to contribution rather than non-contribution). Defaults do not affect fully rational people but they are known to affect the behavior of some. For those affected, it is better that they contribute than they do not (or so it is claimed). Another example is the location of food in a canteen. Likewise this does not influence the choices of the fully rational person, but it does affect those people given to behavioral biases. When left to the canteen manager this leads to displays that encourage the choice of the high salt and sugar foodstuffs because they give immediate gratification to the customer and so increase the chances of their likely return. Such foodstuffs tend to store up long-term health problems but this has no obvious material consequence for the canteen manager and so will not guide his or her display decisions. For this reason, there should be intervention to encourage the more prominent display of fruit and vegetables. This is Sunstein and Thaler's "nudge" toward healthy eating.

The difficulty that Hirschman would have with this argument (and that I have) is not so much that it presumes that governments know what is in the interests of those individuals who are affected by "nudges," but that these people's interests have a particular form. In the two examples, they presume that if those affected by "nudges" were fully rational they would choose to contribute to a pension fund and avoid fatty and sugary food. This may or may not be right. This is part of the problem. But what really matters for my argument is that this casts the "nudge" as a form of compensation for what is a defect in decision making. In other words, they interpret the behavioral evidence on anomalies in decision making (relative to the standard utility maximizing models) as evidence of a form of malfunctioning. The fully rational agent is not subject to such anomalies. They have well behaved utility functions which they maximize. However, if as I have argued in the section "Preferences Do Change", much of the evidence on behavioral anomalies is best understood as evidence that we are unsure of our preferences and that to some degree we are always engaging in creative decisions with respect to Mill's "experiments in living," then these anomalies speak to our rationality in a different and deeper sense. They are not something that necessarily or obviously requires rectification.

Of course, this is not to doubt that there are some anomalies that arise from defects in the way that we process information. Confirmation biases are an obvious example. It does not serve our interests to be guided by such biases, however those "interests" are understood. But not all anomalies fit into this category. Some arise because we are engaging in that process of reflection on our preferences that Hirschman describes. This is the complication that Hirschman wishes to introduce and which Sunstein and Thaler seem not to countenance.

The question that is begged by opening up the space of creative reflection in the domain of welfare economics is whether any kind of intervention might follow from this. It is in the spirit of Hirschman's commitment to Mill-like experiments in living that people should be equipped to engage in such reflective change. If preference change is to be embraced, then it is important that a person feels in charge of this process and not at the mercy of some other persons' interests as they carefully manipulate the "choice architecture" for this purpose. But how can one be in charge in this sense if the thing with which one is identified (one's preferences) are changing?

This is a version of a question that Bianchi (2014) poses with respect to aesthetic preferences. There are, I think, two parts to the answer. One is a developing refrain in this paper. Such change must in some sense be *small* to be satisfactory because otherwise it threatens the integrity of the person who is changing. Bianchi provides some experimental evidence from psychology in support of this in the context of her argument. The other is that one needs some kind of anchor that constrains the changes that occur. Bianchi uses the seven types of narrative for this purpose when discussing the specific case of creativity with respect to aesthetic preferences. More broadly, what seems to be required are resources for thinking. This is what the seven narratives supply in her account of creativity. They are a resource for thinking. This is not the place to discuss what such resources might be. Mill in *On Liberty* and in *Essays of Representative Government* gives some pointers. For example, some minimum material resources, an education, the scope for discussion and the opportunity for participation in collective decision making all seem important. The comment I wish to make instead is that if such resources are important for the sense of individual autonomy and control over life as a changing process, then this is something that is important for all individuals. One cannot distinguish on the basis of valuing the individual in this sense between one individual and another.

This means that a behaviorally informed public policy of the kind that might appeal to Hirschman would not simply be a list of "nudges." It would be concerned with ensuring that all people had the resources for thinking. This is because we are more complicated than the parsimonious account of us as utility maximizes.

CONCLUSION

I have argued that behavioral economics provides some ready support for Hirschman's proposed complications in economics. In this sense, he was a behavioral economist. However, he would, I suspect, have recoiled from the application of these behavioral insights to welfare economics that have come to be known as "nudging." Instead, a summary of the argument here is that Hirschman believed, like Mill, that individuals become individuals, that is distinct persons, through a process of idiosyncratic learning-by-doing. What matters therefore is that people have the resources to engage such processes of "learning-by-doing." That Hirschman reminds us in this and other ways of the importance of "learning-by-doing" is one of his great contributions.

NOTES

1. There are several comprehensive surveys of decision-making anomalies (from the perspective of the standard expected utility maximizing model) that have been documented in experiments: see Rabin (2002), Camerer (2003), Pesendorfer (2006), DellaVigna (2009).

2. I want also to suggest that the centrality of learning-by-doing to Hirschman helps explain, in part, his bias toward incremental change, but more on this later.

3. Henrich et al. (2010) is one of the classic experimental studies where in a cross country study of 16 countries market integration is associated with more generosity in ultimatum games.

4. The details of the experiment can be found in Corr, Hargreaves Heap, Seger, and Tsutsui (2014).

5. There is also a difference in whether the first or second mover's decisions create the boost to joint pay-offs.

6. This was, of course, the logic behind another of Hirschman's colleagues at Harvard, David Riesman's argument, drawing explicitly on the analogy with monopolistic competition and marginal product differentiation, that people engaged in marginal differentiation in modern societies like that of the United States where peer pressures are a key mechanism underpinning social order.

REFERENCES

Bianchi, M. (2014). The magic of storytelling: How curiosity and aesthetic preferences work. *Economics: The Open-Access, Open-Assessment E-Journal*, *8*(44), 1–30. Retrieved from http://dx.doi.org/10.5018/economics-ejournal.ja.2014-44.

Bowles, S., & Polania-Reyes, S. (2012). Economic incentives and social preferences: Substitutes or complements? *Journal of Economic Literature*, *50*(2), 368–425.

Camerer, C. (2003). *Behavioral game theory*. Princeton, NJ: Princeton University Press.

Cheng, T., Oswlad, A., & Powdthavee, N. (2016). Longitudinal evidence for a midlife nadir in human well-being. *Economic Journal, forthcoming*.

Corr, P., Hargreaves Heap, S., Seger, C., & Tsutsui, K. (2014). *Personality, pro-sociality and the in-group bias: An experiment*. UEA Working Paper.

DellaVigna, S. (2009). Psychology and economics: Evidence from the field. *Journal of Economic Literature*, *47*(2), 315–372.

Falk, A., & Kosfeld, M. (2006). The hidden costs of control. *American Economic Review*, *96*(5), 1611–1630.

Fershtman, C., & Gneezy, U. (2001). Discrimination in a segmented society: An experimental approach. *Quarterly Journal of Economics*, *116*, 351–377.

Hargreaves Heap, S. (1980). Choosing the wrong natural rate: Accelerating inflation or decelerating employment and growth. *Economic Journal*, *90*, 611–620.

Hargreaves Heap, S., Tan, J., & Zizzo, D. (2013). Trust, inequality and the market. *Theory and Decision*, *74*(3), 311–333.

Henrich, J., Ensminger, J., McElreath, R., Barr, A., Barrett, C., Bolyanatz, A., ... Ziker, J. (2010). Markets, religion, community size and the evolution of fairness and punishment. *Science*, *327*(5972), 1480–1484.

Hirschman, A. (1977). *The passions and the interests: Political arguments for capitalism before its triumph*. Princeton, NJ: Princeton University Press.

Hirschman, A. (1982). Rival interpretations of market society: Civilizing, destructive, or feeble? *Journal of Economic Literature*, *20*(4), 1463–1484.

Hirschman, A. (1984). Against parsimony: Three easy ways of complicating some categories of economic discourse. *American Economic Review.*, *72*(2), 89–96.

Oswald, A. (1997). Happiness and economic performance. *Economic Journal*, *107*, 1815–1831.

Pesendorfer, W. (2006). Behavioral economics comes of age: A review. *Journal of Economic Literature*, *44*, 712–721.

Rabin, M. (2002). A perspective on psychology and economics. *European Economic Review*, *46*(4–5), 657–685.

Stigler, G. J., & Becker, G. S. (1977). De Gustibus Non Est Disputandum. *The American Economic Review*, *67*(2), 76–90.

Sunstein, C., & Thaler, R. (2008). *Nudge: Improving decisions about health, wealth and happiness*. New Haven, CT: Yale University Press.

Titmuss, R. (1971). *The gift relationship: from human blood to social policy*. New York, NY: Pantheon Books.

SPANNING EXIT AND VOICE: ALBERT HIRSCHMAN'S CONTRIBUTION TO POLITICAL SCIENCE

Peter John and Keith Dowding

ABSTRACT

The article reviews the contribution of Hirschman's Exit, Voice and Loyalty *(EVL) to research in political science. The argument is the framework of exit and voice offers greater understanding of a range trade-offs that exist in politics, in particular over collective action and citizen responses to dissatisfaction, which have implications for institutional design as well as for the functioning of democratic processes. The paper summarizes the EVL model and discusses how it may be elaborated. The main part of the article reviews applications to research literatures on political participation, responses to oppressive regimes, political party and interest group membership, and reports a number of formal treatments. The applications have been useful and illuminated a number of research problems, but overall they are modest in their impact in political science. The article suggests that the potential range of impacts*

Research in the History of Economic Thought and Methodology, Volume 34B, 175–196

ISSN: 0743-4154/doi:10.1108/S0743-41542016000034B007

could be much greater as EVL can show how individual choices are made in politics and are constrained by its institutions.

Keywords: Hirschman; exit; voice; loyalty; political science

INTRODUCTION

As research careers become more and more specialized, we come to appreciate the sheer range of a scholar such as Albert Hirschman. Not only did he work across several disciplines, he saw linkages between them and constructed new understandings by thinking beyond the frameworks scholars normally use. In what is considered to be his most famous work, *Exit, Voice and Loyalty* (1970), this intersection is at its most simple and cogent. As an economist (though an unusual one: Adelman, 2013; Dowding, 2015), Hirschman was preoccupied with exit and efficiency as part of the market mechanisms of competition. He counter-poses to this economically common process the concept of voice, more familiar to political scientists for whom participation and representation are core elements. Hirschman examines these two means of demonstrating dissatisfaction with services or an organization, and considers how they interact and inter-relate. His main concern is that increasing the opportunities for exit can reduce voice, and in some contexts can weaken, rather than strengthen, the signal from consumers or citizens. However, his third category – loyalty – can attenuate the exit–voice trade-off.

Hirschman's idea – often called EVL – has attracted much attention (though his specific framework and the relationships between exit, voice and loyalty are rarely examined). His influence can be detected in many areas, which include consumer behaviour, public administration (John, 2016) and employment studies, as well as political science (see Dowding, John, Mergoupis, & van Vugt, 2000). This article is a review of the application of Hirschman's ideas in political science. The aims are to examine how pronounced and distinctive is this contribution and to consider whether there could be a more extensive use of EVL in the discipline. Political science is broadly concerned with how political systems represent interests, solve problems and overcome social conflict. Its central concerns are the interest group struggle, collective action and coordination problems. At its core is the role of institutions in those processes and how office holders respond to multifarious demands. Hirschman was notoriously sceptical of the problems of collective action and that might affect the applicability of his account; yet his arguments are closely related to core concerns of political science. He understood that voice in collective political situations differs from voice in private market contexts. As Dowding and John (2012) argue, Hirschman's framework may be elaborated rather than undermined by understanding how collective action problems impact upon his concepts. Indeed, as we shall show, the use of EVL by political scientists has been productive for illuminating key problems in politics. But we also argue that the use of EVL could go much further.

EXIT, VOICE AND LOYALTY

Hirschman's starting point is how people act when they are dissatisfied. As an economist, Hirschman naturally assumes that when dissatisfied with a product consumers move to another: this is exit. His work in the developing world made him revise this viewpoint. He saw the Nigerian railway system getting worse as consumers shifted to road transport and decided that this occurred because leavers were also those who previously complained. Voice was being traded for exit to no good effect. The satisfied consumer does not need to voice or exit and can rationally conserve energy by doing nothing.

In a political context, dissatisfied citizens are ones who are unhappy with changes to a service they depend upon or with public servants, either professional or political. Such dissatisfaction might be ideological, accidental or due to falling standards. It can occur even when the organization has acted well and to the limit of its resources and powers; more usually dissatisfaction reflects a general change in organizational performance so that more than one citizen is affected, and occurs when citizens make comparisons with other organizations. This is what Hirschman calls decline, which can happen to any organization, as Hirschman makes clear in the first sentence of the book: 'Under any economic, social, or political system, individuals, business firms and organizations in general are subject to lapses from efficient, rational, law-abiding, virtuous, or otherwise functional behaviour' (1970, p. 1).

In other words, it is to be expected that, just like individuals, organizations from time to time systematically make mistakes or lose sight of their mission. Hirschman was very interested in the idea – promulgated by

Becker and others (1970, pp. 10–14; Becker, 1962) – of slack, which implies that a lack of efficiency could be in the interest of organizations and their leaders. The public sector can suffer from slack due to the absence of competition. Unless the state itself fails, the public sector cannot go out of business or face renewal through competition. The question to ask is whether there is a mechanism that keeps public managers alert and responsive to consumers and citizens. Hirschman considers both exit and voice as possible candidates.

Exit is an essential part of Hirschman's framework. It is one of the responses to dissatisfaction and represents an element of consumer choice: citizens can obtain better services by exiting. Exit in the private market is simply switching products; applied more broadly to public services it could include switching to a private sector provider or moving within or outside the jurisdiction of a provider. For the economist, exit is an essential means to improve the efficiency of the market by giving signals to producers provide desired products. Hirschman recognized that choice is constrained by monopoly provision and also by consumer inertia and information deficit. For the public choice advocate, the solution is to free up the market by introducing competitive mechanisms to increase the number of suppliers or encouraging citizens to buy services from the private sector (Le Grand, 2007). It is possible to set up autonomous service-providing units and disseminate information about their performance. Consumers will benefit from quasi-markets because new units of production or service provision respond to demand and existing public organizations will need to improve services to retain their users. Hirschman's 45-year-old book is even more relevant today, as the privatization and marketization of welfare services have grown apace across the world (see John, 2016).

Hirschman's account of exit has important differences from standard economic approaches. For him, exit is a last-resort option that individuals do not really want to take. Not only is exit costly for the individual, it is also fateful for the organization that loses loyal supporters who by voicing could help it deliver perform effectively. If exit happens all at once, the organization can go out of business or fail, so preventing any chance of recovery. Consumers usually want to give only a signal to exit, which can alert the organization to remedy its performance, but without the drastic course of action of leaving being taken. In this way, consumer responses can be helpful to the organization by assisting recovery. In contrast to the public choice approach, Hirschman is sympathetic to organizations rather than suspicious of them: in each organization there is inbuilt intellectual capital and a cadre of workers with experience who help deliver effective services. It is just that public organizations need the occasional jolt to improve their performance, and this is where voice comes in handy.

Voice is a response to dissatisfaction and involves 'kicking up a fuss' (Hirschman, 1970, p. 30). It encompasses a wide range of activities:

> any attempt at all to change, rather than to escape from, an objectionable state of affairs, whether through individual or collective petition to the management directly in charge, through appeal to a higher authority with the intention of forcing a change in management, or through various kinds of actions and protests, including those that are meant to mobilize public opinion. (Hirschman, 1970, p. 30)

In this way, voice is richer than exit as it conveys more information to the producer and can indicate what the organization can do to put things right (Hirschman, 1981). There are two ways that voice can be silenced. First, the 'alert' consumers exit and, second, those left behind are less educated so their voice is less effective. The most alert are more likely to both voice and exit. Hirschman believes this is a particular problem for publicly produced services, which at the time he wrote often included railways, as well as education and health. Encouraging private schools and health care will lead to a decline in the quality of state provision, as the private and political voice that ensures the quality of public services will be lost.

Hirschman claims that voice needs to be implemented carefully, not excessively, or else there will not be an effective response. Voicing is an 'art' (1970, p. 43). The organization also needs time to respond (1970, p. 33). It needs to be serious in its response: consumers will wait before exiting, basing their responses on past experiences as well as the ones in the current period; but if the response is not forthcoming they will take the exit option from which there is no return. Citizens update their beliefs, and lack of a response to voice will eventually reach a threshold triggering their exit.

Hirschman's main argument is that exit can reduce voice, a problem especially when introducing competition in the public sector. However, he also recognized that it is the threat of exit that makes voice effective, something he thought was demonstrated by the break-up of the Eastern bloc (Hirschman, 1995). In many circumstances, without the threat of exit, voice could simply be cheap talk. However, it should be noted that, in the public service context, voice is not cheap talk even if a service is a state monopoly. Even if exit from a nationalized service is impossible, citizens retain threat potential. In a democracy, they can voice their disquiet and threaten not to vote for any candidate who will not act to improve service quality. In that context, voting can be seen as a form of exit. (In another context, as we see below, voting can be seen as a form of voice.) Either way, however, it is the threat potential of withholding one's vote that gives power to the voice option.

A number of scholars have puzzled over the third concept of loyalty. In Hirschman's view, consumers balance the certainty of exit against the probability that their voice might be responded to. Low responsiveness might incline them to exit. Their loyalty or attachment to the organization gives them hope that voice might indeed be responded to and that it is worth waiting for the organization to put matters right. Loyalty might also increase responsiveness because loyal customers might be more likely to be listened to. Loyalty also helps retain those customers who are most likely to exit. These people are the most quality-conscious so are able to provide feedback and agitate to improve the product. Hirschman talks about the affection that customers often have for the organization from which they buy products or services. Loyalty, then, might be seen as a psychological disposition that inclines people more to voice and less to exit.

The notion of loyalty has been extensively criticized, most notably by Barry (1974), who thought it performed no empirical role. Most researchers believe that loyalty is a slippery concept and hard to operationalize; for example, union membership is taken to be a measure of loyalty in the literature on employee quits, but it is not clear whether it precisely measures the concept. It is also less clear how loyalty affects voice: in general terms, loyalty is more likely to increase voice, as the loyal consumer is more likely to trust the organization and so put forward a point of view; but loyalty on its own might not increase the efficiency of the organization if customers are too trusting and hence passive.

Dowding and John (2012) discuss this problem, arguing that loyalty should be conceptualized as a form of social investment made by individuals in communities and social relationships (see also Lyons, Lowery, & DeHoog, 1992), which is particularly relevant for public organizations that have a stake in local communities. Social investment is akin to social capital, as it comes from forming social networks and trusting others in a particular environment to which individuals become more attached over time. This can make more comprehensible the idea that loyalty dampens exit. The voluminous literature on social capital then comes to bear, showing the powerful impact on outcomes (Putnam, 2000). This mechanism for public service improvement partly relates to lower transaction costs, which is outside the EVL framework, but it also comes from the link from social capital to participation and then to performance. The operation of social bonds is consistent with Hirschman's framework, in particular on the limits on exit.

Dowding and John (2012) extend Hirschman by examining multiple exit and voice opportunities. The latter is particularly important in political contexts. Individual voice is where people voice personally with regard to specific issues. If parents have a problem with their local school, they can take up a particular complaint with the teacher or principal concerned, their school board or local authority, with a local or national politician or even with the education department. Similarly, with health providers there are a number of possible targets for individual complaints. People rarely compliment providers individually unless invited to do so through surveys or questions, but individual positive voice is possible.

People can also voice collectively by means of a collectively organized response through some pressure group or political party. Such action is even more likely if there is a perceived threat to local schools or health-care providers. Finally, people can use other democratic means, notably their vote, to support candidates they think will enable superior provision of health care or education. This might be by voting for school boards or governors, local authority members on health boards or local or national politicians who they believe will work to provide the kind of services they want.

The collective–individual voice distinction is important, since it will affect expectations about the exit–voice trade-off. Individual voice should only occur with dissatisfaction, whilst collective voice is often about defending existing levels of provision, so might occur only if exit is a future option. If future exit is difficult, then collective voice seems the only option, yet suffers from the collective action problem. Loyalty as seen in social investment should, according to Dowding and John, correlate strongly with collective voice. But if exit is made easier – that is, tax incentives are offered for going private in health, education or security, or regulation of schools, health centres and private security is not as effective as in the public sector – then both individual and collective voice might decline, to the detriment of the efficient and effective production of public services. That, certainly, was Hirschman's argument and Dowding and John (2012) found some evidence for it.

Of course, measuring efficiency is especially problematic. Whilst simple measures looking at cost, output and profit levels can give some relative judgements of efficiency in competitive markets, for goods such as education and health care other techniques are required. Objective measures in education are problematic, since educational attainment is relative, and needs change over time. Objective measures such as mortality and morbidity rates over time or across countries give some measure of effectiveness and efficiency in health care relative to cost; but they are crude and capture only part of the demand for health care. Technical advance drives much of the changing output of health and that is orthogonal to efficiency in organizational structure. Data Envelopment Analysis, a more sophisticated parametric technique, requires careful data collection and studies are not always comparable across sectors (for a review, see Hollingsworth, 2003). There is no extant work that really demonstrates the comparative efficiency of exit versus voice procedures, only studies of the inter-relationship of the two, sometimes mediated by loyalty. In the next section, we consider studies in political science that have used EVL as they appear in respective subareas and ask how the insights of EVL have pushed forward knowledge in these areas.

POLITICAL BEHAVIOUR

There are large numbers of political scientists who study political behaviour, which is concerned with why people participate in politics, the determinants of party choice, turnout, and other political variables. EVL offers the insight that the availability of exit may affect participation, which may be a function of institutional design. However, other features of the social support system may help prevent exit from having too much of an effect. Several studies argue that the facility to move jurisdictions will cause a reduction in turnout. Hirschman directs attention to the build-up to the moving decision, because exit opportunities or their prospect depress voice. Loyalty, which Hirschman regards as mediating or softening the exit–voice trade-off, may be conceived as a form of social investment. It is here that it is possible to apply Hirschman's arguments to voting intentions and throw further light on the determinants of voter turnout.

The effect of geographical mobility on turnout has already been demonstrated without Hirschman's insights, first by Squire, Wolfinger, and Glass (1987), who show that voters who have newly arrived in an electoral district are less likely to vote than those who have been there for some time. There are two effects argued for in the literature, therefore: registration costs and local social capital (Rosenstone & Hansen, 1993, p. 157). Highton (2000) distinguishes between residential moves – where a person has simply moved home – and community mobility, where a person moves from one community to another.

EVL has added to research on mobility by placing citizen acts in a more general framework. Dowding, John, and Rubenson (2012) argue that a citizen's decision to geographically exit in the near future will lower the probability of her voting now, since she will be less affected by the decision. In keeping with Hirschman, they further argue that loyalty, in the form of social investment in the community, will positively affect the probability of voice. Using Roper survey data, they provide empirical evidence for this, with high levels of social investment completely washing out the exit–voice trade-off. In a separate dataset (Dowding & John, 2012), they confirm the importance of social capital in the vote–move process, and show that the type of voice differentially affects the relationship to exit.

Earlier survey-based studies of the inter-relationship between exit and voice also appear in other studies of participation, such as those by Orbell and Uno (1972) and Sharp (1984, 1986). In particular, Sharp's (1984) study remains one of the most thorough. The study analyses the probabilities of having voiced, conditional on intentions to exit. The analysis was on those whites who considered the performance of their local government problematic, and considered two types of voice. The first was contacts with local government officials, which she calls 'individualistic' participation; the second was working with neighbours to solve problems, which is called 'communal' participation mode, following Verba and Nie (1972). Sharp stresses that definite intentions to move were associated with a large drop in the 'communal' mode of participation among those with less education: '[t]he better-educated may indeed have more mobility potential, but this does not interfere with their inclination to use voice when local government violates their preferences' (Sharp, 1984, p. 74).

Another take on exit–voice mechanism comes from Schaltegger and Küttel (2002) using evidence from Swiss cantons. The Leviathan hypothesis (Brennan & Buchanan, 1980) and yardstick competition suggest that exit opportunities means that local and state governments are often forced by competitive forces to mimic the fiscal policies of their neighbouring governments, though transaction cost still leaves governments able to act independently of the public. Schaltegger and Küttel argue that fiscal autonomy and enhanced voice through direct democracy means that governments are less likely to mimic their neighbours' policies. Using annual expenditure and tax data from 1980 to 1998, they find governments do tend to follow their neighbours, so mimicking occurs, and that the more fragmented canton and the stronger the fiscal autonomy of the local authorities the smaller the size of government. However, voice, in the form of direct democracy, also decreases the size of government and reduces mimicking behaviour. In terms of the Tiebout or Leviathan hypothesis that exit increases the control of government by citizens, they show that enhanced voice is even more effective, not only does it ensure smaller government, but it also increases variation across communities, an effect we should expect if governments follow citizen's preferences rather than simply copy their neighbours.

COMPARATIVE POLITICS

In the area of comparative politics, there is a great deal of literature that uses the EVL framework, but it does so rather casually without really looking at the interactions between exit and voice or considering the effects of loyalty. We ignore work that simply uses Hirschman's label to examine that work that uses Hirschman theoretically. These studies all examine how lack of voice affects exit, and then how the opening up of regimes or organizations affects voice. The literature in comparative politics falls into main camps: first, those looking at cross-border migration, especially in oppressive regimes and how revolution or rebellion affect exit, and then exit–voice; second, those that examine exit and voice within political organizations, either political parties or organized interest groups.

Exit, Voice and Oppression

Hirschman's (1995) own essay on East Germany compares the 40 years of private exit from public action, due to the high cost of collective voice under communism, with the return to voice enabled, he suggests, by collective exit – the mass exodus of people from the GDR to the West. Pfaff and Kim (2003) follow up Hirschman's work examining the GDR situation more thoroughly (see also Pfaff, 2006) by analysing 214 East German counties municipalities in search of what lay behind protest in East Germany in the revolution of 1989–1990 before the unification of East and West. The puzzle is what causes protest when so many people had exited from the regime in the years since the Second World War (1945–1989). Like Hirschman, they do not find the expected negative relationship between voice and exit. Did exit in fact stimulate voice? Here, they are interested in Hirschman's (1970, p. 39) elaboration that 'the effectiveness of the voice mechanism is strengthened by the possibility of exit'. Pfaff and Kim highlight the costs of voice, not just in contemporary East Germany, but also because of the collective action problem. They argue that people overcame the collective action problem through a signalling game that shifts the trade-off between exit and voice. People leaving can signal discontent to those who are left. The exiting crisis can create the conditions for effective opposition to the regime, but this needs to be at a significant level to make an impact, while at the same time exiting above a certain level erodes the actual participants in protest, just as Hirschman says. Pfaff and Kim (2003) argue that the strength of the signals in part depends on the nature of the networks of those exiting and the means by which information diffuses into the networks of potential protestors.

Pfaff and Kim (2003) regress the degree of voice that occurred in counties/municipalities after the onset of the East German revolution in September 1989–March 1990 on the level of prior exit they had experienced, seeking to map the shape of the relationship controlling for loyalty, economic grievances, past social movement activity and state reactions to protest. The Communist regime provided accurate measures of voice, through state records of protests, and also of exits. But conceptualizing loyalty with aggregate data is rather difficult. Pfaff and Kim use Communist Party membership as a measure, and indicators of perks from working in the tertiary sector and the amount of research and higher education in these places, on the basis that these are sources of networks seeking to promote the regime. These measures are problematic because they may not be tracking loyalty, but something else, such as private side-payments. Pfaff and Kim find that prior exit predicts voice, and that this is also non-linear: as exit increases so the effect of voice decreases. At some higher point, exits start to undermine the protest potential through erosion of the networks. Loyalty had no impact except for those in the tertiary sector (though it is hard to make an inference with such a poor measurement). Overall, this research shows that the exit–voice trade-off tends to happen either under certain conditions or more at the individual level. When issues of collective action are involved, the exit–voice trade-off may disappear or even, as in this case, reverse.

Colomer (2000) compares the strategy of Cuba under Fidel Castro and the United States with the strategies of the East and West Germany under the cold war. He argues that Cuba has an incentive to allow dissidents to leave to reduce internal voice pressures, though these incentives are constrained by not wanting to lose highly skilled workers. The United States would like to encourage voice in Cuba, but at the same time due to internal pressures was happy to enable migration from Cuba in contrast to economic migrant from other Caribbean and Latin American nations. Colomer notes a paradox that the US exceptional migration policy gave Cuba a strategic advantage. Cuba had incentives to stimulate emigration in sequential waves, specifically allowing not only dissidents but also criminals to leave, thus forcing the United States to close its borders.

O'Donnell (1986) and Scott (1986) each examine the relationship between repression and voice or exit tendencies. O'Donnell's is a subtle account of the nature of oppression and different reactions to it. Some repress their own feelings or turn their anger to other objects; some use horizontal voice to whisper to those around them, and others more directly challenge authoritarian rule. Such voices do seek to undermine authoritarian regimes. Scott (1986) examines the reaction of slave owners in Cuba to Spanish attempts to end slavery through the lens of EVL.

Ådnanes (2004) also examines exit across nation borders, treating it as the desire to emigrate, with voice referring to political commitment. She explores these concepts in a survey of 560 Bulgarian university students, using regression on the scales of the underlying factors (thought the analysis is not that clearly reported). She runs regressions to predict exit and voice, finding that voice does not predict exit, but she does not test whether exit predicts voice. One powerful variable that positively predicts voice and negative exit is 'hopelessness', which is a measure that predicts depression, and consists of questions about what someone thinks is going to happen in the future. The decision to exit is also the result of political attitudes, such as degree of conservatism (negative predictor), which may relate to the act of exit specified here: leaving a transition country. The paper claims that the concepts of voice and exit should be brought together, which is somewhat puzzling given the use of different measures and predictors.

Okamoto and Wilkes' (2008) is another migration study that is more closely related to Pfaff and Kim (2003) in two ways. First, it is about the intersection of rebellion against a regime and emigration. Second, it looks at the implication of the EVL framework for collective action, so is an advance on empirical studies. Okamoto and Wilkes use Dowding et al.'s (2000) argument that the different nature of individual and collective voice will have varying relationships to exit. They operationalize these as differences in costs versus opportunities, arguing that:

> fight (rebellion) will be a substitute for flight (emigration) when the costs of exit are high or when the opportunities for exit are few. Conversely, flight (emigration) will be a substitute for fight (rebellion) when the costs of voice are high and the opportunities are low. (Okamoto & Wilkes, 2008, p. 351).

Like many recent EVL studies, Okamoto and Wilkes take a dynamic approach, using measures taken in 1990 and 1999. They use the *Minorities at Risk Project*, which has information on 275 groups across the world and collects aggregate data. They use two dependent variables: rebellion and emigration associated with the minority at risk. They model opportunities and costs of exit (past immigration, kin across international border, regional base, regional autonomy movement and a physical barrier/water border). They find these predict emigration. Similarly, they model the opportunity and costs of voice (mountainous terrain, past rebellion, and per capita income). Bar per capita income, these are significant predictors. A nice feature of this paper is that it also seeks to find out when there is both rebellion and exit. They show that minority groups with opportunities for emigration were less likely to participate in rebellion and groups with opportunities for rebellion were less likely to emigrate. The costs of exit were important, because groups with a regional base were less likely to emigrate. The cost of voice was not a factor. Okamoto and Wilkes find no evidence that voice will be the preferred option when the condition promotes both exit and voice. The limitation of the research is that the costs and benefits of exit and voice are hard to model as they both arise from collective action, which is not linked back to the opening discussion of this issue. The only collective action factor is that of having a regional base, which may provide better opportunities for rebellion because of proximate social networks. In this case, there is a fuller application of EVL.

Political Organizations

Hirschman's framework has been applied to group and party membership and behaviour, which is where members make choices to voice or exit. Eubank, Gangopadahay, and Weinberg (1996) examine responses to Achille Occhetto's 1990 proposal to reform the Italian Communist Party. They suggest that discontent should lead to exit, and examine this by comparing votes across different internal and external forums. Those voting against motions to exit the Party were more loyal, confirming that loyalty inhibits exit. Lifelong members were loyal, whilst the Marxist ideologues left. Whilst the argument is plausible, the model suffers ecological inference issues.

Kato (1998) examines parliamentarians' behaviour within parties in the Japanese House of Representatives. In the 1990s, widespread corruption was addressed by institutional reforms, not only of parliamentary and electoral procedure, but also of political parties, causing strife within the two largest parties, the Liberal Democratic Party (LDP), and the Social Democratic Party (SDP) (formerly Japan Socialist Party JSP). This led to greater exit and voice opportunities. Kato examines the voice activity of parliamentarians during debates within each party. He examines the exit of some members leaving the major parties to form new ones. He finds that members who exit are more likely to have previously used voice than who do not exit, which may be another example of the noisy exiters. He also finds that personal characteristics, particularly a person's political history, predict voice and exit. The organizational rules of the parties also have an independent effect on exit. Kato recognizes that the inter-relationship found between voice and exit cannot be generalized too far as contextual factors are also important. He has no data on satisfaction and we only conclude that those who voice and exit are more dissatisfied because of their behaviour. Contrary to his claims, his results are consistent with Hirschman's framework through the way in which different relations between exit and voice are discussed.

Pettit (2007) compares the Danish Socialist People's Party, the Danish Social Democrats and the British Labour Party to examine the idea that the control leaders have over policies means that voice is ineffective, causing exit to be the only option for party members. But these parties differ in the extent to which exit is a viable option. Pettit argues that Labour members have no party to go to, so they will try to use the party conference to voice, with a correspondingly greater attempt by party leaders to limit the exercise of voice. This is an explanation of conflict. The test is through case studies, which makes it hard to tease out these relationships. Voice and party control may be a feature of the traditions of the parties or of other factors, such as party competition, rather than exit and voice. The paper makes strong claims about exit and voice, but without the evidence to back them up. Nor is there an examination of a change over time to illustrate the theory.

Whiteley and Seyd (2002) use Hirschman's ideas to examine party members exiting in relation to high levels of voice in an examination of what they call 'high-intensity participation'. The same or rather similar factors leading to dissatisfaction cause high-intensity members to voice even more, whilst low-intensity members choose to exit. Weakening the incentives to participate leads to lower efficacy, causing some to participate less and others to exit.

The EVL framework has been applied to relationships across parties, examining what causes members of a coalition to leave. Langston (2002) uses the case of Mexico and three defections by candidates running against the government. Three factors created the conditions for exit: the remova-lof voice within the coalition, a change in the economic context and the lowering of the costs of forming new political parties. Exit happens when the costs change – voice is more costly, exit less so. She also highlights how actors can voice grievance before leaving the coalition. This paper shows how the metaphor of exit and voice can be a useful way to help interpret changes to the party system. One of the strengths of that piece is that it compares across time, but it is not clear how much the EVL framework adds to the story described.

Using case studies from Mexico, Spain and Venezuela, Burgess (1999) broadens the gaze from parties alone to look at the relationship between unions and parties through the lens of EVL. She examines the strategic choices made by trade union leaders in response to disaffection with their coalition parties. She proposes that 'voice and exit constitute points along a path of alliance change, and that loyalty interacts with authority structures to affect the pace and direction of change' (Burgess, 1999, p. 105). The paper focuses on loyalty and how it is constructed, defining it as historically constructed expectations and adherence to codes of conduct. Burgess takes a longitudinal approach, seeing loyalty as something that needs to be renewed. She also splits up voice into norm-based and norm-breaking varieties, with the latter aimed at challenging the norms without leaving the coalition. She sees a continuum from norm-based voice to norm-breaking voice to exit. Burgess argues that exit is much more costly than voice because of the costs of severing ties. Loyalty also makes it hard to break ties as well. Overall, the piece is persuasive and has an attractive dynamic element. But it is not clear that there is a distinction between the voice categories suggested or that they are necessary.

Barakso and Schaffner (2008) focus solely on interest group membership and their variable voice opportunities. They code the bylaws of 114 US national membership organizations according to voice procedures, and argue that when members face few barriers to exiting a group, there are few democratic procedures, and vice versa. They assume that interest group leaders will try to be autocratic; they ideally do not want voice in order to keep their groups 'taut'. But when exit is not an option, organizations have more voice procedures. To find out what influences the extent of democratic governance, Barakso and Schaffner perform a regression using measures of barriers to exit, which are whether it is a professional organization or a union (seen as having fewer exit opportunities), which is positive and significant in their analysis. In addition, they code for advocacy organizations, on the ground that they should have more loyal members, though they find no relationship here. Other covariates that are positive and significant are age, log of membership size and organizational levels. So the basic hypothesis works, even if the exit opportunity measures are rather crude. It would be better to have an indication of how many alternative organizations there are (there could be lots of trade unions, e.g., which would invalidate this measure).

Overall, these studies show that the exit and voice framework can be used to illuminate key relationships that appear in politics, whether it is exit from an oppressive regime or membership of parties and interest groups. There is a variation in the extent to which these studies incorporate EVL, and the best of them are based on tests of the exit–voice trade off using a variety of data sources available. Yet these are largely simple tests and do not explore more complex relationships. The next stage of work in political science covers a field of work that can deal with more complex specifications.

FORMAL MODELS IN POLITICAL SCIENCE

Recent studies have attempted to specify Hirschman's framework more formally in game-theoretic terms. Doing so is more complex than his simple argument might appear. Those who have attempted to do so concentrate upon the exit and voice relationship, to the virtual exclusion of loyalty. Gehlbach (2006) presents a simple general complete information game-theoretic model analysing the relationship between exit and voice. The game is within some organization (a club or a nation, e.g.). It assumes that exit is costly in the sense that the joint payoff to the leadership and membership is greater without exit. Payoffs are between 0 and 1, with payoff x to membership and $(1 - x)$ to the leadership. The leaders have the freedom to set policy to the extent members can exit. Gehlbach then assumes that the members can organize collectively to bargain with leaders to achieve Nash equilibrium such that gains of this trade are split equally. Without collective organization, leaders offer a take-it-or-leave it deal which citizens can either accept (in silence) or exit. There are costs of organizing.

The results show that payoffs for members once organized must be higher to ensure they do not exit. This then specifies the Hirschman voice argument that members gain more when they voice. In the model exit never occurs, the leadership always offering enough to preclude it, and thus 'silence' emerges endogenously just as it seems to in much of organizational life. (Most people neither exit nor voice most of the time.) Members choose to organize if their payoff from sharing the surplus is greater than the cost of organizing plus cost of exit (payoff of the take-it-or-leave it offer).

So here exit will reduce voice when the exit payoff is large (costs of exit are low). However, it is still the case that voice is most powerful when exit is easiest. As Gehlbach (2006, p. 402) puts it, 'Voice and exit are complements once voice has been established, but are substitutes when seen from the perspective of the decision to exercise voice to begin with.'

On loyalty, Gehlbach (2006) shows that it leaves members worse off when it is defined as a tax on exit – it makes members more reluctant to leave – but increases welfare when it is a voice subsidy when it also increases the propensity to voice. Both aspects of loyalty might be present with the tendency to suffer in silence and the desire to improve the organization even though other alternatives are available.

Gehlbach's model tends to the descriptive rather than explanatory – that is, it specifies more formally some of the relations in Hirschman rather than formally deriving testable hypotheses that allow variation in organizational form; and, as he recognizes, it abstracts some important features from Hirschman, such as heterogeneity in membership. It also assumes that voice is collective rather than individual which, as we shall argue, has important behavioural consequences. He does not apply his argument empirically beyond illustrating it by using Hirschman's (1995) account of East Germany. Nevertheless, it is an important and useful first attempt to formalize Hirschman.

Slapin (2009) also formally models the exit–voice relationship, though in his case, voice is a very strong condition of veto, and applies it to the European Union. The use of exit over voice depends on the relative costs of exit for the exiting nation and the remaining members of the federation; and the costs of caving into veto or excluding the recalcitrant state. He does not consider any of Hirschman's hypotheses directly concerning the relationship between increasing voice by reducing exit or the effects of loyalty. In reality, veto is a much stronger condition than voice, making his model not really relevant to Hirschman's framework.

Clark, Golder, and Golder (2015) have a more complete model of EVL with each component a separate behavioural category. As they recognize, this means their approach is closer to the social-psychological 'Exit, Voice, Loyalty and Neglect' approach of Rusbult, Zembrodt, and Gunn (1982) (see Lyons et al., 1992 for a political science application). They examine a three-stage game with a move from the citizen, then a governmental response followed by the citizen's move. The citizen can either exit or show loyalty, the government can respond or ignore, and the citizen can then exit or show loyalty again. Citizens can voice, but they pay a cost. Governments can respond to voice, but only at the first stage; thereafter citizens must decide whether to remain loyal or exit. In this model, voice only counts if exit is plausible.

Clark et al. (2015) model two types of government, those that are dependent on citizens and those that are autonomous. A dependent government is one that values a citizen's loyalty more than the benefits it gains directly from her; but an autonomous one values what it can seize from its citizens more than anything else. So only the former values the citizen's investment. There are two types of citizens: those who have a credible exit threat and those who do not. The model shows that, contrary to Hirschman's claims, only dependent governments respond positively when citizens have a credible threat potential. Citizens without credible exit threats have no hold over government, and where governments are autonomous the credible exit threat also has no effect on government. Clark et al. argue that their model shows we can see citizens' types from their actions, but it is more difficult to see government types since both ignore citizens with no credible exit threats. Like others, they apply this model to the collapse of the GDR.

Extending the model, they argue that conflicts between citizens and government (i.e., mass protest) will only occur if citizens are not powerful (they have no exit threat) or if government fails to understand citizen demands. They suggest this undermines arguments that influence over policy increases with greater lobbying and that those with no exit potential are more likely to voice. They suggest their model supports Marxist accounts of the state, where soft-voice capitalists have far more power than the noisy proletariat. They apply their model to modernization theory and the resource curse and to the role of foreign aid in the economic performance of governments. Whilst the results of the formal model are interesting, how far models with a simple structure can fully model complex relationships is open to question. In the model, the citizen tends to be a single actor, which obscures a major problem for voice activity, the collective action problem, which means that citizen's behaviour will not be revealed as easily as the authors suggest. Nevertheless, these political science applications develop Hirschman's ideas and elaborate EVL in productive ways.

CONCLUSION

We have examined why the EVL framework has been of interest to political scientists. Empirically, applications are sparse and they have not provided dominant themes in any part of the discipline; rather, they have been a niche application. EVL has mainly been applied to political behaviour, both voting and collective action and party switching. However, the implications of Hirschman's EVL argument for political science are dramatic, far more so than most commentators have realized.

The manner in which a country sets up its key political, economic and social institutions will have a major effect on how preferences are revealed. If certain services, such as security, health or education, were only provided at the national level, then the only way preferences could be revealed would be through voice. The only competition would be at the level of political competition through the ballot box. Given other assumptions, we should expect the preferences of the median voter to prevail with greater homogeneity across the levels of provision. Some heterogeneity and other forms of provision can be introduced if services are broken down into different jurisdictional levels with some form of geographical competition. Once private suppliers come into the picture, far greater homogeneity will emerge; but once this form of exit is opened up, it is highly likely that the loudest and most effective voices, both individual and collective, will leave public provision. These voices then act, not to maintain state provision of services but to downgrade them, as they would see few individual benefits from their tax dollars (although they might perceive collective benefits). Citizens may also feel less loyal to private providers so exit velocity is enhanced even further.

Mainstream political science examines the relationship of institutions upon political behaviour. Since those institutions will also reflect and help determine the preferences of the political community, the efficiency calculations across possible scenarios are problematic. Hirschman's work helps us to examine the relationship of political institutions and behaviour. Economics can broadly be thought of as examining private good provision, and politics as public good provision. Of course, this distinction is too simple, but the major ways in which citizens traditionally have input into political processes is through collective behaviour, and democratic government provides goods (both public and private goods) by rules that treat citizens equally. Authoritarian governments do not always need to maintain the same kind of loyalty from citizens, and these factors mean that the inter-relationship of exit and voice differ across the domain. Some game-theoretic work (Clark et al., 2015) recognizes these effects, and also acknowledges the difficulties that strategic interactions cause for empirical work that tries to interpret preferences from social, economic and political behaviour. Most work in the area of EVL is influenced by the exit possibilities for revealing above and beyond voice (e.g., Warren, 2011). Clark et al.'s (2015) application of EVL dynamics to issues such as the resource curse, and their interpretation of the effects of pressure group activity, whilst underspecified, shows that there are clearly areas where application of EVL could prove enormously fruitful.

Despite the multitude of citations in the 45 years or so since the book was published, Hirschman's work has not been truly appreciated in political science. A growing interest, particularly in developing the theory more completely and formally, might see further, more theorized, applications in the future.

REFERENCES

Adelman, J. (2013). *Worldly philosopher: The odyssey of Albert O. Hirschman*. Princeton, NJ: Princeton University Press.

Ådnanes, M. (2004). Exit and/or voice? Youth and post-communist citizenship in Bulgaria. *Political Psychology*, *25*, 795–815.

Barakso, M., & Schaffner, B. F. (2008). Exit, voice, and interest group governance. *American Politics Research*, *36*, 186–209.

Barry, B. (1974). Review article: "Exit voice and loyalty". British Journal of *Political Science*, *4*, 79–107.

Becker, G. (1962). Irrational behaviour and economic theory. *Journal of Political Economy*, *70*, 1–13.

Brennan, G., & Buchanan, J. M. (1980). *The power to tax: Analytical foundations of a fiscal constitution*. Cambridge: Cambridge University Press.

Burgess, K. (1999). Loyalty dilemmas and market reform: Party-union alliances under stress in Mexico, Spain and Venezuela. *World Politics*, *52*, 105–134.

Clark, W., Golder, M., & Golder, S. (2015). *An exit, voice, and loyalty model of politics*. Unpublished paper. Retrieved from http://mattgolder.com/files/research/evl.pdf

Colomer, J. M. (2000). Exit, voice and hostility in Cuba. *International Migration Review*, *34*, 423–442.

Dowding, K. (2015). Albert O. Hirschman: *Exit, voice and loyalty*. In S. Balla, M. Lodge, & E. Page (Eds.), *Oxford handbook of the classics of public policy and administration* (pp. 256–271). Oxford: Oxford University Press.

Dowding, K., & John, P. (2012). Exits, voices and social investment: Citizens' reaction to public services. Cambridge: Cambridge University Press.

Dowding, K., John, P., Mergoupis, T., & van Vugt, M. (2000). Exit, voice and loyalty: Analytical and empirical developments. *European Journal of Political Research*, *37*, 469–495.

Dowding, K., John, P., & Rubenson, D. (2012). Geographic mobility, social connections and turnout. *Journal of Elections, Public Opinion and Parties*, *22*, 109–122.

Eubank, W. L., Gangopadahay, A., & Weinberg, L. B. (1996). Italian communism in crisis: A study in exit, voice and loyalty. *Party Politics*, *2*, 55–75.

Gehlbach, S. G. (2006). A political model of exit and voice. *Rationality and Society*, *18*(4), 395–418.

Highton, B. (2000). Residential mobility, community mobility, and electoral participation. *Political Behaviour*, *22*, 109–120.

Hirschman, A. O. (1970). *Exit, voice, and loyalty responses to decline in firms, organizations and states*. Cambridge, MA: Harvard University Press.

Hirschman, A. O. (1981). Exit and voice: Some further distinctions. In A. O. Hirschman (Ed.), *Essays in trespassing: Economics to politics and beyond*. Cambridge: Cambridge University Press.

Hirschman, A. O. (1995). Exit, voice and the fate of the German democratic republic. In A. O. Hirschman (Ed.), *A propensity to self-subversion*. Cambridge, MA: Harvard University Press.

Hollingsworth, B. (2003). Non-parametric and parametric applications measuring efficiency in health care. *Health Care Management Science*, *6*(2), 203–218.

John, P. (2016). Finding exits and voices: Albert Hirschman's contribution to the study of public services. *International Public Management Journal*, Early view. Retrieved from http://www.tandfonline.com/doi/full/10.1080/10967494.2016.1141814

Kato, J. (1998). When the party breaks up: Exit and voice among Japanese legislators. *American Political Science Review*, *92*(4), 857–870.

Langston, J. (2002). Breaking out is hard to do: Exit, voice, and loyalty in Mexico's one-party hegemonic regime. *Latin American Politics and Society*, *44*(3), 61–88.

Le Grand, J. (2007). *The other invisible hand: Delivering public services through choice and competition*. Princeton, NJ: Princeton University Press.

Lyons, W. E., Lowery, D., & DeHoog, R. H. (1992). *The politics of dissatisfaction: Citizens, services, and urban institutions*. Armonk, NY: M. E. Sharpe.

O'Donnell, G. (1986). On the fruitful convergence of Hirschman's *exit, voice and loyalty* and *shifting involvements*: Reflections from the recent argentine experience. In A. Foxley, M. McPherson, & G. O'Donnell (Eds.), *Development, democracy and the art of trespassing: Essays in honor of Albert Hirschman*. Notre Dame, IN: Notre Dame Press.

Okamoto, D. G., & Wilkes, R. (2008). The opportunities and costs of voice and exit: Modelling ethnic group rebellion and emigration. *Journal of Ethnic and Migration Studies*, *34*(3), 347–369.

Orbell, J. M., & Uno, T. (1972). A theory of neighbourhood problem solving: Political action vs. residential mobility. *American Political Science Review*, *66*, 471–489.

Pettit, R. T. (2007). Challenging the leadership: The party conference as a platform for dissenting membership voice in British and Danish parties of the left. *Scandinavian Political Studies*, *30*, 229–248.

Pfaff, S. (2006). *Exit–voice dynamics and the collapse of East Germany: The crisis of leninism and the revolution of 1989*. Durham, NC: Duke University Press.

Pfaff, S., & Kim, H. (2003). Exit–voice dynamics in collective action: Analysis of emigration and protest in the East German revolution. *American Journal of Sociology*, *109*(2), 401–444.

Putnam, R. (2000). *Bowling alone. The collapse and revival of American community*. New York, NY: Simon & Schuster.

Rosenstone, S., & Hansen, M. (1993). *Mobilization, participation and democracy in America*. New York, NY: Macmillan.

Rusbult, C. E., Zembrodt, I. M., & Gunn, L. K. (1982). Exit, voice, loyalty and neglect: Responses to dissatisfaction in romantic involvements. *Journal of Personality and Social Psychology*, *43*(6), 1230–1242.

Schaltegger, C., & Küttel, D. (2002). Exit, voice, and mimicking behavior: Evidence from Swiss cantons. *Public Choice*, *113*, 1–23.

Scott, R. J. (1986). Dismantling repressive systems: The abolition of slavery in Cuba as a case study. In A. Foxley, M. McPherson, & G. O'Donnell (Eds.), *Development, democracy and the art of trespassing: Essays in honor of Albert Hirschman*. Notre Dame, IN: Notre Dame Press.

Sharp, E. B. (1984). Exit, voice and loyalty in the context of local government problems. *Western Political Quarterly*, *7*, 67–83.

Sharp, E. B. (1986). *Citizen demand-making in the urban context*. Birmingham: University of Alabama Press.

Slapin, J. B. (2009). Exit, voice and cooperation: Bargaining power in international organizations and federal systems. *Journal of Theoretical Politics*, *21*(2), 187–211.

Squire, P., Wolfinger, R. E., & Glass, D. P. (1987). Voter mobility and turnout. *American Political Science Review*, *81*(1), 45–66.

Verba, S., & Nie, N. (1972). *Participation in America*. New York, NY: Harper and Row.

Warren, M. E. (2011). Voting with your feet: Exit-based empowerment in democratic theory. *American Political Science Review*, *105*(4), 683–701.

Whiteley, P., & Seyd, P. (2002). *High-intensity participation: The dynamics of party activism in Britain*. Ann Arbor, MI: University of Michigan Press.

EFFICIENT INSTITUTIONS: THE ROLE OF EXIT AND VOICE☆

Maurizio Franzini

ABSTRACT

Hirschman has repeatedly stated that Voice is better than Exit as citizens or clients response to dissatisfaction with the service provided by organizations of various nature. He also maintained that all too often Exit was preferred to Voice and the negative result would be that services of worse quality will be supplied in the system as a whole.

Unfortunately, Hirschman never formalized his powerful categories and his fascinating ideas. The paper is an attempt to fill this gap; it also aims at showing how helpful Hirschaman's approach can be in the endeavour to design efficient institutions.

This paper provides a definition of efficiency convenient for our purposes and presents a model where both Exit and Voice can be necessary in order to achieve efficient results, given that the decline of organizations can have several different originating factors. Then it identifies the analytical conditions under which Exit is spontaneously chosen by citizens or

☆This paper builds upon and extends my previous work on Hirschman's categories (Franzini, 1999)

Research in the History of Economic Thought and Methodology, Volume 34B, 197–215

ISSN: 0743-4154/doi:10.1108/S0743-41542016000034B015

clients despite being less efficient than Voice. The paper shows that the use of Exit when Voice would be more efficient is not as general as Hirschman seemed to imply but it can arise under well-specified circumstances. In its final part, the paper suggests how institutions should be designed in order to prevent such inefficient results.

Keywords: Exit; Voice; inertia; institutions; efficiency

INTRODUCTION

In a number of writings (1970, 1982, 1986), Hirschman has maintained that when the quality of a service (or product) supplied by an organization[1] declines, the best response should be Voice rather than Exit. Voice (*V*) is defined as 'any attempt to change, rather than escape from, an objectionable state of affairs' (Hirschman, 1970, p. 30), while Exit (*E*) is the choice to no longer use that service and, most likely, to go to some other supplier.

Hirschman was also convinced that despite its positive effects, *V* was underutilized. In *Exit, Voice and Loyalty* (1970), he affirms that the facility of E can atrophy *V*,[2] and in later works, he makes sharper statements, such as: '... in some situations, the proper balance of institutional incentives ought to be adjusted so as to strengthen voice in relation to exit. I now find that my advocacy of voice was not exaggerated, but, on the contrary, be too timid' (Hirschman, 1981, p. 214).

Hirschman's categories have been a tremendous (and justified) success. They have also aroused a broad debate among scholars belonging to different disciplines about various issues, in particular, regarding the proper meaning of *V*, the reasons why people make or do not make use of *V*, and the relationship between *V* and E, that is if they are substitutes, complements or maybe both (Dowding-John, 2012). Some attempts have also been made to give stronger analytical foundations to Hirschman's statements, particularly those referring to the relationship between *E* and *V* (Gehlbach, 2006).

Very few attempts have been made, at least to the best of my knowledge, to understand the implications of Hirschman's categories for the design of an efficient institutional setting. Indeed, the suggestion to encourage *V* is of relevance for the institutional design, and if *V* is to be encouraged, this must be because the institutional design is not producing desirable results according to some criterion of evaluation that Hirschman does not specify. Therefore, his analysis could appear analytically defective. In this paper, I submit a criterion for defining efficient institutions with respect to the decline of organizations and analyse the specific role that *E* and *V* can have in an efficient institutional setting. More precisely, the questions I will address are the following:

(a) How can we define an efficient institutional setting when the issue is clients' reactions to the decline of organizations?
(b) What should be the correct balance between *E* and *V* in such a setting?
(c) Under what conditions will the underutilization of *V* denounced by Hirschman arise? Can it be interpreted as a sort of institutional inefficiency?
(d) If this is the case, how could the inefficiency be corrected without generating other negative consequences?
(e) What is the role of Loyalty (mentioned by Hirschman alongside *E* and *V*) and of Inertia (largely neglected by Hirschman) in an efficient institutional setting?

In my analysis, a crucial role will be played by the motivations of the managers who are responsible for the quality of the performance of their organization. Those motivations are usually overlooked in the debate on *E* and *V*, but they are important. I will draw a distinction between opportunistic managers and managers who are more reactive to the satisfaction of the organization's clients.

In the end, this paper is an attempt to use Hirschman's extraordinary intuitions as a guide for the design of efficient institutions (and for understanding which difficulties have to be overcome to implement these designs).

The paper starts with a presentation of economists' traditional position in favour of *E*, which is basically viewed as an effective sanction against opportunistic suppliers, and its conflict with Hirschman's view of the importance of *V*. I will stress the apparently limited role that Hirschman ascribed to opportunism. Then, assuming that managers can be, but not invariably are, opportunistic, I will present a simple model where both *E* and *V* can be necessary for achieving efficient results. I will also submit a definition of efficient institutions based upon the notion of vital or non-vital organizations. I will then analytically identify the conditions under which *E* and *V* will be used in an efficient manner and, in contrast, the circumstances that generate inefficiencies of the Hirschman-type (too much *E* and too little *V*). Then, I will analyse how these inefficiencies can be remedied and the role of Loyalty and Inertia, as previously mentioned. In the conclusions, I will summarize the answers to the questions listed above.

EXIT OR VOICE? HIRSCHMAN VERSUS ECONOMISTS

The basic idea regarding the virtues of *E*, as viewed by economists, goes back to Adam Smith's 'invisible hand'. According to this view, if the seller's performance worsens, the buyer should turn to another supplier, therefore choosing *E* and inflicting on the seller a sanction that consists of less revenues. If many buyers act in this manner, the sanction will amount to the expulsion of the seller from the market due to his or her default. The worsening performance may be due to several originating factors; one is opportunism by the managers, loosely defined as behaviour (successfully) geared to obtain personal advantages at the expenses of their clients. Economists tend to assume that opportunism is widespread; therefore, *E* should be powerful enough to prevent it.

In perfectly competitive markets, the assumption is that *E* is both extremely powerful and easily accessible. As Williamson once stated, in such markets 'individual buyers and sellers bear no dependency relation to each other. Instead, each party can go its own way at negligible cost to another' (Williamson, 1991, p. 17).

Considering that such markets are rare in the real world, a more sophisticated analysis of the efficacy of *E* in the market has been proposed in recent decades by various strands of the so-called New Institutional Economics. A common feature of these approaches is the focus on rents or quasi-rents,[3] which are considered as much more common in the market than usually assumed. This implies that *E* can be costly because leaving the partner of the transaction results in losing the benefits that comprise the rents. An example is efficiency wage, which allows the workers to enjoy a rent or any other situation in which asymmetric information about the characteristics of the object of transaction leads to the creation of rents.

In general, *E* can be costly in many real markets, and this is good news for opportunists. Faced with this problem, most economists would argue that the best action is to reduce the cost of *E*, while others would call our attention to the more complex contractual arrangements of the real world which have, among others, the purpose of contrasting opportunism in a world of positive *E* costs.

This type of gentle obsession with opportunism seems not to be shared by Hirschman. In a rather neglected sentence, he states: 'The performance of a firm or an organization is assumed to be subject to deterioration for unspecified, random causes which are neither so compelling nor so durable as to prevent a return to performance levels, provided managers direct their attention and energy to that task' (Hirschman, 1970, pp. 3–4). In addition, somewhere else he examines cases of 'recuperable deterioration' (see also Hirschman, 1993) caused by factors not imputable to a rational strategy by the managers. To improve their performance, managers must, as discussed in the quotation, direct their attention and energy to those factors and not receive sanctions. This is exactly what V will accomplish according to Hirschman.

This different view on the role of opportunism is sufficient to understand why Hirschman advocated V (it is necessary in the case of 'recuperable deterioration'), whereas most economists would be in favour of E (sanctions are necessary against opportunism).

However, what if real-world organizations can deteriorate due to both opportunism and 'recuperable deterioration'? This double possibility is a challenge for an efficient institutional setting. It is also the framework within which I will develop my analysis.

A SIMPLE MODEL: FIRST ASSUMPTIONS

The problem of reactions to the worsening performance of an organization will now be analysed based on a rather simplified model.

The first assumption is that the quality of the good (q) or service provided by 'our' organization depends on the effort of the organization's managers (e), a stochastic variable (ε), and other variables (K) related to the endowments of the organization, which are given in our analysis.

$$q = q(e, \varepsilon, K)$$

Let us assume that our organization (but not its rivals) suffers an external idiosyncratic shock that brings the quality of the service to $\underline{q}$, down from the previous level and also below the quality supplied by the best rival competitor (q_0), formally:

$$\underline{q} < q_0$$

As a consequence, the clients will suffer a loss if they do not exit. Moreover, if our organization does not react to the decline so that low quality persists, the loss will be suffered in subsequent periods, as long as the service is demanded.

Assuming that the utility of the clients depends only on the quality of the service, the immediate loss in terms of utility will be:

$$D = U(q_0) - U\left(\underline{q}\right)$$

Indeed, after the negative shock, clients have different options, including Exit, Voice and Inertia. Their choice depends on a number of variables and circumstances. Let us consider the most important for framing the choice between *E*, *V* and I.

(a) *V* is indispensable for ameliorating q. Should amelioration occur automatically, *V* would not perform any useful function, and its advocacy would not be supported.
(b) The magnitude of amelioration (Δq) is, in general, related to the intensity of *V*. To make things simpler, I assume that the intensity of *V* (and its related cost, if any) is given, while Δq depends on the reaction to *V* by the managers, which I will analyse in more detail below. If amelioration occurs, the new quality is $\overline{q}$, which can also be higher than q_0, the quality supplied by the best rival. In this case, our organization is able to deliver a competitive advantage:

$$CA = U(\overline{q}) - U(q_0)$$

(c) Adaptation and amelioration require time. Let us conventionally state that this requires 1 period, and let us assume that the clients expect to use the organization's service for $n + 1$ time periods. This implies that if they do not exit and *V* is effective, they will suffer a loss in the first period equal to *D*, and a hypothetical advantage in the remaining n periods equal to the advantage over the best rival, *CA*.
(d) To make the presentation simpler and more consequential, I will initially assume that neither *V* nor *E* are costly. Subsequently, I will introduce

the costs, c_v and c_e, which can be either monetary or opportunity costs, respectively. By assumption, both of these costs are constant, which is consistent with the previously introduced hypothesis that V is of a given intensity.

(e) Clients are strictly self-interested and aim to maximize their own inter-temporal well-being. Therefore, they care only about D, CA, c_v and c_e. I also assume that the price of the service is given and independent from q. Loyalty could fit into this framework as a further argument for the utility function of the clients that make them prefer their old organization despite some material disadvantage. I will show in the final part of the paper how loyalty can help remedy some specific institutional inefficiencies.

(f) Further simplifying assumptions are as follows: (i) The clients have no inter-temporal preferences; therefore, their rate of discount of future advantages (CA) is equal to zero. (ii) Clients are not in conflict among themselves; rather, they share the same preferences and do not free ride.[4] Therefore, it is possible to treat the entire set of clients as if they were in fact simply one client. (iii) Clients have complete information regarding the effects of V on q and any other relevant variable. Designing an efficient institutional setting is a difficult task, even if these complications are set aside.

The implications of removing some of these assumptions will be briefly discussed at the end of this paper.

CHOOSING BETWEEN EXIT AND VOICE

Clients decide their reaction based on a calculation that takes into account both the costs and results of alternative strategies.

Their choice set includes E, V and Inertia. The latter, as Barry (1974) noted many years ago, has not been sufficiently analysed by Hirschman; however, it can be very important.

E allows the clients to enjoy, for all $n + 1$ periods of use of the service, the utility associated with the quality supplied by the best rival.

V yields a worse result than E during the adaptation period and a better result in the subsequent n periods.[5]

Finally, I imply that the quality enjoyed across all the periods deteriorates.

If neither Exit nor Voice costs exist, the three payoffs are:

$$\begin{aligned} P(E) &= (n+1)U \\ P(V) &= \underline{U} + n\overline{U} \\ P(I) &= (n+1)\underline{U} \end{aligned}$$

Taking into account D and CA, as defined above, the preceding equation can be rewritten as follows:

$$\begin{aligned} P(V) &= U - D + n(U + \mathrm{CA}) \\ P(I) &= (n+1)\,U - (n+1)D \end{aligned}$$

In comparing the three alternatives, if no costs exist, I is always dominated by both E and V. This is quite obvious, given that I results in the lowest q across all periods of use of the service.

When comparing $P(E)$ and $P(V)$, E will be chosen if

$$\begin{aligned} &(n+1)U > U - D + n(U + \mathrm{CA}) \\ &D > nCA \end{aligned}$$

The meaning of this condition is straightforward: E will be preferred if the loss during the adaptation period is larger than the future advantage.

Of course, V will be chosen when

$$D \leq nCA$$

How can we evaluate this behaviour? What are its implications for Hirschman's advocacy of V?

To answer this question, we have to develop a criterion of evaluation.

VITAL ORGANIZATION AND EFFICIENT INSTITUTIONAL SETTING

I now introduce a definition of an efficient institutional setting, based upon the notion of a vital organization.

An organization is vital if it can deliver to its clients, in the long run, advantages of such a magnitude as to more than compensate for the damage they suffer by not exiting. In other words, an organization is vital if $nCA \geq D$.

Therefore, efficient institutions are those that do not allow non-vital organizations to prosper and, conversely, shield vital organizations from the risk of disappearing; clients should be driven by such an institution to choose *E* when the organization is non-vital and *V* when it is vital. Not meeting this rule of behaviour would imply inefficiency of one type (non-vital organizations survive) or another (vital organizations may die).

The behaviour of the clients according to our analysis precisely brings about this result; *E* is chosen when $nCA < D$ (i.e. organizations are non-vital), and *V* is the selected option when $nCA \geq D$ (i.e. organizations are vital). We have a type of 'invisible hand' driving the clients to behave how efficiency would direct.

This result also has some important implications for Hirschman's advocacy of *V*:

(a) *E* can perform a positive role, that is not allowing non-vital organizations to survive;
(b) Sustaining *V* has no particular justification in this case; it will be exerted precisely when efficiency demands it. Advocating *V* in other cases also means that it should be used with non-vital organizations.

This result depends on two assumptions: (i) that there are both vital and non-vital organizations and (ii) that both *E* and *V* are free. I will now show how the first hypothesis is related, among other things, to the assumptions we make on the motivations of the managers running the organization. Subsequently, I will show that when *E* and *V* are costly, Hirschman's advocacy of more *V* may be perfectly justified.

THE MANAGERS AND THEIR MOTIVATIONS

The behaviour of managers is a crucial determinant of the likely effects of *V* on the organization's performance. It may have been overlooked or not properly analysed in the debate on *E* and *V*. For instance, in the model proposed by Gehlbach (2006), one of the few attempts to provide analytical foundations to Hirschman's categories, the assumption is that managers will react in such a manner as to make their clients' payoffs invariably better with *V* rather than with *E*. This is the consequence of having framed the problem in a context of pure bargaining, which does not seem to be the best manner to approach organizational problems.

My general assumption is that the utility of managers depends on their effort, their compensation (*w*), and the clients' satisfaction (*cc*). The latter intends to represent a type of commitment by the managers to their clients, a sort of altruism that departs from the traditional idea of invariably and strictly self-interested individuals. Of course, this effect could be absent, as we shall see. If this is the case, the effectiveness of *V* would be weakened.

This can be represented as follows:

$$U = U(e, w, cc)$$

Higher effort results in lower utility, higher compensation results in higher utility and higher client satisfaction results in higher utility per se, that is not mediated by the effect on compensation, if any.

Suppose the managers have no commitment, and their compensation is not at all related to the quality of the service provided by their organization, that is their compensation is not formally dependent upon *q*, however measured (and this would be a direct effect of *q* on *w*), and the managers will not suffer a material loss if their clients leave the organization because they are dissatisfied with the quality supplied (and this would be an indirect effect of *q* on *w*). The latter is more than an abstract possibility in today's world, not only in the public, but also in the private sphere. One example among many others involves the managers of several financial companies.

In this extreme situation, managers will behave opportunistically, and their effort will not be higher after the decline in quality; they do not care at all about the quality of the service and the well-being of their clients. This is a peculiar form of opportunism. However, opportunism is a matter of degree, not an on-off situation. A higher sensitivity of *w* and *cc* to *q* results in lower opportunism, as I interpret it. In a situation of extreme opportunism, *V* is totally pointless.

In contrast, *V* is indispensable for improving *q*. In fact, *V* can activate a reaction through the commitment channel. When the dissatisfaction of their clients is known, the committed managers experience a loss of utility; they will react to it by expanding their effort in a measure that makes the marginal disutility of the extra effort equal to the marginal utility of the 'altruistic' concern for the clients' satisfaction, which depends on three variables: the effect of the extra effort on *q*, the effect of the increased *q* on the clients' satisfaction, and finally, the effect of the increased client satisfaction on the managers' utility. This is a type of cultural or value channel.

The other channel is a material channel. V can be interpreted, as many have noted (in particular, Dowding-John, 2012), as a threat to E, and this, in turn, could drive the managers to generate a higher effort if they anticipate a loss in their compensation. Additionally, in this case, the strength of the effect will depend on the marginal disutility of effort in comparison to the combined effect of q on w and of w on U.[6]

The final impact of V on q, and therefore the magnitude of what I have called CA, depends on the intensity of these various effects. I will attribute all of these effects to V without entering into the debate about what V really is and how it should be better understood. This debate is interesting, but it seems to me that the important point is whether V can engender a positive reaction by the managers regardless of the channel, either material, cultural or any other that could be added. For example, one could include in the V the type of cooperation between clients and producers that today is important for some technologically sophisticated products, where often competent clients are an asset for the firm, and as a consequence, their V can greatly contribute to the quality of the product or service supplied.

One important implication of the preceding is that V could not be activated because the clients know that the managers are opportunistic (or too much so). Recalling Hirschman's important statement on the role of E as a cause of atrophy for V, one could also add that opportunism by managers has a similar effect, independent from the ease of E. This point will become clearer in the next sections, in particular when discussing the role of Inertia.

THE IMPLICATIONS OF COSTLY EXIT AND VOICE

Let us now introduce the hypothesis that both E and V are costly. Their costs are c_e and c_v, respectively, representing both monetary and opportunity costs. The simplifying assumption is that they are fixed. This hypothesis excludes, in particular, the possibility that by putting more effort into V, clients can obtain a higher CA. Indeed, in a more complex analysis, it could be assumed that $CA = CA(c_v)$, with $CA' > 0$. Here, however, the only relationship that exists between CA and c_v is that the former will not materialize unless the latter is borne by the clients.

The payoff of E is now equal to the utility that the clients enjoy from the quality of the service supplied by the best rival for $n + 1$ periods minus the cost of exit:

$$P(E) = (n+1)U - c_e$$

However, after taking into account its cost, V yields the following payoff:

$$P(V) = U - D + n(U + \mathrm{CA}) - c_v$$

Comparing the two payoffs leads to the conclusion that E will be preferred to V if:

$$U + n(U + \mathrm{CA}) - D - c_v < (n+1)U - c_e$$

which simplifies to:

$$c_v - c_e > nCA - D$$

The meaning of this condition is very simple; if the cost of V exceeds the cost of E by more than the advantage of V over E (represented by $nCA-D$, i.e. the extra advantage enjoyed for n periods less the loss during the time necessary for adaptation), then E will be preferred by clients.

Fig. 1 offers a representation of this situation in the P–D plane. D' is the level of D such that E and V are indifferent, that is it is equal to $nCA + c_v - c_e$. When $D < D'$, V will be chosen, while E is preferred when $D > D'$. Therefore, a high D (i.e. a large negative initial shock) makes it more likely that E will be chosen.

IMPLICATIONS FOR EFFICIENCY

Positive E and V costs can have important implications for efficiency. In fact, they make it possible both that vital organizations will not survive because clients will choose E and that non-vital organizations will survive because V (or, in the more complete analysis of the next section, Inertia) will be the chosen option. Moreover, including those costs into the analysis

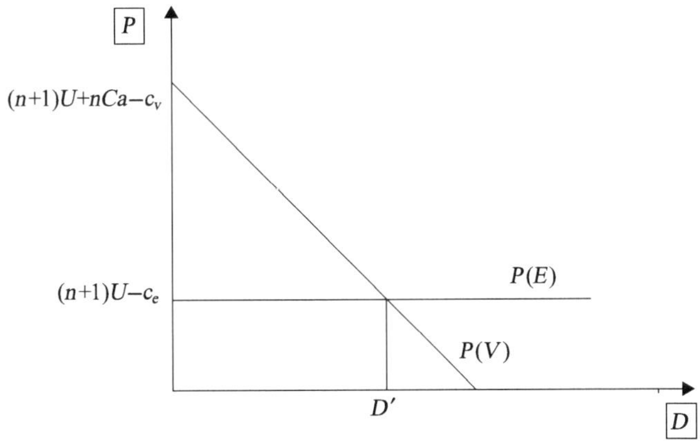

Fig. 1. The Choice between E and V when Both Are Costly.

allows identification of a situation in which the famous Hirschmanian advocacy of *V* is fully justified

Our benchmark situation is when $c_e = c_v$. In this case, the clients' choice between *E* and *V* will not be dislocated from its efficient configuration by the costs of the two options. As shown in the previous analysis, the choice between *E* and *V* will depend only on *D* and *nCA*; *E* will be the choice when $D > nCA$, that is the organization is non-vital, and *V* will be chosen when the opposite holds, and the organization is vital.

However, when the costs of the two options diverge, inefficiencies can arise. The first possible case is when:

$$nCA > D \quad \text{but} \quad nCA < cv - ce + D$$

so that *E* is chosen, even if the organization is vital. Of course, such a situation is possible if c_v is sufficiently larger than c_e.

The second (opposite) case occurs when:

$$nCA < D \quad \text{but} \quad nCA > cv - ce + D$$

V will be the choice, even if the organization is non-vital. This result is made possible by a much larger c_e with respect to c_v.

Inefficiency of the first type seems to be the principle that Hirschman had in mind, a vital organization from which the clients exit. Advocating

V in this case is more than justified because it encourages vital organizations to survive. If E is extremely easy, as recommended by a large number of economists, the consequences in this case would be very negative. It is difficult to determine how frequent in the real-world situations similar to this occur. However, from an institutional point of view, the question is: what could be done to remedy this inefficiency?

Hirschman's answer would likely be to raise the costs of E. Another solution, at least up to a certain point, is raising CA even further, through changes, that are also institutional in their nature and that affect the variables to which managers are, or should be, reactive; this means that opportunism should be made less effective. Finally, the solution could consist of Loyalty, the famous third item in the Hirschmanian trilogy.

An interpretation of Loyalty could be the following: the clients' utility does not depend only on the quality of the service that they receive (and on its price) but also on the identity of the supplier of the service. In particular, their utility is positively related to a type of continuity of the relationship with the supplier, which matters in itself. The impact of this effect on the clients' utility could be strong enough to compensate for some disadvantage in the quality of the service and allow a vital organization to survive despite that the balance of all of the material benefits and costs is tilted towards E.

However, these three remedies have different side effects. I am referring to the possibility that they may have negative implications for the second case above, which cannot be excluded when vitality is not generally guaranteed across organizations or through time.

In fact, raising c_e too much furthers the chances that a non-vital organization will survive. Additionally, the same effect could occur due to an overly strong loyalty effect. Indeed, the endeavour should be to raise c_e to the point where it is equal to c_v and no more. This will eliminate the distortionary effect of both costs.

Improving CA, in contrast, may have no negative implications because it increases the chances that non-vital organizations become vital. It is a way of saying that it is a very good thing if opportunism becomes less intense.

THE IMPORTANT ROLE OF INERTIA

I have thus far not considered Inertia (I), which could be the third option for clients, in addition to E and V. When c_e and c_v are positive, I should not be dominated by either E or V, as was the case when those costs were absent.

Comparing the three payoffs in this new setting results in $P(I)>P(V)$, and therefore I will be the choice, if

$$n(\text{CA} + D) < c_v$$

Moreover, $P(I)>P(E)$ and, again, I will be chosen against E if

$$(n + 1)D < c_e$$

Let us assume that the two costs are equal, so that the choice between E and V will be consistent with efficiency. Suppose, in particular, that the organization is vital so that V will be preferred to E. The problem is that c_v could be so high as to make I a better choice than V with the consequence that either I will prevail or E will in the end prevail if the cost of exit is sufficiently low, as in the condition above.

The opposite is also possible; a non-vital organization that survives despite E is preferred to V because the cost of exit is too high. Raising higher fences against exit could have also this negative implication.

Inertia, therefore, could be a rather disturbing element.

THE IDEAL INSTITUTIONAL SETTING

By combining all of the pieces of the analysis performed in the previous sections, the following conclusions can be drawn about the conditions for an efficient institutional setting, that is a setting where E applies to a non-vital organization and V is raised against a vital organization.

The first condition is that $c_e = c_v$.

The second condition is that

$$c_v = c_e \leq \min\{(1 + n)D; n(\text{CA} + D)\}$$

The latter condition ensures that I will not yield a higher payoff than either E or V. Implementing such an ideal setting can be an out-of-reach task. In particular, it could be extremely difficult to know which will be the CA and D to be taken into account when the institutional setting applies to many different organizations, and moreover, the rules have to last for a relatively long time span. All of these information suggest that a wise strategy could be a rather rough rule-of-thumb: keep both c_e and c_v as low as possible and as close to zero as possible.

CONCLUDING REMARKS

In this paper, my first goal was to set up an analytical framework that allows evaluation of Hirschman's famous advocacy of *V* against *E*.

An important step has been to define a criterion for evaluating the desirability of both of these options. The criterion I have suggested is a sort of institutionally efficient setting where vital organizations (as I have defined them) adapt, due to *V*, to new external circumstances, whereas clients exit from non-vital organizations.

I have argued that in the absence of both *E* and *V* costs, this efficient situation will be brought about by the choices made by self-interested and well informed clients. A type of 'invisible hand' will be working in this case.

If this is the situation, there seems to be no room for complaining about *E* being too easy and responsible for displacing *V*. *E* will be chosen when organizations are non-vital, and this can easily occur in a world where the managers of the organization behave opportunistically. Indeed, this seems to be the assumption that most economists make about the causes of the decline in the quality of services offered by an organization. However, Hirschman, as I have recalled, referred to situations where opportunism was absent and deterioration was always remediable due to the effort of the managers. The conclusions reached in this paper show that when *E* and *V* are not costly, no reason exists to worry about *E*. If opportunism is absent, and if the clients have this information, *E* will never be chosen.

A further implication is that in an efficient setting, it is opportunism that justifies *E* and (rationally) prevents *V*. In such a setting, opportunism, but not *E*, is the enemy of *V*.

Introducing positive costs for *E* and *V* radically changes this picture. Two cases are possible: if the cost of *V* is sufficiently higher than the cost of *E*, clients may exit from vital organizations. The opposite could occur if the cost of *E* is sufficiently higher than the cost of *V*; non-vital organizations would not be abandoned by their clients.

The inefficiency arising in the first case is the type of inefficiency that Hirschman had in mind. An interesting result is that for such an inefficiency to manifest itself, positive and differentiated costs of the two options, with $c_v > c_e$, are necessary.

Loyalty does represent a possible solution to this inefficiency, and this may explain why Hirschman listed it alongside *E* and *V*, despite that it belongs to a different conceptual dimension. Loyalty can favour *V*, and if opportunism is low, so that organizations are vital, efficiency will be enhanced.

Another remedy is represented by a higher cost of *E*, and this is a remedy that seems consistent with the Hirschman analysis. However, if opportunism is not absent, raising this cost too much could have the negative implication that non-vital organizations will survive. The target should be to make the cost of *E* exactly equal to the cost of *V* to restore the 'invisible hand' mentioned previously.

Further and rather serious complications arise if we introduce Inertia as a third possible option by the clients. Inertia is a rather frequent type of behaviour, and it acts against efficiency because it allows non-vital organizations to survive when *E* is better than *V*, and it causes vital organization to not survive because it can defeat *V* but, in turn, can be defeated by *E*.

As I have shown, to exclude the possibility that Inertia may be preferred to either *E* or *V*, the costs of these two options need to be sufficiently small. This could be difficult to achieve because the threshold not to be surpassed may not be known in advance. Therefore, the conclusion is that the aim should be to maintain the costs of *E* and *V* not only as close to each other as possible but also as close to zero as possible. Contrasting opportunism is, however, an important supporting strategy; it will broaden the range of vital organizations and simultaneously enhance the attractiveness of *V*.

Indeed, going back to the Hirschman-type inefficiency and relaxing the assumption that the clients are well informed, we can say that the presumption that opportunism is widespread favours *E* and leads to its selection, even when *V* could be better. Currently, this presumption is a concern for public organizations that may be widely considered as more opportunistic than they really are, at least in some countries. Opportunism, even if only expected, can deter *V*; this can occur jointly with *E* and also independently from it, as in is the case when I is chosen instead of *E*. The first step to reverse this situation, along with the beliefs it nourishes, should likely be not to raise the cost of *E*, but to fight opportunism as fiercely as possible.

NOTES

1. The organization we refer to may be a private firm, a private club, a political party or a public body. Therefore, the service it supplies does not always generate

market exchange. In this paper, I will use the term "clients" to indicate both clients and members.

2. The idea that *E* is the enemy of *V* has been reconsidered by Hirschman, outlining – in diverse circumstances – more complex relationships between the two options (Hirschman, 1993).

3. According to the definition given by Milgrom and Roberts (1992, p. 269) a quasi-rent 'is the portion of earnings in excess of the minimum amount needed to prevent a worker from quitting his or her job or a producer from exiting its industry'.

4. Hirschman draws our attention to free riding and argues, in particular, that it can hamper the use of *V*. Indeed, if *E* is costly and the organization can change its behaviour after a number of clients have left, then *E* can also be vulnerable to free riding. The importance Hirschman attaches to free riding when analysing the limited recourse to *V* is, however, not easy to reconcile with the arguments he uses elsewhere to dismiss the relevance of the phenomenon (Hirschman, 1981, p. 214; 1982, chapter 5).

5. I am assuming that clients first Exit and then re-enter the organization after its adaptation. This would be a type of free riding, and no adaptation would actually occur if such behaviour were adopted.

6. Obviously, if the managers knew themselves of the dissatisfaction of their clients and were sufficiently committed and/or sufficiently worried about their future compensation, *V* would not be necessary and would not be activated by informed clients.

REFERENCES

Barry, B. (1974). Exit, voice, and loyalty. *British Journal of Political Science*, *4*, 79–107. Reprinted in Barry, B. *Democracy and Power*, Oxford, Clarendon Press, 1991.

Dowding, K., & John, P. (2012). *Exits, voices and social investment. Citizen's reaction to public services*. Cambridge: Cambridge University Press.

Franzini, M. (1999). Opportunism and adaptation in economic and political markets. In S. Bowles, M. Franzini, & U. Pagano (Eds.), *The politics and economics of power*. London: Routledge.

Gehlbach, S. C. (2006). A political model of exit and voice. *Rationality and Society*, *18*, 395–418.

Hirschman, A. O. (1970). *Exit, voice and loyalty*. Cambridge, MA: Harvard University Press.

Hirschman, A. O. (1981). *Essays in trespassing. Economics to politics and beyond*. Cambridge: Cambridge University Press.

Hirschman, A. O. (1982). *Shifting involvements. Private interest and public action*. Princeton, NJ: Princeton University Press.

Hirschman, A. O. (1986). Exit and voice: An expanding sphere of influence. In A. O. Hirschman (Ed.), *Rival views of market society and other recent essays*. New York, NY: Elizabeth Sifton Books.

Hirschman, A. O. (1993). Exit, voice, and the fate of the German democratic republic. *World Politics*, *45*, 173–202. reprinted in Hirschman, A. O. (1995). *A Propensity to Self-Subversion*, Cambridge, MA: Harvard University Press.
Milgrom, P., & Roberts, J. (1992). *Economics, organization and management*. Englewood Cliffs, NJ: Prentice-Hall.
Williamson, O. E. (1991). Comparative economic organization: The analysis of discrete structural alternatives. *Administrative Science Quarterly*, *36*, 269–296.

PART II
ESSAYS

ROBERT FRANKLIN HOXIE: THE CONTRIBUTIONS OF A NEGLECTED CHICAGO ECONOMIST☆

Charles R. McCann, Jr. and Vibha Kapuria-Foreman

ABSTRACT

Robert Franklin Hoxie was of the first generation of University of Chicago economists, a figure of significance in his own time. He is often heralded as the first of the Institutional economists and the impetus behind the field of labor economics. Yet today, his contributions appear as mere footnotes in the history of economic thought, when mentioned at all, despite the fact that in his professional and popular writings he tackled some of the most pressing problems of the day. The topics upon which he focused included bimetallism, price theory, methodology, the

☆Portions of this essay were presented at the 12th annual Summer Institute for the Preservation of the History of Economic Thought, held at the University of Richmond, 24–27 June 2011. We gratefully acknowledge the comments of the participants and those of an anonymous reader. Vibha Kapuria-Foreman wishes to thank Colorado College and the Chapman Fellowship Foundation for supporting her work.

Research in the History of Economic Thought and Methodology, Volume 34B, 219–304

ISSN: 0743-4154/doi:10.1108/S0743-41542016000034B008

economics profession, socialism, syndicalism, scientific management, and trade unionism, the last being the field with which he is most closely associated. His work attracted the notice of some of the most famous economists of his time, including Frank Fetter, J. Laurence Laughlin, Thorstein Veblen, and John R. Commons. For all the promise, his suicide at the age of 48 ended what could have been a storied career. This paper is an attempt to resurrect Hoxie through a review of his life and work, placing him within the social and intellectual milieux of his time.

Keywords: Robert F. Hoxie; American Institutionalism; labor problems; labor economics; scientific management

JEL classifications: B15; B31

INTRODUCTION

On June 23, 1916, the front page, section two, of the *Chicago Daily Tribune* carried the following disturbing headline:

> *Professor R. F. Hoxie*
>
> *Takes His Life*
>
> University of Chicago Student of Labor Problems
>
> Cuts His Throat.

The story continued:

> Robert Franklin Hoxie, associate professor of political economy in the University of Chicago, committed suicide yesterday.
>
> Prof. Hoxie had been for years the subject of a severe depression, his associates said yesterday upon learning of his death. He was constantly in charge of a physician.
>
> While worry over the justice of his economic conclusions was not a direct cause of his act, his desire to view labor problems scientifically was regarded as the keynote of his career. He has been charged with bias resulting from labor affiliations and socialistic leanings. He denied this, and seemed overanxious to maintain a position of scientific neutrality in his studies.
>
> ...
>
> There was an inquest in the afternoon, at which it was determined that the professor had taken his own life in a fit of insanity. (*Chicago Daily Tribune*, June 23, 1916, p. 15)

So ended the life and promising career of one of the outstanding students of the American labor movement, esteemed by the Columbia University historian of economics Joseph Dorfman as "perhaps the finest analytical mind that the United States produced in the field of labor" (Dorfman, 1958, p. 6). Dorfman was not alone in his assessment. Columbia University economic historian Carter Goodrich similarly granted that "Hoxie possessed the keenest and most rigorous mind that has ever worked upon the problems of American labor organization" (Goodrich, 1932, p. 525). Among Hoxie's contemporaries, economist Alvin S. Johnson's comment is telling: "I know of no other contemporary economist who displayed so intense a zeal to understand the living facts of his science" (Johnson, 1916, p. 248). Likewise, John P. Frey, labor activist and editor of the *International Molders' Journal*, remarks, "His mental poise was that of the true scientist, but coupled with this was a keen love of justice, deep human sympathy, and a rare ability to grasp and understand the underlying motives which influence men" (Frey, 1916, p. 893). University of Chicago philosopher James Tufts' observation perhaps best sums up for the times the general academic opinion of Hoxie:

> To a mind at once sympathetic with human zeal and scientific in method such as that of Professor Hoxie, the great need seemed clearly to be, not smoothing over conflicting issues with pleasant optimism, but penetrating to the roots of the matter, analyzing the complex of economic and broadly human factors, and making sure that each side should understand both its own and the other's point of view. [His was an] attitude of relentless analysis, frank statement, and scrupulous fairness ... (Tufts, 1916, p. 440)

Surprisingly, accepting Dorfman's comment as a legitimate appraisal of Hoxie's standing in the field of labor economics, little has been written on his life and accomplishments. Selig Perlman's *A Theory of the Labor Movement* (1928) makes no mention of Hoxie's approach to the study of labor. Joseph Schumpeter in his massive *History of Economic Analysis* (1954) has not a single entry on Hoxie; nor does Henry Spiegel's *The Growth of Economic Thought* (1971). There have been, of course, efforts at recognizing Hoxie's accomplishments – notable are the essays by Fishman (1958) and McNulty (1973), tracing the Veblenian roots of his work, and Nyland (1966), documenting the role of Hoxie in preparing a report for the Commission on Industrial Relations. Bauder (1943) includes Hoxie's *Trade Unionism in the United States* as one of three "systematic interpretations" of the labor movement that have been highly influential, the other two being Selig Perlman's *Theory* and Sidney and Beatrice Webb's *History of Trade Unionism* and *Industrial Democracy*. Mark Perlman (1958) covers

Hoxie's contributions to labor economics in his chapter on "Unionism as a Psychological Reaction" and so acknowledges the importance of his analytical approach to the labor question. But these appraisals have been, for the most part, confined to examinations of specific aspects of his work. No significant effort has thus far been made to examine the whole of Hoxie's works so as to place them within the context of his times. Doing so allows one to draw a much more complete picture of a brilliant intellect, an economist whose reputation in his own time was secure but who, given circumstances some beyond his control, has since faded into near complete obscurity.

BIOGRAPHICAL SUMMARY

Life and Career

Robert Franklin Hoxie[1] was born April 29, 1868 in Edmeston, N.Y., the son of Solomon Hoxie[2] and Lucy Peet Stickney. His undergraduate education began at Cornell University in 1891, but in 1892 he left for the University of Chicago, following J. Laurence Laughlin when the latter was invited to head the newly established Department of Political Economy. The next year, Hoxie became a Fellow of Political Economy at Chicago (PhB, 1893), a position he held until 1895. He served as acting professor of economics at Cornell College, Iowa, until 1898, when he removed to Washington University in St. Louis, leaving in 1901 for Washington and Lee University in Lexington, Virginia. In 1903, he returned to Chicago to continue his graduate education (PhD, 1905), while simultaneously serving as an instructor in political economy and finance (1903–1905) then economics (1905–1906) at Cornell in Ithaca, New York.[3] While at Cornell, he lectured on Modern Socialism, Elementary Political Economy, and Problems of Organized Labor (1904–1905 academic year), and Elementary Economics, Labor Problems – American Labor Conditions, Problems of Organized Labor, and Contemporary Socialism (1905–1906).[4] Mark Perlman (1958, p. 37) observes that while at Cornell, Hoxie "greatly expanded the economics curriculum in the areas of trade unionism and socialism. Before his arrival these fields had been cursorily treated in a single problem course, 'The Modern Regime'." In 1906, he secured an appointment at Chicago as an instructor in political economy, becoming assistant professor in 1908 and associate professor in 1912.[5] His courses there included History of Political Economy, Socialism, and Labor Unions (beginning 1907–1908 and continuing), The Constructive Program of Trade Unionism and Research Course in Labor Problems (1908–1909), and later, taking over from John Cummings, the course on Economics of Workingmen (1910–1911).[6] By 1915, his course load focused almost exclusively on labor issues – Labor Conditions and Problems, Trade Unionism, Labor Research, Scientific Management and Labor – the single exception between the courses on History of Political Economy.[7] On June 22, 1916, Hoxie, who had long suffered from depression,[8] and had expressed concerns over the reaction to his book, *Scientific Management and Labor*, took his own life.[9]

Influences

Walton Hamilton notes that Hoxie was the first person to have identified himself as an "institutional economist" (Hamilton, 1916, p. 863, n.5), although he was "sensitive" to the influence of numerous intellectual traditions, some of which "wrote themselves indelibly into his work; others fascinated him for a time; and still others furnished convenient statements of economic truth and untruth against which to protest" (p. 857). In a survey of Hoxie's economics, Hamilton cites three men who exerted profound influence on his professional development: J. Laurence Laughlin, Frank Fetter, and Thorstein Veblen.[10] Laughlin, of whom Hoxie was an early disciple, following him from Cornell to Chicago, was the voice of the establishment, "the representative of the best traditions of classical doctrine"; from 1892 until 1916 he served as chairman of the Department of Political Economy at Chicago. The focus of analysis was the competitive market, with order imposed through natural laws. Adhering to the orthodoxy, he was opposed to "doctrinaire refinements," and believed "that economics must vindicate itself in its application to the everyday affairs of life" (p. 857). Laughlin Hoxie regarded as the "most competent expounder" of the classical doctrine, and his influence held sway during Hoxie's formative years, 1891–1896 (p. 862). Evidence of Laughlin's influence may be seen in Hoxie's (1893a, 1893b) "The Compensatory Theory of Bimetallism," in which he offered a diagrammatic refutation of Stanley Jevons' justification for a bimetallic standard, echoing the view of Laughlin. While he would never completely reject the classical economic doctrine, his protestations to the contrary notwithstanding, Hoxie had become keenly aware "that the assumptions of theory did grievous violence alike to the common-sense of the times and to the economic world of reality ..., " thus leading him to conclude "that the methodology of orthodox economics was out of harmony with the dominant intellectual thought of the times" (Hamilton, 1916, p. 864).

New assumptions were needed, a new methodological approach to render economics relevant. In his 1901 *Journal of Political Economy* essay, "On the Empirical Method of Economic Instruction," Hoxie seeks to identify the requirements for such a methodology so as to secure a place for economics within the sciences. In so doing, he first needs to identify the place of economics within the sciences, achieving this by dividing the sciences into two exclusive classes: the first, consisting primarily of the mathematical and physical sciences, is concerned with fixed relations between material objects and thus is taxonomic, while the second, a class including the biological sciences, has as its primary concern the study of processes of cumulative change and evolutionary adaptation (Hoxie, 1901, p. 484). Economics, concerned as it is with the study of society and social processes, is not in essence (or perhaps better, should not be considered to be) a mere taxonomic discipline, as it had become within the neoclassical framework, but is, on the contrary, one more closely associated with the biological sciences; it is not a science of "fixed material and relationship," but rather one of "developing material and relationship." In Hoxie's terms,

> the economic organization might differ essentially from a true biological organism, and it might fall far short of being in the truest sense an organic entity, still as soon as the theory of evolution was comprehended, it was evident that economics must become a science, not of the greatest production of wealth, or greatest economic welfare, a science founded solely upon universal and immutable laws of nature and human nature, nor a science of economic normalities, taxonomic merely, but a study of life, of the life process and genesis of the economic organization, essentially cognate with the biological sciences. (Hoxie, 1901, p. 486)

Further evidence of the shift in perspective may be found in Hoxie's (1905) dissertation, "An Analysis of the Concepts of Demand and Supply in Their Relation to Market Price," and two essays derived therefrom which appeared in the *Journal of Political Economy* in 1906 – "The Demand and Supply Concepts: An Introduction to the Study of Market Price." His statement of purpose establishes at the outset the need for a reassessment of the basic conceptual apparatus of political economy:

> The present work has been undertaken in the belief that the existing status of economic theory calls urgently for the restatement of economic concepts and for the revision of fundamental economic problems. In the world of business and industry most essential changes have been wrought out in the past half-century. The rapid subjugation of nature by social forces; the growing predominance of the pecuniary or acquisitive over

industrial motivation; the progressive concentration of pecuniary authority and discretion as illustrated in the development of monopolies and in the increasing directive power of small groups of financial agents; the growing importance of the time element in economic activity resulting from the roundaboutness of the modern industrial process and a transition from money to credit economy – these and other manifestations of economic development have, especially of late, altered in some of its fundamental aspects the material of economic speculation. (Hoxie, 1906a, pp. 337–338)

Here Hoxie singles out for special mention the works of Laughlin, Fetter, and Veblen, and employs, to some extent, arguments identifiable in each, while seeking an alternative to the reigning orthodoxy.

The break with the classical doctrine was, in a sense, the result of Hoxie's desire for economics to be relevant, and to this end, Fetter's economics initially seemed to offer the answer. Fetter, whom Hoxie met while at Cornell, was founder and chief protagonist of the American psychological school – the "modern school" – which concentrated on the motivations and actions of the individual. Here, attention was given to the empirical study of economic activity, from which could be formulated "a wonderfully logical and coherent system" (Hamilton, 1916, p. 857). Fetter, according to Hoxie, had an affinity for the Austrian approach to value theory, as "a true and consistent interpretation of economic activity." That the adherents of the Austrian school did not succeed in their endeavor was due not to their insistence on "a purely psychic explanation of economic phenomena in terms of utility," but rather "because they could not wholly emancipate themselves from the older [classical] economic notions" (Hoxie, 1905, p. 210). To Fetter, economics was "essentially the study of value," and so his perspective was the search for a single, consistent, unifying theory of value. True to the Austrian tradition, Fetter sought "a uniform measure for estimating the value of commodities and the means of production," desiring "to attain the Austrian ideal of bridging over the gap between the theory of value and the theory of distribution" (p. 211).[11] In Hoxie's view, Fetter had succeeded in his quest:

Starting from certain fundamental value conceptions, which merely happen to be Austrian, he has made the whole theory of economics to appear as an ever-widening application of these conceptions to the explanation of economic phenomena, – each successive explanation resting upon its predecessor, all forming one complex expression of a single value concept, the final result being but the logical development of the first simple premises. (Hoxie, 1905, p. 211)

Consider the value of a consumption good. It is not the case that a good is valued for its want-satisfying capacity, as if such were essential to the nature of the good. Rather, a good has value to the extent that an individual's *gratification* is seen as being dependent upon that good in satisfying a *specific* want; it has no value otherwise. The "subjective valuation," then, of any good is determined by its marginal utility or marginal use (Hoxie, 1905, pp. 215–216). Marginal utility, in turn, is determined by the scarcity of the good "in conjunction with the law of diminishing marginal utilities." This Hoxie argues is little more than one of "the familiar conclusions of the Austrians" (p. 216).

Price, or "objective exchange value," is determined by subjective valuations, again, a conclusion familiar to the Austrians. "It does not go for its explanation behind these valuations; but, in assuming them in the market, it assumes the conditions of utility and scarcity, or utility and cost, which underlie them." Fetter's dispute with the Austrians rested on their refusal to extend the analysis to production, instead reverting "to the classical notions of Rent, Capital, and Interest, – notions altogether inconstant with the theory thus far developed" (Hoxie, 1905, pp. 216–217).

Thus, as Hamilton concludes, for Hoxie, "Fetter's system appealed to his demand for relevancy by its conscious recognition of business agents and activities, by the striking similarity of its concepts to those of the industrial world, and by the appearance of a genetic method of treatment which its skilful historical introductions conveyed. Its reduction of actuality to psychological terms gave its conclusions a sense of finality." This method of analysis "convinced Hoxie that he had found here the unity which he sought" (Hamilton, 1916, p. 867).

Yet Fetter's influence was short-lived, as Hoxie's "increasing demand for the genetic could not be stayed by Fetter's historical introductions, which Hoxie was coming to see were quite apart from the main body of his doctrines." The American capitalist system could not be condensed to a mere "scheme of values," but rather must be understood as "a scheme of social arrangements," the nature of which could not comport with Fetter's system (Hamilton, 1916, p. 868). Something more was needed, an approach that could explain the workings of capitalist society in a manner that the classical approach had seemingly failed to do. As Alvin Johnson so well phrases it:

> It was easy to dive into one of those schools of doctrine; many of us did it unawares, and ever after the clash of tremendous economic interests, the noisy progress and dramatic defeat of real economic ideals, have sounded in our unheeding ears as a faint murmuring from a distant sphere. Not so Hoxie. For as long as it profited he was a classical of the classical. He revelled in Historismus while it was worth while, and manipulated margins with the most famous of the marginal utilitarians. But while he was joyously flexible in his treatment of the accredited doctrines, their value faded out.

They came to seem to him matters of small import. For his change of heart, probably due in any case, Hoxie himself gave credit to Veblen. (Johnson, 1916, pp. 248–249)

Veblen's approach held much promise for Hoxie in his search for a means to the understanding of the complexity of the economic environment and would eventually, and for a time, for him win the day.[12] Classical political economy had certainly by the end of the nineteenth century developed into "a systematized body of knowledge based upon the laws which were supposed to underlie the greatest production of wealth or the greatest economic welfare." The laws of classical political economy "were supposed to be derived from nature and human nature, and were therefore considered universal and immutable." Economics had transformed into "a science of universal economic normalities," a "taxonomic" science (Hoxie, 1901, p. 484). Veblen offered an alternative to the orthodoxy. Veblen stood as the firebrand, the critic of the industrial system and the economics that seemed to lend its support.[13] He exposed "the importance of the technical and the pecuniary aspects of social life, coining terms in which others could voice with unction their criticisms of the economics of the schools, and formulating principles that could be incorporated into the methodology of the 'coming' economics" (Hamilton, 1916, p. 858). As "the iconoclastic critic of both economic theory and social institutions," Veblen "impressed Hoxie with the conception of the economic process as one of evolutionary change, the general importance of the economic environment in the shaping of attitudes and states of mind, and the particular significance of the cultural impact of the machine process in creating distinct and quite different points of view in the worker and the employer" (McNulty, 1973, p. 454). Veblen's 1898 essay, "Why Is Economics Not An Evolutionary Science?," offers an insight into the nature of the problem while providing little more than a critique, essentially the outline of a proposed methodology; a program for the reconstitution of the discipline never really materialized.[14] In his 1901 "On the Empirical Method of Economic Instruction," Hoxie embraces Veblen's methodological critique of the economics discipline, which "impelled him to the conclusion that the methodology of orthodox economics was out of harmony with the dominant intellectual thought of the times," his specific target being the abstract nature of the orthodox approach (Hamilton, 1916, pp. 864–865).[15] Yet, as Leslie Fishman suggests, Veblen's influence was limited, as Hoxie remained, with respect to the theory of price, firmly within the neoclassical Marshallian camp: "With the tools of modern economics Hoxie was fully familiar. He could dissect a market in terms of supply and demand as neatly as an experienced surgeon completes an appendectomy. Hoxie saw no contradiction between marginalism as a guide to price analysis and Veblenism as a guide to evolutionary economics" (Fishman, 1958, pp. 226–227).

In his 1901 essay, "Industrial and Pecuniary Employments," Veblen again proves a source of inspiration, identifying a distinction that would become central to Hoxie's work on the subject of labor problems. There, Veblen distinguishes the role of the businessman as speculator or undertaker from those "who are mechanically engaged in the production of goods," that is, the industrial worker.[16] In Veblen's terms,

> The business man enters the economic life process from the pecuniary side, and so far as he works an effect in industry he works it through the pecuniary dispositions which he makes. He takes thought most immediately of men's convictions regarding market values; and his efforts as a business man are directed to the apprehension, and commonly also to the influencing of men's beliefs regarding market values. The objective point of business is the diversion of purchase and sale into some particular channel, commonly involving a diversion from other channels. The laborer and the man engaged in directing industrial processes, on the other hand, enter the economic process from the material side; in their characteristic work they take thought most immediately of mechanical effects, and their attention is directed to turning men and things to account for the compassing of some material end. (Veblen, 1901, pp. 205–206)

In sum, the worker, the industrial laborer, is "on the whole, occupied with production of goods; the business men, on the other hand, are occupied with the acquisition of them" (Veblen, 1901, p. 210). This distinction in attitude between the productive and the acquisitive classes – between labor and capital – is the source of industrial conflict.

Joseph Dorfman argues that Veblen's contrast between the industrial and the pecuniary interests persuaded Hoxie of the inevitability of class conflict (Dorfman, 1949, p. 451).[17] Hoxie's stance on the issue may be found in his discussion of Commons' 1908 essay "Is Class Conflict in America Growing and Is It Inevitable?" (1908a). Commons holds that with the advent of the "art of industrial psychology," treating labor as essentially an input on par with capital, there developed among workers a class-consciousness where none had previously existed. Self-consciousness is an essential aspect of individuality. Class-consciousness emerges as a result of attempts to eliminate individuality, to identify the individual with the group – "when his individuality is scientifically measured off in aliquot parts and each part is threatened with substitution by identical parts of other men, then his sense of superiority is gone. He and his fellow-workmen compete with each other, not as whole men, but as units of output." To Commons, this reduction of the individual to a member of a collective creates a sense of solidarity with the group, "the essential thing in class conflict" (Commons, 1908, p. 759). But to Commons, conflict is not inevitable, so long as the "public" – the "third class, which is not a class" – refuses to consent. "[T]he public at large is too big and too exposed for the wire-pulling of classes." It "does not consent that one class shall have an advantage over another," nor does it "favor either radicals or reactionaries." This "third class" has the *potential* to exercise its political will over the parties which legislate in support of one or the other of the warring classes, possibly "through direct nomination, direct election, initiative, or referendum." So long as fairness and honesty are guaranteed, there is hope that class conflict may be ameliorated. "Class antagonism will not disappear as long as there is wealth to distribute, but it can be transferred to the jury of the people." Should this become a reality, "we may expect social classes to state their case in the open and to wait on the gradual process of education rather than plunge into battle" (pp. 764–765).

Hoxie identifies the basis of this divergence in perspective between labor and the owners of capital as the result of environmental influences which serve to inculcate in members of the group distinct felt interests: "In order that classes and class conflict may develop, it is necessary only that the membership of different groups should believe their essential interests to be diverse, and a sufficient cause for belief in difference of essential interest is to be found in differences of materio-economic group discipline" (Hoxie, 1908a, p. 776). As an example, Hoxie offers the Veblenian distinction (mention of which he had made in his 1906 *Journal of Political Economy* essay):

> We have in the United States at least two recognized systems of materio-economic environment. I refer of course to what are commonly known as the working class or industrial environment and the capitalist-employing class or pecuniary environment. In essential respects these environments are diverse, and each subjects those who come most fully and exclusively within its control to a fairly definite and characteristic intellectual and moral disciplinary influence. (Hoxie, 1908a, p. 776)

The material environment of the laborer is one governed by "invariable laws," whereby material transformations are brought about through the application of physical force. These same "invariable laws" that govern the industrial process work to alter the relations "between the man and the material." It is no longer the case that man merely transforms material; on the contrary, it is man "who must conform in time, in place, in action to the laws governing the character of the material and the character of the available force" (Hoxie, 1908a, p. 777).

More importantly, the nature of the productive process ultimately determines the relations between men. The action of the industrial laborer "as an individual is controlled by the character of the machinery with which he works; the individual machine stands definitely related by mechanical necessity to the whole machinery of the individual, industrial process; and thus to the machinery of related process, so that the worker finds himself and his fellows definitely related to one another in a huge machine-process by virtue of these same general invariable laws which characterize the world of material things." These "invariable laws" are to the worker "blind" and "unmoral." As to the capitalist (the "pecuniary worker"), "the physical force and blind law which permeate his world operate not directly upon him in his vital activities but upon his agents. His primary concern is not with physical but with pecuniary results – with the control and acquisition of pecuniary energy. His world is therefore dominated primarily by spiritual force." As opposed to the "invariable laws" that govern the material productive process itself, the capitalist confronts a "variable human will." Thus, the industrial worker and the capitalist businessman are so fundamentally differently constituted as to "make it impossible for the members of the industrial and pecuniary classes to agree in regard to truth, justice, and virtue in many concrete cases" (Hoxie, 1908a, pp. 777–778).[18] Class conflict, therefore, is "inevitable ... unless something should happen to alter essentially the disciplinary situation – either to obviate entirely or partially the differences in discipline which now exist, or to neutralize their effects" (p. 779).

Yet Hoxie was not sanguine about such an obviation. The differences among the classes "seem to be a necessary aspect of the developing life process in society. Without these differences no division of labor, no specialization, no development of efficiency and individuality could exist. To obviate them we should have to accept the simplicity, stagnation, and atrophy of the small communistic community." Nor is the solution to be found in Commons' assertion of the capacity of the "third class" as something of an impartial spectator. To Hoxie, the notion of a disinterested third party is simply a fantasy, as "there is no third discipline unrelated to the disciplines of the fighting classes." The public are, to one extent or another, influenced by the disciplines of one or another of the combatants. Their loyalties, such as they may be, are assured "by similarity in point of view and therefore by sympathy and assumed likeness of interest," and so "there can be no large, homogeneous disinterested third class, whose members can agree upon a formula for the settlement of class disputes" (Hoxie, 1908a, p. 780).

While Hoxie professes affinity with Veblen's theory of the nature of the labor-capital conflict, later he was to break with Veblen,[19] proclaiming Veblen's theory of society as "fairly closely allied with that of the socialist. Like that, it sees society as made up of warring classes, mainly the employing and working class; like that, it is evolutionary – it sees these classes as the result of a process of evolution; like that, it lays immense stress upon the economic factor as a determinant of classes and class conflict" (Hoxie, 1917, p. 365).[20] In addition, while Veblen's theory comports with modern notions of nonteleological evolution, with psychological ideas of nonrationality (man "is a bundle of inheritances, propensities, prejudices and instincts"), and with sociological notions ("no natural rights, no natural order, no natural law as distinct from social order and social law, nonharmony of interests, no absolute right and wrong"), the environment is granted too great a place "as a formative force."[21] While the ability of the individual to react upon his environment directly to affect change it severely limited, he can nevertheless do so indirectly, through education and a reorientation of social arrangements. Here, Hoxie invokes the "progressive-uplift theory," which "postulates a fundamental and ultimate harmony of interests in society." Classes and class conflicts exist, but these are viewed "as the temporary outcome of lack of sufficient social interaction, knowledge and understanding" (p. 367).

> Science and democracy, however, are gradually overcoming these deficiencies. As science increases the knowledge of social facts, forces and relationships, as democracy, especially through universal education, develops, and particularly as the practices of industrial democracy, especially through collective bargaining, spread, there evolves a common social viewpoint, and a real social will of the people destined to do away with classes and class conflict, and to substitute in their place social justice and social harmony in the pursuit of general well-being. (Hoxie, 1917, p. 367)

Interestingly, Hoxie offers that a solution to the conflict between labor and capital lies in a "third party," consumers, "unbiased in its viewpoint, standing for social justice, and representing the true social will, a party already capable in ordinary cases of acting as mediator and arbiter between the warring classes." With the expansion of the knowledge base and the democratization of society, "this third party will gradually control the warring classes and absorb them. The social will will then be supreme, and social harmony will prevail." To Hoxie, the achievement of this end is dependent upon "a constant extension of social control in the form of legislation and public opinion in the support of the weaker warring class – the workers" (Hoxie, 1917, p. 368).[22]

Hamilton, in his memorial tribute, does not mention the significance to Hoxie of Commons, the University of Wisconsin Institutional economist. Yet Commons, perhaps more than any other individual save Veblen, was responsible for the ultimate direction of Hoxie's life and career. Hoxie wrote to Commons in October 1906 regarding his desire to undertake a study of unionism. As the situation in Chicago at the time was "too large and too complex" for a study of unionism as a whole, Hoxie instead sought to limit his focus to the details of a single trade, to attack the problem "one trade at a time." To avoid duplication of effort, covering the same ground in which Commons and others may be engaged, he inquired as to whether Commons was indeed involved in any such studies. Commons, in response, noted that, while he had been in discussion with Jacob Hollander to "divide the field" in such a manner, nothing had as yet come of it, and suggested Hoxie contact Hollander or George Barnett.[23]

In addition, it was Commons who recommended Hoxie undertake the investigation into the effect of scientific management on labor, the work for which Hoxie is perhaps best known. Commons was especially antipathetic to scientific management as promoting a "machinery theory of labor," by which labor's value was determined not through the workings of supply and demand, but through "the quantity of its product." Scientific management to Commons was, in effect, "the engineer's theory of economy and output," with the laborer little more than "an operating organism to be economized" (Commons, 1919, p. 14). It "carries to the final limit that disintegration of the workman's skill and its transfer to the employer, which began a hundred and fifty years ago with the inventions of power machinery, the steam engine, and division of labor," and expropriates from the worker his property right in labor (pp. 15–16). One may conclude from Hoxie's approach to the subject that Commons' desire to justify his preconceptions influenced, if only indirectly, the direction of his work and precipitated his later actions.[24]

Contributions

Hoxie is today perhaps unfairly portrayed as a labor economist, due to his work on the classification of functional types of trade unionism. His two books – *Scientific Management and Labor* (1915) and *Trade Unionism in America* (based on notes and lectures on trade unionism; published posthumously in 1917) – and many journal articles serve to promote this image. Yet this characterization has tended to neglect his contributions to economic theory and economic history, made early in his career. One need only note some of his *Journal of Political Economy* articles on theory, policy, and method to make the point:[25] "The Compensatory Theory of Bimetallism" (1893a); "The Silver Debate of 1890" (1893b), "Adequacy of the Customs Revenue System" (1894); "Fetter's Theory of Value" (1905); "The Demand and Supply Concepts: An Introduction to the Study of Market Price" (1906b); and "Historical Method versus Historical Narrative" (1906c).

Beginning in 1907, Hoxie began writing on the problems of labor, publishing a series of articles (all in *The Journal of Political Economy*, of which he served as associate editor), including "The Trade Union Point of View" (1907b), "The Failure of the Telegraphers' Strike" (1907c), "President Gompers and the Labor Vote" (1908c), "The Truth About the I.W.W." (1913b), "Trade Unionism in the United States" (1914a, 1914b), and "Scientific Management and Labor Welfare" (1916c).[26] This corpus of work seems to have served to define him as an economist interested primarily in the study of trade unionism and the workplace, and to have branded him a "labor economist." It also may have been the reason for his selection as a participant in the study of labor problems undertaken by the United States Commission on Industrial Relations. Yet such a conclusion as to his brand would do injustice to Hoxie as a political economist. His own definition of the science of political economy is telling in this respect:

> Without wishing to dogmatize, I should venture to assume that this science deals with human activity and the social process from the standpoint of market choice or market valuation. Moreover, as thus conceived I should not hesitate to affirm that there is no single matter of fact within the whole realm of social activity that does not conceivably lie within the field of political economy; for there is no single social fact, from the esoteric cogitations of the social philosopher down to the mudsills of human experience, that may not in some way directly or remotely affect human choice in the market. (Hoxie, 1907a, p. 746)

EARLY WORKS

Many of Hoxie's early writings dealt with the silver question and bimetallism, and the tariff, issues which had become important politically. In "The Compensatory Theory of Bimetallism" (1893a), Hoxie (as noted above) takes issue with Jevons' model concerning the efficacy of a bimetallic standard, specifically the analogy of two connected water reservoirs seeking a level mean. As Hoxie defines it, the compensatory theory states that

> [w]hen two metals are constituted legal tender to an unlimited amount, and coined indifferently in unlimited quantities at a fixed ratio of value, any cause that tends to change the ratio of value of the two metals in the market from the mint ratio will, at the same time, through the operation of Gresham's Law, result in a compensatory action, – an increase in the demand for the cheapened metal and a decrease in the demand for the dearer metal, – which will tend to bring the market ratio of the two metals back to the mint ratio. (Hoxie, 1893a, pp. 273–274)

This conclusion, Hoxie reasons, is predicated on the validity of three conditions: the two metals "are equal in regard to their capability for satisfying monetary desires," the action "involves a concurrent circulation of both gold and silver," and the action "is then unlimited in its power, acting at all times and under all circumstances" (Hoxie, 1893a, p. 274). However, the first of these conditions is demonstrably false, as the preference for gold is far greater than the preference for silver. As to the remaining two, Hoxie demonstrates diagrammatically that, with an influx of silver, not only would the market ratio not return to its mint value, as the two metal are not homogeneous, but the influx would completely push gold out of circulation, resulting in a single, silver standard, a "lower standard, which is naturally the one liable to the most violent fluctuations" (p. 276).

In "The Silver Debate of 1890," Hoxie again addresses the issue of bimetallism, in this instance reporting on the politics behind the passage of the Sherman Act, allowing for the free coinage of silver. Advocates had made their case based on the need to inflate the economy, and to rescue debtors and the silver miners, but had ignored any arguments regarding the deleterious effects on the economy as a whole of a bimetallic standard. Opponents did not disagree in principle, only over the method to achieve an end desirable to all. In so doing, the economic arguments were virtually completely disregarded. While proponents and opponents had, on previous occasions, opposed the free monetization of silver, on economic grounds, Hoxie concludes that the motivation for the change of position "is easy, when one understands the American habit of treating economic problems as political questions," a conclusion he regards as being "proved beyond reasonable doubt." First, the country had experienced a (localized) economic depression, nothing particularly severe, rather "one of the frequent disturbances which come of necessity to rapidly growing countries." As a political expedient, the politicians argued that the culprit was, as it had been argued following the Panic of 1873, the demonetization of silver. "The public learned to vociferously demand legislation at the first sign of distress, and the politicians found themselves obliged to comply with the demands, to save the whole monetary system from destruction" (Hoxie, 1893b, p. 577). Therefore, while the economic arguments may have been well known, the politics of the matter decided the outcome.

The second issue concerned the political legislative process itself. Even those opposed had little to offer in rebuttal when the argument was phrased in such politically popular terms. The silver would become monetized, the gold standard would be maintained. That the argument was specious, there was no doubt, but it was the politically acceptable compromise. Hoxie's commentary on the matter extends beyond the single issue at hand, and still rings true today:

> From this study it must be concluded that, economically considered, the debate shows a deplorable weakness, and points to a need among our public officials, as well as among the people, for greater attention to economic studies. Considered socially, it emphasizes this fact, that so long as economic problems are treated by the American people, as the legitimate prey of political parties, no consistent financial policy, or relief from present financial and economic governmental errors is to be expected. (Hoxie, 1893b, p. 587)

THE TRADE UNION POINT OF VIEW

Due in large part to the influence of Veblen, Hoxie's ultimate dismissal of economics as a science of generalizations that in isolation was of little value in the analysis of the conditions of modern society led him to the study of trade unionism.[27] The "union problem" is one of tremendous complexity that cannot be understood by confining analysis to a single dimension, but requires a more holistic, comprehensive approach. "It is not a mere question of wages and hours, of shop conditions and the narrow economic rights of employer and employee, and it cannot be solved by a mere resort to economic theory." Rather, the union problem "is a complex of economic, legal, ethical, and social problems which can be understood and met only by knowing the facts and the genesis of the viewpoint of organized labor in all its reach, diversity, contradictoriness, and shifting character, and by considering this viewpoint in relation to developing social conditions and social standards" (Hoxie, 1914a, p. 205). For Hoxie, trade unionism was pervasive, affecting to some extent virtually every aspect of society and economy; its "influence is effective in a greater or less degree in determining every feature and standard in our industrial, political, social, ethical, and religious life" (Hoxie, 1917, p. 5).[28] Unionism had an impact upon production (limiting hours of work, determining the types of machinery employed, setting the terms governing labor-management relations, etc.);

employer rights; distribution and profit rates; standards of ethical conduct (including claiming priority of class over the individual, the acceptance of the use of violence as a negotiating tactic, and the "minimizing" of property rights); and the social welfare. In myriad ways, not always immediately observable or proximate to the situation, unionism is the perhaps the most omnipresent force in society (Hoxie, 1917, pp. 3–4).[29]

The *problems* of unionism thus stated, Hoxie proceeds to the question of the *psychology* of the group. Social groups may be identified with respect to the distinguishing features of their membership – their "common viewpoint in regard to some vital social matter or series of such matters." The significance of the group lies in its ability to affect the "social will." As "each group has its standards of right, justice, rights and welfare, with respect to the matters with which it is most vitally concerned," each must strive to attain its ends even as against groups with competing or conflicting aims (Hoxie, 1917, p. 7). An important influence in shaping the group ideal is the social and institutional environment within which the group functions, the mechanism which "very largely molds human nature and desires, sets limits to social accomplishment, and at any time determines what can be done by society and how the fundamental environing forces must be dealt with in order to accomplish the socially possible." As the disparate groups interact within the constraints imposed by the environment, the social will is formed (p. 8).

Insofar as one accepts this as an explanation of group behavior, it becomes abundantly clear that, in order to comprehend the social condition, one must first ascertain the motivation of the disparate groups vying to influence and to control the social will, for only then will it be possible "to take any decided steps toward the effective solution of the multitude of harassing social and labor problems which confront us" (Hoxie, 1917, p. 8). Thus the study of trade unionism, and the labor movement generally, which to Hoxie is in its influence and impact the most encompassing and effective of the social groups, seemed ideal as a means to understand the social problem as a whole. As Hamilton phrases it,

> Hoxie found in trade unionism the problem for which he was seeking. In the more general "labor problem" he found the "economic factors," which are the ultimate recipients of income in theoretical discussion, replaced by creatures of flesh and blood struggling in their several ways for shares of the world's goods. In the more particular problems of trade unionism he found involved in this conflict, not only the laws of value underlying "the distributive process," but practically the whole scheme of our social conventions. And, as he watched the struggle proceed, he saw that the world of ideas was an inseparable part of it. Accordingly it was in trade unionism that he attempted to study developing society. (Hamilton, 1916, p. 876)

Method of Analysis

In his Introduction to *Trade Unionism in the United States* (1917), published posthumously from notes and previously published essays, Hoxie addresses the necessity of employing the scientific method in the study of the trade union movement, in an effort to arrive at means to "the control of unionism as it touches upon vital social and economic interests." In order to determine whether in fact unionism can be altered and, if so, the conditions under which this may be effected, one must undertake "a genetic study of unionism" to allow "an understanding of how it came to be what it is" (Hoxie, 1917, p. 19). To achieve this end, the investigator must proceed in as dispassionate a manner as possible, engaging the subject with an unbiased "scientific attitude." Only is this way is it at all possible that the investigator may have a chance of succeeding in "putting aside as far as possible all passion and prejudice, all preconceived notions in regard to the object of study, all beliefs and feelings; seeking only for the truth and being willing to follow it to whatever conclusions it may lead." The truth, he notes, is not "objective," but rather "is a reflex of this thing upon our consciousness; and, therefore, to our apprehension is determined largely by the quality of our mental furniture .... On the quality, therefore, of the existing beliefs, feelings, prejudices, presuppositions, depends the judgment as to the facts. As soon as prejudice enters in, we will slight, or overemphasize, or be unable to see things" (Hoxie, 1917, p. 21).[30]

As applied to the study of trade unionism, such an approach is essential, since the student of trade unionism is "specially prone to prejudice, preconception and partisanship when unionism is in question," this due to the fact that "unionism is a storm center of the most universal and vital controversy in existence – the struggle for a living." The very notions of labor and the union movement "not only touches the individual personally in his most vital concerns, but especially arouses group prejudices – the most bitter and the hardest to eradicate, because they are not the result of the thought of the individual, but are inherited and bred in the bone, and are therefore largely unconscious" (Hoxie, 1917, p. 22).

To apprehend the psychology of the *group*, one must begin with an appreciation of the psychology of the *individual*. Hoxie's approach focuses on the interests and motivations of the worker. In so doing, he rejects the rational actor model as granting too great a role to self-interest "as the motive of rationality and rational action." Emotion, if it "is ever present in the rational human being ... is never allowed to enter as a disturbing factor into his calculation or to influence his subsequent action." Such motivations as "fear, hate, anger, revenge, love of wife, home, country, love of approbation, desire for power or prestige" are granted "only after being translated into terms of utilities and disutilities." All action is calculated and deliberative (Hoxie, 1917, p. 362). Hoxie does not deny that man is rational in his deliberations, only that the standard model is far too restrictive; he merely argues that men "are not altogether rational, that they are moved by love and hate, fear and prejudices, habits and propensity, apart from and often in opposition to the dictates of rationality." Should the economist begin to accept this notion of human behavior, which is "not only in line with common observation but with modern psychology," that is, if the assumption that action is dictated by rational self-interest is rejected, then the "whole classical economic structure with its assumption of harmony of interest in society topples down" (p. 363).

The Psychology of the Worker

The state of scholarship on the nature of trade unionism at the beginning of the twentieth century was quite poor; what little there was of any significance was "either fragmentary or hopelessly superficial or hopelessly partisan." Indeed, as a subject of academic inquiry, "little attempt has been made at a serious, general and scientific study of it" (Hoxie, 1917, p. 1). In a series of articles published in the *Journal of Political Economy*, beginning in 1907 and continuing through 1914, Hoxie approached the subject of trade unionism afresh, differentiating union types not merely with respect to structure, but also taking into account their functional nature, and incorporating analysis of the psychological bases of their existence.[31] Attempting an analytical study of trade unions by focusing simply on structure is a rather pointless task, as it allows little in the way of interpretation as to motivations, political, social and economic, or the psychologies and social philosophies of the memberships.

In his 1907 "The Trade-Union Point of View," his first published essay on the issue of trade unionism, Hoxie addresses the issue of conflict between organized labor and the owners of capital, specifically whether there exists a distinct trade union perspective. This requires him to consider charges leveled by employers that trade unionists routinely reject the property rights of employers, deny the validity of contract, and, while demanding shorter working hours and higher wages, "reduce the efficiency of labor and the extent of the output" (Hoxie, 1907b, p. 345).

To appreciate the significance to labor of the trade union, one must begin by understanding the psychology of the laborer. Here, as we discussed above, the influence of Veblen on Hoxie is most evident. In Hoxie's estimation, the psychology of the laborer cannot be understood within the classical model of the rational actor, and so his relation to the employer *qua* producer cannot be such that the two operate on the same plane. The employer, sustained in his beliefs by a "middle-class philosophy of rights," which grants that proprietary rights derive from production, sees no need to question "the existing order of things" but instead tends "to regard his business prerogatives in the light of natural rights." It is only reasonable that he would view the laborer, in his role as union member, as possibly "the deluded tool of self-seeking and unscrupulous leaders" (Hoxie, 1907b, p. 346).

Yet the laborer is incapable of viewing the employer in the same light, despite his acceptance as well of the philosophy of natural right; specifically, his social and economic conditions preclude him from perceiving the employer as a producer. For Hoxie, the laborer "is not rational in the sense that his response to any given mental stimulus is invariable and is uniform with that of all other men." He is more "the product of heredity and environment." The laborer, "like the rest of us,"

> is a bundle of notions, prejudices, beliefs, unconscious preconceptions and postulates, the product of his peculiar heredity and environment. These unconscious and subconscious psychic elements necessarily mix with and color his immediate impressions, and they together limit and determine his intellectual activity. What is or has been outside his ancestral and personal environment must be either altogether incomprehensible to him, or else must be conceived as quite like or analogous to that which has already been mentally assimilated. He cannot comprehend what he has not, or thinks he has not, experienced. (Hoxie, 1907b, p. 347)

Among those incomprehensible notions is that of property ownership. Custom, ethics, spirituality, the force and sanction of law, "are altogether in the background," the dominant element being "blind physical causation." In his daily activity "the machine and the machine process ... dominate the worker, and the growth in size of the industrial unit renders his economic relationships ever more impersonal withdraws farther from his knowledge the directing and controlling spiritual forces .... He tends to become mentally blind to spiritual, legal, contractual, and customary forces and their effects." As a result, the laborer cannot recognize the claims of the employer to the value of the product. "The only kind of production which he can recognize is the material outcome of physical force – the physical good." Any value otherwise inferred "is to him merely an invention of the employing class to cover up unjust appropriation." On equity grounds alone, then, the rightful owner of the product is the laborer, the ultimate source of its existence (Hoxie, 1907b, pp. 348–349). That this interpretation is Veblenian in nature Hoxie readily admits (p. 348, n.3).

While rejection of the validity of the employer's argument for ownership rights of the output of the firm or industry is sufficient cause for the employer to conclude that his interests and those of the unionist cannot coincide, the "more serious charge," according to Hoxie, is that the worker as unionist denies the sanctity of contract. To the employer, the very nature of the capitalist production process, with its myriad interdependencies, is such "that the failure of a single individual to perform his contract obligation may possibly involve hundreds of others in financial ruin and the members of a whole commonwealth in temporary economic distress." The labor contract is, then, absolutely essential to the functioning not merely of the enterprise but of the system as a whole. "It is not so much a personal virtue with him [the employer] as an evolutionary necessity" (Hoxie, 1907b, pp. 350–351).

Thus, to the employer, failure to abide by the labor contract demonstrates the "perversity" of the laborer, and is evidence that he cannot and should not be granted a say in the operation of the enterprise. Yet to the unionist, there is a moral obligation that transcends the sanctity of the labor contract, this being fidelity to the union brotherhood. He perceives no direct relation between work and remuneration, as the wage he receives corresponds "not to the physical result of his efforts, but to its economic importance," and so he sees "labor as one thing in its effects and another thing in its reward." He realizes that he is little more than a commodity, and so "the sharper the competition between himself and his fellows, the lower the rates are likely to be." He thus sees as a "moral duty" a fellowship with other workers who share his circumstance. The remedy he finds in combination, in the union. The conclusion, then, follows: "*Proneness to breach of contract, therefore, is seen to be a natural and inevitable outcome of his life and working conditions. It is a thing to be remedied, if at all, only by changing conditions* ..." (Hoxie, 1907b, pp. 351–353; emphasis in original).

The third of the charges against the unionist is the deliberate sabotage of the business function. To this charge Hoxie finds some validity. "Unions constantly are demanding higher wages and better conditions of employment, coincident with shorter hours, limitation of the numbers of workers, handicapping of machine introduction, and more or less direct restrictions on individual output." The employer finds this behavior irrational, as in so doing, the worker harms only himself. After all, greater productive efficiency results in greater output and thus a greater share for both the employer and the worker (Hoxie, 1907b, p. 354).

But such a view as that of the employer Hoxie sees as naïve, since it assumes that the increase in aggregate factor shares brought about by an increase in aggregate income will redound to increases in the respective shares of the individual enterprises. The worker, however, tends not to view labor in the aggregate, but rather focuses on his own and his fellow workers' concerns. While he is cognizant "of co-operation within his trade," he has not developed class-consciousness; the very notion of "labor as a whole" appears to the trade unionist as "a mere academic conception." It may very well be "that labor as a whole may gain while the individual laborer starves." Further, he believes that the greater the income of the individual enterprise, more often than not, the lower the wage rate, and *vice versa*. In this conclusion there is, in Hoxie's estimation, some merit. Hoxie holds as true "that the wage-rate of any class of laborers is not determined by the conditions which exist in the particular establishment in which they work, but by the conditions which prevail in their trade or 'non-competing group'." The wage for the industry as a whole is determined competitively in the labor market. Increasing the productivity and hence the output of the individual firm may indeed be profitable for the workers in that firm, but should the productivity increase be spread throughout the industry, with a resulting increase in total output, the competitive outcome will be a reduction in the price of the output and a reduction in wages. So, let the union restrict worker efficiency. By reducing productive efficiency and reducing output in the industry as a whole, "the value of the product per unit" will increase, and "the employer [will] then be forced to increase the reward which goes to each unit of labor effort without any necessary decrease of his own profit, but rather out of the increased price which outside labor has been forced to pay for the products of the group." This Hoxie sees as an example of "monopoly squeeze," a "*perfectly reasonable outcome of the conditions as they exist*" for the worker (Hoxie, 1907b, pp. 355–357; emphasis in original).

Hoxie's conclusion could very well have been written by Veblen himself and demonstrates the validity of his contention of a unique trade union perspective. The laborer's demands are neither "stupid" nor "perverse," as the employer may conclude, but rather "are apparently the inevitable outcome of the peculiar circumstances of his life and work." They are, in fact, "quite reasonable." It should come as no surprise "that men circumstanced differently as to both inheritance and present environment are bound to reach quite different conclusions as to rights, morality, and sound economic policy." Nor should it seem outrageous that the circumstances of the owners of capital and the suppliers of labor are so "radically" different as "to be altogether incapable of mutual understanding." Neither should it be assumed that these differences reflect a "lack of morality or intelligence on the part of either class." Rather, accounting for such circumstances gives rise to this "distinctive trade-union view-point which must be reckoned with, as a matter of fact in connection with all practical labor problems" (Hoxie, 1907b, p. 359).

So for the worker, for the union as well. The "spiritual basis" of the union "is the natural and inevitable outgrowth of the conditions under which the laboring class has for generations lived and worked." Unions cannot, therefore, be suppressed without the worker suffering the same fate. Additionally, worker and employer, labor and capital, are too far apart in their apprehensions of the conditions of industrial life for there to be any immediate solution to their differences (Hoxie, 1907b, p. 361).

In his comments on the 1908 presidential election, in which Samuel Gompers, president of the American Federation of Labor, supported the Democratic Party candidate, William Jennings Bryan, who subsequently lost to the Republican, William Howard Taft, Hoxie again approaches his analysis from the perspective of the psychology of the worker. The rationale behind Gompers' decision to enter the political contest is, to Hoxie, unclear. It may have been that, as a Socialist, Gompers had as a "hidden aim" a desire "to draw the workers as rapidly as practicable in the direction of class-conscious political action," thus leading at some future date "to a united independent labor party." Alternatively, the decision may have been something of an expedient, "forced upon the leaders of the federation by the imperative demand for a positive policy promising immediate results of a visible nature" (Hoxie, 1908c, p. 693).

In support of the latter motive, Hoxie reiterates his claim "that the dominant motive of the average wage-worker must ever be to secure the greatest possible immediate pecuniary results from his toil." So long as the union could achieve for him these aims through the process of collective bargaining, he was satisfied with the direction it was taking. The union required no "grand philosophy," nor did it need to "inspire the workers with hopes of a future in which opportunity and development figure chiefly." Rather, the union simply needed to appeal to the workers' desire, as Hoxie quotes Gompers, for "'more, more, more', *more now*" (Hoxie, 1908c, pp. 693–694; emphasis in original).

The labor movement at the beginning of the twentieth century seemed in peril. The Sherman Antitrust Act of 1890, designed as a means by which to curtail industrial cartels and monopolies, was employed against members of the American Railway Union for interfering with interstate commerce during the Pullman strike of 1894; an economic recession – the Panic of 1907 – pushed the unemployment rate from three to eight per cent; businesses had begun to act in support of one another during labor disputes; and legal decisions were favoring employers over unions in disputes. The perception of a hostile political and economic environment thus provided the ideal milieu for unions, especially the American Federation of Labor and its leadership, previously apolitical and even anti-political (as Hoxie contends), to enter the political arena.[32]

Gompers decided to throw the support of the AFL to Bryan over Taft, a more expedient alternative than supporting the Socialists, who had in his estimation little chance of victory, or running as a candidate on a Labor Party ticket.[33] Yet Gompers' tactic was doomed from the outset. In Hoxie's estimation,

> It was early evident that the bulk of the socialists would stand by their party candidates; that the non-federated unions would pursue their own political ways as usual, and that even the votes of the Federationists would be hopelessly scattered. ... Undoubtedly, however, the leading rôle was again played by the spirit of business unionism and by the conflict between this spirit and its socialist antitype. (Hoxie, 1908c, p. 695)

Specifically, Gompers had counted on the support of an organized and monolithic union movement, coalescing around a developing class-consciousness. Yet the degree of worker solidarity required for such a cooperative endeavor was not forthcoming. The advances made by individual unions are made not by cooperation with other unions, but by the establishment by a *particular* union of favorable working conditions for its members. Allegiance, then, is not to labor as a class, but rather to ones fellow workers; to extend such commitment to labor in general is to lessen its impact and to threaten the security of any advances. "In the struggle to secure these conditions, entangling alliances with weak unions are often a hindrance, and, when secured, their maintenance is easily jeopardized by the attempt to secure them for others" (Hoxie, 1908c, p. 696).

Despite the fact that workers had not as yet developed a class-consciousness, there may be instances when such becomes manifest. Such may be the case "when members of the working class appear to attempt a middle-class pose." Gompers' failure to gain the support of the very unionists he had counted on to elect his candidate may very well have been the result of his "attempt openly to commit unionism as such to the support of a middle-class party." He appears to have taken as an article of faith that "labor" was monolithic, that the workers and the unions to which they belonged, despite the diversity of interests and objectives, nonetheless shared a common perspective and a unity of social, economic, and political interests and purpose. In the end, however, Hoxie concludes that the worker "is to an extent the slave of the need for immediate results." His political choices will redound to one simple observation: "whose election will best assure work and pay now and in the immediate future." Thus can Hoxie conclude, "*There is in America today no 'labor vote'*" (Hoxie, 1908c, pp. 699–700; emphasis in original).

Trade Unionism: Structure and Function

In Hoxie's view, unions arose as workers perceived a commonality of interests with others "similarly situated economically and socially," and so possessed of "a common interpretation of the social situation and a common solution of the problem of living," much as may be seen in the genesis of any other social collective. It was not until the eighteenth century in the United States that the trade union came into existence; prior to that, labor organizations were in the nature of craft guilds, "workmen who combined in themselves the functions of laborer, master and merchant," their function being "to license, or otherwise limit the number of legal craftsmen, to regulate the quality of work, and to maintain customary prices" (Hoxie, 1917, p. 78, n.2). Trade unions – labor unions – emerged only after the roles of worker and employer came to be seen as distinct, for then, "the employers took advantage of the breaking down of the old customary and legal trade and labor regulations, especially of apprenticeship regulations, to utilize the competition of 'illegal' men in attempts to lower wages and increase the hours of labor." The workers countered by establishing labor combinations and exclusionary rules as means to the regulation of wages, conditions, and hours (p. 79).[34] In sum, the emergence of the labor union.

> goes back in its genesis ultimately to the common needs and problems of the wage-workers; it arises immediately out of the consciousness of the common or group character of those needs and problems; it exists for common action looking to the betterment of the living-conditions; it appears primarily as a group interpretation of the social situation in which workers find themselves, and a remedial program in the form of aims, policies, and methods; the organization and the specific form or structure which it

takes are merely the instruments which the group adopts for propagating its viewpoint and putting its program into effect. (Hoxie, 1914b, pp. 468–469)

While Hoxie insists that "unionism itself is so pragmatic and therefore so protean as to warrant the rejection of all attempts to characterize and judge it as a whole," he nonetheless considers that "it has seemingly developed along certain fairly distinct general lines giving rise thus to types sufficiently definite to allow of legitimate generalization." To this end, he identifies union types with respect to *structure* and *function* (Hoxie, 1914a, p. 206). The functional union type is essentially "a specific case of group psychology, ... a social interpretation and remedial program held by a group of wage-workers." By contrast, the structural union type "is simply one of the organic methods by means of which the functional types seek to maintain discipline among their members and to put into effect their programs of action." In terms of analogy, "the structural type is related to the functional type somewhat as government is related to the nation. It is altogether a subordinate and dependent manifestation" (Hoxie, 1914b, p. 470).

In terms of structure, Hoxie identifies four such union types: the *craft union*, the *trades* (or *crafts*) *union*, the *industrial union*, and the *labor union*.[35] The first of these, the craft union, "is an organization of wage-workers engaged in a single occupation, ... [which] may be limited strictly to one simple task or may include a number of closely allied tasks or crafts." Each member of a craft union is capable of performing multiple tasks as required by the occupation, but the focus is on a specific craft, which may represent "but a fraction of the work of a given industry" (Hoxie, 1914a, p. 207). Hoxie dates the appearance of the craft union between 1798 and 1827, brought about through "the development of a master-workman-retailer and especially of the jobber and merchant middleman" which led to a differentiation between masters and journeymen and the development of the wage system. Craft unions came into being "because of the coming of capitalistic conditions, an employing class, general market, labor competition, strategic advantage of the masters with a tendency to lower wages, to bring in inferior workmen, the lengthening of hours," and the realization that such an organization had become, by that time and in those circumstances, "natural and possible" (Hoxie, 1917, p. 82). Modern examples are the United Brotherhood of Carpenters and Joiners, and the International Brotherhood of Electrical Workers.[36]

The *trades* (or *crafts*) *union*, by contrast, "is a *federation* of unions in different crafts or industries," the individual unions retaining a degree of independence. This type is typically referred to as a trades council or labor federation (Hoxie, 1914a, pp. 207–208). The trades union appears between 1827 and 1837, with the expansion of markets and "manhood suffrage, which stimulates to the correction of social and political evils, mainly inflated money and the high cost of living, educational and assumed political inequalities" (Hoxie, 1917, pp. 83–84). Between 1866 and 1874, the craft union amalgamations reappeared, more politically active than previously, regaining prominence once again by 1890. An example of a federation of craft unions is the American Federation of Labor (AFL) (p. 87).

The *industrial union* is distinct from the crafts union in that its organization is with respect to the industry, not the task. The purpose of the industrial union is "to unite into one homogeneous organic group all the workers, skilled and unskilled, engaged in turning out and putting on the market a given finished product or series of closely related products." The form of the industrial union varies with the specific industry under consideration, "but the essential test of industrial unionism seems to be that the industrial scope or area of the workers' organization shall be coterminous with that of the capitalistic enterprise or series of closely related enterprises" (Hoxie, 1914a, p. 208). An example of this type of union is the United Mine Workers.[37]

Finally, the *labor union* is an organization of workers without respect to craft or industry. Its appearance coincides with the erosion of the craft form of enterprise and the formation of employer associations and business trusts. It is simply representative of labor as labor, the exemplar being the Knights of Labor (Hoxie, 1914a, p. 209, 1917, pp. 86–87).

In sum, Hoxie offers the following generalization with respect to the structural types of unionism:

> Craft unions tend to be businesslike, selfish, nonidealistic, nonpolitical, nondemocratic; trades unions tend to be group-conscious and political; labor unions tend to be idealistic, moralistic, theoretical, political, but nondemocratic; industrial unions tend to be class-conscious, socialistic, and theoretical. (Hoxie, 1917, p. 88)

Having identified structural types, Hoxie next classifies unions with respect to *function*, the "primary and essential expression" of unionism (Hoxie, 1914b, p. 466).[38] The first of these is the *business union*, an "essentially trade-conscious rather than class-conscious" form, the interest of which is the craft worker and not the working class. Its primary concern is with the securing of "higher wages, shorter hours, and better working conditions, regardless for the most part of the welfare of the workers outside the particular organic group, and regardless in general of political and social considerations except in so far as these bear directly upon its own economic ends."[39] The business union is generally conservative in outlook, "in the sense that it professes belief in natural rights and accepts as inevitable, if not as just, the existing capitalistic organization and the wage system as well as existing property rights and the binding force of contract." It tends to exclusivity, preferring the apprentice system as a means to limit membership to the more highly skilled,[40] and manages conflict through collective bargaining, generally eschewing strikes, unless such may enhance its bargaining position (Hoxie, 1914a, pp. 212–213).[41]

The second functional type is *friendly* or *uplift unionism*, the purpose of which is "chiefly to elevate the moral, intellectual, and social life of the worker, to improve the conditions under which he works, to raise his material standards of living, give him a sense of personal worth and dignity, secure for him the leisure for culture, and insure him and his family against the loss of a decent livelihood by reason of unemployment, accident, disease, or old age." It is generally conservative, democratic, and inclusive, accepting of the existing economic and social order while seeking reform from within, favoring the co-operative form of business organization, collective bargaining, and, when necessary, political action. Such conflicts as may arise between labor and capital are not indicative of a failure of the institutions of capitalism; conflict is not endemic, but remediable. Worker education, employment security, and the provision of mutual insurance protection were among the demands secured by uplift unionism.[42] The Knights of Labor represents for Hoxie an example of this type (Hoxie, 1914a, p. 213).[43]

Revolutionary unionism is the third type of functional unionism. This type is profoundly radical, "distinctly class-conscious rather than trade-conscious," declaring "the complete harmony of interests of all wage workers as against the representatives of the employing class" as it "seeks to unite the former, skilled and unskilled together, into one homogeneous fighting organization." The demands of the industrial classes take priority over those of the pecuniary. The revolutionary union is profoundly anti-capitalist in outlook, opposed to individual ownership of the means of production and the wage system itself, and eschews collective bargaining and labor contracting (except when expedient) in favor of direct action.[44] Two varieties of revolutionary unionism are the *socialistic* and the *quasi-anarchistic*, the former viewing the union and socialist movements as class-based and so consistent in aims, while the latter opposes all forms of political order, and employs direct confrontational action (including violence and industrial sabotage) as it seeks "a society based upon free industrial association" (Hoxie, 1914a, pp. 214–215). The socialistic variant is exemplified by the Western Federation of Miners, while the quasi-anarchistic form finds expression in the International Workers of the World (I.W.W.). With respect to the latter, Hoxie describes it as "the bug-bear of American syndicalism," the character of which is "for the most part compounded of a species of anarchistic idealism and a blind, instinctive impulse to react somehow against capitalism and capitalistic society in the absence of the ordinary organic, financial, and political means and opportunities" (Hoxie, 1914d, p. 140).[45] Hoxie finds the membership drawn from "the desperate elements of the working class, the men who have not developed and cannot develop, under the existing system, organic discipline and constructive ability." They abhor such democratic niceties as majority rule and believe "organic strength and action" to be tantamount to oppression. The leadership of the organization, by and large, consists of "men who have deliberately discarded all constructive ideals, deliberately thrown off social restraint, and, in the spirit of the mediaeval knight or the revolutionist of the well-to-do classes in Russia, have constituted themselves the personal avengers of the wrongs of the working class," undermining the effectiveness of the union as viable organization dedicated to the betterment of the conditions of labor (Hoxie, 1913b, pp. 792–794).[46]

Lastly, there is *predatory unionism*, a "wholly pragmatic" form, the purpose of which (to the extent that such may be determined) is the securing of "immediate ends" through "the ruthless pursuit of the thing in hand by whatever means seem most appropriate at the time, regardless of ethical and legal codes or the effect upon those outside its own membership." The securing for its members every possible advantage over the employer appears its sole aim, yet its practices tend toward the anarchistic. Sub-categories of predatory unionism are *hold-up unionism* and *guerrilla unionism*. The former, while appearing to be a form of business unionism and so "masquerading" as conservative, in fact "has no abiding principles and no real concern for the rights or welfare of outsiders." It is profoundly corrupt and monopolistic, even conspiring with employers to eliminate rivals and exclude workers from other unions. The latter differs from the former in that "it operates always directly against its employers, never in combination with them," and is "secret, violent, and ruthless, seemingly because it despairs of attaining what it considers to be legitimate ends by business, uplift, or revolutionary methods." The International Association of Bridge and Structural Iron Workers, members of which were accused of dynamiting the *Los Angeles Times* building in 1910, killing 21employees, is Hoxie's exemplar of the guerrilla type (Hoxie, 1914a, pp. 215–216).[47]

A fifth functional type, *dependent unionism*, Hoxie mentions in a footnote, suggesting its relative unimportance to his taxonomy. The existence of this type "is dependent wholly or in large part upon other unions or upon the employers." These tend to be specialty unions, corresponding to a specific goods market, and "could not exist except for their labels." Dependent unions tend to be conservative in outlook and employer-dominated (Hoxie, 1914a, p. 216, n.1).

Having identified the structural and functional types of unionism, Hoxie then proceeds to the question as to whether such types actually exist. With respect to structural types, there appears to be no question – those familiar with the study of labor and the union movement readily acknowledge the existence of the identified types. With respect to function, once it is accepted "that the union is in essence an expression of group psychology we realize that it will get its specific character not merely from environmental conditions but from these in conjunction with the temperamental characteristics of the workers concerned, and that consequently union variants are likely to appear with a variation in either of these factors." The labor movement in the United States is not homogeneous. Unions develop distinct perspectives consistent with the demands of the industries with which they must deal and the temperament of their leadership, and factional conflicts periodically give rise to changes in approach. Even within the same industry, unions should not be presumed to have similar aspirations, political and economic aims, or methods of bargaining, as their interests need not coincide (Hoxie, 1914b, pp. 470–471). Thus, economic and environmental explanations are insufficient to account for the observed functional differences among American labor unions. What Hoxie proposes is a more pluralistic approach, one consistent with the works of University of Michigan sociologist Charles Horton Cooley, Yale sociologist and economist William Graham Sumner, University of Chicago sociologist William Isaac Thomas, and French social psychologist and criminologist Gabriel Tarde, which incorporate an understanding of the psychology of the group. One must account not merely for economic considerations, but as well political, social, and traditional attitudes, "in the sense of the whole body of transmitted sentiments, ideas, and precepts moral, religious, and customary." Social psychology, in contrast to economics, allows for the accounting of differences in "temperament and aptitudes, both personal and racial, which show themselves as between different races and individuals in relatively permanent and conflicting feelings, ideals, and attitudes."[48] These are subjective factors that had been all but ignored in the received body of union scholarship. "It is these temperamental differences plus environmental influences that at any moment cause individuals to differ in respect of what is good and bad, right and wrong, just and unjust; which mold and color their social interpretations, and thus, through the primal forces of association, bring about psychological groups with diverse and conflicting viewpoints and programs of action" (pp. 473–474).[49]

Unions and Socialism

The emergence of the Socialist Party in American politics also held fascination for Hoxie, especially its association with trade unionism. From 1908 until 1912 he published in the *Journal of Political Economy* a series of articles on the Party itself and on Socialism as a phenomenon. In the first of these, "The Convention of the Socialist Party" (1908b), Hoxie notes the "startling heterogeneity of representation" at the convention held in Chicago in May 1908. Instead of wage-laborers, a natural constituency, he found the delegation to be composed of "farmers, lawyers, editors, small enterprisers, politicians, professional organizers, professional agitators, and ministers and ex-ministers of the gospel." As an explanation for the lack of representation of working men, Hoxie offered that it was, at least in part, the result of "the comparative poverty of the actual wage workers in the party and the difficulties which they naturally meet with in quitting work for propagandistic purposes." While wageworkers may agree with the objectives of the Socialists, maintaining their livelihoods was a much higher priority. In addition, a more significant reason was that Socialism as a political movement in the United States "is by no means correctly represented as a mere movement of the working class and that it is neither to be understood nor judged by the mere study of Marxian or any other socialist philosophy." Rather, Socialism "is, like most new movements resting to any considerable degree on sentiment, a loadstone for the most diverse elements in society; that it has drawn to itself, along with intelligent and constructive middle-class leaders, a generous quota of cranks, mystics, and mere agitators" (Hoxie, 1908b, p. 442).

For the most part constructivist and moderate, the leadership of the Party understood that their movement, to succeed, must recruit from the membership roles of the trade unions. To succeed as a viable alternative in the American political system, the Socialist Party must make explicit a declaration of principles "supported both by the revolutionary and constructive or practical socialists, that would satisfy the industrial unionists in and out of the party" while also persuading the trade unionists that the Party has the wherewithal to secure "for the worker immediate amelioration of his condition and amelioration without interference with the direct policy and methods of unionism and craft autonomy." Yet the more radical elements, supportive of *industrial* unionism as against *trade unionism*, sharply disagreed. While ultimately the constructivists won the day, referring in the end only to "organized labor," Hoxie expresses reservations that the Party and the Socialist movement in general can succeed in bringing the trade unionists into the fold. "Trade-unionism does not take seriously from the socialist party mere general assurance of appreciation and co-operation. Its officers and members want to be shown that *immediate* advantage will result to *them* before they take serious steps toward any alliance with the socialists" (Hoxie, 1908b, pp. 443–444; emphasis in original).

Dissension manifested in the Party platform, with the more revolutionary elements forcing compromise wording with respect to farmers (assuring them that, to protect the interests of the smallholder, Socialism would secure the nationalization of industry), on the issue of immigration (finessing the demands for restrictions to protect the American worker with the purity of the socialist commitment to the working class as a whole), and on the place within the movement of the Christian Socialists (declaring in the end that Marxian Socialism – the materialist conception of history – is ultimately incompatible with religious doctrine). Hoxie sees this internal dissension as problematic to the future of the Party. If the Socialist Party has any possibility of being a viable political force in American politics, it "must be purified by the elimination of certain elements which breed only dissension within and distrust without." The "ignorant, doctrinaire, ultra-revolutionary, semi-anarchistic element," in the guise of agitators such as Bill Haywood and Eugene Debs, threatens any future success of the Party; when this "element" fails in its efforts at establishing itself as a viable political party,

> these men and their like fasten themselves like leeches upon the most revolutionary party existing and, by the power which extravagant appeal to class consciousness has upon the minds of the rank and file, they make themselves popular heroes, force the real party leaders unwillingly to support their outrageous and destructive actions, and damn the party in the minds of reasonably conservative men by assuming to act as its mouthpieces and spokesmen. (Hoxie, 1908b, p. 446)

Hoxie identifies three measures that were taken in an effort to "purify" the Party: the marginalization of the more divisive elements, the insertion into the party constitution of a clause calling for the expulsion of any member who professes "direct action" as opposed to "political action" as a means to the accomplishment of the Party's interests, and a rejection of any union with the more radical Socialist Labor Party. A fourth measure called for a more centralized executive authority – as it is, there is simply "too much democracy and untrammeled individualism in the party organization." This centralization the Party achieved by amending the constitution to allow election of the executive committee by the national committee. In this way might be lessened "the cumbrous tyranny of the rank and file which has heretofore put a brake upon the party machinery" (Hoxie, 1908b, pp. 447–448).

In his conclusion, Hoxie appraises Socialism and the Socialist movement as "a conscious, organized struggle *for* the social domination of the working class," its aspiration being "to reconstruct the political and legal fabric in the interests of this class" (Hoxie, 1908b, p. 448; emphasis in original).[50]

One of the difficulties with the acceptance by labor of Socialism and Socialist parties has been the parties' alliances with and seeming acceptance of ultra-revolutionary elements. For Hoxie, the American labor movement – trade unionism – views as anathema such efforts at control as being akin to an external imposition, one at odds with the nature and aims of the movement. American trade unionism

> is not a made-to-order affair; it is not imitative of anything to be found abroad, nor is it the objectification of any general social theory. It is a means, slowly forged by experience, of meeting the immediate needs and solving the immediate problems of the American workers. It has been developed by the trial-and-error method. It is experimental, opportunistic, pragmatic. And if you will look back over the past century and a quarter you will find that this is the only kind of labor organization that has survived and *worked* in this country. (Hoxie, 1914d, p. 143; emphasis in original).

Given the historical development of American trade unionism, it is quite evident that "socialism, before it could make any successful appeal to American workmen, had to cut loose from the ultra-revolutionists, thrust its theories into the background, and develop a program for meeting immediate needs and problems" (Hoxie, 1914d, p. 143). Socialism had, in other words, if it were to become as effective political force, to appreciate the unique psychology of the American worker and to structure its message to his purposes and demands.

THE COMMISSION ON INDUSTRIAL RELATIONS

In the closing decade of the nineteenth century and the opening decades of the twentieth, much of the effort of industrial management was directed to the "problem" of labor, focusing on the incentive wage and time management as means to produce greater worker efficiency. The evolution of the industrial firm itself created the conditions for which this form of management seemed ideal. As the firm became larger and more complex, the "managerial hierarchy" of the firm expanded apace. The managers of the firm in pursuit of ever more efficient means of production saw the solution in the specialization of tasks. Such methods as were employed, however, were typically trial-and-error. Far from producing the results intended, this overspecialization actually had the perverse effect of interfering with the efficient functioning of the organization, and led to strained relations between labor and management. What was needed was a means by which tasks could be evaluated and labor roles assigned to the end of producing a more efficiently organized firm.

Scientific Management as a Solution to the Problem: Taylorism

In 1895, Frederick Winslow Taylor read before the American Society of Mechanical Engineers a paper entitled "A Piece-Rate System," in which he argued that, through the use of greater efficiencies in task management, the "wage problem" and hence the "labor problem" might be solved – piece-rates could be replaced by fixed wages, based on efficiency. This was followed in 1903 by *Shop Management*, which laid the foundations of the new field of "scientific" management,[51] the purpose of which was to reorganize the *entire* productive apparatus of the firm on a rational, scientific basis.[52] Other systems soon followed, including Harrington Emerson's *Efficiency as a Basis for Operation and Wages* (1910), and Henry Laurence Gantt's *Work, Wages, and Profits* (1910). Taylor continued refining his treatment of the subject, publishing in 1911 *The Principles of Scientific Management*, which eventually became the standard reference; Louis Dembitz Brandeis (later a justice of the U.S. Supreme Court) published *Scientific Management and Railroads* that same year, essentially an edited portion of a brief presented to the Interstate Commerce Commission (3 January 1911). In 1912, Frank Bunker Gilbreth published *Primer of Scientific Management*, which included a Preface by Brandeis.[53]

In essentials, scientific management, as presented by Taylor et al., is a comprehensive approach to the promotion of systemic industrial efficiency, an approach developed by the engineer.[54] It is not "scientific," as that term is generally understood.[55] As Forrst Cardullo, a Cornell University mechanical engineer, defines it, scientific management[56].

> aims at the careful investigation of every problem of the industrial world in order to determine its best solution. It is not content to rely upon records, or upon the judgment of the most experienced workman. It brings to its aid all the resources of science. Every possible method of performing a piece of work is carefully analyzed and the best elements of all of the methods combined in order to form a new method. Having established the best methods of work, scientific management then instructs the workman how best to perform his task, and offers an incentive to do it in the prescribed manner. (Cardullo, 1912, p. 51)

Scientific management, especially in the form advanced by Taylor, offers a means by which the inefficiencies in production and management brought about by competition may best be ameliorated – without recourse to legislative interference. As Bruce Kaufman notes, Taylor's solution was to allow "the visible hand of the scientist and engineer to supplement and replace the invisible hand of the market" (Kaufman, 2008, p. 111). The Taylor system requires for its successful application the complete reorganization of the workplace and a change in perspective of the labor-management relation. The entire production system was to be evaluated and standardized. Every aspect of the organization was to be scrutinized, the process reduced to a set of scientifically adduced rules, capital equipment standardized throughout the workplace, logistics streamlined for more efficient coordination, and workers trained to ensure a thorough familiarity with the new production processes and techniques. Above all, labor-management cooperation was to be secured, with the worker "given as far as possible the highest class of work for which his brains and physique fit him" (Taylor, 1903, p. 1347; also Nyland, 1996, pp. 986–988).[57] Through the application of such methods of control, output could be dramatically increased, efficiencies realized, and the "labor problem" finally addressed.

Yet, despite the promise of increased industrial efficiency through the employment of methods designed to produce a more competent allocation of capital and labor, scientific management, for many reasons, some having little to do with the process as envisioned by its promoters, did not live up to the claims of its proponents. Its detractors, first and foremost among them the leaders of organized labor, voiced their objections to the methods as they were employed in the industrial workplace. These objections and others, respecting scientific management's effects on industrial labor conditions in general, became of great concern to the political class, and ultimately proved significant in the charges of and the conclusions reached by the Congressional investigative commission.

Precipitate to Reform

On 1 October 1910, two dynamite bombs were detonated at the offices of the *Los Angeles Times*.[58] The blast ruptured natural gas lines located under the building and ignited barrels of printer's ink that had been stored in the alley.[59] Twenty people died in the explosion[60] with as many as one hundred injured, the blast and resulting fire destroying the building. So horrendous was the carnage that it was labeled the "Crime of the Century." Additional explosive devices were discovered the next day, unexploded, at the home of the editor of the *Times*, General Harrison Gray Otis, a vehement critic of organized labor, as well as the home of the secretary of the Merchants and Manufacturers' Association, Felix J. Zeehandelaar. Immediately, suspicion turned to elements associated with organized labor, as the *Times* was seen as having opposed union efforts at organizing the city's construction industry. Such a conclusion was not entirely without support – exactly a month earlier, a package of dynamite had been discovered near the annex of the Alexandria Hotel, and eight days later, another device was uncovered near the Los Angeles County Hall of Records (both of which had been erected by nonunion workers, the latter by employees of the Llewellyn Iron Works).[61] The front page of the *Times* on Sunday, 2 October, laid blame on "the Enemies of Industrial Freedom and of This Paper." "Must Blame the Unions" headlined an accompanying page one article, noting that the governor, William Gillett, himself had so maintained (Los Angeles Times, October 2, 1910, p. 1). Otis, in particular, sounded the alarm:

> I knew well enough beforehand the desperate nature of the conspiracy against my newspaper and the desperate character of some of the conspirators; yet I could not believe, until I was forced to believe, that they would go to the extremes to which they did go in the use of dynamite, resulting in the blowing up of the building and its subsequent destruction by the resultant conflagration.
>
> . . .
>
> O you anarchist scum, you cowardly murderers, you leeches upon honest labor, you midnight assassins, you whose hands are dripping with the innocent blood of your victims, you against whom the wails of poor widows and the cries of fatherless children are ascending to the Great White Throne, go mingle with the crowd on the street corners, look upon the crumbled and blackened walls, look at the ruins wherein are buried the calcined remains of those whom you murdered. (*Los Angeles Times*, October 2, 1910, p. 2)

Samuel Gompers and other union officials denied any such involvement by organized labor; others, such as Eugene V. Debs, asserted the management of the *Times* may have been responsible. Focus quickly fell on members of the International Association of Bridge and Structural Iron Workers, who had been suspected of a series of dynamitings in the Los Angeles area and elsewhere.[62] On 14 April 2011, James B. McNamara and Ortie McManigal, members of the Iron Workers' union, were arrested in Detroit; on 22 April, John J. McNamara, secretary-treasurer of the union, was arrested at his office in Indianapolis. The three were extradited to Los Angeles on 26 April to stand trial for the bombings. McManigal confessed, implicating the McNamara brothers in the crime. Initially, the unions insisted the brothers were innocent of the charges; famed defense attorney Clarence Darrow was retained to lead the defense effort. Public opinion sided with the McNamaras. Alternative theories were offered by union officials, the Socialist press, and others as to the source of the explosion, including a gas leak at the plant and a conspiracy orchestrated by Otis.[63] A Grand Jury, however, concluded otherwise, declaring "that the explosive used was one of high power, such as nitro-glycerine, or a product of nitro-glycerine ...." Similar devices had been discovered at the Otis and Zeehandelaar homes. Further, the Grand Jury determined that the testimony of witnesses showed "that the perpetrators and instigators of this terrible catastrophe have been members of labor unions and officials and organizers therein, and, moreover, intimately associated and connected with certain leaders and high officials of labor unions," while absolving the labor organizations themselves of any complicity (Final Report of the Los Angeles County Grand Jury).

As it became clear that the case could not be won – they had allegedly admitted guilt to journalist Lincoln Steffens – Darrow sought a plea bargain, hoping to gain some leniency in sentencing, but the prosecution demanded the McNamara's admit guilt in open court.[64] (Darrow himself had been accused of bribing a juror, which, although he denied the charge, created an additional obstacle). On 1 December 1911, James McNamara pleaded guilty to the bombing and the deaths of the twenty employees of the *Times*, while John McNamara pleaded guilty to a separate incident, the dynamiting on 25 December 1910 of the Llewellyn Iron Works.

The bombing outraged the public, leading to calls for a federal investigation into the underlying causes of industrial unrest. Writing in a special issue of *The Survey*, a publication of the Charity Organization Society of the City of New York, "The Larger Aspects of the McNamara Case," Columbia University economist Edwin R. A. Seligman condemned both "the extreme conservatives in the capitalist class who push their individualism to the point of opposing labor unions as such, and who are endeavoring wholly to eliminate organized labor from the industrial field," and "the extremists in the labor ranks, like the Socialists, who incessantly preach the inevitability of class conflict and the coming of the social revolution" (Seligman, 1911, p. 1419). University of Wisconsin sociologist Edward Alsworth Ross declared, "[o]rganized labor must pitilessly rid itself of the terrorists," while adding, "how laborers fare in their dealings with employers is not *their* question only; it is *our* question." He then advocated "the free use of rational laws to better the lot of labor," and included among these, limitations on the "vast influx of immigrants, which obliges American workingmen to sell their labor in an open market, while the rest of us dispose of our services in a naturally protected market" (Ross, 1911, p. 1425; emphasis in original). In that same special issue, Hoxie opined that the bombing "was not merely the isolated act of an irresponsible pervert, but was the outcome of conditions which inhere in the American industrial and social situation." The solution involves instructing workers on the difference between unionism and "predatory unionism," and how to discriminate between the two, and instructing the employer on "the modern theory of rights," such that he is "wrenched loose from his narrow feudalistic absolutism." In addition, political action may be necessary, including the establishment of "a strong labor party which can be depended upon to voice labor's attitude and to work effectively for remedial legislation in its interests" (Hoxie, 1911b, pp. 1425–1426).

The Commission

The social reformers' demands for an investigatory commission resulted in a petition, organized by members of the Committee on Standards of Living and Labor of the National Conference of Charities and Corrections, printed in *The Survey* and presented to President William Howard Taft on 30 December 1911. Among the twenty-eight signatories were businessman Henry Morgenthau, Rabbi Stephen S. Wise, Minister John Haynes Holmes (a co-founder of the NAACP and the ACLU), social reformer Florence Kelley, economist Edwin Seligman, banker and philanthropist George Foster Peabody, lawyer Louis D. Brandeis, and the Reverend Lyman Abbott.[65] (The petition was reprinted in *The Chautauquan* (March 1912) and several union publications, including *The Bricklayer, Mason and Plasterer* (March 1912) and *The American Federationist* (February 1912), by which time the number of signatories had increased to forty-one, and included such figures as activist Jane Addams, economists Thomas Nixon Carver, Frank A. Fetter, Irving Fisher, Simon N. Patten, Jeremiah W. Jenks, and Alvin S. Johnson, sociologist Edward Alsworth Ross, and legal scholar Ernst Freund.) Accepting the guilt of the McNamaras, there is still the question as to "what happened, is happening, and may happen to workmen who did not and would not use dynamite as a method to secure their ends." The laws respecting labor, as they perceived them, had been enacted to account for conditions of a different age and time, but the changes in the American industrial landscape that had taken place since had "been dominated by the readily mobilized forces and influences controlled by capital." This domination of the legal process by the owners of capital is, in part at least, responsible for the "serious distrust which has come to be felt by great masses of workers toward the fabric of our law and the structure and control of the machinery through which we apply it." Justice for the industrial worker demands equal protection of the laws, to ensure to them the same legal defenses enjoyed by the owners of the means of production. To this end, the petitioners requested the establishment of a commission the purpose of which would be to investigate the conditions of labor, the legal status of trade unions, the state of labor law, the costs of strikes and other actions of organized labor, the relations of unions and employer associations, and the arbitration system. In summation, the petitioners offer a plea:

> Today, as fifty years ago, a house divided against itself cannot stand. We have yet to solve the problems of democracy in its industrial relationships and to solve them along democratic lines. On the same vitality, the same idealism, the same constructive justice of the people which stood the stress of Lincoln's time, we ground our confidence in petitioning the President and Congress of the United States to appoint a commission to investigate, study, and consider the grave problems of internal statesmanship herein set forth. (Petition to the President, 1911, pp. 1430–1431)

President Taft made a formal request to Congress on 2 February 1912. On 23 August 1912, the United States Congress passed legislation,[66] signed by the President, authorizing the establishment of the United States Commission on Industrial Relations to investigate labor conditions in American industrial plants and to examine the entire scope of industrial relations. The next step would prove to be far more difficult, as it involved the selection of the members of the Commission.[67] Political considerations were, as one might expect, to determine the composition. On 17 December 1912, Taft submitted to the Congress his list of nominees. The list included three representatives of labor – James O'Connell and John B. Lennon, both of the American Federation of Labor, and Austin B. Garretson, a member of the Order of Railway Conductors; three representatives of business – Ferdinand C. Schwedtman, an engineer and businessman from St. Louis, Adolph Lewisohn, a financier from New York, and Frederic A. Delano, president of the Wabash Railroad (and uncle of Franklin D. Roosevelt); and three at-large representatives of the public – Charles S. Barrett, a Democrat from Georgia, president of the Farmer's National Union, George B. Chandler of Connecticut, an agent of the American Book Company, and, as Chair of the Commission, Senator George B. Sutherland, a Republican from Utah. But Taft was unable to get the nominees through the confirmation process before the end of his term, as the Democrats effectively filibustered the nominations. Woodrow Wilson took office in March 1913 and, with suggestions from all quarters and mindful of the political repercussions of his decision, on 26 June announced his selection of nominees for the Commission. He retained Taft's appointees representing the interests of labor (as they were Democrats and pro-union) as well as Frederic Delano, and nominated five others, all considered amenable to Senate Democrats – two representatives of management (Harris Weinstock, a businessman from California, and Samuel Thruston Ballard, a flour mill owner from Kentucky) and two at-large members representing the public (Democrat party fund-raiser Florence Harriman and University of Wisconsin economist John R. Commons). (On 17 March 1915, Delano resigned to take a position at the Federal Reserve Board, and was replaced by Richard H. Aishton, president of the Chicago and Northwestern Railway Company.) The ninth member of the panel was the Chairman, labor lawyer Frank P. Walsh of Kansas City,[68] who was offered the position by Wilson after it had been turned down by Louis Brandeis.

The task of the Commission, as established in the Congressional authorization, was quite wide-ranging, encompassing virtually every aspect of the labor question, as well as an unrelated charge respecting limitations on Asian immigration. As expressed in the Statute, its mandate was to

> inquire into the general condition of labor in the principal industries of the United States including agriculture, and especially in those which are carried on in corporate forms; into existing relations between employers and employees; into the effect of industrial conditions on public welfare and into the rights and powers of the community to deal therewith; into the conditions of sanitation and safety of employees and the provisions for protecting the life, limb, and health of the employees; into the growth of associations of employers and of wage earners and the effect of such associations upon the relations between employers and employees; into the extent and results of methods of collective bargaining, into any methods which have been tried in any State or in foreign countries for maintaining mutually satisfactory relations between employees and

employers; into methods for avoiding or adjusting labor disputes through peaceful and conciliatory mediation and negotiations; into the scope, methods, and resources of existing bureaus of labor and into possible ways of increasing their usefulness; into the question of smuggling or other illegal entry of Asiatics into the United States or its insular possessions, and of the methods by which such Asiatics have gained and are gaining such admission, and shall report to Congress as speedily as possible with such recommendation as said commission may think proper to prevent such smuggling and illegal entry. The commission shall seek to discover the underlying causes of dissatisfaction in the industrial situation and report its conclusions thereon. (Statutes at Large, 1912, Ch.351, p. 416)

Among the charges assigned the Commission on Industrial Relations was an examination of the effects on labor of scientific management. While scientific management had not been a factor in the violence in Los Angeles, it had been of consequence in strike actions and had been the focus of previous Congressional hearings. On 11 August 1911, workers at the federal arsenal at Watertown, Massachusetts, members of the International Molders' Union, went on a "sanctioned strike" to protest the imposition of the Taylor system "and the discharge of a member who had resented the imposition of unjust and humiliating conditions upon him," such being the use by an efficiency expert of a stopwatch.[69] With assurances that the strikers and the discharged workers would be reinstated, on 18 August the strike ended (Frey, 1911, p. 695). Yet the actions of the workers were to have significant consequences in regards to the Taylor system of scientific management – the House of Representatives established a Special Committee to investigate the charges, and held hearings on the matter from 4 October 1911 to 12 February 1912. The unanimous conclusion of the Special Committee, submitted on 9 March 1912, was that neither the Taylor system or any other of the systems of scientific management had been in application for a long enough period to have had any determinable effect "on the health and pay of employees" or "on wages and labor cost" (Report of the Chief of Ordnance, U.S. Army, 1913, Appendix I, p. 80). Thus, no recommendation for legislative action was made.[70]

The newly organized Commission on Industrial Relations would continue the inquiry begun earlier by the Special Committee of the House. The decision to include scientific management among the topics of investigation was the idea of Charles V. McCarthy, of the Wisconsin Legislative Reference Library. McCarthy had come to the Commission following the resignation of economist William Jett Lauck, and sought to expand its scope, increasing the number of research divisions from four to nine, each under the direction of an expert in the area (Adams, 1966, pp. 205–206). The Research Division would then function as an independent fact-finding arm, similar in nature to McCarthy's "Wisconsin Idea." One area of special interest was that of the impact of scientific management. McCarthy convinced Commons that the Commission should be given a more complete knowledge of the workings of the Taylor system and other approaches to scientific management, to be made aware of the positive contributions (Nyland, 1996, pp. 997–998). Commons himself had believed this issue to have been "at that time, the most 'irrepressible conflict' before the Commission" (Commons, 1934, p. 178). Through four days of hearings on the subject in April 1914, the Commission heard testimony by representatives of management and labor respecting the claims of the proponents and opponents of scientific management. Following the hearings, the Commission authorized a more exhaustive investigation, to be undertaken under the supervision of Hoxie,[71] accompanied by Robert G. Valentine, an "Industrial Counselor" who (ostensibly) represented the interests of the employers and the scientific managers (but was, in fact, the choice of Commons), and John P. Frey, editor of the *International Molders' Journal*, nominated by the American Federation of Labor to represent the interests of labor. In all, from January to April 1915, a total of thirty-five "shops and systematizing concerns" were investigated, and interviews were conducted with experts in scientific management and employers, "almost without exception, those designated by authorities on scientific management, such as Messrs. Taylor, Gantt, and Emerson, as the *best* representatives of the actual results of scientific management."[72] Any "defects and shortcomings pointed out hereinafter are, therefore, characteristic of the system under the most favorable conditions."[73] The report by Hoxie, Valentine, and Frey on the impact of scientific management was "agreed upon without exceptions" (Commission on Industrial Relations, 1915, p. 209; emphasis in original).[74] The Commission, however, chose not to print it.

Hoxie presented to Commons at the commencement of his investigation "an outline analysis and questionnaire of the whole subject, indicating the points to be investigated," which Commons later described as having been "as comprehensive and detailed an outline of an investigation" as he had seen, before or since (Commons, 1934, p. 179).[75] Yet before Hoxie's investigation could be completed, he and others whose appointments had been made by McCarthy and secured by Commons were dismissed by Walsh. As told by Adams, the reason for the dismissals centered on a dispute between Walsh and McCarthy over funding and whether research or continued Congressional hearings should have priority. With the Commission in need of additional funds from Congress to continue its investigations, which, given the political climate and the fact that Congress had already authorized additional funds, could not be guaranteed, McCarthy suggested focusing on research and curtailing the hearings. This Walsh rejected, opting instead to terminate McCarthy and his Wisconsin Idea specialists (Adams, 1966, pp. 208–209).[76]

Another reason given for the dismissals, this by Nyland, centered on Walsh's disenchantment with Commons' perceived support of the employers and McCarthy's willingness to listen to the position of the advocates of scientific management, specifically Taylor – Commons had appointed McCarthy as Director of Research in June 1914, and McCarthy had insisted, as had Hoxie, on cooperating with Taylor in the investigation. Commons, while sympathetic to the demands of labor, held that the respective roles of employer and employee must be separate – the responsibility for production must rest solely with the employer[77] – and in the bargaining process, they must meet as equals; the role of the State should be restricted to that of arbiter of labor disputes, favoring the interests of neither labor nor capital. This, as he himself recognized, essentially placed him in league with the employer representatives.[78] Further, Commons by this time had become fearful of the socialistic influences that seemed to be gaining support within the unionist movement, which threatened what he believed were the very ideals of the movement.[79] Walsh, on the other hand, decidedly pro-union, was intent upon making the Report not an investigation into scientific management, but rather an indictment of the capitalist production system, "to expose the oppression workers suffered under capitalism" (Nyland, 1996, pp. 1003–1005).[80]

Hoxie's dismissal had a devastating impact on his mental health, and Commons was concerned for his welfare. As Commons describes the events that followed:

> After his dismissal from the Commission, he [Hoxie] came to me at Madison, with all of his manuscripts, his notes, and his outline. He was in a nervous and incoherent state of mind. I was immediately alarmed. I went over all his material with him, explaining that he had the first really scientific study of scientific management, and it would be a serious misfortune if he did not publish as much of it as was already prepared. I promised to get a publisher for him, but he was worried about the share of the costs imposed upon him. Practically all of his notes on unfinished parts of his outline we eliminated. He went home seemingly cheerful, and put together what was already prepared, although he was anxious because he dreaded criticism in that he had not finished a complete piece of scientific work according to his ideals of workmanship. I think I made a mistake, which ended in his suicide. (Commons, 1934, p. 179)

Commons did succeed in convincing D. Appleton and Company to publish "what I thought were the high-grade pieces of work left unfinished by the staff of the Industrial Relations Commission" (Commons, 1934, p. 179). The extended study, despite Hoxie's apprehensions and under pressure from Commons, was published in 1915 under the title *Scientific Management and Labor*.[81]

HOXIE'S REPORT: SCIENTIFIC MANAGEMENT AND LABOR

Prior to the hearings conducted by the Commission on Industrial Relations, Hoxie published a piece in *The Survey* with the title "Springs of Conflicting Action," in which he restates the charge of the Commission:

> The mandate is specific and inclusive. It directs the commission to inquire into the most vital objective aspects of the labor problem, including labor conditions generally, the individual relations between employers and employes, the growth and methods of unions and employers' associations, the effect of these conditions, relations, and associations on public welfare, the methods for avoiding labor disputes and maintaining satisfactory relations between employers and employes, and the methods, rights and powers of the community in dealing with the labor problem. (Hoxie, 1913a, p. 580)

While in the achievement of these ends the Commission "will doubtless perform a useful social service," it will nonetheless, should it confine itself to these and these alone, "fail signally of meeting the most vital want of the community and the demands of those who wrought most intelligently for its creation" (Hoxie, 1913a, p. 580). The wants and needs of the community as Hoxie interprets them are two – "the eradication of the industrial evils which beset our working people," and "the ridding of American society from industrial warfare, ... seen especially in the McNamara incident and in the rise in this country of syndicalistic organization, ideals and methods." Addressing these wants and needs demands not merely a recitation of facts regarding employment, wages, hours, productivity, safety, and the right to work, and the motives behind the need of workers to organize, to control the output of the firm and the industry, to limit entry into the profession, and to burden the employer with "minute regulations and restriction," facts objectively ascertained, but as well "a profound study of the causes of these facts." Conflicts between labor and capital are due not to "ignorance, selfishness or perversity" on the part of one or the other, but "are due largely to contradictory notions of rights and justice, which inevitably develop in the diverse industrial environments created for worker and employer by modern machine industry" (p. 580). The problem to which the Commission must address itself, then, is not a labor problem or a management problem, but a *social* problem.

The Objective of Hoxie's Report

In the Preface to *Scientific Management and Labor* (1915), Hoxie states his research objective quite clearly: "The discussion which follows is for the most part an attempt to test Mr. Taylor's claims respecting scientific management in its relations to labor, the claims of Mr. Gantt and Mr. Emerson being considered only in so far as they differ from those of Mr. Taylor." The expressed purpose is not "to uphold or to condemn scientific management or either party to the controversy concerning it," but rather is "simply to discover and to set forth the facts and the truth, in the hope of dispelling misconceptions and misunderstandings, that a basis may be found for constructive effort in the interests of all concerned" (Hoxie, 1915, pp. v-vi). Again, as he proved in his work on trade unionism, Hoxie's professed standard is to approach the study of the impact on labor of scientific management with the dispassionate objectivity of the scientist.[82] As such, the emphasis is to be upon "the possible benefits of scientific management, its actual results thus far in practice, together with their causes, and its fundamental relation to labor welfare." Hoxie is not, however, so naïve as to believe that his audience would accept his statement without reservations, or that, in places, his personal feelings would not color his professional judgment. Though acknowledging that, in proceeding along the established lines, the "treatment may give to particular portions of the study an air of partisanship," one should consider the work in its entirety. Approaching the study with an open mind, "the unbiased reader will reserve judgments to the end" (p. vi).

Hoxie did not, however, notwithstanding his best efforts, regard *Scientific Management and Labor* to be "a complete consideration of all the important phases of the subject," despite the perceived need for just such an effort. Specifically, he admits at the outset that "[s]ome vital matters have been discussed very briefly and one very important topic – unfounded and unproved trade union charges against scientific management – has been omitted altogether" (He does, however, express a hope to address in a follow-up study "all aspects of the subject fully and to present the specific evidence which is necessarily omitted here ...") (Hoxie, 1915, p. vi).[83] It may well have been the failure to produce a more comprehensive work, to address matters considered beyond the scope of the inquiry, which proved troublesome for the study and for Hoxie himself.

The study itself was to be governed by two standards. First, scientific management was to be judged by its *results*, not by its *claims* or by the charges of its opponents. The proof rather would lie in the manner in which the system of industrial management was in fact applied, and not with whether the application was faithful and true in every particular to the ideal. "Scientific management ... is like any other thing in the social or material world. It is what it is in fact, and not what the ideals or theories of its advocates or opponents would have it to be." Even granting Taylor's admonition, "that if any principle of scientific management which he has laid down is violated, scientific management ceases to exist," the principle itself must nonetheless be judged by its *effects*, especially as they pertain to the welfare of the workers (Hoxie, 1915, pp. 4–5).

The second standard, consistent with the first claim, regards the *features* of scientific management that must be considered part and parcel of the technique, whether acknowledged by the theorists and advocates or not. In other words, account must be taken of the shared characteristics of the establishments adhering to scientific management principles, characteristics that may or may not correspond with the ideal. Thus, as an example, if the establishments employing the methods of scientific management stress "welfare work," and "eliminate the spirit and the means for the expression of democracy, then welfare work must be considered a part of scientific management, and the absence of democracy a feature of it" (Hoxie, 1915, p. 5).[84] Taylor may disagree vociferously with such a portrayal, but ultimately the proof lies in the application.

Claims of Management

Hoxie begins the investigative portion of his study by delineating the arguments made by the proponents of scientific management, specifically as it had been developed by Taylor. Acknowledging important differences between the systems of Taylor, Gantt, and Emerson, he justifies his decision to focus attention on the Taylor system on the grounds that it was the most complete, it had been applied with the greatest consistency and fidelity, and "it is to the Taylor system that organized labor has most generally and most strenuously objected." Taylor was, after all, the acknowledged founder of scientific management, having literally written the book on the subject, and the Taylor system had come to be accepted as "scientific management par excellence," Taylorism and scientific management seeming synonymous (Hoxie, 1915, p. 7).

Taylor had asserted that the "labor claims of scientific management" amounted to forty general points. Hoxie, in an effort to simplify so as to minimize superfluity, reduces this classification to six generalizations:

(1) *Definition*: "Scientific management is a system devised by industrial engineers for the purpose of subserving the common interests of employers, workmen, and society at large, through the elimination of avoidable wastes, the general improvement of the processes and methods of production, and the just and scientific distribution of the product."
(2) *Principles*: There exists a "harmony of interests" between management and labor, such that both recognize that lower labor costs redound to higher wages and better working conditions.
(3) *Relation to Fact and Law*: In insisting on the employment of scientific principles in the management of organizations, "the government of fact and law" replaces "the rule of force and opinion," establishing "a code of natural laws equally binding upon employers and workmen."
(4) *Character of Scientific Management*: Scientific management is not only "scientific," but is also "democratic." The use of time and motion analysis uncovered "the great mass of laws governing the easiest and most productive movements of men." This "great code ... completely controls the acts of the management as well as those of the workmen." Reward is based on efficiency and individual effort; workers with different capacities are assigned tasks that take advantage of these differences. The selection procedure provides a more effective basis for the allocation of resources dedicated to training. As performance is standardized, worker fatigue is reduced; as workers are deemed individuals and not simply part of a collective, arbitrary decisions (of foremen or union bosses) are replaced by the rule of law. Grievances are settled through recourse to "the great code of laws which has been developed and which must satisfy both sides." The workplace as a result becomes more democratic.
(5) *Efficiency*: As it increases productive efficiency through standardization, scientific management promotes expanded training, which allows the workers to increase their skills and hence become more proficient at their tasks and "rationalizes" the management function, resulting in the elimination of waste. With standardization, training can focus on instilling in workers "traditional craft knowledge," skills that had atrophied

under the old system of industrial management. Each worker becomes responsible for his own task, promoting a greater sense of individual accomplishment.

(6) *Labor welfare*: Scientific management "tends to prevent the degradation and displacement of skilled labor"; rewards employees for suggesting better techniques of shop management; opens opportunities for promotion; provides workers with intellectual and physical stimulation, "and promotes their self-reliance and individuality"; prevents the imposition of arbitrary work rules; increases wages, while reducing hours of work; provides a spirit of community between management and labor; makes trade unions and collective bargaining unnecessary, as protection of the workers is a priority, and thus lessens the chance of strikes and industrial unrest. (Hoxie, 1915, pp. 8–11)

Claims of Labor

In contrast to the claims of management, which were for the most part accepted as a reasonable representation, trade unions did not have a coherent and agreed-upon position regarding scientific management; Hoxie finds unions to be anything but united in their attitude, but rather they appear "essentially opportunistic," with their organization "little more than a loose affiliation of sovereign bodies." This attitude evidently derives from his earlier analyses of the trade union movement. He does, however regard the executive council of the American Federation of Labor, by this time the dominant representative voice of mainstream unionism, as uniquely able to "claim the right to voice the prevailing sentiment of organized labor in America." Although the executive council did not have a prepared statement regarding objections to scientific management, Hoxie was able to prepare such a statement with their participation, contributions, and approval (Hoxie, 1915, pp. 13–14).

Hoxie synthesizes the labor position, as he had that of management, into six general claims:

(1) *Definition*: Organized labor understands "scientific management" to refer to specific "efficiency systems" that had been designed in the manner suggested by Taylor, Gantt, and Emerson. Labor further distinguishes "scientific management" from "science in management," supporting the latter insofar as it is concerned with reductions in waste and the promotion of greater efficiencies in production, the use of

improved machinery to the end of greater output, and more efficient management practices.

(2) *Labor welfare*: Scientific management, as the unions understand it, "is a device employed for the purpose of increasing production and profits; and tends to eliminate consideration for the character, rights and welfare of the employees." It is seen as dehumanizing workers and reducing them to the status of adjuncts of machines and tools. By speeding up the production process, it drives workers to the limits of their energy and holds each worker to unrealistic standards without regard to human variability and legitimate delays. Through extreme specialization, it "degrades" and "displaces" the skilled worker, placing him in direct competition with the unskilled, thus reducing the bargaining power of labor; it replaces the daily wage with piece-rates and bonuses, and holds to a standard unrelated to the cost of living; it demands longer hours, but instills uncertainty of employment; and finally it reduces tasks to "monotonous routine," which has the effect of suppressing initiative and stunting intellectual development.

(3) *Industrial democracy*: Scientific management is profoundly undemocratic, as it produces "industrial autocracy," to the extent that fairness is defined by the employer. The skills, judgment, and knowledge of the workers now become the property of the manager; workers have little say in task management or wage setting; grievances go unheard; cooperation and group solidarity disappear; and union cohesion and collective bargaining are destroyed.

(4) *Scientific nature of scientific management*: Scientific management is inherently "unscientific," as it "deals with human beings as it does with inanimate machines," and thus "violates the fundamental principles of human nature by ignoring habits, temperament, and traditions of work and tends to minimize the acquired skill of the workers." It offers no scientific justification for task assignments or for the calculation of the wage rate. Further, it regards production only, and so does not take into account distribution, and thus "violates and indefinitely postpones the application of the fundamental principle of justice to distribution."

(5) *Efficiency*: Scientific management is "fundamentally inefficient," as the emphasis is on quantity of output, and not quality.

(6) *Worker solidarity*: Scientific management destroys worker solidarity, which exacerbates the problem of labor unrest. Harmonious and cooperative relations among workers devolve into group antagonism. (Hoxie, 1915, pp. 15–19)

Benefits of Scientific Management

Before reporting on the results of his investigation into shops employing scientific management techniques, Hoxie proffers a "critical examination" of the benefits that might entice forms to institute such measures, benefits Taylorists claim as consequences of its proper application. Wage increases, improvements in the conditions of work and in standards of living, and in the overall economic progress of society as a whole were all directly attributable to increased productive efficiency and the expansion of industrial output. This, he avers, is undeniable. While unions may achieve some gains in wages, working conditions, and living standards through collective bargaining, "the community as a whole, including all classes of labor, can consume more and live better only through an increase in the goods produced." To achieve the increased level of output, firms must seek to lower the costs of production, one method of so doing being to reduce the costs of labor. This was the mantra of the scientific management movement, specifically as expressed by Taylor and the promoters of the Taylor system. Lower labor costs allow higher wages as a consequence of lower production costs, which results in an increase in industrial output and in overall living standards. One must conclude, then, that scientific management has the *potential* to produce benefits not merely to the employers, but to the workers and to the nation and society at large. "In so far, then, as scientific management affords opportunities for lower costs and increased production without adding to the burden of the workers in exhausting effort, long hours or inferior working conditions, it creates the possibility of very real and substantial benefits to labor and to society" (Hoxie, 1915, pp. 20–21).

The difficulty manifests in implementation. Scientific management cannot simply be incorporated into an antiquated production system; there needs first to be standardization and enhancement of the capital equipment and a reorganization of the managerial and production structures before its methods can be applied effectively to the promotion of labor efficiency. This includes the rearrangement of the production process so as to avoid delays (such as the establishment of continuous straight line production), the elimination of wasted motions and activities, improved inventory control, stock, purchasing, and sales management, and better accounting methods, all of which promise great possibilities for increased production at lower cost "without any necessary addition to the burden of the workers in exhausting effort, long hours or inferior conditions of employment" (Hoxie, 1915, pp. 21–22).

In addition to the efficiency advantages obtained through an improvement of the capital stock and a reorganization of the methods of production, by standardizing tasks and rates of pay, scientific management holds the possibility of improving the conditions of workers and their relation with management; this is, in a sense, one of its chief goals. For labor to decry "scientific management" while lauding "science in management" is merely an evasion, as "scientific management, at its best, is not only a systematic search for scientific productive methods, but is broad enough to include all that science in management demonstrates to be productively most efficient." This is true, "its peculiar methods of dealing with labor" notwithstanding. The very nature of the process of standardization in tasks as well as rates of remuneration and efficiencies in production redounds to the benefit of labor (Hoxie, 1915, p. 23).

The proponents of scientific management have "incessantly proclaimed the doctrine that only through the strict maintenance of rates and standardized conditions of employment, and through fair and liberal dealing with labor, can employers hope to escape from the slough of inefficiency and the evils of cut-throat competition" (Hoxie, 1915, pp. 23–24). While the views of management and of organized labor at times seem almost diametrically opposed, with the institution of standards seen as reflecting a trade-off between equity and efficiency, labor demanding that, despite the changes in the methods of production, existing standards and conditions be maintained, all the while scientific management experts insisting upon "progressive alteration," it is nonetheless the case that "the adherence of scientific management to the ideal of the strict maintenance of standard conditions of work and pay as long as the efficiency conditions are not altered, marks a distinct advance in the interests of labor over the ideals which have been apt to govern the relations of employers to organized labor" (p. 24).[85] Even if, in practice, scientific management does not live up to the claim of its proponents, Hoxie argues, this calls not for its rejection as a principle of management, but rather for "intelligent social action to eliminate that which is detrimental and to supplement and control that which is beneficial to all." Scientific management, after all, "is not one rigid and indivisible whole which must be accepted or rejected as it is, but is rather an experimental and developing entity, which can be modified and molded if its character and implications are thoroughly understood" (p. 25).

The Application of Scientific Management Principles

Hoxie's research revealed divergences between the principle and the performance, the assumptions of the scientific managers "completely shattered by first-hand study of the facts." The examination of shops and plants[86] demonstrated to Hoxie the "manifold diversity" and "striking incompleteness" of the *practice* of scientific management from the *theory* of scientific management (Hoxie, 1915, p. 26). This proved to be a critical concession, one that Taylor himself had insisted would validate his claims of inconsistencies in the empirical application of his principles. Hoxie could find among the shops investigated not one

> which could be said to represent fully and faithfully the Taylor system as presented in the treatise on 'Shop Management'; no representative of the Gantt system was encountered, complete and unmixed with alien elements; no shop was discovered wherein the Emerson ideals were completely demonstrated and held full sway, and no two shops were found in which identically or even approximately the same policies and methods were established and adhered to throughout. (Hoxie, 1915, p. 26)

Since this failure to adhere to the principles as set forth by the leading theorists of scientific management was found in shops specially designated as representative by Taylor, Gantt, and Emerson, the actual variation in practice had to be truly immense. "It would appear in fact that scientific management in practice is never fully installed, the system never wholly conformable with the ideals and principles laid down by the leaders, and that each management has to some extent at least its own peculiar viewpoint and its own peculiar policies and methods which prevail in the installation and operation of the system" (Hoxie, 1915, p. 26). While, in general, the *ideals* of scientific management may be seen to be acknowledged by the managers of the enterprises, in practice, certain integral elements were delayed, neglected, or incompletely applied, while others were stressed out of proportion.[87]

Hoxie then spends the next 88 pages detailing what appear to be the claims of the proponents of scientific management and the manner in which they diverge from practice in the shops under investigation.[88] Among the topics are: (1) failure to adhere to the order and completeness of the process by which the principles are installed; (2) retention of the old foreman structure; (3) retention of the old practices of employee selection and hiring; (4) failure to apply scientific methods of training and "occupational adaptation" such as would allow workers to be assigned those tasks for which they are most qualified and proficient; (5) subjective and arbitrary application of time and motion studies, allowing a great degree of diversity, inaccuracy, injustice, and prejudice in application; (6) failure to implement scientific rate making (which replaces the bargained wage with a combination of base or day wages and efficiency wages, based on the specific task in question); (7) failure to safeguard the welfare of the workers by providing protection from over-exertion resulting from inadequate training, the use of substandard, inadequate or obsolete equipment, and inattention to the problem of worker fatigue in task setting; (8) failure to provide adequate opportunities for promotion; (9) setting of unrealizable goals for which failure to meet resulted in punitive measures; (10) arbitrary and more rapid discharge of workers; (11) an autocratic mentality on the part of employers and managers, contrary to the claims of scientific management as promoting industrial democracy (Hoxie, 1915, pp. 25–112).

In general, Hoxie's investigation concludes that scientific management shops provided good safety and sanitary conditions, workers were not over-speeded, and arbitrary disciplinary authority was absent. Thus to a limited extent, at least, the claims of the proponents of scientific management appear to have been confirmed. Overall, Hoxie is not completely dismissive of the *promise* of scientific management, acknowledging "the great possible benefits of the movement," especially in respect of labor. Nor is he completely convinced of the legitimacy of the trade unionists objections. Scientific management as a practical method of industrial organization "is still in its infancy or early trial stages," and so it must be understood "that immaturity and failure to attain ideals in practice are necessary accompaniments to the development of any new industrial or social movement." Through continued evaluation of procedures, the application of scientific management may be greatly improved and its value to management and labor realized (Hoxie, 1915, p. 113).

Yet, notwithstanding his positive opinion as to the *potential* of scientific management, Hoxie warns of the need to eliminate "certain potent causes of present evil." First among these is the desire to apply the principles "outside their natural sphere." To do so implies a preconception of industrial homogeneity, and ignores the fact that "there is no single necessary or logical line of industrial development," and "no perfectly uniform set of conditions and problems in different industries or even in different shops with the same general productive output." Given that dissimilar industries will have specialized organizational and industrial production structures, one cannot expect to apply methods of scientific management without an adequate understanding of the specific problems inherent in each industry and in each shop within an industry; there is no one-size-fits-all approach to management. It "is not a ready-made garment to which it can be made easily to conform, but must be worked out by the slow and painful process of cut and try" (Hoxie, 1915, p. 113). Much of the worker resentment, notes Hoxie, is due to the inability of the managers to understand the nature of the production process and the need to tailor scientific management methods to the peculiarities of their specific operations. Blame for this indiscriminant employment of scientific management Hoxie lays at the feet of Taylor himself. Taylor's system was designed as "a system of control for application to the machine shop where the dangers of overspeeding and overfatigue are not as great as in some other industries and the human factor requires relatively less consideration in the setting of the task" (p. 114). While Taylor may have cautioned against an indiscriminant application of his methods, insisting upon the need to modify procedures in light of the peculiarities of the work environment, nonetheless,

> being an enthusiast, he proceeded at once to broad generalizations, based on his machine shop experience. He believed that he had discovered industrial laws and methods of universal applicability. And being also an idealist, he failed to distinguish between what might be and what is. His personality and his claims fired a relatively large following who, without much understanding of the subtler labor problems involved, proceeded to attempt the universal application of his methods, and these have been followed by a less intelligent and less worthy set of imitators. (Hoxie, 1915, p. 114)

A second source of "danger and evil to labor in the application of scientific management" results from the fact that the "systematizer" – the developer of the methods of scientific management – cannot control the manner in which the methods are employed. The "ideals" of the theorist and the professional may be quite opposed to the need of the manager for immediate increases in output and profit, and the financial position of the firm may not be such as to allow an adequate application of the methods.

> In such cases, which are deplorably many, the systematizer must usually forego, to a great extent, the careful preliminary improvement and standardization of machinery and processes, the adequate organization of the accounting and sales departments, and the careful development of a functional staff, things which the best authorities agree should precede the definite handling of the labor problem, and proceed immediately to task and rate setting, with results varying greatly from his mature designs and entailing almost inevitably unintended positive errors and injustices where the laborers are concerned, and absence or immature application of the means and methods designed by him for their protection and welfare. (Hoxie, 1915, p. 115)

Third, the methods of scientific management itself are such as to put efficiency and economy over the interests of labor in terms of priority. There may be little concern that "simple and crude tests" may lead to "glaring injustices" or even "open labor protest." The expert may "halt the work of installation far short of conditions which would make good the labor claims of scientific management, and content themselves with 'making allowances' which 'in their judgment' are sufficient to offset any evils and injustices which might arise out of the crudity of their tests and studies" (Hoxie, 1915, pp. 116–117).

Fourth, scientific management has become a "movement" which "is cursed with fakirs." Due to its success, there has emerged "a crowd of industrial patent medicine men," offering quick fixes under the name of "scientific management" which have nothing whatever to do with the actual procedure, to the detriment of management and labor alike. Lacking standards, scientific management as a means for industrial and social improvement has been tainted by association with charlatans (Hoxie, 1915, p. 118).

Even more fundamentally, the sponsors and supporters of scientific management have been and continue to be profoundly ignorant of the "broader humanitarian and social problems which it creates and involves, especially as these touch the character and welfare of labor" (Hoxie, 1915, p. 118). There are many reasons for this, including "the newness of their approach to the questions involved," and an ignorance of the methods of the social sciences. To this latter Hoxie devotes particular attention. The practitioners of scientific management "seem to be developing their economic and social theories, in fact, almost wholly on the basis of their own experience and of the simple, fundamental and general assumptions which economists and social scientists generally have tried out and abandoned."

> Problems which are to the modern social scientists complex and enormously difficult – at present unsolvable – appear to them simple, and they rush to solutions, conclusions and claims, deduced from narrow, absolutistic assumptions, which have no warrant in fact. This awakening to economic and social problems by the engineers and scientific management employers is, in itself, a most hopeful sign. They are close to the practical problems of industry. Their efforts seem bound in the end to correct economic errors and to enrich economic thought. But, in the present, the tendency is to rush in boldly with crude statements of 'laws' and 'solutions' and claims that could be made good only on the basis of much that social science at its best has as yet not attained. (Hoxie, 1915, pp. 119–120)

Impact of Scientific Management on Labor Welfare

Distilling the "inherent characteristics of scientific management and its more ultimate effects upon labor and labor welfare," Hoxie views the use of scientific management principles as having a deleterious effect, primarily as a result of specialization of tasks. "Functional foremanship," for example, reduces the worker to a mere appendage of the machine. Where once the worker could exercise initiative and call on his skills and knowledge in operating and maintaining the machinery of his trade, performing "manual and mental labor as the result of his craft knowledge and skill," under scientific management, he is little more than "a machine tender," working with a process designed to "discourage experimentation." In every phase of the process, tasks are handled by specialists, functionaries, each focusing on one specific aspect. "Functional foremanship projects the managerial activity down into every phase of the shop work," maintaining "a more equal division of the work between the management and the men by taking from the latter many of the activities which they were formerly obliged to perform" (Hoxie, 1915, pp. 123–124).[89]

Time study, as an adjunct to functional foremanship, serves also to the specialization of the productive process. As "the chief cornerstone of all systems of scientific management," time study is applied in an effort to reduce operations as far as possible to their simplest, most elementary actions, and by so doing, allow for the most efficient operation. With operations reduced to their most elementary motions, the way is cleared for the replacement of the worker with machinery designed to perform the simplified tasks (Hoxie, 1915, pp. 124–125).

This reduction of tasks to their most elementary functions has the added effect of producing such an extreme specialization as to induce permanent, task-specific occupations – workers are no longer able to shift between tasks without risk of losing earnings, and the firm finds it difficult to reassign workers without risk of disruptions to the process. "Stimulation" is achieved through the wage structure, designed to maximize worker proficiency. Switching between tasks may result in a loss to the worker of earnings, as such may result in a decline in the overall efficiency of the line. In addition, "craft knowledge," as traditionally instilled through the apprentice system, becomes absorbed into the management of the enterprise. "The whole system, in its conception and operation, is pointed toward a universally specialized industrial régime." Finally, with its tendency "to break down existing standards and uniformities set up by the workmen, and to prevent the establishment of stable conditions of work and pay," scientific management produces a state of constant change, the introduction of new and better methods of production leading to the need for even newer and better methods. This Hoxie sees as "the special purpose and mission of this special instrument and central feature of scientific management" (Hoxie, 1915, pp. 126–127).

Yet for all the negative consequences of scientific management, Hoxie sees it as "by no means a unique force." It is simply part of a natural progression of the process of industrial growth, in which "the progress of machine industry and specialization have gone hand in hand." The increased specialization is "merely a part of the price which we have to pay for the conquest of nature and industrial development" (Hoxie, 1915, p. 128). What he finds most troubling is that scientific management, by insisting upon such extreme job specialization as to allow tasks to be performed even by the unskilled, may have the effect of destroying unionism and collective bargaining. Unskilled workers are averse to organization, which is essential for collective bargaining to be effective.[90] In addition, the dynamic of the machine process made possible by scientific management makes it difficult for there to be established any uniform conditions and standards such as would allow for worker classification, essential to the ability of the union to bargain collectively. "When the employer can constantly initiate new methods and conditions and reclassify the work and the workmen, he can evade all efforts of the union to establish and maintain definite and continuous standards of work and pay." Specifically, time and motion studies invite reclassification of tasks and workers. Combined with the "systematization of craft knowledge" and the breakdown of the apprentice system, scientific management leads perhaps inevitably to the demise not only of collective bargaining but of the trade unions as well (pp. 129–130).[91]

With respect to the impact on the worker, it appears to Hoxie as "inevitable" that the importation of methods of scientific management will lead to "the progressive degeneration of craftsmanship and the progressive degradation of skilled craftsmen," absent some other means for their continuation. The long-run impact is uncertain, but in the transition, wages must be realigned, as skilled workers are forced into competition with the unskilled and semi-skilled; this "leveling" will occur as the unskilled become more efficient and their wages increase as a result. But such efficiencies become difficult to sustain when the apprenticeship system no longer serves its former function. While scientific management in its role as systematizer of the knowledge of the productive process "tends enormously to add to the strength of capitalism," it also has the potential to make more uncertain the security of employment (Hoxie, 1915, pp. 133–134).

In the end, Hoxie sees trade unionism as persisting, even with the expanded use of the techniques of scientific management; scientific management cannot, despite the claims of its proponents, prevent strikes and other organized actions on behalf of labor. He further maintains that, given the continued existence of industrial unions and the persistence of the threat of strikes, scientific management will be regarded as "a constant menace to industrial peace." "So long as present-day unionism exists, and unionists continue to believe, as they seem warranted in doing, that scientific management means the destruction of their organizations or their present rules and regulations, unionism will doubtless continue to oppose it energetically whenever and wherever opportunity affords" (Hoxie, 1915, p. 135).[92] Yet scientific management is but the latest development in the evolution of capitalist system of production, and so "is like the progressive invention of machinery in its effect upon workers and social conditions and welfare generally." Throughout its historical development, the industrial system has witnessed the shift from the craftsman to the specialized laborer, from the skilled to the semi-skilled. Scientific management aims to continue along this evolutionary road, to include the unskilled. The solution, as Hoxie sees it, is "social supplementation and increased knowledge." This will require "a frank recognition of the trend of events and for some method of putting back into the worker's life the content which he is losing as the result of increased specialization and the abandonment of the old apprenticeship system" (Hoxie, 1915, pp. 135–136).

Reviews

Scientific Management and Labor was the only book published by Hoxie in his lifetime, and he was reluctant to do so. Only because of the insistence of Commons did he relent and agree to submit the work for publication. His apprehension proved well-founded. Hoxie's book produced only a limited number of contemporary commentaries, but these proved significant in that the general tone of one in particular may very well have led to his depression and ultimately to his suicide. Here, we will briefly mention five such reviews. Dexter Kimball's review in the *Journal of Political Economy* is generally positive but at the same time guarded. A professor of industrial engineering at Cornell University, Kimball acknowledges that Hoxie's book represents the first such attempt at evaluating scientific management "from the viewpoint of a trained economist who has had an unusual opportunity to study these new methods at first hand and as they exist in actual operation," and as such is "a most important addition to the literature of this much-debated subject" (Kimball, 1916, pp. 194–195). Hoxie's study shows that scientific management alone is but "a means of increasing productive capacity and does not carry with it a single regulative principle that automatically tends to protect the individual worker against certain results that ensue from its introduction ...." Thus one must conclude "that the distribution of the benefits flowing from improved methods cannot be left to chance, since these methods themselves afford no protection to the worker during the period of readjustment following the introduction of more economic methods." Labor cannot rely for the correction of abuses merely on the "personal good-will" of the managers (pp. 196–197). *Scientific Management and Labor* is not, then, on the whole, a study "overfavorable to scientific management," and, while its conclusions may be criticized as having "been deduced from personal opinions rather than from actual personal knowledge of the new methods," yet at the same time it must be acknowledged, with Hoxie, that any "shortcomings" as may be "are not inherent in the system but are the result often of ignorance on the part of those who are introducing these new and as yet poorly understood methods" (p. 197).

Predictably, John Commons, in his review in *The American Journal of Sociology*, finds much to praise in *Scientific Management and Labor*. Here, Commons clearly lays out his perception of the extent of the threat scientific management poses to workers. Commons believes that the progress of industry had stripped skilled workers of their craft knowledge and power and transferred it to the owners of the machinery and to the unskilled workers. Scientific management represents an effort by the owners of capital to capture "the remainder of the skill which the craftsman still retains in his head and hand not yet transferred to machinery." The desire on the part of the owners of capital is to reduce the skill sets to their most elementary motions, and by so doing rob the craftsman "of his trade secrets and personal skill, on which his bargaining power and trade union depended." Further, by introducing "new and ingenious methods of payment" into the workplace, scientific management instills in the worker a feeling of alienation from his fellow laborers, undercutting worker solidarity and effectively substituting a "scientific psychology into working-class psychology." This, in Commons' view, strikes at the very heart of "distributive democracy" (Commons, 1916, pp. 688–689).

For Commons, the "scientific laws" Taylor claimed to have discovered are little more than assertions, "the same *ipse dixit* which in former days was known as 'divine law' and latterly as 'natural law.' They simply stop further discussion and that ends it." With this conclusion, Commons notes, Hoxie agrees completely. The tenets of scientific management are not objectively defined at all, but rather the result of individual judgment, and so are capable of varying with the whims of the various practitioners of the craft (Commons, 1916, p. 690).[93]

Lastly, Commons addresses Hoxie's distinction between the "democracy of science" and "democracy of equality of bargaining power." The former is "impersonal," and requires a system which is "'naturally' harmonious." If this is the true state of affairs, negotiation and bargaining become unnecessary, as each party recognizes a commonality of interests. The latter, by contrast, is what is needed in the industrial workplace, as it reflects more accurately the relative strengths and positions of workers and owners, and recognizes the essential place of the collective bargaining right. With this scientific management cannot deal (Commons, 1916, pp. 691–692).

Charles W. Mixter's[94] review for the *American Economic Review* is the most negative of the group, and the most controversial. Mixter argues that Hoxie seems interested not so much in the effects of scientific management on the *individual* laborer as in matters of industrial democracy and *collective* labor, and so Hoxie had chosen to include matters of only tangential importance, matters outside "the usual prerogatives of management under the entrepreneur type of industrial society" (Mixter, 1916, p. 374). Hoxie does not, for instance, compare scientifically managed shops with other shops (except incidentally), but rather with the labor "claims" of scientific management as elucidated by Taylor.

While Mixter finds that, when focused on the area of shop management, much of the criticism in Hoxie's book is well taken, he thinks Hoxie makes too much of the finding that scientific management is not as "scientific" as it is represented to be; this assertion is merely a statement of the obvious, that in an effort to create an appeal for a new method, one conceals it in the costume of scientific language. Further, contrary to Hoxie's representation, that scientific management requires for its success that "the methods of work in a shop are kept in such a constant state of flux that there is little or no opportunity for collective bargaining," Mixter contends that, in fact, scientific management confers on the production process a degree of stability and standardization and thus *expands* the possibilities for collective bargaining (Mixter, 1916, p. 374).

Mixter argues further, contrary to Hoxie, that scientific management principles are not "inherently inimical" to collective bargaining. Going further, he insists that "the standardization of operations which obtains under scientific management makes for greater stability than exists generally in industry, and affords unusual opportunity for definiteness of contract." The difficulty rests not with the workers, but with the union: under scientific management, "it is difficult for a union, most of whose members are outside scientific management shops, to legislate for unfamiliar conditions," and "to keep up its membership in a shop where workmen receive at the hands of the management exceptionally high pay and satisfactory general conditions of employment," Unions have a penchant for "leveling," that is, for creating of workers a homogeneous mass through which bargaining may better be achieved. This is threatened by the employment of scientific management principles, as the result is *greater* differentiation. Thus Mixter notes that, should the union decide to engage in "differentiated" bargaining, no conflict with scientific management would be seen (Mixter, 1916, p. 375).

Hoxie, Mixter contends, has a predisposition towards the union point of view, accepting the basic premise of the "solidarity of labor."[95] "Throughout [*Scientific Management and Labor*] there runs a quasi-syndicalist assumption of the virtual part-ownership of labor in industry; and hence the main indictment of the whole situation is not that individual workmen are oppressed under scientific management methods, but that 'industrial democracy' has a hard time of it" (Mixter, 1916, p. 375). He argues that there appears to have been, from the "misconceptions and misunderstandings" evident in the presentation, a *political* motive behind the study, that the book was intended "to arouse the antagonism of organized labor toward scientific management" (p. 376).

The biggest criticism by Mixter relates to the methodology employed by Hoxie. The study should have been limited to those shops which had employed the Taylor system, and none other. Although Mixter acknowledges that Hoxie had found that Taylor shops adhered to Taylor principles with greater fidelity than any of the rival shops pursuing scientific management, the broad conclusions about scientific management are based on a review of *all* shops claiming to have employed the principles of scientific management. This Mixter finds inappropriate: "Only cases of failure to live up to real Taylor principles on the part of real Taylor shops would constitute damaging findings of an investigation" (Mixter, 1916, p. 376).

Columbia University professor of economics Robert Murray Haig reviewed *Scientific Management* for the *Political Science Quarterly*, assessing it a "real contribution in a field where some reliable information was badly needed," this despite his general misgivings as to the overall value of the work of the Commission on Industrial Relations (Haig, 1916, p. 641). Hoxie finds, notes Haig, that the labor claims of Taylor and others are not substantiated by the evidence. There is in the plants under investigation "no general adherence to the order of installation laid down by Taylor, the eagerness for immediate results operating to preclude this." In all, Hoxie's conclusion is that the Taylor approach – simplified as time and motion study and task setting – "is not really scientific but, on the contrary, the methods and results 'are the special report of individual judgment and opinion'." In addition, it is clear that "scientific management in practice is found to be essentially undemocratic and to contain elements which tend to weaken the organizations of the workmen" (pp. 641–642).

Despite his agreement with the general conclusions, Haig notes two major criticisms of Hoxie's approach. The first is that the plants selected may be an unrepresentative sample of those in which scientific management principles had been applied. Although Hoxie had acknowledged Taylor's contention that all his tenets of scientific management must be in place before its effectiveness can be judged, he did not employ this as a criterion for selection. This could certainly introduce a bias into the study: "Professor Hoxie is still under the necessity of making sure that the plants whose fruit he is judging are essentially of the scientific-management type and not ordinary plants to which a mere twig or two of scientific management has been grafted. Although the shops visited are said to have been designated as representative, it is difficult to believe, after reading the account of the conditions in the shops, that the adherents of the strict 'Taylor' school would recognize them as even faintly resembling purely scientific-management shops" (Haig, 1916, p. 642).

More fundamentally, Hoxie's methodological approach sets up scientific management for failure, while being less critical (or more charitable) of the claims of labor:

> The treatment consists, in the main, of an examination of the "labor claims" of scientific management. Among them are included those of the strictest "Taylorites," in spite of the fact that many plants of which they would not approve were accepted for the tests. The result is that claim after claim is shown to be "unfounded" and the impression is given that the merits of the case are with the labor side. Had the labor "claims" been treated in a similar manner, they would probably have yielded a similarly depressing series of negative results. (Haig, 1916, pp. 642–643)

In contrast to the reviews of Mixter and Haig, Alvin S. Johnson's review in *The New Republic* emphasizes the scientific and methodical nature of Hoxie's investigation. "Professor Hoxie has sought to introduce objectives standards for determining the relevancy of concrete inquiries. It is his endeavor to subject scientific curiosity to social control, in order that investigating energy may be confined to work that promises to be fruitful" (Johnson, 1915, p. 127). Here is yet another definition of scientific, namely, that the investigator pursues questions of social significance rather than just "the slaking of idiosyncratic curiosity" (p. 126). In this regard, Hoxie clearly succeeded, as the social significance of *Scientific Management and Labor* is beyond question. Johnson concludes by stating that Hoxie's study is a major contribution because it not only provides evidence of the potential for good from new industrial processes but also the need for monitoring and control necessitated by its possibilities of evil.

Epilogue

Robert Hoxie in his study of scientific management and labor succeeded in establishing two important results. First, organized labor indeed had cause for concern that the systematic use of scientific management practices would ultimately have a negative impact on the process of collective bargaining and thus on the unions themselves. Second, no shop among those investigated had actually applied the Taylor or Gantt systems of management in the manner stipulated by the proponents and so the results on the investigation could not serve as an indictment of the system. In fact, Hoxie demonstrated that the very term "scientific management" had no clearly defined operational meaning, as the various proposals that fell within the rubric varied widely in critical areas.

Writing in 1917, Jett Lauck and Edgar Sydenstricker conclude that the "investigation and analysis carries with it the weight of official authority" and therefore the conclusions drawn must be carefully considered (Lauck & Sydenstricker, 1917, p. 237). Yet while much has been written about the history of scientific management, and the events which led to an investigation and a reappraisal of its methods with respect to their effects on labor, the place in this history of Hoxie's work for the Commission on Industrial Relations and the subsequent publication of his extended study, *Scientific Management and Labor*, have received scant attention; Chris Nyland's essay (1996) is perhaps the most comprehensive examination of the machinations involved and the roles played by Commons and Hoxie. Most often, in references to the work of the Commission, Hoxie's participation and his subsequent published study are mentioned in passing, as historical facts without context or import.[96]

Yet Hoxie's work was at the time of significant importance as regards the debate over the effectiveness and equitability of these new methods of industrial control – in their impact on industrial efficiency and the consequences of this for the welfare of the worker. This is especially so in terms of the *political* debate. The focus of Hoxie's work may be seen as having been at once determined by and employed as a means of securing a particular political agenda, one which sought to bolster the claims of labor against the owners and managers of industrial enterprises. Hoxie's own role in support of this agenda appears to have been minimal, the agenda itself having been determined by the Commissioners and especially by one of the leading advocates of labor, John R. Commons. In bringing to light – in effect highlighting – the negative qualities of scientific management, Hoxie's study served as grist for the mill of those opposed to *any* measures designed to transform the structure of the enterprise, or thought to alter the relationship of employer to employee or to interfere with the ability of labor to organize against the owners of capital.

In addition, the politics of the Commission on Industrial Relations and the reaction to the recommendations of the Hoxie Report brought to light the divisions within the labor movement itself. While some labor advocates were quite willing to listen to the arguments advanced by the proponents of scientific management – after all, Taylor and others were within the orbit of the Progressives, who invoked the specter of science as the means of producing industrial efficiency through social control – and so were interested in offering constructive advice in an effort to ameliorate the excesses of this new system of industrial management, others cared little for negotiation, opting instead for confrontation as the means to the establishment of better labor conditions and greater labor control of industry. In the end, scientific management appears to have prevailed, transforming itself into Human Resource Management and Efficiency Management, the more undesirable aspects of the former system having been modified or eliminated, while the desire for labor control of the industrial workplace has been weakened significantly.

Finally, Graham Adams, Jr., in his otherwise excellent study of the Commission on Industrial Relations, *Age of Industrial Violence*, offers but a nod to Hoxie and others who worked in the Research Division, merely acknowledging that their contributions served to "diffuse" the influence of the Commission through the years that followed. Still, he regards Hoxie's *Scientific Management and Labor* "as by far the most important single book that emanated from the Research Division," a work that "rose to the status of a classic in modern economics" (Adams, 1966, p. 223). Perhaps such is itself testament to the consequentialness of Hoxie's work – that his contribution is even today better known than the product of the Commission itself.

CONCLUSION

As an economist and social scientist, Robert Franklin Hoxie made significant contributions to his chosen fields of research. His writings were well-regarded in his own time and his intellectual achievements praised by his contemporaries. While his name is today almost exclusively associated with his contributions to labor economics – a field practically non-existent prior to his work on the subject – the totality of his published work suggests an intellect unconstrained. He was never completely satisfied with any single approach to a topic, and was more than willing to question orthodoxy, open to new approaches should the standard models and methodologies prove inadequate to the task. Yet in the final analysis, it was the *politics* associated with Hoxie's attempts to apprehend and to advance a solution to the "labor problem" that would ultimately prove decisive in determining his fate. His studies of labor unions and labor-management conflict brought him renown; this, in turn, led to his involvement, the extent perhaps unbeknownst to him at the time, in a political struggle to which he was ill prepared. He became essentially a pawn in a contest between rivals with personal agendas, with the final product being, to him, incomplete, a compromise instead of the more comprehensive and critical piece of research he envisioned. Moreover, the negative commentaries on his work proved to be too much to bear.

Noting Hoxie's intellectual transformations, methodological and doctrinal, the philosopher George Herbert Mead concludes that "[t]here was one constant characteristic of all his changes of theory and shifts of standpoint. They were always moving away from what he considered irrelevant theory and description toward the living economic experiences which became the goal of his interest" (Mead, 1917, p. 114). This made Hoxie not a mere theoretician, but a reformer as well, albeit one without prejudice or preconceptions.

> He came indeed with no recipe for the healing of social ills. He was in no sense a partisan in social struggles. He met and comprehended men on both sides as he could not if he had come with a parti pris. But his passionate determination to understand was born of no intellectual curiosity or academic ambition. It sprang from the profound belief that scientific comprehension is the indispensible precondition of intelligent solution of the problems of the social as well as of the physical sciences, and his passion was for their solution, not merely for their understanding. (Mead, 1917, p. 116)

What better epitaph could a scholar wish?

NOTES

1. Biographical information may be found in Hamilton (1916, 1932), Goodrich (1932), Perlman (1958), and an unsigned obituary from the *University of Chicago Magazine*, July 1916.

2. Solomon Hoxie was primarily a dairy farmer and cattle breeder who achieved business success importing Holstein cattle from Europe. A devout Quaker and Republican who greatly admired Abraham Lincoln, from all appearances he lived an exemplary life. A biography was written by his daughter, Jane. (Hoxie, 1922).

3. From The Ten-Year Book of Cornell University (1908, p. 35).

4. See the Cornell University Register, January (1905a, 1905b) May 1905, January (1906).

5. See *Twenty-Five Years of the Department of Political Economy, University of Chicago*, by Laughlin (1916, p. 7) for the dates of Hoxie's appointments.

6. While at Harvard, Cummings, a staunchly-conservative neoclassical economist, wrote a lengthy (thirty-one page) critical review of Veblen's *Theory of the Leisure Class* for the *Journal of Political Economy*. See Cummings (1899).

7. See the *Annual Register* of the University of Chicago (1908, 1909, 1911, 1915). Hoxie's Introductory Lecture on the Nature of the History of Political Economy was published in *Research in the History of Economic Thought and Methodology* in 2006. (See Luca Fiorito and Warren J. Samuels, Eds., 2006)

8. Hoxie's sister, Jane, writes that one of her brothers "was very delicate and, during the early years of his life, suffered from almost chronic invalidism. The father was untiring in his attention to this child, repeatedly nursing him through periods of well nigh hopeless illness" (Hoxie, 1922, p. 26). While no name is given, the allusion is most probably to Robert. Alvin Johnson, in Pioneer's Progress (1952, p. 204), states that Hoxie suffered from polio as a child.

9. The Institutionalist Clarence Ayres had desired to work with Hoxie at Chicago, but Hoxie's suicide prompted him to alter his plans and to shift his focus from economics to philosophy and ethics. See Hodgson (2004, p. 345). We wish to thank an anonymous reader for suggesting this passage.

10. Hamilton notes also the influence of Herbert J. Davenport and Alvin S. Johnson, but such influence "cannot be so definitely particularized as can that of the three mentioned above" (Hamilton, 1916, p. 858, n.2).

11. Hoxie identifies "four fundamental concepts" upon which rested Fetter's economics: psychic income, "the sole source or basis of value"; diminishing marginal utility; diminishing returns, a principle of universal applicability, as per John Bates Clark; and time value (Hoxie, 1905, pp. 211–214).

12. Dorfman remarks that "when Veblen had a proper foil, such as Robert Hoxie, or when he felt in the mood, he could talk for hours on almost any topic" (Dorfman, 1945, p. 247). Veblen's influence was profound indeed. Yet such was reciprocal: "Veblen was deeply moved by the death of Hoxie, and when he was asked about his influence on Hoxie he replied that it was about the same as Hoxie's influence on him" (Dorfman, 1945, p. 354). We wish to thank an anonymous reader for pointing out this passage.

13. Alvin Johnson appraises Veblen's influence on Hoxie thus: "What seems in the end to have been Veblen's most significant contribution to Hoxie's development was the exposure of traditional economic science as an unconscious apologetic of things as they are. All the premises of the traditional logic are derived from the facts of money-making enterprise. 'Labor', 'capital', 'land', as manipulated in economic science, are not the raw physical facts, but the facts involved in a system of relations that are fully real only when every laborer has his employer, every field its tenant. Thus economics assumes in its premises a specific economic system, not very old, not at all universal and apparently not imperishable, and this system it reproduces in its conclusions, *sub specie aeternitatis*. What practical consequences might follow from this criticism of the accepted doctrine need not concern us here. They never

greatly concerned Veblen. The theoretical consequence is evident. The traditional science is not a glass through which you see reality clearly. It is a more or less opaque medium, in which all outlines are distorted and by which much that is most significant is effectually concealed" (Johnson, 1916, p. 249). Johnson, in his autobiography, opines that "Hoxie loved Veblen with a love that passeth understanding" (Johnson, 1952, p. 205). For his part, Veblen held Hoxie in high esteem: "Veblen commented to John H. Urie, a student who lived with him in 1916–1917, that his outstanding 'pupils' were, in order, Mitchell, Davenport, and Hoxie" (Dorfman, 1945, p. 311).

14. On Veblen's "unfulfilled" promise, see Rutherford (1998).

15. Yet, notes Hamilton, Hoxie's "protest is peculiar in view of his search for relatively general truths and his own use of abstract concepts. It is difficult to think of an economist whose categories are more highly abstract than Hoxie's" (Hamilton, 1916, p. 865, n.2).

16. Veblen admits this distinction is not a novel one, but "has, of course, been possible from the beginning of economic theory, and, indeed, the distinction has from time to time temporarily been made in the contrast frequently pointed out between the proximate interest of the businessman and the ulterior interest of society at large. What appears to have hindered the reception of the distinction into economic doctrine is the constraining presence of a belief in an order of Nature and the habit of conceiving the economic community as an organism. The point of view given by these postulates has made such a distinction between employments not only useless, but even disservicable [sic] for the ends to which theory has been directed" (Veblen, 1901, p. 203).

17. See as well the discussion in McNulty (1973), especially pp. 464–466.

18. In his response, Commons addresses only the comment of Hoxie: "Mr. Hoxie has gone several flights above me on industrial psychology. He has added pecuniary psychology. I think he has made an important contribution to the discussion but has not changed the outcome. You will notice that his psychology is based very definitely upon the industrial facts themselves. It follows accurately, like the reflection in a mirror, the mechanical fact on the one hand which makes one class, and the pecuniary fact that makes the other class. All that I can see that he has added is his method of tracing the operation of class interest from the occupation into the mind of the man" (Commons, 1908, pp. 781–782).

19. Rutherford (1998) notes that, while Hoxie's trade union work was motivated by Veblen's views, he had by 1908 begun to diverge from Veblen, arguing against the view that unionism was monolithic in its perspective on labor. See Rutherford (1998), pp. 474–475.

20. McNulty suggests that Hoxie's attempt to distance himself from Veblen led to self-doubt and ultimately to suicide. "Hoxie's disenchantment with Veblen evidently finally undermined his faith in his own work. Long subject to ill health and recurring emotional depressions, he confided to a colleague and friend shortly before his death that he feared his work was 'rotten with Veblenism', – 'diseased', as he put it, by the Veblenian premise of a uniquely 'industrial' trade-union viewpoint irreconcilably at odds with the 'pecuniary' outlook of employers" (McNulty, 1973, p. 476). Chris Nyland ascribes the suicide to his discomfort with *Scientific Management and Labor*, its reception (particularly Charles Mixter's review in

the *American Economic* Review), as well as denial of promotion at Chicago (Nyland, 1996, pp. 1006–1010). "Mixter's review was published in June 1916, and the charges appear to have had a devastating effect on Hoxie. He went into a deep depression that lasted through June 23" (p. 1010). Clearly the date is incorrect, as Hoxie died June 22, 1916 (*Chicago Daily Tribune*, June 23, 1916, p. 15).

21. McNulty (1973) presents a more complete review of the Veblenian influence on Hoxie's economics.

22. Daniel Ernst concludes, "Hoxie thus leapt from one branch of the dilemma of liberal pluralism to the other, from moral relativism to an anxious assertion of absolute (if minimal) standards to be enforced by a disinterested public. With more courage than logic, he concluded that well-meaning citizens should not await the millennium of universal consensus but immediately embark on programs of social betterment" (Ernst, 1993, p. 73).

23. Papers of John R. Commons: Correspondence and General Correspondence 1859–1911. Box 1, Folder 1, Reel 1. Wisconsin Historical Society.

24. This has been more than adequately documented by Nyland (1996).

25. McNulty also notes this change in emphasis: "From 1893, the year of his first publication, through 1906, his interest focused on money, the tariff, and colonial policy, as well as on general value theory. His first article on trade unionism appeared in 1907. From then, until his death in 1916, all of his work was in the field of labor organization" (McNulty, 1973, p. 462).

26. In addition to his work in the above-listed areas, he published in the same journal four articles on Socialism in the United States: "The Convention of the Socialist Party" (1908b), "The Rising Tide of Socialism" (1911a), "The Socialist Party in the November Elections" (1912a), and "The Socialist Party and American Convention Methods" (1912b).

27. Hoxie prefers "trade unionism" to "unionism", as the latter "is the result of a universal social tendency – the tendency of men of similar temperament and similar environment and interest to get together for common action," while the former "is distinguished from other forms of unionism simply by the fact that it is the unionism of the wageworkers, but it does not differ essentially in fundamental purpose and method from the unionism of other social classes and groups" (Hoxie, 1917, p. 358, n1).

28. "The business man, even though he may employ nonunion men, must understand it, if he is not to become involved in harassing and ruinous difficulty, for unionism has ways of making its force felt far beyond the realm of its membership. The consumer is never free from its influence and effect; the politician must seek its support or find a way to escape from its influence; the lawyer must know its purpose, contentions and force, if he is to serve his clients effectively; the social worker cannot proceed, apart from consideration of its aims and attitudes, the preacher must consider it in working out his plans and prophecies if he is to be more than a mere exhorter; even the teacher finds himself forced to work with or against it. There is apparently no occupation into which any individual may enter where unionism may not appear as a factor that must be taken account of" (Hoxie, 1917, pp. 5–6).

29. "In short, it would appear that unionism has its finger in practically every social pie that is baking. It concerns itself in innumerable ways with the processes of

production and distribution and with the welfare of the consumer. Where it is strategically located it can, if it will, paralyze our whole economic activity as such. It is a force affecting definitely the number, training and general efficiency of our productive laborers, the organization of the labor market, the shop, the problems of living, discipline, promotion and discharge, the hours of labor, the employment of women and children, the organization of industrial enterprise and the general and specific methods of production, the use or neglect of new industrial machinery and processes, the quantity and quality of the productive output, the modes of payment which may be employed, the cost of production of commodities and the prices which we must pay for them, the problems of industrial accident, disease and death, and the method and extent of compensation which society shall pay therefore, the certainty and continuity of employment, the community problems of housing, cleanliness, health, and recreation, the character of our educational system, the standards of political honesty and efficiency, the character of our legislation, not only on industrial but on all social matters, the enforcement and legal interpretation of our laws, the extent of drunkenness and vice, the general ethical and religious standards of the community, and hundreds of other matters with which the community and every individual in it is vitally concerned" (Hoxie, 1917, pp. 4–5).

30. In his 1906 "Historical Method vs. Historical Narrative", Hoxie concludes "that in reality all scientific investigation is undertaken in furtherance of some definite, vital human interest", and so "all scientific investigation is bound to be highly selective. We do not seek to understand the existing situation as a whole – that would be impossible – but we seek to understand the present in its relation to the interest at stake, the problem in hand" (Hoxie, 1906c, p. 569).

31. E. H. Downey concludes that Hoxie's essays on the nature of the trade union movement were "the first attempt at a systematic interpretation of unionism in the United States" (Downey, 1914, p. 170).

32. While the AFL had been active in the mid-term Congressional elections of 1906, the Presidential election of 1908 afforded them an opportunity to effect change to the benefit of labor. Gompers' rationale for the decision to support a candidate he explained in testimony to Congress in 1913:
"The war that had been declared upon us by the officers of the National Association of Manufacturers; the suits that were begun against us in 1907; the decision of the court holding that the Sherman Antitrust law did apply to associations of workers and that they could be mulcted in damages for any injury or loss that an employer or businessman might claim was due to the normal activities of workers; the injunction proceedings brought by the Buck's Stove & Range Co.; the proceedings in contempt against Mr. John Mitchell, Mr. Frank Morrison, and myself – all these aroused an interest and an activity among the workers of the country in that campaign that were very marked, and we were more generally active in that campaign than in any preceding" (Gompers, 1913, p. 1009).

33. "The socialist dream of future felicity will not mate with the unionist demand for immediate results. From the Federation point of view, therefore, union with the forces of socialism promised no cure for the ills which beset Mr. Gompers and his followers. Nor obviously could any cure be sought in independent political action. Such action as surely as socialist fusion runs counter to the business-union ideal" (Hoxie, 1908c, p. 695).

34. "Here appears what may be taken as a hypothetical general principle of unionism, if there is such a thing. The union organization tends to parallel the capitalistic or employers' organization. It attempts to cover the industrial field within which there is labor competition with respect to work, wages, and conditions of employment" (Hoxie, 1917, p. 80).

35. Hoxie identifies as well two variants that seem not to belong to any of the four structural forms. These are the *compound craft union*, or *amalgamated craft union*, "a centralized, homogeneous organization of the workers in a number of related crafts", and the *quasi-industrial federation*, "a federation of industrially related craft and compound craft unions." Each overlap with the above-mentioned structural types and so are not considered as distinct. Hoxie (1914a, pp. 209–211).

36. The Socialist labor activist Debs (1909a) regards craft unions as being conservative in nature, and generally in league with the capitalist employers. The employers, by and large, accept the unions because they lend stability. "To organize along craft lines means to divide the working class and make it the prey of the capitalist class" (Debs, 1905, p. 8).

37. Debs argues that the United Mine Workers had been ineffective in respect of the welfare of its members due to the fact "that they are not organized upon the basis of the class struggle." Specifically, the Executive Board, in negotiations with the mine operators, "will fix things that are out of joint and settle matters generally. They will arrive at mutually satisfactory conclusions. They will harmonize beautifully. And when they do harmonize, it will be in the interests, not of the miners who do the work, who dig the coal, who produce the wealth, but in the interests of the operators who own the mines and exploit the slaves of the pits" (Debs, 1909a, p. 6).

38. As Commons observes, "The merely economic interpretations, he [Hoxie] holds, may indicate an orderly succession of unionism from one stage of industry to later stages, but the psychological – or as he calls it, the functional – analysis of unionism gives contradictory group interpretations, pluralistic rather than monistic. The underlying group psychology, which differs so widely for different groups, springs from the political, religious, traditional, educational, circumstances into which individuals are thrown and from their own attitudes and aims." In Commons' view, "[t]he outstanding contribution which Hoxie makes to the study of unionism is psychological" (Commons, 1918, p. 396).

39. One of business unionism's "fundamental principles" is what Hoxie identifies as the Principle of Uniformity. "This principle requires that all the men doing the same work use the same kind of tools and materials, work normally the same length of time, and at the same speed, turn out the same quantity and quality of goods, and receive the same rate of wages." The union can then limit labor-market competition by establishing a minimum standard wage rate, a maximum hourly work day and week, and "uniformity in the conditions and rate of work," as well as "minute specifications of standards in regard to all the incidents of work and pay, from which no deviation can normally be allowed." Collective bargaining provides the enforcement mechanism for securing these standards; the apprenticeship system and the "closed shop" are necessary to control hiring of outside workers; job classification is essential to limit the introduction of new workers not bound by union rules (Hoxie, 1914c, pp. 602–605).

40. "[T]hough it may, where immediate circumstances dictate, favor a broadly inclusive policy – when, for example, the unregulated competition of the unorganized and unskilled seriously threatens to sweep aside the trade barriers and break down the standards of wages, hours, and shop conditions which it has erected. Under these circumstances it tends to develop a broad altruism and to seek the organization of all the workers in the craft or industry" (Hoxie, 1914a, p. 212).

41. It is this form of unionism which Debs identifies as "old unionism," the functional equivalent of the craft union. See Debs (1905, 1909a, 1909b). Philip Taft argues that business unionism – pure unionism – was "the first type of cooperative activity carried on by workers in the United States" (Taft, 1963, p. 37). McNulty concludes that, in his discussion of business unionism, Hoxie shows a break with Veblen, as the business union seeks harmony with the employer, its membership pursuing pecuniary benefits from such an arrangement (McNulty, 1973, p. 469). Later, he concludes that, in fact, business unionism offered "a reflection of the sort of dichotomy Veblen had drawn … In a sense, then, business unionism presented a microcosmic example of precisely the kind of division that Veblen had posited. Not in this institution did Hoxie find any reason to challenge the Veblenian model" (p. 472).

42. Hoxie notes that, according to a "friendly critic", business unionism and uplift unionism are not "distinct and independent types, but rather two varieties of one type more comprehensive than either." The suggested alternative designation is *bargaining unionism* or *constructive business unionism* (Hoxie, 1914a, p. 213, n.1).

43. One group of workers for whom the Knights had no place was the Chinese, going so far as to advocate passage of the Chinese Exclusion Acts (1882). A letter from the Executive Committee, published in *The Journal of United Labor* – the house journal of the Knights – for August 15, 1880, begins "We are cursed here with Chinese competition. It stands around us and before us in all its appalling misery and degradation to the white Christian laboring-classes" (Executive Committee, 1880, p. 39).

44. In a letter to A. J. Portenar of the Department of Labor, dated 10 June 1914, Hoxie observes, "I can hardly agree with you that it is only a few Socialists who stand in opposition to the business unions and the pragmatic business union progress. Aside from well defined groups of predatory unionists, mainly in local bodies, I have become convinced by observation and inquiry, that there are between 500,000 and 800,000 men who can be called revolutionary unionists … and I find that many of the revolutionaries are men of age, experience and substance." Portenar pointed out "that Professor Hoxie expressed this view in reply to my assertion to the contrary. But because of things I have seen and heard, I am now inclined to give much more credence to his opinion" (Portenar, 1919, p. 121).

45. That the I.W.W. is assuredly not in the syndicalist camp is "proved unequivocally" by the fact that it "is a flat failure, and, far from being the grim, brooding power which it has been pictured, is a body pathetically weak in membership, without consistent leadership, organically chaotic, and torn by apparent irreconcilable internal conflict resulting from a discrepancy of fundamental ideals" (Hoxie, 1914d, p. 140).

46. "The Industrial Workers declares that the workers must make themselves the masters of the tools with which they work; and so a very important function of this new union is to teach the workers, – or, rather, have them teach themselves – the

necessity of fitting themselves to take charge of the industries in which they are employed when they are wrested, as they will be, from their capitalist masters" (Debs, 1905, p. 16). "This involves a revolution, and this means the end of the capitalist system, and the rearing of a working class republic ..." (p. 28). A few years after this acclamation, Debs, one of the founders of the I.W.W., severed his connection with the group, regarding it as having become anarchistic.

47. Leonard Lecht notes that "Professor Hoxie's typology serves to provide the criteria which set apart the Teamsters as the most prominent example of predatory unionism in the contemporary American scene" (Lecht, 1959, p. 216).

48. Cherry (1976) offers this passage and one other as evidence of Hoxie's "explicit use of racial arguments" (p. 157). It is clear in this instance, however, that Hoxie merely referenced the subjective factors identified by the social psychologists, especially Cooley, without necessarily accepting their overt racism. Consider his discussion of the problem of syndicalism. Hoxie opines that the American workmen "are not conscious revolutionists, but are optimistic opportunists." The attitude of American labor is one of preference for the satisfaction of present wants, the solution of present problems, and the amelioration of existing conditions. They are, as well, averse to radical change and "speculative theorizing." The constitution of the American worker "is the outcome partly of the racial character of American workmen, and partly of American economic and social conditions. The hardheaded, tradition-bound, empirical element predominates in our labor movement, just as it does in our business affairs, in law and politics, and in our social ideals and affairs generally, and this characteristic, perhaps racial, has been reinforced by the fact that the economic and social conditions have for generations been such that the workers *could* see hope ahead in gradual betterment through constructive industrial and political action. The labor movement thus given character has assimilated and Americanized foreign accretions, just as in general we have assimilated and Americanized the immigrant, socially and politically" (Hoxie, 1914d, pp. 143–144; emphasis in original). Hoxie in these passages uses race to refer to the American *type*, as distinguished from other national types.

49. In his 1909 *Social Organization*, Cooley addresses the topic of labor unions and the psychology of the worker. Labor unions arose "out of the urgent need of self-defence, not so much against deliberate aggression as against brutal confusion and neglect." While the "primary function" of unions is "group-bargaining," they have been influential in furthering legislation to ameliorate the conditions affecting labor, and have served to promote "spheres of fellowship and self-development" among the laboring class. This latter Cooley sees as a vital contribution: "To have a we-feeling, to live shoulder to shoulder with one's fellows, is the only human life; we all need it to keep us from selfishness, sensuality and despair, and the hand-worker needs it even more than the rest of us. Usually without pecuniary resource and insecure of his job and his home, he is, in isolation, miserably weak and in a way to be cowed and unmanned by misfortune or mere apprehension. Drifting about in a confused society, unimportant, apparently, to the rest of the world, it is no wonder if he feels 'I am no link of Thy great chain', and loses faith in himself, in life and in God. The union makes him feel that he is part of a whole, one of a fellowship, that there are those who will stand by him in trouble that he counts for something in the great life. He gets from it that thrill of broader sentiment, the same in kind that

men get in fighting for their country; his self is enlarged and enriched and his imagination fed with objects, comparatively, 'immense and eternal'." Beyond this, the union, as a democratic and disciplinary association, "is perhaps the chief guaranty of the healthy political development of the hand-working class – especially those imported from non-democratic civilizations – and the surest barrier against recklessness and disorder" (Cooley, 1909, p. 287).

50. Ira Kipnis, in his bibliographic citation of Hoxie's article, holds that Hoxie was "[v]ery sympathetic to the Right wing of the Socialist Party (Kipnis, 1952, p. 447).

51. Drury (1915, pp. 15–16) contends that the term "scientific management" originated with Louis Brandeis, in hearings before the Interstate Commerce Commission, 13 July 1910.

52. Nelson (1974) presents an efficient examination of the Taylor system, arguing for its comprehensiveness as a "refinement and extension" of systematic management.

53. The above-listed books on scientific management were all published by The Engineering Magazine.

54. Note Thorstein Veblen: "[T]he keeping of the balance in the comprehensive machine process of industry is a matter of the gravest urgency if the productive mechanism is to proceed with its work in an efficient manner, so as to avoid idleness, waste, and hardship. The management of the various industrial plants and processes in due correlation with all the rest, and the supervision of the interstitial adjustments of the system, are commonly conceived to be a work of greater consequence to the community's well-being than any of the detail work involved in carrying on a given process of production" (Veblen, 1904, p. 18). On the connection between Veblen and the scientific managers, see Knoedler (1997).

55. At the Summer Institute, June 2011, David Colander, Deirdre McCloskey, and David Levy all noted the distinction between the methods and practices of the engineer and the scientist.

56. Henry Gantt summarizes it thus: A "systematized business" operates with a regular and established routine; orders "proceed, from the office to the different departments, through to the shipping department, and in many cases they have a proper sequence worked out, so that the method of filling the order is not entirely left to the subordinates." "Scientific" management, on the other hand, "comes when each of those steps has been thoroughly investigated, each of the steps through which the work shall proceed, from the point at which it originates, to the point that it comes out of the works, when each of the steps has been investigated by the best expert available, be it a mechanic or whatever other person he may be. When that has been done, when each of those steps through which the work has progressed has been studied in detail, and a specific, definite route has been laid out, reduced to writing, and the returns come to the office to show how this work has progressed each day, from the time it is issued from the office; and when any failure to live up to these instructions is immediately reported back to the office, and a proper person who knows how it should be done goes out and helps the work along – does not wait until it is three or four or five days late and then go out and make a row – but as soon as it is one day late, he goes out and tries to remove the obstacle so that it can proceed, and perhaps catch up with the other work that

has gone before it – that is scientific management" (as cited in Brandeis, 1911, p. 7).

57. "To summarize, then, what should be aimed at in all establishments is:

1. That each workman should be given as far as possible the highest grade of work for which his ability and physique fit him.
2. Each workman should be called upon to turn out the maximum work which a first-rate man of his class can do and thrive under.
3. Each workman, when he works at the best pace of a first-class man, should be paid from 30 per cent. to 100 per cent., according to the nature of the work which he does, beyond the average of his class" (Taylor, 1903, pp. 1347–1348).

58. Details of the bombing and subsequent trial may be found in Adamic (1931), Adams (1966), McCartin (1997), and Irwin (2013).

59. "So great was the power of the explosion that parts of the concrete base of the alley were pulverized into fine dust, much of the concrete was broken, fractured and precipitated with tremendous violence into the basement, killing one of the workmen directly under the spot. Supporting I-beams of structural steel, one of them a twelve inch I-beam, were cut off as if by a pair of gigantic shears; others were buckled, kinked and fractured in a fashion not attributable to fire or weight" (Final Report of the Los Angeles Grand Jury, 1911, p. 4).

60. Some accounts place the number at 21.

61. See Adams (1966, p. 7) and Stevens (2009, p. 70).

62. Adamic asserts that, between 1905 and 1910, members of the Iron Workers' union "dynamited about 150 buildings and bridges in the United States and Canada – or at least most of those explosions can reasonably be ascribed to the doings of official union terrorists" (Adamic, 1931, p. 197).

63. An article in the *International Socialist Review* by "Unionist" identifies the victims as "DESPISED workingmen." Noting that, at the time of the explosion, Otis "was conveniently out of the city," the building itself had been "very heavily insured," the paper reaped "thousands of dollars worth of FREE ADVERTISING," and no capitalists had been injured in the blast, the author asked, "WAS THIS A HUGE CONSPIRACY AGAINST UNION LABOR in Los Angeles?" The article further questioned whether dynamite had caused the explosion or had it been caused by an accumulation of gases from the combustible materials used in the printing process. This, so the argument goes, would have made the *Times* culpable and would have lessened the prospects of collecting damages from the insurance company. Thus, given these claims, the author concludes that "OTIS was the CHIEF beneficiary of the disaster," and so "it would be well to do some INVESTIGATING in HIS DIRECTION" ("Unionist," 1910, pp. 262–266; emphases in original).

64. Adams states that the prosecution seemed aware of Darrow's defense strategy "almost instantaneously," and in fact they had infiltrated the defense team, while Darrow had, as well, placed his own agents among the prosecution and so he was aware of the strength of the prosecution's case (Adams, 1966, p. 15.)

65. Among other signatories, businessman and socialite William J. Schieffelin, humanitarian Lillian D. Wald, Owen R. Lovejoy of the National Child Labor Committee, sociologist Samuel McCune Lindsay, the Reverend J. Howard Melish,

civil rights activist and NAACP co-founder Henry Moskowitz, editor Arthur P. Kellogg, Minister Frank Oliver Hall, Minister and Orientalist John P. Peters, economist and welfare advocate Edward T. Devine, director of the Russell Sage Foundation John M. Glenn, writer and economist John A. Fitch, journalist and secretary of the New York Association for Labor Legislation Paul Kennaday, social reformer John A. Kingsbury, journalist and social reformer Paul U. Kellogg, social reformer John Collier, author and activist Robert Erskine Ely, Minister Frank Mason North, social worker James Bronson Reynolds, and Charles B. McFarland.

66. The United States Congress entertained several resolutions directed at the application of the "Taylor system" of shop management. A Report of 24 June 1911, an accompaniment to House Resolution 90, entitled "'Taylor System' of Shop Management," concludes that any such system "which may be applied in Government work should be thoroughly investigated so that whatever there may be good in any of them may be approved and applied and whatever there may be bad may be condemned and eliminated" (U.S. House of Representatives, 1911, p. 12). Another, of 9 March 1912, "Taylor and Other Systems of Shop Management," concludes that, while "[a] great amount of good work" may have been done in respect of industrial efficiency, nonetheless, "neither Mr. Taylor nor anyone else has presented to this committee a system so complete and perfect as to justify a recommendation that it be imposed in its entirety in any Government shop" (U.S. House of Representatives, 1912a, p. 1).
On another matter related to the "excesses" of Taylorism, on 15 July 1912, the U.S. House of Representatives considered House Resolution 23505, "A BILL TO regulate the method of directing the work of Government employees," which states, in part: "*Be it enacted by the Senate and House of Representatives of the United States of America in Congress assembled*, That it shall be unlawful for any officer, manager, superintendent, foreman, or other person having charge of the work of any employee of the United States Government to make or cause to be made with a stopwatch or other time-measuring device a time study of the movements between the starting and completion of any job of any such employee" (U.S. House of Representatives, 1912b, pp. 1–2).

67. Adams (1966, pp. 25–74) presents in great detail the drama involved in the selection of the commissioners. This section draws heavily on that presentation.

68. David Montgomery identifies Walsh as having been "an active Democratic politician with close ties to the Midwest's network of single taxers, the Catholic benevolent order of the Knights of Columbus, proponents of woman suffrage, movements to reform municipal government and to suppress commercial prostitution, advocates of Irish independence, and trade unionists." As head of the Commission, he "played an increasingly aggressive and partisan role, overriding both the representatives of business and the self-styled impartial social scientists selected by John R. Commons to make the commission the tribune for the oppressed American worker" (Montgomery, 1987, pp. 360–361).

69. "[T]he Executive Board gave its official sanction to strike if any member was discharged for refusing to do more work than seemed fair for a day's work, or for refusing to work under conditions which were humiliating in their nature, such as having some whipesnapper [sic] standing over him with a stopwatch, timing every

movement and endeavoring from these accumulated timing records to set the definite time in which the job must be finished" (Frey, 1911, p. 695).

70. In his testimony before the committee, Brigadier General William Grozier, Chief of Ordnance, U.S. Army, states, "At the Watertown Arsenal, when this strike was precipitated, I fancy that the authorities had been lulled to sleep by the smoothness with which the operation of installing this system had proceeded. Some time studies had been made in the machine shop. We had been working for two years on the systemization features, and one day when the time study feature was attempted in the foundry there was a strike. "I do not believe that the Government employees as a rule think they are badly treated. I do not think they would consider, if they were left to themselves, that the Government was contemplating treating them badly. I think it may be possible that somebody, considering that there was some disadvantage to him in the introduction of this system, thought it worth his while to endeavor to stir up the employees into a state of dissatisfaction with it and opposition to it" (U.S. House of Representatives, 1912a, p. 1221).

71. In an obituary published in *The University of Chicago Magazine*, July 1916, the claim is made that Hoxie "had recently been burdened by unusual expenses connected with special reports for the Walsh Industrial Relations Commission," which perhaps contributed to his suicide.

72. Hoxie notes that "about one hundred and fifty scientific management leaders, systematizers, employers, managers, time study men, labor leaders, and other authorities on the subject were consulted as individuals" (Hoxie, 1915, p.4). Among those listed, in addition to Taylor, Gantt, and Emerson, are Louis D. Brandeis (later Associate Justice of the U.S. Supreme Court), the labor leader Samuel Gompers, Carl G. Barth, and James Hartness (inventor, entrepreneur, and, later, governor of Vermont)

73. A concise description of Hoxie's method of analysis in his studies of scientific management and labor problems in general is given in Frey (1916).

74. In a eulogy published in *The University of Chicago Magazine*, James Tufts asserts, "It was evidence of the scientific impartiality of the work that the experts representing the two sides of the issue concurred in the conclusions as well as in the statement of their respective positions" (Tufts, 1916, p. 440).

75. "As printed it covered one hundred and sixty-five pages of his book, with only one hundred and thirty-seven pages devoted to the text" (Commons, 1934, p. 179).

76. The Research Division continued to function, under the direction of Basil Manly.

77. Note Commons: "I consider that production is the business of the employer, and that, if a union turns itself mainly to production, it can do so only by becoming its own employer – that is, by becoming a cooperative society" (Commons, 1911, p. 463).

78. "On the Industrial Relations Commission I eventually found myself in the hateful predicament of separating myself from my three labor colleagues. I finally drafted an independent report, signed by Mrs. Harriman and myself, and approved, with reservations on secondary boycott and representation of the public in labor disputes, by the three employer representatives" (Commons, 1934, p. 167).

79. "The Railway Brotherhoods, not members of the American Federation of Labor, were represented on the Commission by the head of the conductors' organization, Mr. A. B. Garretson. They were then, I thought, being carried away by what afterwards came to be known as the 'Plumb Plan' of representation of 'labor' on the boards of directors of the railway corporations, as well as by the illusion of investment of their funds and the operation of such outside activities as banks, coal mines, office buildings, or even land speculation. I considered these schemes destructive of unionism, because they dissipated the strike funds and took labor over to the side of capitalists with a minority vote, leading them, by way of politics, into socialism or communism" (Commons, 1934, p. 168).

80. "The political program of Walsh and Garretson, I argued, would not only get business into politics but it pointed toward communism and socialism" (Commons, 1934, p. 169). "To the practical business man in the midst of the conflict, 'socialism' meant any movement or opinion, even trade-unionism, bent on reducing his profits or reducing his control over his own business" (p. 170).

81. Hoxie neatly summarizes the argument in Hoxie (1916a).

82. "In making this study, the effort has been to avoid personal bias, and to view all matters purely from the standpoint of fact and cause. The purpose of the investigation has been to lay foundations for the judgment of scientific management, not relative to an absolute ideal, but relative to the alternative which would exist without it. There is no desire to uphold or to condemn either party to the controversy, least of all to foment contest. The prime objects are to lay bare the facts of the actual situation and to dispel misunderstandings, as a starting point and basis for reasonable control and constructive effort. Any criticisms of scientific management which follow must be understood in this light" (Hoxie, 1915, p. 6). Nyland concludes that Hoxie's report, while "accepted as Gospel," nonetheless "was seriously compromised and must be considered to have little scientific value" (Nyland, 1996, p. 988).

83. Nyland concludes: "All charges laid against the Taylorists were published in the report, but only those for which some evidence could be found were actually discussed. As a consequence, the Taylorists were charged publicly with a great many crimes, found innocent of none and guilty of many. The overall impression left by this imbalance is that all important union accusations had been sustained." Nyland further argues that Hoxie was less-than-candid in claiming to present a more balanced follow-up report, as he accepted Valentine as an advocate for the scientific managers, thus giving the study an air of bipartisanship. "As structured, it constituted a damning indictment of scientific management that depicted Taylor as an idealist with little commitment to scientific rigor and a tool of management who aimed to both deskill workers and destroy collective bargaining" (Nyland, 1996, pp. 1007–1008).

84. Cf. Commons: "There are many attractive and important contributions which the efficiency engineers are making towards the solution of labor problems. Their careful study of the human element in production is notable, appearing in the greatest variety of applications under the name of 'welfare work'" (Commons, 1911, pp. 471–472).

85. "The mere recognition of labor standards is always protective, and when such recognition is accompanied not only by assurances of disaster to follow their

violation, but by the demonstration that their maintenance is an essential factor in the general scheme of efficiency, the labor concerned stands to gain, in the long run, even though the advocates of standardization are not always themselves able to attain the ideal of standardization or are not guiltless of its violation" (Hoxie, 1915, p. 24).

86. The shops visited included the Tabor Manufacturing Company (Philadelphia, Pennsylvania), The New England Butt Company (Providence, Rhode Island), Acme Wire Company (New Haven, Connecticut), The Plimpton Press (Norwood, Massachusetts), The Watertown Arsenal (Watertown, Massachusetts), The Remington Typewriter Company ((Ilion, New York), The Aluminum Castings Company (Detroit, Michigan), Joseph and Feiss, Clothescraft Shops (Cleveland, Ohio), The Westinghouse Electric and Manufacturing Company (Pittsburgh, Pennsylvania), Jones and Laughlin Company (Pittsburgh, Pennsylvania), The German-American Button Company (Rochester, New York), Filene's Specialty Store (Boston, Massachusetts), and Ford Automobile Works (Detroit, Michigan), among others. The last two – Filene's and Ford – are listed as "Other Plants", not Scientific Management plants. (See Hoxie, 1915, pp. 3 4).

87. "The logical distribution of duties according to the Taylor scheme seems more capable of practical fulfillment than the distribution of authority" (Hoxie, 1915, p. 31). In a later essay, published in *The Survey*, Hoxie phrases this somewhat differently: "The *logical* distribution of duties according to the Taylor scheme seems more capable of fulfillment than the *practical* distribution of authority" (Hoxie, 1916a, p. 674; emphasis in original).

88. Clarence Thompson concludes that Hoxie's Scientific Management and Labor "seems to rest on a consideration chiefly of abuses and inadequacies of the movement" (Thompson, 1917, p. 172n.). Thompson's book is dedicated "To the Honored Memory of Frederick Winslow Taylor."

89. "All the extra work is done for him by a series of functional foremen or specialized workmen. The belting connected with the machine is cared for by a special functionary – the belt man; the tools which he uses are brought to him already ground by a specialist who does nothing else; his materials are always at hand, delivered by the move man, who also takes away the product. The laying out and setting up of the work, the feed and speed to be used in doing it, and the mode of handling the material and putting it through the machine are determined by special functionaries and embodied in written instructions, except where the functional foreman is actually present to perform or assist in the initial operation or where the work is so thoroughly subdivided and repetitive that actual instructions are not deemed necessary, and, though the worker may depart in some instances from the instructions given, he does so at the peril of the bonus, premium or higher differential piece rate" (Hoxie, 1915, pp. 123–124).

90. "What this means in increased competition of workmen with workmen can be imagined. Were the scientific management ideal as at present formulated fully realized, any man who walks the street would be a practical competitor for almost any workman's job. Such a situation would inevitably break down the basis of present-day unionism in its dominant form and render collective bargaining as now practiced impossible in any effective sense in regard to the matters considered by the unions most essential. It has been proved by experience that unskilled workers

generally find it most difficult to maintain effective and continuous organization for dealing with complicated industrial situations. But effective collective bargaining, as we have it now, cannot exist without effective organization" (Hoxie, 1915, pp. 129–130).

91. In his last essay on the issue, "Why Organized Labor Opposes Scientific Management," published posthumously, Hoxie reiterates his contention as to the reason behind union opposition: "Scientific management, properly applied, normally functioning, should it become universal, would spell the doom of effective unionism as it exists today" (Hoxie, 1916b, p. 85). This essay is reprinted as Chapter XIII of *Trade Unionism in the United States* (Hoxie, 1917).

92. In "Why Organized Labor Opposes Scientific Management," Hoxie notes five possible explanations, "brought forward both by opponents and advocates of scientific management to account in general and causal terms for the attitude and belief of organized labor" in respect of the process. These are (1) an "ignorance" on the part of labor as to "the true nature, methods, and results of scientific management," (2) a "distrust ... of anything new or different in industrial organization and methods", (3) the propaganda campaign waged by the leaders of organized labor "who fear that if a better understanding is allowed to grow up between the real workers and the employers, their prestige and emoluments will be decreased, and even their positions abolished, and they be reduced again to the ranks," (4) the "crudities of scientific management" in its application and the abuses which followed therefrom, and (5) the notion that the "dominant ideals of trade unionism ... are incompatible with those of scientific management" (Hoxie, 1916b, pp. 66–67).

93. Yet in his 1919 *Industrial Goodwill*, Commons seems to modify his objection: "Mr. Taylor's great contribution to the subject was that of accurately *measuring* the *task* in advance, instead of leaving it to the hit-or-miss, cut-and-try, methods of the old style piece-work practice. Scientific management, applied to labor, is scientific measurement of the laborer's task required to hold the job" (Commons, 1919, p. 13; emphasis in original).

94. In his testimony before the Commission on Industrial Relations, 14 April 1914, Mixter identified his occupation as "time-study man with the Sentinel Automatic Gas Appliance Co., of New Haven" (Commission on Industrial Relations, 1916, p. 835).

95. He points out that both of the assistants appointed by the commission to ensure fairness "were out and out labor men" (Mixter, 1916, p. 376). Nyland (1996) provides support for this lack of balance.

96. For example, Nelson's (1974) summary of the evolution of the scientific management approach affords but a single line to Hoxie, and then on the last page of his essay.

REFERENCES

Adamic, L. (1931). *Dynamite: The story of class violence in America*. New York, NY: Viking.

Adams, G., Jr. (1966). *Age of industrial violence 1910–1915: The activities and findings of the United States Commission on Industrial Relations*. New York, NY: Columbia University Press.

Annual Register (University of Chicago). (1908). July 1907–July 1908. Chicago, IL: University of Chicago.

Annual Register (University of Chicago). (1909). (July 1908–July 1909) Chicago, IL: University of Chicago.

Annual Register (University of Chicago). (1911). July 1910–July 1911. Chicago, IL: University of Chicago Press.

Annual Register (University of Chicago). (1915). Academic Year Ending June 30, 1915. Chicago, IL: University of Chicago Press.

Bauder, R. (1943). Three interpretations of the American trade union movement. *Social Forces*, *22*(2), 215–224.

Brandeis, L. D. (1911). *Scientific management and railroads, being part of a brief submitted to the Interstate Commerce Commission*. New York, NY: The Engineering Magazine.

Cardullo, F. E. (1912). Industrial administration and scientific management: 1: What constitutes scientific management. Machinery 18: 931–935. As reprinted in Clarence Bertrand Thompson, ed. Scientific Management: A Collection of the More Significant Articles Describing the Taylor System of Management. Cambridge, MA: Harvard University Press.

Cherry, R. (1976). Racial thought and the early economics profession. *Review of Social Economy*, *34*(2), 147–162.

Chicago Daily Tribune. (1916). *Prof. R.F. Hoxie takes his life*, *75*(150), 15.

Commission on Industrial Relations. (1915). *Final report of the Commission on Industrial Relations*. Washington, DC: Barnard and Miller, Chicago.

Commission on Industrial Relations. (1916). *Final report and testimony submitted to Congress by the Commission on Industrial Relations created by the Act of August 23, 1912*. Volume I. 64th Congress, 1st Session, Document no. 415. Washington, DC: Government Printing Office.

Commons, J. R. (1908). Is class conflict in America growing and is it inevitable? *American Journal of Sociology*, *13*(6), 756–766.

Commons, J. R. (1911). Organized labor's attitude toward industrial efficiency. *American Economic Review*, *1*(3), 463–472.

Commons, J. R. (1916). Review of Scientific Management and Labor. *American Journal of Sociology*, *21*(5), 688–692.

Commons, J. R. (1918). Hoxie's Trade Unionism in the United States. (Review of Trade Unionism in the United States, by Robert F. Hoxie.). *Quarterly Journal of Economics*, *32*(2), 396–399.

Commons, J. R. (1919). *Industrial goodwill*. New York, NY: McGraw-Hill.

Commons, J. R. (1934). *Myself*. New York, NY: Macmillan.

Cooley, C. H. (1909). *Social organization: A study of the larger Mind*. New York, NY: Charles Scribner's Sons.

Cornell University Register. (1905a). *Series 5, no. 2 (January)*. Ithaca, NY: Cornell University.

Cornell University Register. (1905b). *Series 5, no. 4 (May)*. Ithaca, NY: Cornell University.

Cornell University Register. (1906). *Series 6, no. 2 (January)*. Ithaca, NY: Cornell University.

Cummings, J. (1899). The theory of the leisure class. *Journal of Political Economy*, 7(4), 425–455.

Debs, E. V. (1905). *Industrial unionism: An address delivered at Grand Central Palace*, New York, NY, Sunday, December 10, 1905. Chicago, IL: Charles H. Kerr and Company.

Debs, E. V. (1909a). *Craft unionism: Speech delivered at Chicago*. November 23, 1905; Revised by the Author and Re-issued October, 1909. Chicago, IL: Charles H. Kerr and Company.

Debs, E. V. (1909b). *Revolutionary unionism: Speech delivered at Chicago*. November 25, 1905; Revised by the Author and Re-issued September, 1909. Chicago, IL: Charles H. Kerr and Company.

Dorfman, J. (1945). *Thorstein Veblen and his America*. New York, NY: Viking.

Dorfman, J. (1949). *The economic mind in American civilization* (Vol. 3, pp. 1865–1918). New York, NY: Viking.

Dorfman, J. (1958). Veblen centenary round table: Source and impact of Veblen. *American Economic Review, Papers and Proceedings*, *48*(2), 1–10.

Downey, E. H. (1914). Professor Hoxie's interpretation of trade unionism. *American Journal of Sociology*, *20*(2), 170–180.

Drury, H. B. (1915). *Scientific management: A history and criticism*. New York, NY: Columbia University.

Ernst, D. R. (1993). Common laborers? Industrial pluralists, legal realists, and the law of industrial disputes. *Law and History Review*, *11*(1), 59–100.

Executive Committee (1880). Chinese labor. *Journal of United Labor*, *1*(4), 39.

Final Report of the Los Angeles County Grand Jury. (1911, October 25). *Department of special collections*. Stanford University, 1910, October 13.

Fiorito, L., & Samuels, W. J. (Eds.). (2006). Robert Hoxie's introductory lecture on the nature of the history of political economy [1916]: The history of economic thought as the history of error. *Research in the History of Economic Thought and Methodology*, *24-C*, 49–97.

Fishman, L. (1958). Veblen, Hoxie, and American labor. In D. F. Dowd (Ed.), *Thorstein Veblen: A critical reappraisal: Lectures and essays commemorating the hundredth anniversary of Veblen's birth*. Ithaca, NY: Cornell University Press.

Frey, J. P. (1911). Editorial: The strike at the Watertown arsenal. *International Molders' Journal*, *47*(9), 695.

Frey, J. P. (1916). Robert F. Hoxie: Investigator and interpreter. *Journal of Political Economy*, *24*(9), 884–893.

Gantt, L. (1910). *Work, wages, and profits: Their influence on the cost of living*. New York, NY: The Engineering Magazine.

Gompers, S. (1913). Abstract of President Gompers' testimony before the House Lobby Investigation Committee. *American Federationist*, *20*(12), 997–1031.

Goodrich, C. (1932). *Hoxie, Robert Franklin. Encyclopaedia of the social sciences* (Vol. 7, pp. 524–525). New York, NY: Macmillan.

Haig, R. M. (1916). Review of scientific management and labor. *Political Science Quarterly*, *31*(4), 641–643.

Hamilton, W. H. (1916). The development of Hoxie's economics. *Journal of Political Economy*, *24*(9), 855–883.

Hamilton, W. H. (1932). Hoxie, Robert Franklin. In Dumas Malone (Ed.), *Dictionary of American biography* (Vol. 9). New York, NY: Charles Scribner's Sons.

Hodgson, G. M. (2004). *The evolution of institutional economics*. London: Routledge.

Hoxie, J. L. (1922). *Solomon Hoxie: A biography by his daughter Jane L. Hoxie*. Baldwinsville, NY: C. H. Smith, printer.

Hoxie, R. F. (1893a). The compensatory theory of bimetallism. *Journal of Political Economy*, *1*(2), 273–276.
Hoxie, R. F. (1893b). The silver debate of 1890. *Journal of Political Economy*, *1*(4), 535–587.
Hoxie, R. F. (1894). Adequacy of the customs revenue system. *Journal of Political Economy*, *3*(1), 39-72.
Hoxie, R. F. (1901). On the empirical method of economic instruction. *Journal of Political Economy*, *9*(4), 481–526.
Hoxie, R. F. (1905). Fetter's theory of value. *Quarterly Journal of Economics*, *19*(2), 210–230.
Hoxie, R. F. (1906a). The demand and supply concepts: An introduction to the study of market price. *Journal of Political Economy*, *14*(6), 337–361.
Hoxie, R. F. (1906b). The demand and supply concepts: An introduction to the study of market price II. *Journal of Political Economy*, *14*(7), 401–426.
Hoxie, R. F. (1906c). Historical method vs. historical narrative. *Journal of Political Economy*, *14*(9), 568–572.
Hoxie, R. F. (1907a). Sociology and the other social sciences: A rejoinder. *American Journal of Sociology*, *12*(6), 739–755.
Hoxie, R. F. (1907b). The trade-union point of view. *Journal of Political Economy*, *15*(6), 345–363.
Hoxie, R. F. (1907c). The failure of the telegraphers' strike. *Journal of Political Economy*, *15*(9), 545–547.
Hoxie, R. F. (1908a). Discussion of "Is class conflict in America growing and is it inevitable?" by John R. Commons. *American Journal of Sociology*, *13*(6), 776–781.
Hoxie, R. F. (1908b). The convention of the Socialist Party. *Journal of Political Economy*, *16*(7), 442–450.
Hoxie, R. F. (1908c). President Gompers and the labor vote. *Journal of Political Economy*, *16*(10), 693–700.
Hoxie, R. F. (1911a). "The rising tide of socialism": A study. *Journal of Political Economy*, *19*(8), 609–631.
Hoxie, R. F. (1911b). Unionism and unionism. *The Survey (Special Issue: Larger Bearings of the McNamara Case)*, *27*(13), 1425–1426.
Hoxie, R. F. (1912a). The socialist party in the november elections. *Journal of Political Economy*, *20*(3), 205–223.
Hoxie, R. F. (1912b). The socialist party and American convention methods. *Journal of Political Economy*, *20*(7), 738–744.
Hoxie, R. F. (1913a). Springs of conflicting action. *The Survey*, *30*(18), 580–581.
Hoxie, R. F. (1913b). The truth about the I.W.W. *Journal of Political Economy*, *21*(9), 785–797.
Hoxie, R. F. (1914a). Trade unionism in the United States: General character and types. *Journal of Political Economy*, *22*(3), 201–217.
Hoxie, R. F. (1914b). Trade unionism in the United States: The essence of unionism and the interpretation of union types. *Journal of Political Economy*, *22*(5), 464–481.
Hoxie, R. F. (1914c). The principle of uniformity. In Walton Hamilton (Ed.), *1915. Current economic problems*. Chicago, IL: University of Chicago Press. (From an unpublished lecture, May 17, 1914).
Hoxie, R. F. (1914d). Discussion of "The Problem of Syndicalism" by John Graham Brooks. American Economic Review Supplement, 4:1 (March): 136–144, *Papers and*

Proceedings of the Twenty-sixth Annual Meeting of the American Economic Association, Minneapolis, Minnesota, December 1913.

Hoxie, R. F. (1915). *Scientific management and labor*. New York, NY: D. Appleton and Company.

Hoxie, R. F. (1916a). Scientific management and social welfare. *The Survey*, *35*(23), 673–680. 685–686. (Article is signed "Robert H. Hoxie").

Hoxie, R. F. (1916b). Why organized labor opposes scientific management. *Quarterly Journal of Economics*, *31*(1), 62–85.

Hoxie, R. F. (1916c). Scientific management and labor welfare. *Journal of Political Economy*, *24*(9), 833–854.

Hoxie, R. F. (1917). *Trade unionism in the United States*. New York, NY: D. Appleton and Company.

Irwin, L. (2013). *Deadly times: The 1910 bombing of the Los Angeles Times and America's Forgotten Decade of Terror*. Guilford, CT: Lyons Press.

Johnson, A. S. (1915). A model of scientific investigation. *New Republic*, *5*(57), 126–127.

Johnson, A. S. (1916). Robert Franklin Hoxie. *New Republic*, *7*(88), 248–249.

Johnson, A. S. (1952). *Pilgrim's progress*. New York, NY: Viking.

Kaufman, B. E. (2008). *Managing the human factor: The early years of human resource management in American industry*. Ithaca, NY: Cornell University Press.

Kimball, D. S. (1916). Review of scientific management and labor. *Journal of Political Economy*, *24*(2), 194–197.

Kipnis, I. (1952). *The American socialist movement*, 1897–1912. New York, NY: Columbia University Press.

Knoedler, J. (1997). Veblen and technical efficiency. *Journal of Economic Issues*, *31*(4), 1011–1026.

Lauck, W. J., & Sydenstricker, E. (1917). *Conditions of labor in American industries: summarization of the results of recent investigations*. New York, NY: Funk and Wagnalls Co.

Laughlin, J. L. (1916). *Twenty-five years of the Department of Political Economy*. Chicago, IL: University of Chicago. Privately printed.

Lecht, L. A. (1959). The Teamsters and predatory unionism. *American Journal of Economics and Sociology*, *18*(2), 213–221.

Los Angeles Times. (1910). Twenty-one killed and more injured in the dynamited Times building. *Los Angeles Times*. October 2.

McCartin, J. A. (1997). *Labor's Great War: The struggle for industrial democracy and the origins of modern American labor relations, 1912–1921*. Chapel Hill, NC: University of North Carolina Press.

McNulty, P. J. (1966). Labor market analysis and the development of labor economics. *Industrial and Labor Relations Review*, *19*(4), 538–548.

McNulty, P. J. (1973). Hoxie's economics in retrospect: The making and unmaking of a Veblenian. *History of Political Economy*, *5*(2), 449–484.

Mead, G. H. (1917). Professor Hoxie and the community. *The University of Chicago Magazine*, *9*(3), 114–117.

Mitchell, W. C. (1941). J. Laurence Laughlin. *Journal of Political Economy*, *49*(6), 875–881.

Mixter, C. W. (1916). Review of scientific management and labor. *American Economic Review*, *6*(2), 373–377.

Montgomery, D. (1987). *The fall of the house of labor*. Cambridge: Cambridge University Press.

Nelson, D. (1974). Scientific management, systematic management, and labor, 1880–1915. *Business History Review*, *48*(4), 479–500.

Nyland, C. (1996). Taylorism, John R. Commons, and the Hoxie Report. *Journal of Economic Issues*, *30*(4), 985–1016.

Papers of John R. Commons. Correspondence and General Correspondence. (1859–1911). Microfilm, Box 1, Folder 1, Reel 1. State Historical Society of Wisconsin.

Perlman, M. (1958). *Labor union theories in America: Background and development*. Evanston, IL: Row, Peterson and Co.

Perlman, S. (1928). *A theory of the labor movement*. New York, NY: Macmillan.

Petition to the President. (1911). *Survey*, *27*(13), 1430–1431.

Portenar, A. J. (1919). Reconstruction – A survey and a forecast. *Annals of the American Academy of Political and Social Science*, *82* (March), 111–123.

Report of the Chief of Ordnance, U.S. Army. (1913). *The Taylor system of shop management at the Watertown arsenal*. Washington, DC: Government Printing Office.

Ross, E. A. (1911). Their question and ours. *The Survey (Special Issue: Larger Bearings of the McNamara Case)*, *27*(13), 1425.

Rutherford, M. (1998). Veblen's evolutionary programme: A promise unfulfilled. *Cambridge Journal of Economics*, *22*(4),463–477.

Schumpeter, J. A. (1954). *History of economic analysis*. New York, NY: Oxford University Press.

Seligman, E. R. A. (1911). The reactionary and the radical fanatic. *The Survey (Special Issue: Larger Bearings of the McNamara Case)*, *27*(13), 1419.

Spiegel, H. W. (1971). *The growth of economic thought*. Englewood Cliffs, NJ: Prentice-Hall.

Statutes at Large of the United States of America. (1912) (Vol. 37), Washington, DC: Government Printing Office.

Stevens, E. W. (2009). *Radical L.A.: From Coxey's army to the Watts riots* (pp. 1894–1965). Norman, OK: University of Oklahoma Press.

Taft, P. (1950). A rereading of Selig Perlman's "A Theory of the Labor Movement". *Industrial and Labor Relations Review*, *4*(1), 70–77.

Taft, P. (1963). On the origins of business unionism. *Industrial and Labor Relations Review*, *17*(1), 20–38.

Taylor, F. W. (1895). A piece-rate system: Being a step toward partial solution of the labor problem. *Transactions of the American Society of Mechanical Engineers*, *16*, 856–903.

Taylor, F. W. (1903). Shop management (with discussion). (Paper read before the American Society of Mechanical Engineers). *Transactions of the American Society of Mechanical Engineers*, *26*(1003), 1337–1480.

Taylor, F. W. (1911). *The principles of scientific management*. New York, NY: Harper and Brothers.

Tead, O. (1918). Review of trade unionism in the United States. *Journal of Political Economy*, *26*(7), 762–767.

Ten-Year Book of Cornell University IV: 1868–1908 (1908). Ithaca, NY: Cornell University.

Thompson, C. B. (1917). *The theory and practice of scientific management*. Cambridge, MA: Riverside Press.

Tufts, J. H. (1916). Professor Hoxie's work. *The University of Chicago Magazine*, *8*(9), 440–441.

"Unionist" (1910). The Los Angeles conspiracy against organized labor. *International Socialist Review*, *11*(5), 262–266.

Unsigned. (1916). Robert Franklin Hoxie. *The University of Chicago Magazine*, 8(9), 439.
U.S. House of Representatives. (1911). *"Taylor system" of shop management. 62nd Congress, 1st Session. Report No. 52 (to accompany House Resolution 90)*. Washington, DC: Government Printing Office.
U.S. House of Representatives. (1912a). *The Taylor and other systems of shop management. 62nd Congress, 2nd Session, Report No. 403 (to accompany House Resolution 90)*. Washington, DC: Government Printing Office.
U.S. House of Representatives. (1912b). *Stop watch and bonus in government work. House Reports (Public), 62nd Congress, 2nd Session, Report No. 1001*. Washington, DC: Government Printing Office.
Veblen, T. (1898). Why is economics not an evolutionary science? *Quarterly Journal of Economics*, *12*(4), 373–397.
Veblen, T. B. (1901). Industrial and pecuniary employments. In *Publications of the American Economic Association*. Third series (Vol. 2, p. 190–235). New York, NY: Macmillan.
Veblen, T. B. (1904). *The theory of business enterprise*. New York, NY: Charles Scribner's Sons.

THE MISES-KNIGHT THEORY OF UNCERTAINTY AND ITS IMPLICATIONS FOR ENTREPRENEURSHIP, EQUILIBRIUM, AND THE THEORY OF THE FIRM

Per L. Bylund and G. P. Manish

ABSTRACT

The goal of this paper is to analyze the views of Frank Knight and Ludwig von Mises on the topic of uncertainty and how it influences the theory of individual decision-making and to trace out the implications of the same for the theories of entrepreneurship, equilibrium, and the firm. The paper adopts a historical approach in its analysis of the theory of uncertainty, with an extended discussion of the primary writings of Knight and Mises on this topic. It then uses the insights gleaned from this discussion in order to address issues and topics that have found a prominent place in the modern literature on entrepreneurship, equilibrium, and the firm that draws its inspiration from the Austrian School.

Research in the History of Economic Thought and Methodology, Volume 34B, 305–336

ISSN: 0743-4154/doi:10.1108/S0743-41542016000034B002

The paper offers three main findings: in the realm of entrepreneurship it argues that there can be no theory of the entrepreneur without the concept of uncertainty provided by Knight and Mises, whereas with regard to the theory of equilibrium it focuses on highlighting the concept of an equilibrium with error prevalent in the Austrian tradition and on the implications that an explicit introduction of uncertainty has for the existence of a process of equilibration that pushes the economy toward a state of general equilibrium in real time. As regards the theory of the firm we find that a proper understanding of uncertainty ultimately reverses the direction of any causal explanation of economic organization, making the firm an outcome of dealing with uncertainty rather than a means to do so.

Keywords: Uncertainty; risk; Austrian school of economics; Frank H. Knight; entrepreneurship; equilibrium

INTRODUCTION

Economics has over the course of the last three quarters of a century evolved into a highly mathematical endeavor that seeks to be a "social physics" (see, e.g., Mirowski, 1991; Schabas, 1993). As such, it has increasingly come to rely on formal, streamlined models that purport to measure and predict economic behavior with the utmost precision. As a result of this approach, mainstream economic theory has all but done away with the open-ended uncertainty of economic action. Indeed, the concept is extremely difficult to fit into theoretical constructs that seek to ape the physical sciences and which therefore focus on the study of phenomena thought of as being embedded in a world of quantitatively determined relationships.

Unsurprisingly then, actions occurring without the aid of a unique, additive and fully reliable probability distribution, that is, under "strong" uncertainty (Dequech, 2011), which casual introspection and common sense reveal as commonplace, have put economists in an uncomfortable position. In addition, the mere possibility of structural change that is not predetermined, or action under "fundamental" uncertainty (Dequech, 2011), further serves to reinforce this felt uneasiness; a sentiment that Lucas (1977, p. 224) captured bluntly when he stated that while risk can be dealt with using the standard analytical toolbox in modern economics, "in case of uncertainty economic reasoning will be of no value." Indeed, uncertainty, ignorance, and open-endedness, all of which are defining characteristics of the real world, cannot be fitted into modern economic models.

While the treatment of uncertainty as a no more than marginally important concept facilitates the construction of internally consistent models for the prediction of behavior, the assumption of perfect (or perfectly available or procurable) information that underlies these models implies that they are consigned to focusing on an analysis of human action and choice in a world free of error. However, the widespread impression that doing away with any sort of strong or fundamental uncertainty can nonetheless offer a useful approximation, while taking it seriously would make the whole edifice of economics crumble down, is unwarranted. Instead, such an approach produces internally consistent and mathematically "true" models that are nevertheless unrealistic, inapplicable and thus only limitedly usable, if at all. As a result, theory and reality part ways

We seek in this paper to bring these problems to the attention of scholars by discussing the nature and implications of uncertainty for economic theorizing. Our contribution consists of identifying how placing uncertainty at center stage, rather than treating it as a peripheral and unnecessary complexity, in fact makes room for sound economic theorizing and fundamentally adds to the realism of economic theory. We accomplish this by looking at the treatment of uncertainty in the Austrian school of economics, paying special attention to the concept's integration into the School's theory of subjective value and price. This discussion serves as an illuminating framework and a valuable stepping stone that allows us to then study the implications of this integration for three important areas of economic research: entrepreneurship and economic calculation, the use of equilibrium constructs, and the organizing of production in firms.

The paper proceeds as follows: The next section provides an introduction to the conceptual differences between risk and uncertainty as introduced into economic literature by Frank H. Knight. The following section focuses on the integration of uncertainty into the Austrian theory of value and price, after which we apply the concept to indicate its implications for theorizing in the three areas mentioned above. The final section discusses our findings and implications for economic theory.

UNCERTAINTY AS DISTINCT FROM RISK

The first systematic exposition of a distinction between risk and uncertainty is arguably to be found in Knight's *Risk, Uncertainty and Profit* (1985 [1921]).

The distinction itself is the outgrowth of Knight's far-reaching classification of various notions of probability; and the narrower economic question that leads to this classification is that of the source of profit and loss. With omniscient people, in a state of perfect competition, nothing could "upset the perfect apportionment of product values among the contributing agencies, and profit (or loss) would not arise" (Knight, 1985 [1921], p. 198). Hence, profits and losses must be associated with a lack of perfect foresight. However, the mere fact that people do not predict any contingency is not sufficient for profits and losses to arise. For

> Even though the business man could not know in advance the results of individual ventures, he could operate and base his competitive offers upon accurate foreknowledge of the future if quantitative knowledge of the probability of every possible outcome can be had. For by figuring on the basis of a large number of ventures (whether in his own business alone or in that of business in general) the losses could be converted into fixed costs. Such special costs would, of course, have to be given full weight, but they would be costs merely, like any other necessary outlays, and would not give rise to profit, which is a difference between cost and selling price. (Knight, 1985 [1921], pp. 198–199)

In other words, what we have here is a "probability judgment in the form that a given numerical proportion of X's are also Y's" (Knight, 1985 [1921], p. 214). Knight refers to these sorts of measurable imperfections of knowledge as "risk" (Knight, 1985 [1921], p. 233).

Two methods can be utilized to arrive at judgments that seek to measure the magnitude of risk: the "a priori" or "mathematical" method, and the "statistical" method (Knight, 1985 [1921], pp. 214–215). The first method typically applies to games of chance. For instance, it can be known without throwing a perfect die that the chance of landing a six with it is 1/6. This a priori method, however, is of limited relevance as far as economics is concerned, for it "is practically never met with in business." The second method, on the other hand, "is extremely common" (Knight, 1985 [1921], p. 215).

This second method consists of calculating the proportion of distribution among the possible outcomes which have been discovered by tabulating the results of experience (with as many instances performed as possible of events empirically classified as alike). To provide an instance of when this second method is actually utilized, Knight uses the example of champagne producers (1985 [1921], p. 213). The champagne producer can find out from past experience that a fixed proportion of bottles burst during the production process. Now, while this analysis of experience does not enable him to know which particular bottle will burst over the course of producing a batch of them, it does enable him to convert the monetary loss that results from the bursting bottles into a fixed cost via insurance. As a result, this fixed cost can be accounted for prior to the commencement of production. And thus, despite the imperfect knowledge that the producer has concerning the bursting of bottles, this event no longer contributes to the emergence of profit or loss.

The crucial insight, however, that is the hallmark of Knight's enquiry into the nature of imperfect knowledge, is his conclusion that in many instances in daily life, including business life, "there is no valid basis of any kind for classifying instances," and therefore no basis for utilizing this second method of measuring imperfect knowledge. Stated differently, "the essential and outstanding fact" that dominates practical economic life "is that the 'instance' in question is so entirely unique that there are no others or not a sufficient number to make it possible to tabulate enough like it to form a basis for any inference of value about any real probability in the case we are interested in" (Knight, 1985 [1921], p. 226). As a result, given the impossibility of grouping a set of events into a class, it is impossible in these instances to measure imperfect knowledge in the form of a probability distribution over potential outcomes culled from the observation and analysis of experience.

A typical such instance is that of entrepreneurial decision-making (Knight, 1985 [1921], p. 232). Thus, consider the case of an entrepreneur trying to decide whether or not he should expand production. With limited knowledge of the possible outcomes and no valid basis for classifying the various relevant outcomes that might emerge in the future, he cannot reduce the lack of knowledge that he encounters to a measurable probability distribution and thus cannot take advantage of any calculation of the sort that insurance deals with. As a result, this entrepreneur, and indeed all entrepreneurs, when making "any typical business decision," must necessarily resort to "intuitive judgment" and the aid of "estimates" (Knight, 1985 [1921], pp. 226–227, 229). The future, consequently, is neither foreseeable nor predictable, but can only be imagined.

Knight refers to such unmeasurable knowledge imperfection as "uncertainty" (Knight, 1985 [1921], p. 233). Being irreducible to fixed costs, uncertainty permanently leaves room for errors in judgment and hence the existence of profits and losses. Typical business decisions being based on such estimates, failure to forecast future prices and quantities are perfectly normal and result in bidding up factors of production too much or not enough in relation to their prospective or anticipated marginal value product.

THE USE OF UNCERTAINTY IN THE AUSTRIAN SCHOOL OF ECONOMICS

Value and Marginal Utility

In his path-breaking treatise, *Principles of Economics* (Menger, [1871] 2007), Carl Menger, founder of the Austrian School of economics, divides the world of goods into two broad classes: economic goods that are scarce by nature and non-economic goods that are distinguished by the relative abundance of their supply with respect to the needs that individuals have for them. The scarce nature of economic goods ensures that they bear a very different relationship to human well-being as compared to their non-economic brethren. The latter merely possess the quality of usefulness, or "the general capacity to subserve human weal" (Böhm-Bawerk, [1888] 1930, p. 133), and due to their abundance are never indispensable causes of human well-being. That honor is reserved for economic goods, which, on account of their scarcity, serve as the *conditio sine qua non* for the satisfaction of certain wants. These goods, as a result, possess not only usefulness but also value; they are, in other words, of importance to human well-being in a way that non-economic goods are not.

A simple example can help clarify the difference between usefulness and value. Consider an individual who lives beside a stream that pours forth a 100 buckets of water a day, of which only 10 buckets are required to satisfy his myriad needs. Does any satisfaction, in this scenario, depend on his possession of a bucket? None whatsoever, given that he has far more water than he needs. But if a drought were to reduce the stream to a trickle yielding a mere five buckets of water a day, the scarce nature of water ensures that the possession of a bucket serves as the indispensable pre-condition for the satisfaction of a want. The loss of a bucket, in other words, impairs the individual's ability to satisfy some want and entails a loss in satisfaction, thereby acquiring value.

Thus, the value of goods emerges from their scarcity and the subsequent interaction of the possible ends that can be satisfied with their aid and the available stock of them. Moreover, in any given situation, the value of a unit of a good is determined by its marginal utility. Let us revisit the individual with a supply of 5 buckets of water and with requirements for 10 such buckets.

If this individual were to lose a bucket of water, what is the specific satisfaction of his that is dependent on its possession? He certainly would not be willing to give up his highest ranked end. Instead, the axe would fall on the lowest ranked end amongst those that he currently satisfies. The satisfaction derived from this end is the satisfaction that is contingent on the possession of a bucket. Christening this utility that is dependent on the possession of the marginal unit, which in our case is a bucket of water, as the marginal utility, one can conclude that the value of a good is determined by its marginal utility.[1]

Value, Choice, and Uncertainty

In the Austrian tradition, the concept of value is totally inseparable from concrete acts of choice undertaken by individuals in real time and therefore fundamentally dependent on that individual's valuation, that is, it is strictly subjective. It is a concept that has been crafted and is utilized to understand actual choices that human beings make in specific historical instances. It is thus purely momentary in nature; a result of a scale of ends that the choosing individual draws up at the moment of choice, and on the momentary estimation on his part of the stock of a good at his disposal and its efficacy in the satisfaction of various wants. The value of a good, in other words, is ephemeral; it constantly changes with the individual's estimation of his given situation.

It follows that an individual's assessment of the marginal utility of a good can very well be erroneous. His momentary scale of ends, and thus the assessment of whether an action is "worth it," does not assume perfect knowledge on his part; nor does it rule out mistakes made by him in the assessment of the suitability of a good to serve specific wants. Indeed, as Mises notes, there is no place in the science of economics for "such notions as absolute validity and omniscience," since its "subject matter is erring man." Thus, "An end is everything which men aim at. A means is everything which acting men consider as such" (Mises, [1949] 1998, p. 93).

This focus on the actual choices made by living, erring men makes it possible to integrate issues surrounding imperfect knowledge into Austrian value theory; for deficiencies of knowledge cast their shadow on the value of goods by affecting the prevailing scale of ends of the actor as well as his estimation of the goods at his disposal. Imperfect knowledge is, in other words, reflected in erroneous judgments of marginal utility on the part of choosing individuals.

Significant steps toward such an integration of knowledge imperfections into the theory of choice and subjective value were taken right from the outset by Menger. Duly noting that "error is inseparable from all human knowledge," he went on to claim that "the relative degrees of importance of different satisfactions and of successive acts of satisfaction are [...] matters of judgment on the part of economizing men;" and that, as a result, even individuals "whose conduct is conducted rationally," and who put in a lot of time and thought into drawing up their scale of ends, "are subject to error" (Menger, [1871] 2007, pp. 147–148). Moreover, he argued that what applies to ends applies with equal force to the "question of their knowledge of the magnitudes of the quantities available to them and of the different qualities of goods" (Menger, [1871] 2007, p. 148).

But while Menger did take the first steps in integrating issues surrounding imperfect knowledge and error into the theory of choice, he did not conceive of or develop the distinction between risk and its more radical cousin, uncertainty. Nor did he extend the discussion of imperfect knowledge to the case of interpersonal exchange; his treatment of the issue was restricted to the actions of an isolated individual. The elucidation of the differences between the concepts of risk and uncertainty and the extension of the latter to the realm of interpersonal exchange was the handiwork of Ludwig von Mises.

Mises on Uncertainty and Choice

Imperfect knowledge, for Mises, is inseparable from the very existence of human choice and action. "The uncertainty of the future is already implied in the very notion of action. That man acts and that the future is uncertain are by no means independent matters. They are only two different modes of establishing one thing" (Mises, [1949] 1998, p. 105). Indeed, the assumption of omniscience has no place in a world of choosing men. In a world of perfect knowledge men as we know them would cease to exist. Living, acting man would instead be replaced by "an automaton, reacting to stimuli without any will of his own" (Mises, [1949] 1998, p. 105).

But what, precisely, is the underlying nature of this imperfect knowledge that permeates and infiltrates all of man's actions? Here, Mises largely concurs with Knight. The actions of men are influenced by two distinct types of knowledge imperfections. There is, on the one hand, imperfect knowledge that is measurable and expressible in mathematical language via the calculus of probability and which therefore falls into Knight's category of risk. And there is, on the other hand, what Knight terms uncertainty, or imperfect knowledge that is immeasurable and inexpressible in mathematical language.

Both forms of knowledge imperfections play a role in the choices of men and influence their decisions.

Risk owes its existence to the fact that a number of conditions that affect the potential outcome of a choice are governed by class probability, or a type of incompleteness of knowledge in which "we know or assume to know, with regard to the problem concerned, everything about the behavior of a whole class of events or phenomena; but about the actual singular events or phenomena we know nothing but that they are elements of this class" (Mises, [1949] 1998, p. 110). An excellent illustration of such incompleteness of knowledge is provided by the example cited earlier of the bursting champagne bottles. Similarly, a "fruit dealer may know [...] that one of every fifty apples will rot in this stock; but he does not know to which individual apple this will happen" (Mises, [1949] 1998, p. 109). The "calculus of probability provides a presentation in symbols of mathematical terminology" of precisely this type of numerical "defective knowledge" (Mises, [1949] 1998, p. 108).

The entrepreneur can seek to shield himself from such knowledge deficiencies with the aid of insurance, which characteristically deals with a "whole class of events" (Mises, [1949] 1998, p. 109). Indeed, the basic idea underlying insurance is the "pooling and distribution of risks, not the calculus of probability," which is evident from the "fact that the elimination of hazardous risk by pooling can also be effected without any recourse to actuarial methods" (Mises, [1949] 1998, p. 109). For every business man deals with losses "that regularly occur in the course of business," that is, losses whose amounts are known "as far as the whole class of the various items are concerned," like "any other item in the bill of costs" (Mises, [1949] 1998, p. 109).

Mises here greatly improves on Knight's treatment of risk with a clearer delineation of its underlying nature, which he captures in his definition of class probability. And like Knight he notes that the distinguishing characteristic of risk and the mathematical expression of such knowledge imperfections is the possibility of organizing events into classes that, from the perspective of the acting individual, are considered to be homogeneous.

The phenomenon of uncertainty, however, owes its existence to the inherently subjective nature of human choice. As discussed above, an actor's scale of ends and his assessment of the means at his disposal and their efficacy in satisfying wants are purely momentary phenomena undertaken at a particular time and place. As a result, the marginal utility and therefore the value of a good are also purely momentary and time and place specific in nature. This in itself introduces one source of imperfect knowledge. Furthermore, the fact that in any market the outcome of the actions of one individual are contingent on certain actions undertaken by others introduces another source of imperfect knowledge that affects the choices of individuals.

Now, the fact that the value of a good is ephemeral implies that it is subject to constant, unceasing change. And this implies, of course, that the choices of individuals regarding the goods exchanged on any market are also subject to such unceasing change. As a result, the knowledge that any individual has regarding the actions of others is bound to be defective. For while this individual "may know the motives of [...] acting men, the ends they are aiming at and the means they plan to apply for the attainment of these ends," and may "have a definite opinion with regard to the effects to be expected from the operation of these factors," he, nevertheless, "cannot exclude beforehand that he may have erred in the appraisal of their influence," or indeed that he may have excluded from his consideration certain other relevant factors (Mises, [1949] 1998, p. 112).

Moreover, the very subjectivity of the valuations of individuals implies the lack of any constant relations between the choices of an individual and his immediate external environment. Indeed, it is a primordial characteristic and an ultimate given of human action that individuals placed in an identical environment at the same time or one individual facing an identical situation at different times can make different choices. As a result, the field of human action is governed by a type of knowledge imperfection that is very different from the aforementioned class probability. Instead, the incompleteness of knowledge that an individual has regarding his own future valuations as well as the valuations of others that might impinge on the outcome of his choice can be said to fall into the category of *case* probability (Mises, [1949] 1998, p. 110), the distinguishing feature of which is that it applies not to a class of events but to a particular event; an event that in itself is necessarily unique and stands alone and is incapable of being included in any meaningful class.

This inherent "historical uniqueness or individuality" (Mises, [1949] 1998, p. 112) of all human action implies that an individual seeking to mitigate any knowledge imperfections with respect to it cannot make use of probability distributions and mathematical language. Indeed, "any reference to frequency is inappropriate" when dealing with the lack of knowledge surrounding human action, "as our statements always deal with unique events which as such – i.e., with regard to the problem in question – are not members of any class" (Mises, [1949] 1998, p. 111).

In other words, it is impossible to mitigate the incompleteness of the knowledge of human choices by forming classes of homogeneous events and culling distributions of relative frequency from experience.

Instead, the only method available to deal with such unmeasurable uncertainty is to try and form an understanding of the actions of others; to try to make sense of their choices by attempting to "grasp what is going on in the minds of the men concerned" (Mises, [1949] 1998, p. 118). One can, in other words, try and understand the possible ends that others aim at and the means that they seek to utilize. But such attempts at understanding, while they can shed more light on the particular actions of others, cannot completely remove the imperfect knowledge surrounding them due to the inherent indeterminateness of all human action, that is, due to the lack of any "constancy" or "continuity" in the valuations of men (Mises, [1949] 1998, p. 118).

Thus, in the world of interpersonal exchange, where "acting man is faced with the fact that there are fellow men acting on their own behalf as he himself acts, [...] the necessity to adjust his actions to other people's actions makes him a speculator for whom success and failure depend on his greater or lesser ability to understand the future" (Mises, [1949] 1998, p. 113). Every investment, in other words, "is a form of speculation," for there is, in a world characterized by change and uncertainty, "no stability and consequently no safety" (Mises, [1949] 1998, p. 113).

Implications for the Theory of Market Exchange

Mises improves on Knight's analysis of uncertainty by giving it a solid foundation in the theory of value developed by Menger and Böhm-Bawerk. The concepts of choice, as developed by the early Austrians, were, as we discussed above, capable of incorporating issues relating to uncertainty into the isolated actions of individuals. However, in his treatment of real or "Knightian" uncertainty Mises goes one step further by highlighting how the actions of others influence the valuations of goods in a world of interpersonal exchange. Stated differently, Mises' analysis of uncertainty lays the necessary conceptual foundations for a theory of price formation that gives pride of place to issues related to imperfect knowledge and error.

It goes without saying that any theory of price that accords an important role to uncertainty must differ considerably from the price theory that currently dominates the neoclassical mainstream. For the latter, inspired principally by the works of Walras (1954), Pareto (1971), and Hicks (1939), is essentially a theory of equilibrium prices. It is an analysis, in other words, of error free prices in a world devoid of uncertainty. Indeed, as Knight and Friedrich A. Hayek have argued, the prices analyzed by this theory could only come to be in a world populated by omniscient individuals. For such prices result from a correspondence of the knowledge possessed by individuals, or the "individual sets of subjective data," with the "objective data" that characterizes an economy at a given point in time (Hayek, [1937] 1948, p. 40).

It follows that the construct of equilibrium bears a lot less theoretical importance and weight in Austrian price theory. Static equilibrium is viewed as a purely conceptual tool with no real world significance or empirical relevance. Instead, it serves the function of a "purely hypothetical abstraction," used only "as a means of approaching an understanding of a continuously changing world" (Mises, 1980, pp. 230–231). Moreover, any such inherently dynamic theory must be able to integrate and elucidate the actions and choices of entrepreneurs. For the entrepreneurial function is one that is characterized by uncertainty (Cantillon, [1755] 1959; Knight, 1985 [1921]); indeed, the entrepreneurial function would completely disappear in a world without change and imperfect knowledge. And any theory that provides pride of place to the entrepreneur must have implications for the theory of the firm. The subsequent sections focus on analyzing some of these implications of uncertainty and its explicit integration into a theory of choice for the theory of the entrepreneur, the role of the equilibrium construct and the theory of the firm.

THREE CASES OF THEORETICAL IMPLICATIONS OF UNCERTAINTY

Entrepreneurship under Uncertainty

The entrepreneur has traditionally been endowed with a variety of roles in the history of economic thought, chief among which are those of "uncertainty-bearing," "decision-making," "allocation of resources among alternative roles," "coordinator of resources," and "arbitrageur" (Hébert & Link, 2006, pp. 4–5). With the tendency in the 20th century for economics to focus on Walras-inspired general equilibrium constructs with no uncertainty, the entrepreneur was forced to disappear from the picture, his task being essentially reduced, for the sake of maintaining logical coherence, to the performance of a kind of labor service.[2] Thus, the entrepreneur came to be conceived of as a mere superintendent of the production processes. In the words of Baumol (1968, p. 66), "the Prince of Denmark [was] expunged from the discussion of *Hamlet*." In stark contrast to this trend in the history of economic thought, Knight and especially Mises kept the entrepreneur alive in their conceptualizations of a market economy. For once we leave the world of automatic general equilibrium behind, the entrepreneur rises back into prominence as an uncertainty bearer.

Indeed, since general uncertainty is an endemic feature of the real world and thus unavoidable, all participants, in all their economic functions are necessarily entrepreneurs in this sense. Given that "every action is embedded in the flux of time and therefore involves a speculation, [...] the capitalists, landowners and laborers are by necessity speculators," as indeed is the "consumer in providing for anticipated needs" (Mises, [1949] 1998, p. 254). Nevertheless, the focus of the economist's attention, when theorizing about entrepreneurship must be on the entrepreneur as uncertainty bearer in his execution of the key production decisions of what, how, how much, and where to produce. All of these decisions, it is vital to note, hinge on the future outcomes of the actions of others that manifest themselves in the form of prices and quantities of goods produced and sold. Given that the actions of others are clouded with case probable, unmeasurable uncertainty, the entrepreneur, in making his decisions must rely on his understanding; on his appraisement of the valuations of others, most importantly those of his potential customers and competitors.

Now, in the same way that various actors are unequal in their capacity to handle various laboring tasks, which, in conjunction with the variety of natural resources in their environment accounts for the superior productivity of the division of labor over isolation, some actors will be more capable than others in their ability to bear uncertainty and thus will tend to display better quality of judgments regarding other people's future preferences, actions, and their outcomes. To the extent that the weight of bearing uncertainty can be transferred, through contracts that fix in advance the price and income that the less eager to bear it will earn from their contributions to production processes, those that are more eager and capable to bear uncertainty, what Knight terms "superior judgment," become leaders. They assume a prominent role in economic life in so far and as long as they are successful. In Mises' words, they are those "who are especially eager to profit from adjusting production to the expected changes in conditions, those who have more initiative, more venturesomeness, and a quicker eye than the crowd, the pushing and promoting pioneers of economic improvement" (Mises, [1949] 2008, p. 255).

Such specialists at bearing uncertainty (Knight, 1985 [1921], p. 271) or "entrepreneurs-promoters" are the "driving force of the market" (Mises, [1949] 2008, p. 256). They are the ones that keep the factor markets in constant flux, bidding away factors of production from uses that they estimate to be of lower value to those that in their estimations are expected to yield more revenue.

Economic Calculation

We noted above that the economic problem arises due to the presence of scarcity: the problem of allocating available resources to their highest valued uses (cf. Robbins, 1945, p. 16). Crucially, however, as noted by both Hayek (1945) and Mises ([1949] 1998, pp. 706–707), the problem essentially ceases to exist in a world of perfect knowledge. For in such a world all the available resources would, at every moment of time, be allocated instantly toward satisfying the highest valued ends. Indeed, this would hold true regardless of the underlying institutional framework; both a socialist, centrally planned economy as well as a market-based economy would be characterized by an optimal resource allocation if those making the important production decisions, that is, the central planner in the former case and private entrepreneurs in the case of the latter, were blessed with complete knowledge of the prevailing data characterizing the economy.

Thus, scarcity only becomes a problem of practical significance in a world characterized by uncertainty. And it is in precisely such a world that Mises argued, in his famous contribution that kick-started the "socialist calculation debate" (Mises, [1920] 2008), that a central planner will be unable to make any meaningful decisions regarding the allocation of the available resources. For the central planner will be in a situation similar to that of the head of a self-sufficient household. Given that there is no exchange of producers' goods in a socialist economy he will have to make his decisions of how to allocate resources without the aid of money prices. This, coupled with the fact that the *value* of goods has no unit, that their values thus cannot be compared across heterogeneous products (Mises, [1949] 2008, p. 699) and therefore cannot be measured, which is, after all, merely an implication of its subjective nature, implies that when making a decision with respect to the utilization of a portion of any producer good the planner will need to perform a mental survey of the entire production structure in order to try and form an idea of its value in alternate production processes.

But given the highly complex nature of the production structure in a modern, capital intensive economy, it becomes next to impossible to carry out such a direct imputation of value from consumer goods to producer goods through their technical relationships. Thus, devoid of money prices, which provide a common denominator for comparison and calculation, the planner finds himself unable to make any rational decision regarding the allocation of the factors of production.

In a market-based economy all factors of production are exchanged for money, thereby generating prices for these goods, allowing entrepreneurs to utilize these prices in planning their actions and estimating the outcome. Entrepreneurial bidding for resources in pursuit of profits releases information about value through establishing prices. Money prices thereby serve the purpose of making information about the state of the market's production structure relative consumer preferences available as well as comparable (Hayek, 1945). With money prices one can assess the outcome of one's past actions, assess one's present situation and formulate comparable and therefore meaningful forecasts of the outcomes of various competing choices by comparing monetary expenses and receipts from sales. As a result, entrepreneurs can make decisions regarding the allocation of producer goods anywhere in the production structure without surveying the entire structure in order to obtain information regarding the actual bundles of consumer goods that are contingent on their choice. Thus, money prices, which are outcomes of entrepreneurial undertakings in the market, serve to approximate relative resource scarcities from the point of view of consumer wants satisfaction and present them in terms that allow for comparisons both in space and time.

Economic calculation does not provide the actor with special insights about the future, as the future is neither known (or *can be* known) nor created at the time of action. However, it is a tool of thought in terms of which the decision-makers producing for other people in a market economy can anticipate other people's actions and plan accordingly. It provides the terms in which success and failure are gauged in relation to the clients' (ultimately consumers') needs. In other words, it is the tool of thought of uncertainty-bearing entrepreneurs, a means by which they can use their judgment to lessen the scope of possible outcomes and therefore bring seeming structure to their appraisals. Money prices serve to aggregate knowledge revealed through historic (up to the present) market actions; they also provide a common basis for comparison on which entrepreneurs can rely when acting for future profits. Prices expressed in money connect the market structure of the past and present to the future by forming a bridge between actors' individual valuations.

The Equilibrium Construct

The acknowledgment that the future is strictly uncertain, and that the outcome of individual action is unknown and the path of the market process open-ended, impacts how we can study the economy. In other words, the tools available to the economist are different when studying the real market with entrepreneurship and uncertainty and the streamlined and closed models of modern mathematical economics. The concept of general equilibrium used in the latter loses its empirical validity in the former, but this does not mean there is no place for equilibrium constructs. To the contrary, the Austrian tradition's study of the market process shows the usefulness of theoretical state-of-rest constructs as conceptual tools to illustrate the tendency and workings of the market.

The Plain State of Rest

Consider an imaginary market for horses[3] where potential buyers enter the market with units of money to offer the potential sellers. Each buyer, as he arrives on the market, has a certain valuation that he places on each additional unit of a horse that he wishes to purchase; a valuation that is reflected in the maximum buying price that he is willing to pay for each unit of a horse. Sellers, in turn, enter the market with horses that they wish to exchange for money and like the buyers have, in their minds, certain valuations placed on each horse in their possession that are reflected in their minimum selling prices.

Now, all these maximum buying and minimum selling prices will of necessity be tainted by the stain of uncertainty. There is, to begin with, the uncertainty stemming from each individual's own valuations. Buyer A might very well have overestimated the marginal utility and therefore the value of his first horse. His scale of ends, at the moment that he enters the market, might be erroneous, thereby inflating the importance of the horse to his well-being. Thus, he very well might, if he does indeed purchase a horse based on his prevailing valuations, live to regret his decision to do so.

Seller B, meanwhile, may have overestimated the value of money that he seeks to receive in exchange for his horse. Indeed, given that the basis of the value of money is its pre-existing purchasing power, the momentary marginal utility of a sum of money is necessarily steeped in error and uncertainty. For the goods that can be acquired with a unit of money can only be estimated. Thus, seller B, while forming an estimate of the value of a certain sum of money, must base this valuation on an appraisement of the prevailing prices in other markets; an act that in all likelihood, being inherently speculative in nature, will be fraught with error.[4]

To this first source of uncertainty we must add a second: the uncertainty stemming from the appraisement, undertaken by each participant, of the prevailing valuations of the other potential buyers and sellers. For every buyer (seller), given the fact that he prefers more to less money, would prefer to purchase (sell) each horse at the lowest (highest) possible price and in order to do so will try and form estimates of what this price is. Once such estimates are formed, the buyers and sellers may very well revise their maximum buying prices downward or upward, so as to ensure that they reap the maximum gains from trade. Now, given that they are a result of the understanding formed by each individual of the underlying valuations of the other market participants, these estimations may indeed be erroneous. And as a result buyers could very well hold out for prices that are too low, given the underlying market conditions, and sellers may hold out for prices that are far too high.[5]

What applies in the case of our imaginary horse market applies with equal force in the case of all goods, be they consumers' goods or factors of production. In the case of the latter, the demand side of the market consists of the maximum buying prices of the entrepreneurs. Entrepreneurs, as discussed earlier, base all their decisions on their judgment or understanding of an uncertain future. Their valuations for units of producers' goods will also, therefore, be the result of acts of appraisement of the possible future conditions that will prevail in the market for the product being produced. Needless to say, these momentary maximum buying prices will be filled with error.

These error-filled valuations of potential buyers and sellers throw up reverse valuations that can be exploited via exchange. Indeed, the realized prices that result from these reverse valuations can be conceived of as symptoms of "an economic equilibrium in the distribution of possessions between the economies of individuals" (Menger, [1871] 2007, p. 192), where every willing buyer finds a willing seller and only those potential sellers and buyers who "consider the market price too low or too high respectively" choosing to stay out of the market (Mises, [1949] 1998, p. 245). Stated differently, each price results in the exploitation of all possible gains from trade and thereby in the establishment of a "plain state of rest," or a state in which no market participant, given his prevailing valuations, has any incentive to act (Mises, [1949] 1998, p. 245).[6] It follows, therefore, that the "whole market economy" can be conceived of as a "big exchange or market place," where "at any instant those transactions take place which the parties are ready to enter into at the realizable price" (Mises, [1949] 1998, p. 245).

This conceptualization of realized prices as establishing plain states of rest, or a state of equilibrium with error, follows directly from the Austrian emphasis on analyzing the actual actions that individuals undertake in real time. Indeed, it is vital to note that a realized price only establishes a plain state of rest given the momentary, error-filled valuations that are a result of appraisement and speculation. If, on the other hand, a different set of valuations were considered, the realized price would no longer bring this market to a state of equilibrium. For instance, if all buyers and sellers on our imaginary horse market were to make no mistakes in their estimates of the marginal utility of horses and of money, and were to correctly judge the underlying market conditions both in the present as well as the future, a totally different set of maximum buying prices and minimum selling prices would prevail and the price that brought the market to a plain state of rest (PSR) would no longer eliminate all possible reverse valuations in this changed scenario.[7]

Thus, given their inherently erroneous nature, realized prices are equilibrium prices from one perspective, but are nevertheless symptomatic of the prevalence of a deep disequilibrium. Indeed, such prices are, first and foremost, disequilibrium prices from the perspective of the ultimate facts or the data that underlie each individual market at any given moment in time, that is, the valuations that buyers (sellers) originally had before they tried to form an estimate of the lowest (highest) price that they could buy (sell) at. Moreover, they are also far from being prices that establish a state of general or static equilibrium. Realized prices do not establish a state of equilibrium consonant with the data underlying the entire economic system at any given moment in time. They do not, in other words, succeed in establishing a "final state of rest" (FSR) (Mises, [1949] 1998, p. 246), or a state in which no individual in the economic system has any incentive to act given the underlying valuations of the consumers, the stocks of available resources and the prevailing state of technological knowledge.

It follows, therefore, that realized PSR prices do not go hand in hand with optimality in the allocation of resources. The array of realized prices thrown up by the process of exchange at any given moment in time does not, in other words, establish one price for each good. Nor does it establish a state in which all profits and losses have been eliminated. Both these features, instead, are characteristic of general equilibrium, FSR prices.[8]

It is, nevertheless, vital to note that it is precisely the allowance for the presence of uncertainty and error that lends the construct of the PSR its distinctive realism. Thus, far from being an imaginary construct, it is instead an "adequate description of what happens again and again on every market" (Mises, [1949] 1998, p. 246). The prices associated with the final state of rest, meanwhile, are purely hypothetical in nature, with it impossible for the economist to attribute a "definite numerical value in monetary terms or in quantities of other goods" to them (Mises, [1949] 1998, pp. 246–247). Indeed, given the assumption of perfect knowledge that underlies the latter construct, we can safely conclude that the actual "market price can never coincide with the final price coordinated to the instant in which this market structure is actual" (Mises, [1949] 1998, p. 247).

The Error Correction Process

Taking the uncertainty that bedevils all human action seriously brings into sharp focus the deep and chronic disequilibrium that characterizes economic activity at any given moment in time. Realized prices, while establishing momentary states of rest, do not give rise to an optimal allocation of available resources. The economic problem, at any given moment, remains unsolved.

A thoroughgoing and logically consistent integration of uncertainty into the theory of price formation, however, also leads one to discard the idea that the market system is characterized by a process of *tâtonnement* that takes place in real, historical time. Stated differently, one is forced to abandon the idea that there is any process of equilibration whereby the actual, realized prices tend over time to approach the FSR prices consistent with a state of general equilibrium. This conclusion follows from the fact that the concepts of uncertainty and change are inseparable. Indeed, in a stationary world where the data or the underlying conditions relevant for action reappear unchanged period after period, there would be no problem of a lack of knowledge regarding the future and the concomitant doubt surrounding the outcomes of one's actions would disappear. In fact, in such a world, action or "the conscious striving of thinking man after the removal of uneasiness" would be substituted with mere "automatic reaction" (Mises, [1949] 1998, p. 250). Uncertainty would disappear and along with it all error clouding human choice.

Thus, taking uncertainty seriously implies conceiving of the process of exchange on the market as necessarily open ended in nature. The real world is characterized by the possibility of unceasing change. But any process of *tâtonnement* in historical time assumes that the data underlying the market system remains unchanged through the process of error correction. But given, however, that "through history, the given data change," all that can be said regarding any process of equilibration in historical time is that although "*at every moment* there are tendencies towards an equilibrium, yet *from moment to moment* it is not the *same* equilibrium towards which there is movement" (Lionel Robbins, quoted in Marget, 1966, p. 237, fn. 34).

Thus, it seems as if a thoroughgoing integration of uncertainty into the theory of price formation seems to imply that the market economy seemingly limps from one array of PSR prices to the next, with no mechanism in place to correct erroneous decisions made by entrepreneurs. For how can any such process take place in an open-ended world with ever changing data? All that can be concluded, it appears, is that a general equilibrium with the corresponding FSR prices would be instantly established given the underlying data if all market participants were blessed with perfect knowledge. Only in this unrealistic world would there be any optimality in the allocation of available resources. In the real world, the economic problem lies unsolved and there is no tendency or process via which a solution is approached.[9]

A way out of this intellectual conundrum, however, is provided through a deeper reflection on the nature of entrepreneurship. As discussed above, the bearing of uncertainty is the essence of entrepreneurship (Knight, 1985 [1921]) and entrepreneurs are those who are more willing and able to form an understanding of future market conditions and act accordingly. It is vital, nevertheless, to note that the class of entrepreneurs at any given moment in time is not homogeneous in nature. Instead, the market is characterized by entrepreneurial heterogeneity, with some of those who make production decisions under uncertainty more capable of doing so than others. This, after all, is merely the reflection of a "datum that is a general characteristic of human nature," that is, the fact that "various individuals do not react to a change in conditions with the same quickness and in the same way" (Mises, [1949] 1998, p. 256). Indeed,

> the operation of the market reflects the fact that changes in the data are first perceived only by a few people and that different men draw different conclusions in appraising their effects. The more enterprising and brighter individuals take the lead, others follow later. The shrewder individuals appreciate conditions more correctly than the less intelligent and therefore succeed better in their actions. (Mises, [1949] 1998, p. 325)

This entrepreneurial heterogeneity is reflected in the profits and losses generated via the establishment of PSR prices in historical time. The more capable appraisers, those with comparatively superior judgment, earn the profits (or a higher rate of profit), whereas the less capable ones suffer losses (or earn a lower rate of profit).[10] The result is a re-allocation of the pool of capital available for investment. The better appraisers acquire a greater share of this available pool at the expense of the less capable entrepreneurs. And this, of course, translates into a greater influence of the former on the future course of business affairs, whereas the latter witness a gradual diminution of their influence before they are altogether relinquished of their roles as entrepreneurs.

Thus, the profits and losses thrown up by the prices realized from moment to moment give rise to a selection process whereby the most capable individuals are placed in the role of making production decisions.[11] As a result, the market, via the profit and loss system, has an in-built process, not of error correction, but of error prevention. For, while there cannot, given the constant flux of the underlying data, be a process of correcting past errors over the course of historical time, there is, nevertheless, a process in place whereby future errors are minimized.[12] Thus, while the economic problem is never solved completely due to the endemic uncertainty that characterizes the real world, the resource allocation that the market system throws up from moment to moment is the best that can be accomplished given the inherent frailties of erring man.

The Theory of the Firm

The issue of formal organization in the market is also closely tied to the concept of uncertainty, the unforeseeability of the future, and therefore the costs arising due to imperfect knowledge and lacking forecastability. Ronald H. Coase, the "father" of the modern theory of the firm, noted that "[i]t seems improbable that a firm would emerge without the existence of uncertainty" (Coase, 1937, p. 392). Market uncertainty, as opposed to mere probabilistic risk, is also core to Knight's theorizing on the role and function of the firm (Knight, 1985 [1921]), as mentioned above.

This view is prevalent also in modern mainstream theories of economic organization, thereby making the economic theory of organizations distinct from the common economics literature. Uncertainty is here treated either implicitly as a condition under which economic activity takes place or explicitly as a formal determinant of the need for organization. To Alchian and Demsetz (1972), uncertainty takes the form of necessarily imperfect knowledge that induces workers to shirk, which causes output losses in team production. The firm here emerges as the means by which workers through a separate monitoring function bring about proper incentive structures and thereby maximize their joint output. Similarly, Grossman and Hart (1986) and Hart and Moore (1990) find in centralized resource ownership a means by which the firm can deal with unforeseen situations in the future by establishing decision and control rights ex ante. Uncertainty is furthermore one of three fundamental transactional dimensions that drive integration in firm hierarchy in Transaction Cost Economics (Williamson, 1975, 1985, 1996). It is here a necessary prerequisite for incomplete contracting as well as a reason why opportunistic behavior leads to costly realignment processes under co-specialized contractual relationships.

While these approaches to economic organization acknowledge the importance of uncertainty, the concept is commonly implemented as action under imperfect or asymmetric information and operationalized as incomplete contracting (Aghion & Holden, 2011; Foss, 1996; Hart, 1988; Klein, 2010). This conceptualization's much more limited scope makes it more easily formalizable in predictive models, but this also eliminates many of the important aspects of market action that we noted above by narrowing the scope and interpretation of uncertainty.

Austrian economists have attempted to amend theories of economic organization by introducing uncertainty-bearing entrepreneurship. Foss and Klein (2012), for instance, follow Knight in placing entrepreneurial judgment at the core of the firm. They see formal organizing as a means for imaginative entrepreneurs to conduct controlled experiments to thereby figure out how to deal with uncertain market conditions. Sautet (2000), similarly, sees the firm as a means to "protect against opportunistic behavior" and "to secure the use of inputs that could be used elsewhere by other entrepreneurs" (2000, p. 74, 75); the firm is how the entrepreneur secures capabilities of combined inputs to exploit a discovered opportunity (cf. Kirzner, 1973). Lewin (2011), following Lachmann (1956), places a greater emphasis on the market's evolving capital structure, and sees the firm as a device for plan coordination.

These and other Austrian approaches to the firm have in common that they recognize and deal with at least one aspect of the implications of uncertainty in the market process: lack of or dispersed, imperfect knowledge; changing capital structure; need for coordination; and entrepreneurship as the driver of change (Bylund, 2011). Common to these approaches is the identification of the firm as a form of hierarchical structure that establishes authority and therefore control, which is asserted to be the means with which one can successfully deal with uncertainty. Yet, it is far from obvious why control, and thereby the centralization of decision-making, should help alleviate rather than augment the effect (and frequency) of error in the face of uncertainty. As Bylund (2015, p. 226; emphasis in original) notes, the asserted "solution ... is to centralize decision making and thereby greatly *increase* the risk by augmenting the knowledge problem already present in the market." A central authority may naturally produce decisions for the whole unit *faster*, but there is no reason to assume those decisions are also better. Therefore, the cost of uncertainty might as well increase, and this is perhaps the likely outcome considering the market's fragmented and dispersed "knowledge of the particular circumstances of time and place" (Hayek, 1945, p. 521) that economic actors rely on. It is therefore premature to conclude that the firm as a hierarchical structure is a means for entrepreneurs to deal with or overcome uncertainty.

The implications of integrating economic production within a formal organization in the face of uncertainty appear on two levels of analysis, of which only one is commonly addressed in the aforementioned literature. As the firm is conceived of as authority through control rights, going back at least to Coase's (1937) analysis of the firm as a planned hierarchy (Bylund, 2014a), it alleviates individual resource owners from uncertainty by centralizing it in the hands of an entrepreneur or manager. The uncertainty "internal" to the production process is thus managed through instituting centralized coordination that, in turn, facilitates formal planning. Yet, while this may benefit individual resource owners, it only redistributes the cost of market uncertainty by letting the entrepreneur bear the uncertainty of the full scope of the enterprise; there is no reason to assume the cost of uncertainty is smaller when centralized, unless it is also assumed that the entrepreneur has an innate ability to successfully overcome uncertainty (which indeed is the case with, e.g., Knight's (1985 [1921]) "superior judgment" and Kirzner's (1973) "alertness").

The uncertainty of the market, or what Knight (1985 [1921], p. 227) referred to as the business man's "estimate of an estimate" in pursuing a certain business opportunity, remains intact for the firm. This can only be dealt with by speculating on the structure and magnitudes of future demand as well as the potential economic value thereof. The role of the entrepreneur is then to align the production structure created and adjusted within the firm to the future state of the market in the most valuable way (Bylund & Lacr, 2014), in this sense, the entrepreneur bears the uncertainty of the whole enterprise since its success is ultimately dependent on the quality of his or her judgment. As adjustment of the firm's production structure necessarily takes time, the successful entrepreneur must exercise foresight and be correct in the judgments made. Rather than allowing individual factors to react to price changes and discrepancies, the uncertainty for all factors due to a firm's formal hierarchy is therefore intensified and augmented.

Note that the problem of foresight is not a matter simply of imperfect or asymmetric information, since the market data according to which the entrepreneur is to align the enterprise do not yet exist. The role of the entrepreneur is to partly speculate about the future state of the market, and partly to meet or create it (Alvarez & Barney, 2007). While it is important and perhaps also necessary to experiment with resource combinations, secure their potential capabilities, and protect the combined enterprise from transactional frictions (Coase, 1937; Mahoney & Qian, 2013; Williamson, 1975), these objectives are insufficient reasons for organization as they do not stretch beyond a collection of market contracts. As Jensen and Meckling (1976, p. 310) note, "most organizations are simply legal fictions which serve as a nexus for a set of contracting relationships among individuals." Asserting, as does Coase (1937) and Simon (1951), that the "employment contract" is qualitatively different from market contracts only invokes its legal peculiarity but ultimately fails to provide an economic argument for integrated production. A similar argument can be made for the equally common assertion of authority within the firm (Bylund, 2014b).

As hierarchy only reallocates uncertainty within a production process – even if to those most able to bear it – it can neither supply a definition nor provide a generally applicable rationale for formal economic organization. Rather, it is a category of action that is ever present in the market, the extent or implications of which is unknown and unknowable until the market data have been revealed and are firmly historic. The value of integrated economic organization must therefore be to provide some function in the market process that is otherwise *impossible*, not simply costly, through decentralized market action. This function may be found in the implementation process of previously unknown and untried innovative production structures that bring promise of improved productivity through the use of more intensive divisions of labor and capital, a process that indeed makes use of but is not limited to or defined by the aspects noted above (Bylund, 2016; cf. Holcombe, 1998, 2007). Its very existence here creates new market data, which means it cannot be a means to deal with but instead appears to potentially cause uncertainty for other market actors by subjecting the market structure to the disruptive (and therefore uncertainty-creating) forces of creative destruction (Schumpeter, 1911).

The firm is then not a means by which to manage or overcome uncertainty, but to pursue imagined and yet unrealized, and for this reason highly speculative, especially from the economic viewpoint, novel production structures. In this sense, the firm indeed constitutes a sense of centralized uncertainty-bearing in the entrepreneur, but this is an *effect* of innovating and implementing previously untried productive structures that lie outside the standard market's production possibility frontier – it is not its purpose. Not a means for uncertainty-bearing, the firm brings about market uncertainty through changing fundamental market data by disrupting the market's productive structure and, thereby, forcing it out of its established tendency toward a conceivable equilibrium state (Bylund, 2011, 2015).

This changes the direction of any causal explanation of economic organization, since uncertainty cannot be introduced to explain the firm – but the firm is introduced as a partial explanation for uncertainty. Econometric analyses cannot distinguish between causation and correlation, which means the existing literature may have progressing down the wrong track. Rather than relying on existing economic models to explain economic organization as a means to overcome limited uncertainty, thereby keeping (if not saving) modern economic theory intact, the proper approach may be to identify economic action as inherently uncertain and the firm as a phenomenon for disruption of the existing order – a cause of uncertainty.

CONCLUDING DISCUSSION

In the previous sections, we saw that uncertainty is conceptually distinct from risk. While the distinction is not always acknowledged, its implications in theorizing and applications are important. Due to its bounded set of possible outcomes, often with probabilities and their distribution known ex ante, risk facilitates a simplified and formalized analysis that allows for discrete and objective cost calculations as well as maximizing behavior. To achieve economic efficiency, one need only attempt to maximize functions based on known and knowable data about the market. In contrast, uncertainty is fundamentally unknown and open-ended in terms of its outcomes and therefore limits the actor to rely mostly or exclusively on his or her subjective probabilities, business judgment, or tacit understanding for the market process.

Uncertainty permeates human action and is an important component in any decision or choice. It is not simply a lack of knowledge about the future, as in theories of decision-making under imperfect or costly-to-acquire knowledge, but a category of action (Mises, [1949] 1998). In fact, the data about the future *do not yet exist*, and any actor must therefore speculate about the future states of the market as well as their potential opportunities using his or her judgment about what tendencies may be important, what possibilities should be taken into account, and what market data in the present may be important to consider.

Formal economic models rely on objective data. But this has little resemblance with the situation in which an actor chooses, which can only be subjectively understood. The data are selected as well as interpreted. The actor is always subject to imperfect as well as asymmetric information, and from this subjectively understood situation, he or she values and ranks and then chooses possible and seemingly attainable outcomes. This process is necessarily based on his or her appraisal of possible outcomes, the necessary means for their attainment, and their relative values. The subjectivity of action and the interpretation of market data are important reasons why streamlined, mathematical economic models fail to capture the true goings-on in the market.

The anticipated and aimed-for outcome is as uncertain as the interpretation of data in the starting position. An actor may exercise superior judgment or benefit from luck (Barney, 1986; Demsetz, 1983), and for those reasons come very close to the real future state of the market, and therefore make a profit. Yet, whether this is possible can only be known ex post facto, since future market data do not exist at the time the choice is made or even during the process of implementation. Instead, implementation produces part of the social reality in which the potential fruits of one's actions may be realized (Bylund, 2016; cf. Klein, 2008).

We showed above, in both our discussion on the place of uncertainty in economic theory and its implications for entrepreneurship and calculation, the role of the equilibrium construct, and theorizing on organizing in the market, that this situation bears very little resemblance to the analysis of risk, in which data about the outcomes as well as their relative probabilities is known at the time a choice is made. Very few choices, if any, are made under circumstances that resemble risk but are unaffected by uncertainty. Needless to say, action is predominantly speculative and takes place primarily under "Knightian" uncertainty.

Uncertainty changes not only the cost structure of the market, but also is an important explanans for market structure and the emergence of institutions. Institutions in the form of "rules of the game" (North, 1990; Williamson, 1985), whether formal or informal, are generally instituted as a means to deal with costs of uncertainty. Market standardization can in this sense be understood as, at least in part, a means by which actors self-select behaviors that promote predictability. This is also an argument for formal organizations such as the firm, an argument that we found to be lacking. Uncertainty affects action in the decentralized market as well as in centralized hierarchies, though in different ways, and the costs thereof must be considered when theorizing on resource allocation and means for coordination.

As our discussion above illustrates, espousing uncertainty in a "Knightian" sense rather than probabilistic risk fundamentally changes the economic analysis. In Austrian economics, the recognition of the fundamentally uncertain nature of economic action has placed focus on the market as a dynamic, entrepreneur-driven (Kirzner, 1973; Mises, [1949] 1998; see also Cantillon, [1755] 1959) disequilibrium process of open-ended discovery (Hayek, 1978). It underlies the Misesian argument against socialist economic planning (Mises, 1920, [1936] 1951) and the necessity to have access to reliable money prices for economic calculation and investment. It also emphasizes the heterogeneous nature of resources and their complementary use in elaborate capital structures (Böhm-Bawerk, [1888] 1930; Lachmann, 1947) for the purpose of effective production, which in turn suggests a fundamental complexity of economic production as well as inertia and frictions when exogenous change warrant responses by entrepreneurs (Ebeling, [1978] 1996). And it means that economic actors without exception suffer fundamental ignorance about what the future market holds (O'Driscoll & Rizzo, [1985] 2015), which necessitates speculation and "imagining" the future based on judgment and understanding for both man and market.

As our discussion shows, uncertainty emerges as a crucially important aspect of economic action with implications that fundamentally change our analysis of and understanding for the market's structure, its productive apparatus, and ability to meet consumer wants. Formal models of economic systems can provide insights into maximizing behavior under very specific assumptions, and indicate how exogenous changes affect such behavior. But they fail to address the reality of market action as fundamentally open-ended and consequently speculative, and therefore do not account for the constant adjustments made within the market process as economic actors continuously discover values and ends attainable by individuals acting alone or in concert. We have shown in the discussion above that while conclusions based on streamlined models may indeed indicate probable directions of or outcomes in the real market, they do only that: indicate probable directions. These directions are themselves valid under the assumptions on which the model is based, and are relevant to the empirical market only to the extent these assumptions happen to coincide with actions taken under uncertainty the real market process. In this sense, economic models are blunt tools that can at best produce approximations of barebones economic behavior. To understand the market process, one needs to acknowledge that it is a fundamentally uncertain endeavor.

NOTES

1. For more detailed expositions on the theory of subjective value and marginal utility, see Menger ([1871] 2007, pp. 115–175) and Böhm-Bawerk ([1888] 1930, Bk. III).

2. Revealingly enough, Walras had developed a view of the entrepreneur as an intermediary between production and consumption earning profits or losses. In other words, the Walrasian entrepreneur was an important figure in the explanation of real world markets. However, it did not fit in his most recognized contribution, that is, the representation of the economy through a system of equations whose solution is the features of general equilibrium, including the absence of profit or loss (Hébert & Link, 2006, pp. 64–69).

3. The imaginary construct of a horse market was first utilized by Menger and then by a number of other economists writing in the Mengerian tradition to help elucidate their theories of price formation. See Menger ([1871] 2007, pp. 197–225), Böhm-Bawerk ([1888] 1930, pp. 239–258), and Rothbard ([1962] 2009, pp. 106–161).

4. "A value judgment is, with reference to money, only possible if it can be based on appraisement [...]. Neither a buyer nor a seller could judge the value of a monetary unit if he had no information about its exchange value – its purchasing power – in the immediate past" (Mises, [1949] 1998, p. 408). For detailed expositions of the Austrian theory of the value of money and the determination of its purchasing power see Mises ([1912] 1971, [1949] 1998, pp. 395–475) and Rothbard ([1962] 2009, pp. 233–279, 755–831).

5. For a detailed and lucid exposition of the process by which buyers and sellers appraise the underlying market conditions and adjust their valuations accordingly before concluding an exchange see Wicksteed (1910, pp. 217–237).

6. Marget (1966, pp. 231–247) and Manish (2014) provide more detailed analyses of how momentary valuations give rise to plain states of rest.

7. ... the realized prices which may be sufficient to move successive parts of the stores from the market may not necessarily be the same as the price which would have removed the whole if, again in Marshall's own words, a single price had been "fixed on at the beginning and adhered to throughout." (Marget, 1966, p. 233)

8. For more on the erroneous nature of the allocation of resources at every array of PSR prices thrown up by the exchange process from moment to moment

and on the differences between such an allocation of resources and that which prevails in a state of general or static equilibrium characterized by a set of FSR prices, see Salerno (1994, pp. 97–106) and Klein (2010).

9. Stated differently, taking uncertainty seriously leads one to discard the stationary interpretation of the static equilibrium construct and adopt an instantaneous interpretation of the same instead. For a more detailed exposition of the differences between these two interpretations, see the numerous papers written on the subject by the excellent historian of general equilibrium Franco Donzelli, but especially Donzelli (1993, 2007).

10. For a more detailed treatment of the proposition that the exchange process rewards the better appraisers as compared to the less capable ones, albeit in the imaginary world of a pure exchange economy, see Wicksteed (1910, pp. 222–226) and Manish (2014, pp. 134–136, 146–150).

11. For more on the selective process inherent in the market process see Mises ([1949] 1998, pp. 308–310).

12. Taking uncertainty and subjectivism seriously thus does not lead to the conclusion that the market is inherently kaleidic in nature as alleged by radical subjectivists such as Lachmann and Shackle (Lachmann, 1976, 1986; Shackle, 1972; also see O'Driscoll & Rizzo, [1985] 2015). The market need not, in other words, oscillate between order and chaos; "interspersing its moments or intervals of order, assurance and beauty with sudden disintegration and a cascade into a new pattern" (Shackle, 1972, p. 76). Indeed, the process of entrepreneurial selection at work as the result of the profit and loss system ensures that resources on the market are always allocated more or less in line with consumer preferences despite the fact that the expectations of entrepreneurs are subjective in nature (Manish, 2015). Moreover, the presence of this process precludes the need to integrate the concept of ideal types into economic theory (Koppl, 2002) in order to explain orderly economic activity in an uncertain world with subjective value and expectations.

ACKNOWLEDGMENTS

The authors are greatly indebted to Dr. Xavier Méra for assistance with previous versions of this paper and appreciate the thoughtful comments and suggestions by two anonymous reviewers and the editor. The usual caveat applies.

REFERENCES

Aghion, P., & Holden, R. (2011). Incomplete contracts and the theory of the firm: What have we learned over the past 25 Years? *Journal of Economic Perspectives*, *25*(2), 181–197.

Alchian, A. A., & Demsetz, H. (1972). Production, information costs and economic organization. *American Economic Review*, *62*(5), 777–795.

Alvarez, S. A., & Barney, J. B. (2007). Discovery and creation: Alternative theories of entrepreneurial action. *Strategic Entrepreneurship Journal*, *1*(1–2), 11–26.

Barney, J. B. (1986). Strategic factor markets: Expectations, luck, and business strategy. *Management Science*, *32*(10), 1231–1241.

Böhm-Bawerk, E.v. ([1888] 1930). *The positive theory of capital*. New York, NY: G.E. Stechert and Company.

Baumol, W. J. (1968). Entrepreneurship in economic theory. *The American Economic Review*, *58*, 64–71.

Bylund, P. L. (2011). Division of labor and the firm: An Austrian attempt at explaining the firm in the market. *Quarterly Journal of Austrian Economics*, *14*(2), 188–215.

Bylund, P. L. (2014a). Ronald Coase's "nature of the firm" and the argument for economic planning. *Journal of the History of Economic Thought*, *36*(3), 305–329.

Bylund, P. L. (2014b). The firm and the authority relation: Hierarchy vs. organization. In G. L. Nell (Ed.), *Austrian theory and economic organization: Reaching beyond free market boundaries* (pp. 97–120). New York, NY: Palgrave Macmillan.

Bylund, P. L. (2015). Explaining firm emergence: Specialization, transaction costs, and the integration process. *Managerial and Decision Economics*, *36*(4), 221–238.

Bylund, P. L. (2016). *The problem of production: A new theory of the firm*. London: Routledge.

Bylund, P. L., & Laer, W.v. (2014, August). Implications of discovery and creation: How entrepreneurial opportunities relate to the market process. Paper presented at the Academy of Management meeting in Philadelphia, PA.

Cantillon, R. ([1755] 1959). *Essai sur la Nature du Commerce in Général (Essay on the nature of trade in general)*. London: Frank Cass and Co.

Coase, R. H. (1937). The nature of the firm. *Economica*, *4*(16), 386–405.

Donzelli, F. (1993). The influence of the socialist calculation debate on Hayek's view of general equilibrium theory. *Revue Europeene des Sciences Solicales*, *96*, 47–83.

Donzelli, F. (2007). Equilibrium and *tatonnement* in Walras' *elements*. *History of Economic Ideas*, *15*(3), 85–138.

Dequech, D. (2011). Uncertainty: A typology and refinements of existing concepts. *Journal of Economic Issues*, *45*(3), 621–641.

Demsetz, H. (1983). The neglect of the entrepreneur. In J. Ronen (Ed.), *Entrepreneurship*. Lexington: Lexington Press.

Ebeling, R. M. ([1978] 1996). *The Austrian theory of the trade cycle and other essays*. Auburn, AL: Ludwig von Mises Institute.

Foss, N. J. (1996). *Firms, incomplete contracts and organizational learning*. DRUID Working Papers. Danish Research Unit for Industrial Dynamics, Copenhagen.

Foss, N. J., & Klein, P. G. (2012). *Organizing entrepreneurial judgment: A new approach to the firm*. Cambridge: Cambridge University Press.

Grossman, S. J., & Hart, O. D. (1986). The costs and benefits of ownership: A theory of vertical and lateral integration. *The Journal of Political Economy*, *94*(4), 691–719.

Hart, O. D. (1988). Incomplete contracts and the theory of the firm. *Journal of Law, Economics, & Organization*, *4*(1), 119–139.

Hart, O. D., & Moore, J. (1990). Property rights and the nature of the firm. *Journal of Political Economy*, *98*(6), 1119–1158.

Hayek, F. A. (1945). The use of knowledge in society. *American Economic Review*, *35*(4), 519–530.

Hayek, F. A. ([1937] 1948). Economics and knowledge. In *Individualism and economic order* (pp. 33–56). Chicago, IL: University of Chicago Press.

Hayek, F. A. v. (1978). Competition as a discovery process. *New Studies in Philosophy, Politics, Economics, and the History of Ideas*, *5*, 179–190.

Hébert, R. F., & Link, A. N. (2006). The entrepreneur as innovator. *The Journal of Technology Transfer*, *31*(5), 589–597.

Hicks, J. R. (1939). *Value and capital*. Oxford: Clarendon Press.

Holcombe, R. G. (1998). Entrepreneurship and economic growth. *Quarterly Journal of Austrian Economics*, *1*(2), 45–62.

Holcombe, R. G. (2007). *Entrepreneurship and economic progress*. New York, NY: Routledge.

Jensen, M. C., & Meckling, W. H. (1976). Theory of the firm: Managerial behavior, agency costs, and capital structure. *Journal of Financial Economics*, *3*(4), 305–360.

Kirzner, I. M. (1973). *Competition and entrepreneurship*. Chicago, IL: University of Chicago Press.

Klein, P. G. (2008). Opportunity discovery, entrepreneurial action, and economic organization. *Strategic Entrepreneurship Journal*, *2*(3), 175–190.

Klein, P. G. (2010). *The capitalist and the entrepreneur*. Auburn, AL: Ludwig von Mises Institute.

Knight, F. H. (1985 [1921]). *Risk, uncertainty and profit*. Chicago, IL: University of Chicago Press.

Koppl, R. (2002). *Big players and the economic theory of expectations*. New York, NY: Palgrave Macmillan.

Lachmann, L. M. (1947). Complementarity and substitution in the theory of capital. *Economica*, *14*, 108–119.

Lachmann, L. M. (1976). From Mises to Shackle: An essay on Austrian economics and the kaleidic society. *Journal of Economic Literature*, *14*(1), 54–62.

Lachmann, L. M. ([1956] 1978). *Capital and its structure*. Kansas City, MO: Sheed Andrews and McMeel.

Lachmann, L. M. (1986). *The market as an economic process*. New York, NY: Basil Blackwell.

Lewin, P. (2011). *Capital in disequilibrium: The role of capital in a changing world*. Auburn, AL: Ludwig von Mises Institute.

Lucas, R., Jr. (1977). Understanding business cycles. *Carnegie-Rochester Series on Public Policy*, *5*, 7–29.

Mahoney, J. T., & Qian, L. (2013). Market frictions as building blocks of an organizational economics approach to strategic management. *Strategic Management Journal*, *34*(9), 1019–1041. doi:10.1002/smj.2056

Manish, G. P. (2014). Error, equilibrium and equilibration in Austrian price theory. *Quarterly Journal of Austrian Economics*, *17*(2), 127–153.

Manish, G. P. (2015). *Subjectivism of expectations and the process of error correction: The views of Lachmann and Mises*. Working Paper.

Marget, A. W. (1966). *The theory of prices* (Vol. 2). New York, NY: Augustus M. Kelley Publishers.

Menger, C. ([1871] 2007). *Principles of economics*. Auburn, AL: Ludwig von Mises Institute.

Mirowski, P. (1991). *More heat than light: Economics as social physics, physics as nature's economics*. Cambridge: Cambridge University Press.

Mises, L.v. ([1912] 1971). *The theory of money and credit*. New York, NY: Foundation for Economic Education.

Mises, L. v. ([1936] 1951). *Socialism: An economic and sociological analysis [J. Kahane, Trans.]*. New Haven, CT: Yale University Press.
Mises, L.v. ([1949] 1998). *Human action*. Auburn, AL: Ludwig von Mises Institute.
Mises, L.v. ([1949] 2008). *Human action: A treatise of economics*. Auburn, Al: Ludwig von Mises Institute.
Mises, L.v. ([1920] 2008). *Economic calculation in the socialist commonwealth*. Auburn, AL: Ludwig von Mises Institute.
Mises, L. v. (1980). My contributions to economic theory. In L. v. Mises (Ed.), *Planning for freedom* (4 ed., pp. 224–233). South Holland, IL: Libertarian Press.
North, D. C. (1990). *Institutions, Institutional Change and Economic Performance*. Cambridge: Cambridge University Press.
O'Driscoll, G., & Rizzo, M. ([1985] 2015). *The economics of time and ignorance*. New York, NY: Routledge.
Pareto, V. (1971). *Manual of political economy*. New York, NY: Augustus M. Kelley Publishers.
Robbins, L. (1945). *An essay on the nature & significance of economic science* (2nd ed.). London: Macmillan and Co.
Rothbard, M. N. ([1962] 2009). *Man, economy and state*. Auburn, AL: Ludwig von Mises Institute.
Salerno, J. T. (1994). Ludwig von Mises's monetary theory in light of modern monetary thought. *Review of Austrian Economics*, *8*(1), 71–115.
Sautet, F. E. (2000). *An entrepreneurial theory of the firm*. New York, NY: Routledge.
Schabas, M. (1993). What's so wrong with physics envy? In N. de Marchi (Ed.), Reflecting on the enterprise of *more heat than light* (pp. 45–53). Durham, NC: Duke University Press.
Schumpeter, J. A. ([1911] 1934). *The theory of economic development: An inquiry into profits, capital, credit, interest, and the business cycle*. Cambridge, MA: Harvard University Press.
Shackle, G. (1972). *Epistemics and economics: A critique of economic doctrines*. Cambridge: Cambridge University Press.
Simon, H. A. (1951). A formal theory of the employment relationship. *Econometrica: Journal of the Econometric Society*, *19*(3), 293–305.
Walras, L. (1954). Elements of pure economics *(W. Jaffe, Trans.)*. Homewood, IL: Richard D. Irwin, Inc.
Wicksteed, P. H. (1910). *The common sense of political economy*. New York, NY: Macmillan Company.
Williamson, O. E. (1975). *Markets and hierarchies, analysis and antitrust implications: A study in the economics of internal organization*. New York, NY: Free Press.
Williamson, O. E. (1985). *The economic institutions of capitalism*. New York, NY: Free Press.
Williamson, O. E. (1996). *The mechanisms of governance*. Oxford: Oxford University Press.

THE ROAD LESS TRAVELED: MONETARY DISEQUILIBRIUM, AUSTRIAN CAPITAL THEORY, AND THE "KEYNESIAN DIVERSION"

Scott Burns

ABSTRACT

For nearly 80 years, the field of macroeconomics has largely been shaped by the aftermath of the Keynesian revolution. Many economists have argued that this revolution and the subsequent internal and external disputes it has sparked have had the unfortunate side effect of crowding out much of what was good in macro-level analysis before it, leading to the dissatisfactory state of macroeconomics we have today. In the search for alternative paths for macroeconomics, I focus on two separate but compatible traditions: monetary disequilibrium (MD) theory and the Austrian business cycle theory (ABCT). I argue that scholars in these traditions employed a far richer micro-theoretic explanation for the business cycle well before Keynes's General Theory. *Unfortunately, their ideas were not united in time to mount a sufficient counterattack to*

Research in the History of Economic Thought and Methodology, Volume 34B, 337–363

ISSN: 0743-4154/doi:10.1108/S0743-415420160000034B012

the Keynesian crusade. My goal is to unite the best elements of these two traditions by providing what I believe is the "missing link" that can help connect these alternative paths: free banking theory.

Keywords: Monetary disequilibrium theory; Austrian business cycle theory; quantity theory of money; J. M. Keynes; F. A. Hayek; free banking

JEL classifications: B10; B22; E30; E42; E50; E58; N10

INTRODUCTION: THE KEYNESIAN DIVERSION

What alternative path should macroeconomics take to the one that it has been diverted to by the Keynesian revolution? Economists generally recognize that macroeconomic analysis long predated Keynes. What constituted that orthodoxy, however, remains very much in dispute. According to Krugman (2007), the state of economics in the early 20th century was a lot like Christianity in the 16th century. Prior to Keynes, he argued, macroeconomics was a dormant field "completely dominated by free-market orthodoxy." It was not until Keynes nailed his *General Theory* to the door of the economics establishment that the tyranny of this orthodoxy was overthrown.

Within a few years, Keynes's crusaders had conquered the commanding heights of the academic establishment "as completely as the Holy Inquisition had conquered Spain." The "free-market orthodoxy" that allegedly preceded Keynes had been supplanted by a market failure theory of the business cycle. Subsequent developments like the monetarist counter-revolution and the more radical new classical revolution did succeed in undermining some of these core tenets. But as the rise of new Keynesianism in the 1990s and the revival of Keynes following the recent financial crisis clearly indicate, they failed to deliver a fatal blow to Keynes (Snowdon &Vane, 2005).

Over the years, however, a number of economists have boldly challenged not only the Keynesian reformation but also the new direction that economics embarked upon in its wake (Hayek, 1941; Hazlitt, 1959 [2007]; Hutt, 1963; Knight, 1937; Yeager, 1973). To them, this new path represented a "diversion" from what was right in economics dating all the way back to the classical scholars (Yeager, 1973). The key to true advance in economic theory, they argued, was to rediscover these classical insights.

My core argument in this paper is that there were two classical traditions that did, in fact, provide a much stronger alternative for macroeconomic analysis than Keynes: monetary disequilibrium (MD) theory and Austrian business cycle theory (ABCT). Despite their differences, these scholars provided a far richer explanation for the business cycle that was rooted in superior *micro*foundations that focused more clearly on the role of time, money, and relative prices on individual behavior. These analytical tools set them apart from their Keynesian rivals by allowing them to not only diagnose how central banks could severely disrupt economic activity but also to describe how it would distort the economy's structure of production. Had they combined forces, it is possible that they would have been capable of thwarting the Keynesian offensive. Unfortunately, their ideas were never forged together in time to mount a sufficient counterattack.

My objective here is to sketch out what such a union might look like. Admittedly, the timing of this effort might seem a century too late. But just as the Great Depression laid the intellectual groundwork for the Keynesian revolution, the Great Recession has provided heterodox scholars with an opportunity to challenge the reigning hegemony in macroeconomics. This time around, however, I believe it is essential that we introduce a key *institutional* element that has the potential to better unite Austrian and MD scholars: free banking theory. Once all three of these elements are integrated, I believe that it will be possible for these scholars to offer a more viable road forward for macroeconomics.

"The Road Less Traveled" section provides a brief overview of both MD and ABC theory. "The Path Forward: Austrian Macro and Monetary Equilibrium" section outlines the key similarities and differences between the two schools and makes a case for how they can be reconciled. "Free Banking: The Missing Institutional Link" section discusses what I consider the "missing link" that can connect both schools of thought – free banking theory. "Conclusion" section concludes.

THE ROAD LESS TRAVELED

Monetary Disequilibrium (MD) Theory

It is well known that writers well before Keynes developed theories of the trade cycle.[1] Yet unlike Keynes in his *General Theory*, many of these earlier authors placed a strong emphasis on the role that unanticipated changes in the supply of or demand for *money* play in explaining economic fluctuations. Classical writers dating as far back as John Locke, David Hume, Adam Smith, and Richard Cantillon recognized that unexpected money shocks affected real variables in the short run. Later icons like David Ricardo, Thomas Malthus, Jeremy Bentham, Thomas Attwood, and J. S. Mill as well as leading Bullionist thinkers like Henry Thornton, John McCulloch, and Robert Torrens also recognized the problems associated with unanticipated price level changes – deflation, in particular – stemming from unexpected monetary shocks (Humphrey, 1991).

In the early 20th century, "Old Monetarist" thinkers like Alfred Marshall, A. C. Pigou, Dennis Robertson, and Ralph Hawtrey in England, Irving Fisher, Herbert J. Davenport, H. G. Brown, and Arthur Marget in the United States and Knut Wicksell and Gustav Cassel in Sweden elaborated on these ideas, placing the role monetary factors play at the center of their theory of the trade cycle (Yeager, 1973). Wicksell (1898 [1965]) played a particularly influential role in arguing that unanticipated changes in the money supply could lead to disequilibrium in the capital and commodities markets. Even Keynes attempted to integrate these Wicksellian themes in his *Treatise on Money* (1930 [2011]) before abandoning them in his *General Theory*. Warburton (1950) coined their unifying theme of this tradition – that monetary disturbances can exert a non-neutral impact on real variables in the short run – "the monetary disequilibrium hypothesis."

Leland Yeager did arguably more than any other postwar scholar to elaborate on and systematize MD theory. Yeager founded his approach on the three "essential properties of money" (1968).[2] The first is that money is the economy's "generally accepted medium of exchange." For Yeager and others, this simple insight has profound implications. Money is systemically important precisely because it is so pervasive. In an advanced economy, money represents one side of virtually every market exchange. All purchases of goods are sales of money, and all sales of goods are purchases of money. Since money has no unique price or market of its own, *all* markets are in effect money markets.

The second fundamental property Yeager identifies is that the demand for money is the demand to *hold*, not spend, real money balances. As the economy's most "saleable" good, money's ultimate service is that it provides (near) absolute liquidity for its holders. These real units of purchasing power are, in effect, "available" at a moment's notice if one decides to engage in a spot exchange. This near perfect liquidity is a critical part of Yeager's third essential property: our acquisition of money takes on a "routineness" that is not shared by other goods. Individuals will always accept money in exchange – even if they have no desire to hold it – because they know they can always shed these excess money balances by trading them for goods and services.

Using this "real cash balance approach" approach employed by Yeager (1956) and others before him, *monetary equilibrium* can be defined as the condition that holds when the supply of money balances is equal to the demand to hold them at the existing price level. The most common case of monetary disequilibrium that scholars in this tradition focus on is an excess *demand* for money, where the propagation mechanism is most often an unexpected contraction of the money supply by the central bank. Yeager starts from the foundation of Say's Principle[3] (Leijonhufvud, 1981) to show how an excess demand for money can result in a "general glut" of goods. An excess demand for money implies that individuals are trying to accumulate more real balances than are available at the existing price level. They can replenish their money balances only by selling goods or reducing their spending. In either case, a seller's market prevails. Mutually beneficial exchanges cannot take place until prices endure a slow, often times painful downward adjustment. But since, empirically, prices and wages tend to be "sticky" downward due to a variety of informational and collective action problems,[4] firms respond by reducing output and employment as they see inventories build up. An excess supply of money, in contrast, implies that exchanges take place at the current price level that might not have otherwise occurred as existing money holders shed their excess cash balances. The result is a transitory rise in output, followed by inflation.

Since prices do eventually adjust, MD theory provides only a short-run explanation for economic downturns. In the most prevalent case of an excess demand for money, for instance, prices will gradually decline to restore monetary equilibrium. The severity of the downturn ultimately depends on various regulatory and institutional factors that determine how "sticky" prices are and how quickly they can adjust (Hutt, 1939 [1977]). To avoid this painful adjustment process, Yeager and other scholars in this tradition argue that the central bank should engage in monetary expansion sufficient to offset the excess demand. The increase in the money supply alleviates the excess demand for money without requiring an adjustment in overall prices, preventing a drop in output from taking place. This willingness to intervene in such circumstances places them at odds with the second pre-Keynesian school of thought I will discuss: the Austrian school.

Austrian Capital and Business Cycle Theory (ABCT)

Before Keynes, ABCT as developed by Mises (1912 [1981]) and Hayek (1931 [2008], 1933) was widely regarded as one of the leading explanations of the business cycle. ABCT was grounded in two of the leading traditions in the German language literature. The first was the early Austrian tradition of Carl Menger and Eugen Böhm-Bawerk. Menger laid the foundation for Austrian capital theory in his discussion of the time structure of production and distinction between higher and lower order goods. Böhm-Bawerk built on Menger's notion of higher and lower order goods to develop a more elaborate vision of a capital-intensive structure of production.[5] Like Menger, he argued an economy could grow wealthier if individuals invested their savings in longer and more productive – or more "roundabout" – methods of production. In particular, he emphasized the *heterogeneity* and *multi-specificity* of capital and stressed the relationship between time preference, the interest rate, and the structure of production.[6] The combined influence of Menger's price theory and Böhm-Bawerk's capital and interest theory provided Mises and Hayek with the core microeconomic rationale that underlined ABCT.

The second was the Swedish school led by Wicksell (1898 [1965]). In addition to being a leading influence in MD theory, Wicksell was among the first to stress that there was an intimate link between the money market and loanable funds market. His theory described in detail how the general price level responded to a divergence between the "real" (or "natural" rate, reflecting consumers true underlying time preferences) and "bank" (or "market" rate) interest rate that itself stemmed from disequilibrium in the market for money balances. In Wicksell's story, an unanticipated expansion of the money supply creates an excess supply of money that individuals can either spend on goods and services or lend out on the loanable funds market. This pressure pushes the market rate of interest below the natural rate, leading to a temporary increase in investment expenditure. This disequilibrium in both the money and loanable funds market would only be cured once market forces drove prices and interest rates back up to their new equilibrium values. Any effort by the monetary authority to keep interest rates below their natural level and prolong the expansionary phase would only drive prices and nominal rates higher.[7]

Though Wicksell was influenced by these Austrian scholars, it was Mises and Hayek who ultimately connected his work on money and interest to Menger and Böhm-Bawerk's work on capital theory to form ABCT. ABCT highlights the distortionary effects that a divergence between natural and market rates have on particular prices and markets – namely, the interest rate and loanable funds market.[8] In the case of an unanticipated credit expansion, newly created credit pushes the market rate *below* the natural rate. Interest rates no longer serve as an accurate reflection of consumer time preferences. Firms are misled into investing more resources in early-stage production processes that, thanks to the false interest rate signal, temporarily appear more profitable. This "cluster of errors" in the producer goods industry characterizes the boom; it also explains why the bust is more pronounced in the early stages. The "deepening" of the economy's capital structure is unsustainable precisely because there are not enough real savings to sustain all of these longer, capital-intensive projects. Once this problem reveals itself – either in a credit or real resource crunch – the boom turns to bust. Many resources that were diverted into the earlier stages are revealed to be unprofitable and unsustainable. As such, Austrians stress that these "malinvestments" must be liquidated so that the capital structure can be realigned with consumer preferences. It is for this reason that ABCT is often characterized as a "monetary-malinvestment" theory (Garrison, 1989).

THE PATH FORWARD: AUSTRIAN MACRO AND MONETARY EQUILIBRIUM

Austrian Macro and Monetary Disequilibrium: Similarities and Differences

The preceding analysis revealed that there are a number of similarities between MD theory and ABCT. Both schools derive an enormous influence from Knut Wicksell – particularly his work on the tight nexus between monetary and loanable funds markets. Both provide *monetary* theories of the trade cycle that recognize the non-neutrality of money (at least in the short run) whereby exogenous shocks to the nominal money supply can have real effects on economic activity. Both emphasize the long run self-correcting tendencies that are built into the market process. Lastly, both pin the lion's share of the blame for economic recessions and depressions squarely on the failure of government monetary authorities – not "market failures." Yet in highlighting these points of tangency I do not mean to imply that the two theories by any means perfectly dovetail.

We can best highlight the differences by analyzing each theory in isolation. MD theorists describe the perverse consequences an excess demand for money in the *money market* has on individuals' *real cash balances* and the *general price level* (Yeager, 1956).[9] However, by focusing most of their analytical attention on real cash balances and total spending, they rely on a similar sort of overly aggregated framework that Austrians often condemned Keynes, Friedman, and others for using. "Sticky" wages and prices provide their microeconomic rationale for why markets fail to clear. Yet, while they acknowledge that different relative prices will *by necessity* adjust at different rates, MD scholars provide little explanation of the degree of this stickiness or how that stickiness is distributed between consumer and producer goods all across the stages of production.

By couching their analysis in terms of the *absolute* price level and the total level of consumer spending in the economy, it is all too easy for MD theorists to gloss over the all-important micro-level ramifications of the process by which individuals' real cash balances are restored to their equilibrium levels through slow and painful changes in the general price level. It is also easier for them to largely dismiss what implications MD might have on specific relative prices and specific markets – namely, the interest rate in the loanable funds market. This, in turn, makes it easy for them to neglect the economy's capital structure and the relative distribution of spending and production in the economy. These problems become especially prevalent in terms of understanding both Cantillon and reverse-Cantillon effects – that is, the relative price effects that are associated with either injecting new money or withdrawing existing money from circulation.

In short, MD theorists do a commendable job of describing certain aspects of the business cycle. For instance, they thoroughly describe the spending decisions from the perspective of individuals and firms that result from a disequilibrium in the market for real cash balances. However, like most economists they pay virtually no attention to the economy's time structure of production and relative allocation of capital. They instead focus their analysis on the slow and painful adjustment of the absolute price level over *all* markets – in particular labor and output markets – that results from discrepancies between each individuals' desired and actual cash balances.

The Austrian theory, in contrast, focuses on the distortionary effects of monetary disequilibrium on *relative* prices in *specific* markets through *time*. Austrians specifically stress the important role the interest rate (i.e., the price of time) plays in coordinating savings and investment in the loanable funds market (i.e., the market for time). Rather than limiting their analysis of macro-maladies to the money market, they describe how MD spills over into intertemporal disequilibrium, distorting the role that interest rates play in coordinating the production decisions of entrepreneurs with consumers underlying time preferences. This, in turn, causes distortions the economy's capital structure.

The Austrian emphasis on the link between capital and interest – particularly both the heterogeneity and time element of capital – provides a clear methodological point of departure. Like their MD counterparts, ABCT has its roots in a monetary disturbance. At its core, however, it is primarily a story of *intertemporal discoordination*. This sharp focus on relative prices – especially the interest rate – and the economy's capital structure distinguish Austrians from just about every other school of macroeconomic thought. Importantly, it enables them to also place far more emphasis on Cantillon, or relative price, effects of newly created money, which play a critical role in explaining changes to the economy's capital structure in ABCT. For this reason, Garrison (2001) refers to Austrian theory as "capital-based macroeconomics."

Toward a Synthesis: The Return of the Master(s)

The preceding section outlined some of the key similarities and differences between MD and ABC theory. To summarize, both schools view exogenous monetary shocks as the key causal factor in recessions. Where they diverge is in explaining how this nominal shock is translated into real economic effects. MD theorists tend to focus on the disequilibrium price level in the money market, tracing its effects on individuals' real cash balances and total spending. Austrians, in contrast, tend to focus on the disequilibrium interest rate in the loanable funds market, tracing its effects on a particular type of spending – namely, early-stage capital investment (particularly in interest-sensitive projects). However, these differences in emphasis in no way imply that the two theories cannot be reconciled.

One way to reconcile these apparent tensions is to note that the two theories essentially describe two different cases of monetary disequilibrium. MD theory primarily addresses the problems associated with an excess *demand* for money. It is primarily a story of the *bust* and the painful *deflation* that results from the central bank unexpectedly contracting the money supply and individuals' efforts to restore their cash balances to their desired level. Since the impulse (a negative monetary shock) and propagation mechanism (nominal price stickiness) in this account are both nominal, their prescription is to simply have the central bank increase the nominal money supply. In so doing, they are able to avert a painful and perhaps unnecessary deflation by providing individuals with the real cash balances they desire to hold as a part of their portfolio of wealth.[10]

The Austrian theory, on the other hand, primarily addresses the problems of an excess *supply* of money and the unsustainable effects that result from this relative *inflation*. It is thus a *boom-bust* story that describes both the *boom* that sparks the unwarranted lengthening of the economy's capital structure and the *bust* that inevitably results from these systematic errors. Their first best prescription, then, is for the central bank to avoid the artificial boom in the first place. But once the boom has occurred, their best course of action is to allow the bust to run its course so as not to reflate the bubble. In short, the differing prescriptions Austrians and MD theorists offer often stem from the fact they are ultimately diagnosing two separate illnesses. Horwitz (2006, p. 168) writes:

> The key point for reconciling Yeager's approach with that of the Austrians is to recognize that the former case, that of the insufficient supply, corresponds to the traditional MD theory explanation of depressions, while the latter case, that of the excess supply, corresponds to the Austrian concern with inflation and the possibility that it could generate a business cycle and eventual depression. These two theoretical approaches can fruitfully be seen as *two elements of the same underlying story*. [Emphasis Added]

This insight sheds some light on why modern Austrian and MD theorists seem to offer these widely divergent prescriptions at precisely the same moment of the economic downturn. Virtually all Austrians warn central banks against trying to sustain or re-inflate the credit-fueled bubble by continually injecting new money. Yet, some Austrians have acknowledged that their colleagues can take this liquidationist urge too far – even in the context of their own boom-bust story. The reason for this mistake is that the end of a boom often times coincides with a sharp decline in consumption and a rush for liquid assets as individuals struggle to increase their real cash balances. Many Austrians argue that this is a salutary process because it provides the economy with precisely the real savings it was lacking to fund all of its investment projects. But others – particularly those who are influenced by MD and free banking theory – note that Austrians neglect the fact that these savings cannot automatically be intermediated into investment; they can only be converted into loanable funds through the intermediation of the banking system.

One of the best ways to understand the link between financial intermediation and maintaining monetary equilibrium is to understand how a banking system would ideally respond to changes in the demand for money in the absence of legal restrictions and what the macroeconomic ramifications of this behavior would be, which is the topic of Conclusion section. The short version runs as follows. Absent restrictions on the quantity and composition of their liabilities, banks would have no trouble transferring this credit by simply changing the composition of their liabilities (between notes and deposits, for instance) to satisfy the public's demand for savings and issuing new loans.[11] However, since central banks monopolize the supply of currency – the economy's most basic form of money in today's fiat money context – the banking system cannot itself provide the liquid assets the public desires without forking over some of its scarce reserves. So rather than holding their savings in a form banks can intermediate (by holding bank-issued liabilities like checking or savings deposits), the public's rush for liquidity results in a drain of bank reserves and a collapse in the supply of loanable funds. An earlier excess *supply* of money might eventually give way to an excess *demand* for money. In this case, MD theorists might, in fact, be warranted in calling for the monetary authority to increase the nominal money supply in order to avoid a complete collapse of the money and credit pyramid and the downward spiraling of economic activity that Yeager (1986, p. 370) coined the "Wicksellian cumulative rot."

Many Austrians might fear supporting a continuation of what – at face value – might seem like the very same expansionary credit policies that initiated the boom/bust cycle in the first place. Better to let the excess demand be remedied by a natural – indeed, "healthy" – fall in prices, they would argue, than to risk prolonging these malinvestments and delaying the salutary restructuring process the economy must undergo. But upon closer analysis, this fear may well be misplaced. Far from exacerbating the bust, such palliative action may actually be necessary to prevent precisely the sort of "secondary depression" that Hayek (1978) cautioned against in his retrospective of the Great Depression.[12]

The secondary depression marks the turning point where the liquidity rush (prompted by an uncertain environment) that arises in the aftermath of the bust snowballs into an excess demand for money (and, hence, excess supply of goods). At this point, the economy moves *inside* its new PPF. The economy's problems go from being confined to the malinvested industries to spilling over to otherwise healthy sectors of the economy. In the traditional AS-AD framework, the contagion prompts an inward shift in aggregate demand. As a result, real output and prices are forced to endure a more painful and needless decline than was actually needed for the economy to liquidate malinvested resources and reallocate them appropriately. Echoing Hayek, Lachmann (1978, p. 120) argues avoiding a "secondary deflation … must always be the primary aim of monetary policy." Identifying this situation is admittedly easier said than done. But even if one concedes that the central bank is plagued by various epistemic problems, there is nothing heretical about supporting – at least in theory – expansionary monetary policy that merely seeks to *restore* monetary equilibrium. This is because many of the same pathologies that accompany an excess *supply* of money – relative price distortion, extensive coordination problems, etc. – also accompany an excess *demand* for money. MD theory therefore rescues Austrians from being inconsistent in their analysis of excess supply and demand for money by holding a fatalistic bias in favor of "bad" deflation (Horwitz, 2000, ch. 5).

Whereas MD theory provides a useful framework for Austrians to analyze the specific issue of the secondary depression as well as the more general problems associated with an excess *demand* for money, Austrian price and capital theory can provide useful insights for MD thinkers on the relative price effects that are associated with MD as well as the very real problems associated with an excess *supply* of money. Austrian capital theory, in particular, can be used to supplement their story by pointing out the real effects MD has on the economy's structure of production. These insights are especially valuable for explaining the coordination problems that arise in particular markets – namely, the market for higher order goods – due to an *excess supply* of money.

Many MD theorists tend to downplay these problems relative to the case of an excess demand for money. This is due not only to their near exclusive focus on the money market and individuals' real cash balances but also to their emphasis on "sticky" prices. MD theorists generally agree that prices are sticky downward. Although they provide a roughly parallel explanation for why prices may be sticky upward, it is less clear in their analysis what harmful effects actually result from an excess supply of money aside from a temporary excess demand for goods. This lack of any clear and present danger has caused many to err on the side of supporting inflationary policies. Yet a proper understanding of ABCT, Cantillon effects and the all-important role relative prices play in conveying vital information to entrepreneurs and economic actors across the entire economy should caution them against holding such crude inflationary biases.

This Austrian focus on relative prices also has direct implications for one of the most hotly contested internal debates in the MD camp: the debate over whether or not the goal of monetary policy should be to target a perfectly stable price level. Historically, many leading thinkers in this tradition dating back to Knut Wicksell have argued for targeting zero inflation.[13] Yeager himself was a staunch advocate of zero inflation. He essentially argued that *any* changes in the general price level ought to be regarded as "symptoms or consequences" of monetary disequilibrium (Yeager, 1986, p. 373).

However, a number of scholars in both the Austrian and MD tradition have argued against targeting zero inflation and in favor of a "productivity norm," which would allow the absolute price level to rise or fall with changes in productivity. In this view, a rise in productivity of a particular good that causes a decline in the general price level is not an indicator of MD. It simply reflects the fact that a certain product can be produced more efficiently. The falling price serves as a useful signal to market actors that certain goods are less costly to produce and attain. For this reason, supporters of the productivity norm like Selgin (1997) refer to productivity-induced deflation as benign or "good" deflation.[14] This deflation, they argue, is consistent with monetary equilibrium.

This emphasis on maintaining the integrity of relative prices versus stabilizing the price level (however defined) provided a stark contrast in the policy advice given by Hayek and early monetarists like Irving Fisher throughout the 1920s. Hayek (1935) rebuked the Federal Reserve and other central banks for trying to stabilize the consumer price level instead of allowing prices to fall as technological innovations in particular industries reduced per unit cost of production. A policy of price level stabilization in the face of rising productivity, he argued, would result not in absolute inflation but in "relative inflation" whereby prices are artificially kept higher than they should be. This relative inflation via credit creation, Hayek warned, would ignite the exact same "boom-bust" processes as outright inflation. Price level stabilizationists like Fisher and later monetarists accused the Fed of being too contractionary from 1929 onward because it allowed the price level to plunge by one-third. But they saw absolutely nothing wrong with Fed policy during the boom of the 1920s. Hayek's emphasis on relative prices enabled him to diagnose a threat that others dismissed. This episode provides a microcosm of the virtues of the two respective camps: Austrians provide a compelling explanation for the artificial *boom*, MD theorists, on the other hand, provide an explanation of the *bust* and the avoidable dangers that accompany the "secondary depression." A proper interpretation of the two schools can therefore help macroeconomists develop a compelling explanation of *both* sides of the business cycle: the artificial boom and the resulting bust.[15]

The key lesson for Austrian scholars to bear in mind is that the non-neutrality of money that they all recognize in the case of an excess *supply* of money becomes equally problematic in the case of an excess *demand* for money, as MD theorists note. Just as a credit-driven boom can disrupt relative prices and the economy's capital structure, a deflationary spiral can also disrupt the plans of economic actors. In both cases, the price system is unable to perform its key function of transmitting information about relative scarcities to economic actors. The Austrian emphasis on relative prices also provides a critical lesson for MD theorists. By incorporating the key insights of Austrian price and capital theory, they can gain an appreciation for the real adverse effects that MD has on the economy's relative prices and capital structure. In particular, they can develop a greater understanding of the real dangers that are caused by an excess supply of money. In this sense, Austrian and MD theory can be seen as reinforcing each other and providing economists with more superior *micro*foundations for macroeconomics.[16]

FREE BANKING: THE MISSING INSTITUTIONAL LINK

A proper understanding of both Austrian and MD theory can certainly help guide central bankers and policy-makers to make more informed policy decisions. Still, relying on the same government monetary authorities that often create a crisis to ameliorate the excess supply or demand for money would seem to clash with both schools' general presumption in favor of laissez faire and against the need for government intervention.

From the standpoint of robust political economy,[17] central bankers – like central planners – suffer from two distinct problems when trying to conduct an optimal monetary policy (defined here as maintaining monetary equilibrium) (Boettke & Smith, 2015; Salter, 2013). First, they face an insurmountable *knowledge* problem, for example, how can they tell that they are accommodating the increased demand for money that monetary equilibrium theory implies it should while not reflating the bubble in the way Austrians fear? Second, they face an *incentive* problem, for example, what rules and constraints must be put in place to prevent central bankers from engaging in either too much (or too little) money creation in order to finance government deficits or benefit certain interest groups? These twin problems coalesce to create a more general institutional dilemma: how can the problems associated with MD be alleviated without relying on the wisdom or benevolence of officials at an exogenous, non-market institution like a central bank?

Economists have grappled with this institutional dilemma many times throughout history.[18] Perhaps, the most famous case came during the monetarist counter-revolution in the debate over "rules versus discretion" (Friedman, 1960; Kydland & Prescott, 1977). Friedman and his fellow monetarists made a compelling argument against the Keynesian case for discretion. Yet, the debate did very little to address the fundamental question of whether or not the central bank is itself a necessary component of the money and banking system. At most, it represented a modest institutional turn in macroeconomics.

The best answer to this question is provided by the theory of free banking that has been most developed by Lawrence H. White in (1984) and Selgin (1988).[19] Generally speaking, a free banking system is an institutional framework where government plays no special role in the money and banking system outside of protecting private property and contracts and upholding the rule of law. Banks are free to enter and exit the industry as they wish, competing on a coequal legal status. They are also free to issue their own debt and equity claims in whatever form they wish without any restrictions on the quantity, types, or mix of assets they may hold as backing. This means that private banks can compete for depositors by offering both traditional deposit accounts *and currency* (i.e., bank notes). Since banks are free to issue their own notes, they are fully capable of accommodating their customers' preferences for whatever form of money they would like to hold.[20] In short, a free banking system is one where banking is treated no differently than any other competitive industry. There is no state-sponsored central bank with a monopoly on currency issue, no official lender of last resort, no government deposit guarantees, and no special restrictions on the contractual terms made between banks and their customers (Selgin & White, 1994, pp. 1718–1719). In theory, a free banking system can be built on the foundation of any monetary standard – including central bank-issued fiat money. However, free banking scholars typically assume that the basic reserve money in such a system consists either of some outside commodity like gold or silver (as has historically been the case), or a frozen or computer controlled stock of fiat money (Selgin, 1988).[21]

Free banking scholars acknowledge that no country has actually adopted a theoretically pure free banking system, as described above. Nevertheless, banking historians have studied a number of relatively free or "lightly regulated" banking systems that meet the core requirements of a free banking system: a fair degree of bank freedom, multiple note issuers, and the absence of any sort of government-sponsored lender of last resort (Dowd, 1992, p. 2).[22] The evidence suggests that these systems tend to spontaneously develop certain characteristics that contribute to financial stability. Private clearinghouses, for instance, evolved to keep private money issue in check, monitor their members, and serve as a private "lender of last resort" in the rare case of a liquidity crisis (Dowd, 1993; White, 1984). These systems also showed no tendency toward monopoly or any sort of anti-competitive concentration in the banking sector (Briones & Rockoff, 2005; Schuler, 1992). Generally speaking, these episodes suggest that relatively free banking systems generally enjoyed greater stability, more competition, and greater financial innovation than their more heavily regulated rivals.

The main reason why it is important for Austrians and MD theorists to understand the operations of a free banking system is because there is strong evidence to suggest that it contains certain automatic tendencies that make it very attractive for those who are primarily concerned with maintaining monetary equilibrium. One of the defining traits of a mature free banking system with a well-functioning interbank clearing system is that the supply of bank-issued money tends to respond endogenously to changes in its demand. This is because each bank in its effort to maximize profits faces a strong incentive to accommodate changes in the demand for its money with changes in its supply.

For instance, if the demand for a particular bank's liabilities unexpectedly rises relative to its rivals' (i.e., its velocity of circulation falls), that bank enjoys "positive clearings," or a net gain in its reserve relative to rival banks. The resulting increase the supply of its reserves over and above the level it demands for precautionary reasons sends a direct signal to the bank that its customers are more willing to hold (i.e., abstain from spending) its money as a form of savings, thereby providing it with an additional source of loanable funds. The bank can intermediate these otherwise idle savings into productive investments by expanding its portfolio of interest-bearing loans. By putting more of its money into circulation, the flow of its liabilities entering the clearing system eventually rises, bringing its actual reserves back in line with its desired reserves. The reverse holds when a bank faces a fall in the demand for its liabilities (i.e., its velocity of circulation rises). Such a bank suffers from "adverse clearings," or net loss of reserves to rival banks. This forces them to contract their liabilities to restore actual reserves to their desired level. In this way, the supply of bank-issued money in a free banking system is *demand-elastic*.

We can extrapolate from the case of the individual bank to see what happens across the entire banking system when there is a *general* rise in the demand to hold inside money. In this case, no bank on average gains any reserves relative to its competitors. However, the decline in *gross* clearings causes each bank to reduce its demand for precautionary reserves by reducing the variance in the size of reserve losses (Selgin, 1988, pp. 73–78). Since banks can safely expand their issuance of inside money without risk of dipping below their now lower desired level of precautionary reserves, they can increase their profits by reducing their reserve ratios and issuing more liabilities in exchange for interest-bearing loans. The reverse holds when there is a general fall in the demand for inside money (i.e., an increase in the velocity of the circulation of inside money). In this case, banks – facing a higher risk of adverse clearings – contract their balance sheets to meet their higher demand for precautionary reserves. In this way, the supply of money that is provided by the banking system as a whole is *demand-elastic* (White, 1999, p. 66).

The key benefit of a free banking system, then, is that these micro-level actions on the part of individual banks tend to yield the desirable macroeconomic consequence of maintaining monetary equilibrium. Generally speaking, all banks in a free banking system face a direct incentive to offset changes in the transactions velocity of inside money with opposite changes in its circulation. In terms of the original equation of exchange, MV_T = PT, changes in the transaction demand for money (the inverse of the transactions velocity of inside money, V_T) are met with offsetting changes in its supply, *M*. One unintended virtue of a competitive free banking system, then, is that it has a built-in mechanism for adjusting the supply of bank-issued money in the face of shocks in the demand for it. In so doing, a free banking system contains an automatic tendency to maintain monetary equilibrium.[23] This helps to ensure that the natural and market rate of interest coincide in the market for loanable funds so that ex ante savings and investment are equal and the loanable funds market is in equilibrium. It also upholds Say's Law, so that both aggregate supply and demand as well as our notional and effective demand are equal. The price level in a free banking system would be determined solely by the intersection of the supply of and demand for real money balances. Consistent with the productivity norm, the price level would respond inversely to changes in productivity but *not* changes in the demand for money. In the traditional AS-AD framework, this implies that prices would adjust in response to shifts in aggregate supply but not to shifts in aggregate demand.

The key feature that enables a free banking system to operate so effectively is *competition*. Each individual bank has a profit maximizing incentive not only to prevent its rivals from over-or-under issuing but also to restrain itself from issuing too much or too little money. For instance, any bank that tries to build up its reserves by contracting its balance sheet misses out on the interest revenue it could earn by lending out the loanable funds it has been granted by its depositors. In this case, investors – realizing they could earn a higher return on their deposits at rival banks – will likely withdraw their deposits from the excessively cautious bank and reinvest their savings elsewhere. On the other hand, any bank that thinks that one of its rivals is putting too many notes and loans into circulation can maximize its profits by redeeming that bank's liabilities, thereby gaining new reserves that it can intermediate into interest-bearing loans and investments. In this sense, the interbank clearing system acts like a "chain gang," keeping all of its members in lockstep with one another. Importantly, since no particular bank enjoys any special legal privileges on currency issue, there is no central bank capable of escaping the discipline of this chain gang and leading the entire banking system "pied piper" style into a system-wide over-or-under expansion. A competitive free banking system would therefore go a long way in preventing the sort of *over*expansion of money and credit that ABCT cautions against while at the same time preventing the *under*expansion that MD theorists justifiably fear.

A free banking system is ultimately superior to monetary institutions that rely on heavy government involvement – regardless of whether they are governed by "rules" or "discretion" – precisely because this market competition enables it to *endogenously* overcome both the knowledge and incentive problems that plague government officials and central bankers. Since its money holders are its direct customers, individual banks can take advantage of their localized knowledge to ensure that the new money is injected precisely where it is in greatest demand. Moreover, profit maximizing bankers have an incentive to ensure that the supply of its inside money is equal to the demand for it at all times. A free banking system therefore tends to maintain monetary equilibrium and, in so doing, loanable funds equilibrium. It is this connection between the money and loanable funds markets that is at the center of Wicksell's analysis as well as MD and ABC theory.

A free banking system would also go a long way in preventing the sort of *over*expansion of money and credit that ABCT cautions against while at the same time preventing the *under*expansion that MD theorists justifiably fear. Following Garrison's (1984, p. 200) logic that "it is the 'intersection' of the 'market for time' and the 'market for money' that constitutes macroeconomics unique subject matter," understanding the role and importance of a well-functioning free banking system is an absolutely essential starting point for any macroeconomic theory. In the same way that the theory of free trade is essential for helping us understand the comparative benefits of alternative policy regimes in the realm of international trade, understanding the theory of free banking is essential for conducting research on comparative monetary and banking institutions.[24] In this sense, free banking theory has the potential to connect thinkers in both the Austrian and MD camps. It is for this reason that I consider free banking theory the "missing link" that is needed to connect MD theory and Austrian macro.

CONCLUSION

My core objective in this paper has been to build on the work of earlier scholars to unite the key insights from both ABCT and MD theory under the same banner. Because both traditions place a strong focus on the importance of money and banking institutions, I introduced free banking theory as a "missing link" that has the potential to synthesize core insights from both traditions and unite scholars behind a shared policy prescription. Once this key element is introduced, I believe that scholars in these traditions can work together to provide a compelling alternative for the study of macroeconomics.

The timing of this effort might strike some as being a century out of date. But I believe that just as the failure of the "New Economics" of Keynes opened the door for a lively debate over the future of macroeconomics, the Great Recession of 2009 and the ongoing sluggish global recovery have the potential to spark a reinvigorated conversation over alternative macroeconomic frameworks. Thanks to more recent developments in free banking theory, scholars in these two traditions now have a far better understanding of the critical role an unfettered banking system can play in promoting both monetary and intertemporal equilibrium. By taking time, money, capital and relative prices seriously and incorporating the key insights from free banking theory, I believe that the alternative path outlined here provides the best sort of "microfoundations" for macroeconomics (Horwitz, 2000). As Austrian macroeconomist Garrison notes, sound economic analysis begins with recognizing that: "There are *macro*economic problems, but only *micro*economic solutions." This observation runs directly counter to the mainstream notion that there are only *macro*economic solutions to *micro*economic problems.

Future Austrian and MD scholars will have to build on the work of Garrison (2001), Horwitz (2000), and others to further develop these ideas into a unified, coherent alternative to the prevailing paradigms. Scholars who are interested in free banking, in particular, will need to work out in greater detail how a free banking system would fit into an international financial system and what sort of practical and epistemic problems might arise in transitioning toward a free banking system from our existing international monetary institutions. The best place for reform-minded scholars to start, I would argue, is by reading and building on the ideas of these oft-neglected "mainline" thinkers in the Austrian, MD and free banking tradition (Boettke, 2012). In so doing, they will gain a greater appreciation of the critical role that monetary institutions play not only in promoting microeconomic coordination but also in generating desirable macroeconomic outcomes.

NOTES

1. White (2012), Murphy (2009), and Laidler (1999) have extensively documented some of the macroeconomic theorizing that occurred before Keynes. In fact, the term "macroeconomics" was coined in 1933 by Ragner Frisch more than two years before the *General Theory* was released.

2. Although MD theory shares a great deal of overlap with Friedman's Monetarism, MD theorists take a different approach to explaining economic fluctuations. Most notably, they largely work outside of the Keynesian framework that Friedman employed to deconstruct Keynes's theory from within. Instead, they frame their analysis on each individuals' demand for real cash balances as a way of explaining how changes in the supply of or demand for money can spill over into changes in aggregate spending.

3. Say's Principle is derived from Say's Law of Markets, which maintains that "production is the source of demand." Keynes (1936) misleadingly defined it as "supply creates it own demand." However, Clower and Leijonhufvud's reformulation places Say's Law in its proper context by showing that the law only holds under monetary equilibrium. In this case, aggregate supply and demand are equal at the prevailing price, and notional demand (which is based on the actual value of our labor's marginal product) is equal to effective demand (which is based on our actual ability to command real resources, irrespective of our marginal product of labor). An excess demand for money, however, implies an excess supply (or "general glut") of goods; an excess supply of money implies an excess demand for goods (or "general shortage").

4. The notion that prices are "sticky" – particularly downward – is an idea that long predates Keynes. In fact, it has been shared by virtually all scholars in the MD tradition. Yeager (1997, p. 408) clarifies this position: "By 'stickiness,' we do not mean rigidity; we do not mean that prices are unresponsive to market imbalances. Different prices (and wages), however, are responsive in different degrees." He specifically notes – as many other scholars have argued – that input prices tend

to be far less responsive than output prices. He continues: "Because prices are interdependent, yet necessarily are set in a decentralized and piecemeal manner, it takes time for them to achieve a new equilibrium pattern after a pervasive disturbance. Stickiness in this sense is a fact of reality." His precise logic for why prices are sticky (*ibid.*, pp. 224–229) revolves around collective action problems – what he terms the "who goes first problem" and various informational asymmetries. The latter bears a striking semblance to the "signal extraction problem" that Lucas highlights in his famed "Lucas Island Model."

5. As Garrison (1976) notes, the notion of a two dimensional capital structure featuring a time-intensive structure of production was also laid out around the same time by Jevons(1871) and Cassel (1903). Nevertheless, Böhm-Bawerk's contribution remains the most extensive.

6. Although Böhm-Bawerk felt he was largely building on Menger's earlier work, it has been well-documented that Menger was harshly critical of his work, going so far as to call it "one of the greatest errors ever committed" (Schumpeter, 1954, p. 847, n. 8). Endres (1987), Kirzner (1966, pp. 54–58), and Garrison (1990) speculate that Menger's biggest problem with Böhm-Bawerk's capital theory was that it strayed too far from his emphasis on the role of subjective valuations of individuals.

7. Wicksell had an enormous influence not only on later Austrian theorists but also his fellow Swedes. However, many of Wicksell's Swedish followers like Gunnar Myrdal, Bertil Ohlin, and Eric Lindahl took a far more Keynesian approach. Laidler (1999) argues their emphasis on the simultaneous equality of ex post savings and investment and yet lack of coordination between ex ante savings and investment in a dynamic context is at least partially embedded in the "IS" curve in the popular Keynesian IS-LM framework.

8. The notion of the "natural" rate has been hotly contested in Austrian circles. Hayek (1931 [2008]) largely adopted Wicksell's notion of the natural rate as occurring where the demand for loan capital and the supply of savings are equal. He pointed out that in theory the natural rate would be the rate of interest that would prevail if savings and investment were made *in natura* (via barter). However, he follows Wicksell by arguing that in a *money* economy, the actual (or money) rate may diverge from the equilibrium (or natural) rate. Sraffa (1932) famously critiqued this notion of a single "natural" rate of interest by arguing that in the context of a barter economy with multiple goods there must be multiple natural rates. A number of Austrians have attempted to either defend or update the Austrian theory to account for Sraffa's criticisms (Lachmann, 1986; Murphy, 2010). Mises (1949 [1996]) and Rothbard (1962) defended their position by maintaining that the natural rate is, in fact, a money rate of interest. This is because *money* is the actual good in which time preferences are demonstrated, not a "veil" that is added to a barter economy. It is therefore possible to have a single natural rate of interest because the different rates are quoted in terms of a single commodity (money) that can be equilibrated (Boettke & Newman, 2015, pp. 9–10).

9. Mises himself employed this "real cash balance approach" in *Theory of Money and Credit* (1912 [1981]).

10. Though the typical example is a decrease in the money supply that either originates from or is presided over by central bank, the same effects and policy

recommendations follow from a change in individual's demand for real money balance. An increase in the public's demand for real money balances, for instance, can also spark an excess demand for money unless the central bank quickly responds by proportionately increasing the nominal supply of money.

11. It is worth pointing out that in the example given here, the public is satisfied to hold its wealth in the form of bank-issued, or "inside," money. The liquidity run can better be described as a "currency run." In theory, individuals could run on the banks' reserves asset, be it gold, silver, or any other sort of commodity money that naturally arose in relatively free banking systems, which is a form of "outside" money that is *not* issued by the banking system. This case is admittedly more complex and might, in fact, require some type of "lender of last resort." Historically, however, Selgin (1988) shows that currency runs were far more prevalent, and that relatively free banking systems very rarely suffered from runs on their reserve assets.

12. Hayek (1978, pp. 210–211) explicitly notes that: "such a 'secondary depression' caused by an induced deflation should of course by prevented by appropriate monetary countermeasures." Hayek himself revised his position years later after admitting at the time he erred too far on the side of supporting "liquidationist policies" that very likely prolonged the depression.

13. Selgin (1997) includes Knut Wicksell, Gustav Cassel, and Irving Fisher as prominent scholars in the monetary equilibrium tradition that favored a zero inflation norm. He includes David Davidson, Gottfried Haberler, Ralph Hawtrey, F. A. Hayek, Alfred Marshall, Gunnar Myrdal, Dennis Robertson, and A. C. Pigou as just some of the scholars who argued for some kind of productivity norm as an alternative to zero inflation. He notes that even Keynes flirted with the idea before eventually settling for a full employment target with something like a zero inflation norm.

14. In terms of the AS-AD framework, a zero inflation norm implies that ideal monetary policy would respond to such an outward shift in the LRAS and SRAS curves by increasing the money supply to satisfy individual's increased demand for real money balances promoted by their higher real income, thereby shifting the AD curve outward so that it intersects the new LRAS curve at the previous price level. A productivity norm, in contrast, would refrain from expanding the money supply, allowing the existing AD curve to intersect the new LRAS and SRAS curves at a new, lower price level. The lower price level automatically serves to meet the increased demand in individual's desired real money balances and maintain monetary equilibrium. For more information on the desirability of allowing the price level to fluctuate with changes in productivity, see Selgin (1997).

15. Two caveats apply here. First, many economists reject the notion of a "boom-bust" cycle. This idea is best captured in Friedman's "plucking model," which argues that historical "business cycles" show no signs of a preceding "boom" and in fact only been characterized by "bust." Second, my argument here by no means implies that the bust that follows an unsustainable boom can somehow be avoided by wise policy or that Austrians have nothing to say about the bust. An unsustainable boom necessarily requires a restructuring of capital and labor. Here, the Austrian theory clearly provides useful insights.

16. It should be noted here that in arguing that Austrian and MD theory provide *superior* microfoundations I do not mean to imply that microfoundations are entirely absent from the Keynesian framework or later developments in macroeconomic theorizing. Hoover (2010) has persuasively argued that Keynes's emphasis on microfoundations – that is, how all aggregate behavior is ultimately rooted in the action of individuals – is often overlooked. "It is an underappreciated element of Keynes's appraoch in the *General Theory* that it respects the heterogeneity of individual agents to a degree rarely found in macroeconomics," he writes (Hoover, 2010, p. 12). New Keynesian scholars have also taken seriously the new classical developments in microfoundations in updating Keynes's theory (Snowdon & Vane, 2005).

17. Leeson and Subrick (2006) introduce the idea of "robust political economy." A political system is defined to be "robust" in their taxonomy if it is able to produce social welfare-enhancing outcomes in the face of deviations from ideal assumptions about individuals' knowledge and incentives.

18. As White (2012, ch. 12) and others have documented, the rules versus discretion debate in its broadest terms extends as far back as the British Bullionist debates of the 18th and 19th centuries, which culminated in the passages of Peel's Banking Act in 1844. It continued into the 20th century with proposals by leading economists like Alfred Marshall, Irving Fisher, and others to establish some sort of rule for stabilizing the price level in the context of a commodity standard. The most pioneering work of this topic in the context of a fiat money regime, however, came in Henry Simons' (1936) article on "Rules versus Authorities in Monetary Policy," which had a profound influence on Friedman and other Chicago economists.

19. Though White and Selgin have arguably done more than any other scholars to develop and formalize the *theory* of free banking, it would be unfair to characterize them as its sole "inventors." The core ideas of free banking theory originated during the Bullionist debates with the leading thinkers of the "free banking" school such as H. B. Parnell, J. W. Gilbart, and G. P. Scrope (Schwartz, 2008). Most of the ideas can also be found in rudimentary form in Mises' *Theory of Money and Credit* (1912 [1981]).

20. White (1999, pp. 11–14) distinguishes between *inside money* – money issued by banks in the form of bank liabilities (e.g., bank notes and deposits that are included in M2) – and *outside money* – money that is *exogenous* to the banking system. Historically, this has consisted of either commodity money like gold or silver or, as is the case in our modern context, central bank-issued fiat money. Banks can accommodate changes in the demand for inside money, but not outside money.

21. The issue of how a fiat money would be managed without allowing for discretion raises its own issues. Selgin (2013) addresses how such rules-based "quasi-commodity" money might be designed in practice.

22. For more on the mechanics and performance of historically free banking systems, see: White (1984), Schuler (1988, 1992), Briones and Rockoff (2005), and Dowd (1992).

23. White (1999, ch. 3) and Selgin (1988, ch. 2) provide a more detailed informal explanation of how this process unfolds at the microeconomic level. Sechrest (2008) shows this result using a formal model.

24. The historical record indeed indicates that relatively free banking systems enjoyed more financial stability and were less vulnerable to macroeconomic fluctuations (Dowd, 1992; Schuler, 1988).

ACKNOWLEDGMENTS

The author would like to thank Peter J. Boettke, Lawrence H. White, Kevin D. Hoover, Daniel J. Smith, Patrick Newman, the editor and two anonymous referees at RHETM, and the participants at the Graduate Student Paper Workshop at George Mason University for their helpful comments. The usual caveat applies.

REFERENCES

Boettke, P. J. (2012). *Living economics: Yesterday, today, and tomorrow*. Oakland, CA: The Independent Institute.

Boettke, P. J., & Newman, P. (2015). *The Keynesian liquidity trap: An Austrian critique*. Working Paper No. 15–52. Department of Economics, George Mason University.

Boettke, P. J., & Smith, D. J. (2015). Evolving views on monetary policy in the thought of Hayek, Friedman, and Buchanan. *The Review of Austrian Economics*, *29*(1), 1–20.

Briones, I., & Rockoff, H. (2005). Do economists reach a conclusion on free-banking episodes. *Econ Journal Watch*, *2*(2), 279–324.

Cassel, G. (1903). *The nature and necessity of interest*. London: Macmillan and Co.

Dowd, K. (1992). *The experience of free banking*. London: Routledge.

Dowd, K. (1993). *Laissez-faire banking*. London: Routeledge.

Endres, A. M. (1987). The origins of Bohm-Bawerk's 'Greatest Error': Theoretical points of separation from Menger. *Journal of Institutional and Theoretical Economics*, *143*, 291–309.

Friedman, M. (1960). *A program for monetary stability*. New York, NY: Fordham University Press.

Garrison, R. W. (1976). *Austrian macroeconomics: A diagrammatical exposition*. Menlo Park, CA: Institute for Humane Studies.

Garrison, R. W. (1984). Time and money: The universals of macroeconomic theorizing. *Journal of Macroeconomics*, *6*(2), 197–213.

Garrison, R. W. (1989). The Austrian thory of the business cycle in light of modern macroeconomics. *The Review of Austrian Economics*, *3*(1), 3–29.

Garrison, R. W. (1990). Austrian capital theory: The early controversies. In B. J. Caldwell (Ed.), *Carl Menger and his legacy in economics*. Durham, NC: Duke University Press.

Garrison, R. W. (2001). *Time and money: The macroeconomics of capital structure*. New York, NY: Routledge.

Hayek, F. A. (1931 [2008]). *Prices and production*. Auburn, AL: Ludvig von Mises Institute.

Hayek, F. A. (1933). *Monetary theory and the trade cycle*. New York, NY: Sentry Press.

Hayek, F. A. (1935). *Prices and production* (2nd ed.). London: Routeledge.

Hayek, F. A. (1941). *The pure theory of capital*. Chicago, IL: University of Chicago Press.

Hayek, F. A. (1978). *The denationalization of money – The argument refined: An analysis of the theory and practice of current currencies* (2nd ed.). London: Institute for Economic Affairs.

Hazlitt, H. (1959 [2007]). *The failure of the new economics*. Auburn, AL: Ludwig von Mises Institute.

Hoover, K. D. (2010). *Microfoundational programs* (pp. 1–59). Retrieved from SSRN http://ssrn.com/abstract = 1562282.

Horwitz, S. (2000). *Microfoundations and macroeconomics: An Austrian perspective*. New York, NY: Routledge.

Horwitz, S. (2006). Monetary disequilibrum theory and Austrian macroeconomics: Further thoughts on a synthesis. In R. Koppl (Ed.), *Money and markets: Essays in honor of Leland B. Yeager* (pp. 166–185). New York, NY: Routledge.

Humphrey, T. M. (1991). Nonneutrality of money in classical monetary thought. *Economic Review*, *77*, 3–15.

Hutt, W. H. (1939 [1977]). *The theory of idle resources*. Indianapolis, IN: Liberty Press.

Hutt, W. H. (1963). *Keynesianism – Retrospect and prospect*. Chicago, IL: Regnery.

Jevons, W. S. (1871). *The theory of political economy*. London: Macmillian and Co.

Keynes, J. M. (1930 [2011]). *A treatise on money: The pure theory of money and the applied theory of money*. London: Martino Fine Books.

Keynes, J. M. (1936 [1973]). The general theory of employment, interest and money. In E. Johnson & D. Moggridge (Eds.), *The collected writings of John Maynard Keynes* (Vol. 7). London: Macmillan.

Kirzner, I. M. (1966). *An essay on capital*. New York, NY: Augustus M. Kelley.

Knight, F. H. (1937). Unemployment: And Mr. Keynes's revolution in economic theory. *The Canadian Journal of Ecnomics and Political Science*, *3*(1), 100–123.

Krugman, P. (2007). *"Introduction," in John Maynard Keynes, the general theory of employment, interest, and money*. New York, NY: Palgrave MacMillan.

Kydland, F. E., & Prescott, E. C. (1977). Rules rather than discretion: The inconsistency of optimal plans. *The Journal of Political Economy*, *85*(3), 473–491.

Lachmann, L. (1978). An interview with Ludwig Lachmann. *Austrian Economics Newsletter*, *1* (3).

Lachmann, L. (1986). Austrian economics under fire: The Hayek-Sraffa duel in retrospect. In W. Grassl, B. Smith, & W. G. Smith (Eds.), *Austrian economics: Historical and philosophical background* (pp. 210–224). New York, NY: New York University Press.

Laidler, D. (1999). *Fabricating the Keynesian revolution: Studies of the inter-war literature on money, the cycle, and unemployment*. Cambridge: Cambridge University Press.

Leeson, P. T., & Subrick, J. R. (2006). Robust political economy. *Review of Austrian Economics*, *19*(2), 107–111.

Leijonhufvud, A. (1981). *Information and coordination: Essays in macroeconomic theory*. Oxford: Oxford University Press.

Mises, L. v. (1912 [1981]). The theory of money and credit *(H. E. Batson, Trans.)*. Indianapolis, IN: Liberty Fund.

Mises, L. v. (1949 [1996]). *Human action: A treatise on economics*. San Francisco, CA: Fox & Wilkes.

Murphy, A. E. (2009). *The genesis of macroeconomics: New ideas from Sir William Petty to Henry Thornton*. Oxford: Oxford University Press.

Murphy, R. M. (2010). *Multiple interest rates and Austrian business cycle theory*. Retrieved from http://consultingbyrpm.com/uploads/Multiple%20Interest%20Rates%20and%20ABCT.pdf.2010

Rockoff, H. (1974). The free banking era: A reexamination. *Jounal of Money, Credit and Banking*, *6*(2), 141–167.

Rothbard, M. N. (1962). *Man, economy and state*. Los Angeles, CA: Nash Publishing.

Salter, A. W. (2013). Not all NGDP is created equal: A critique of market monetarism. *Journal of Private Enterprise*, *29*(1), 41–52.

Schuler, K. (1988). Free banking: A bibliographic essay. *Human Studies Review*, *6*(1), 1–22.

Schuler, K. (1992). The world history of free banking. In K. Dowd (Ed.), *The experience of free banking* (pp. 7—47). London: Routledge.

Schumpeter, J. A. (1954). *History of economic analysis*. Oxford: Oxford University Press.

Schwartz, A. J. (2008). Banking school, currency school, free banking school. In S. N. Durlauf & L. E. Blume (Eds.), *The New Palgrave dictionary of economics* (2nd ed., Vol. 6). Basingstoke: Palgrave Macmillan.

Sechrest, L. J. (2008). *Free banking: Theory, history, and a Laissez-Faire model*. Auburn, AL: Ludwig von Mises Institute.

Selgin, G. A. (1988b). *The theory of free banking: Money supply under competitive note issue*. Washington, DC: Cato Institute.

Selgin, G. A. (1997). *Less than zero: The case for a falling price level in a growing economy*. London: Institute for Economic Affairs.

Selgin, G. A. (2013). *Synthetic commodity money*. Department of Economics, University of Georgia.

Selgin, G. A., & White, L. H. (1994). How would the invisible hand handle money? *Journal of Economic Literature*, *32*(4), 1718–1749.

Simons, H. C. (1936). Rules versus authorities in monetary policy. *Journal of Political Economy*, *44*, 1–30.

Snowdon, B., & Vane, H. R. (2005). *Modern macroeconomics: Its orgins, development and current state*. Northampton, MA: Edward Elgar Publishing.

Sraffa, P. (1932). Dr. Hayek on money and capital. *Economic Journal*, *42*(165), 42–53.

Warburton, C. (1950). The monetary disequilibrium hypothesis. *American Journal of Economics and Sociology*, *10*(1), 1–11.

White, L. H. (1984). *Free banking in Britain*. Cambridge: Cambridge University Press.

White, L. H. (1999). *The theory of monetary institutions*. Oxford: Blackwell.

White, L. H. (2012). *The clash of economic ideas: The great policy debates and experiments of the last hundred years*. Cambridge: Cambridge University Press.

Wicksell, K. (1898 [1965]). Interest and prices *(R. F. Kahn, Trans.)*. New York, NY: Augustus M. Kelley.

Yeager, L. (1997). *The fluttering veil: Essays on monetary disequilibrium*. Indianapolis, IN: Liberty Fund.

Yeager, L. B. (1956). A cash-balance interpretation of depression. *Southern Economic Journal*, *22*(4), 438—447.

Yeager, L. B. (1968). Essential properties of the medium of exchange. *Kyklos*, *21*(1), 45–69.
Yeager, L. B. (1973). The Keynesian diversion. *Western Economic Journal*, *11*, 150–163.
Yeager, L. B. (1986). The signifiance of monetary disequilibrium. *Cato Journal*, *6*, 369–399.

PART III
FROM THE VAULT

J. M. KEYNES'S LECTURES ON FISHER IN 1909☆

Carlo Cristiano

ABSTRACT

Marshall, Pigou, and Keynes on one side of the Atlantic, and Fisher on the other, had different approaches to the quantity theory of money. But they shared its basic framework, with the result that theoretical discussions did not prevent some degree of mutual support on policy proposals. If a divergence there was, at this stage, this pertained the feasibility of Fisher's proposals, because Fisher's enthusiasm for reform could find no match at Cambridge. This notwithstanding, and although in varying degrees, Marshall, Pigou, and Keynes were sympathetic with Fisher's battle for "stable money." Indeed, a fragment from the Keynes Papers shows that, at a very early stage of his career, Keynes paid great attention to Fisher's empirical research on the relationship between "Appreciation and interest," taking the relation between nominal and real rates of interest as a possible explanation of the trade cycle. For some time at least, this widened the common ground upon which Fisher's proposals for "stable money" could find some support at Cambridge.

Research in the History of Economic Thought and Methodology, Volume 34B, 367–401

ISSN: 0743-4154/doi:10.1108/S0743-41542016000034B003

Keywords: Fisher; Keynes; quantity theory of money; interest rates; trade cycle; monetary reform

INTRODUCTION

In 1908, John Maynard Keynes obtained a post as lecturer in the Cambridge Economics Tripos.[1] During the tenure of his lectureship he produced a large amount of papers, including reading lists, notes from reading books, and detailed plans of courses on several topics.[2] The course on "Money, Credit and Prices," given for the first time during the Lent Term of 1909, included a lecture on "Appreciation and interest. The relation between Money, the Rate of Interest, and the Rate of Discount." Fourteen pages of handwritten notes on this subject were prepared by Keynes, together with a few other pages of accompanying material, which are now extant in the Keynes Papers (KP).[3] As Keynes himself tells us in the opening page of the file, the subject occupied him for two days – the 25th of February and the 1st of March 1909. Exception being made for the part on the rate of discount, the notes for these lectures were based on the contents of Fisher's homonymous book (Fisher, 1896) as restated and expanded in chapters V and XIV of *The Rate of Interest* (Fisher, 1907). The notes on Fisher were not included in the selection of "Keynes's Early Lectures" in vol. XII of *The Collected Writings of John Maynard Keynes* (CWK), nor, to the best of my knowledge, is there any trace of this archival material in the secondary literature. These papers are reproduced here for the first time. By way of introduction, the following sections are a brief survey of what has been ascertained so far on the reception of Fisher's early monetary thought at Cambridge.

The Quantity Theory

The names of Fisher and of his Cambridge contemporaries Alfred Marshall, A. C. Pigou, and J. M. Keynes are commonly associated with the versions of the quantity theory of money known as the Fisher's transaction approach and the Cambridge cash-balances approach. These pieces of analysis are usually presented as not irreconcilable but nonetheless rival, the main issues being priority of publication, empirical verification, and explanatory power. This standard narrative is firmly rooted in Fisher's *The Purchasing Power of Money* (Fisher, 1913 [1911], henceforth *PPM*), Keynes's review of *PPM* in the *Economic Journal* of September 1911 (Keynes, 1911), and Pigou's article on "The Value of Money" in the *Quarterly Journal of Economics* of November 1917 (Pigou, 1917). While *PPM* contained the most successful presentation of the equation of exchange ever published,[4] Marshall's pupils insisted that Fisher's monetary theory was correct as far as it could go, but that the Cambridge approach was a better instrument of analysis, created by Marshall well before the publication of *PPM*. However, even though Keynes and Pigou were firmly convinced that Marshall's monetary theory was to be preferred, it still remained true that the cash-balance approach had never seen the light in any published work.[5] While Keynes (1911) denounced this awkward state of affairs, Pigou (1917) provided a remedy. Therefore, if *PPM* had at least one consequence at Cambridge, it was that it led the younger generation of Cambridge economists to fill an important gap in Marshall's published works. From then onward, Fisher's equation of exchange served as a foil to Pigou's equation as put forth in the 1917 article (and vice versa). Even today the two versions of the quantity theory are still commonly presented in economics and history of economics textbooks with the same two formulae – $MV + M'V' = PT$ and $P = kR/M$ – that can be found in Fisher (1913 [1911]) and Pigou (1917), or slight variations on them.

The two versions of the quantity theory presented analogies as well as differences. The main difference is that while Fisher insisted on the velocity of circulation of money (V), and thus on money actively employed in transactions, the method that Marshall taught his pupils focused on the fraction of the money income that was retained from circulation in the form of individual cash balances. The latter was therefore a theory of the demand for money. For Pigou (1917), this was "a somewhat more effective engine of analysis," one that could shed some light on individual decisions rather than focusing on the "accidental and arbitrary" parameter offered by the "velocity of circulation" (1917, p. 54).[6] From Fisher's standpoint, on the other hand, empirical and theoretical analysis of the velocity of circulation was probably inevitable. The staunch opposition to the quantity theory that Fisher had to face in his country consisted largely in statistical confutations based on a very naïve version of the theory, in which any divergence between movements in the quantity of money and the level of prices was taken as proof that the quantity theory was wrong.[7] It was therefore crucial to identify the specific circumstances in which the relation between the quantity of money (M) and the level of prices (P) could be expected to hold, and then to prove that, when these conditions are satisfied, a causal nexus linking P to M actually exists.[8]

It is evident from his article of 1917 that it was very important for Pigou to promote the Marshallian tradition while at the same time providing some support to Fisher on his national battleground. One of the American economists that launched an attack on Fisher was B. M. Anderson, and Pigou (1917) referred to Anderson (1917) as the book that had prompted him to write: a book which was "mainly vigorous controversy," based on the wrong assumption that "the 'quantity theory' [should be] defended and opposed as tho it were a definite set of propositions that must be either true or false." As a way out from this view, Pigou proposed that "the formulae employed in the exposition of the theory are merely devices for enabling us to bring together in an orderly way the principal causes by which the value of money is determined." Finally, Pigou clearly stated that there could be no doubt, among the "competent writers," as to the nature of these "principal causes" – and it is clear from the article that he included Fisher, and not Anderson, among the competent authors. Indeed, Pigou was at pains to make it very clear that he did not consider Fisher's equation of exchange logically wrong, showing that his own formulation was mathematically equivalent to that of *PPM*.

What was completely different was the situation in which Fisher and the Marshallians found themselves. Keynes (1911) found in the complete absence of any controversy on money the main reason why no systematic exposition of the British (Marshallian) "oral tradition" had ever appeared. Quite simply, no one had ever felt the need to publish it. And even though Keynes was perhaps less circumspect than Pigou in claiming British priority and superiority on the subject, compared to the opposition that Fisher was facing in the United States, his review seems a favorable one. Albeit with some regret, Keynes had no hesitation in presenting *PPM* as the standard textbook on monetary theory. He did have some serious reservations, especially about Fisher's account of the transmission mechanism connecting variations on the quantity of money with price-movements and, to a lesser extent, the use of index numbers, but none of these criticisms could be seen as destructive, nor were they meant to be so.

At the analytical level, however, there was at least one more important and well-recognized difference. Unlike the Cambridge men, Fisher reasoned more in the terms of general equilibrium analysis.[9] Following this method, he looked for the normal (equilibrium) conditions in which the direct relation between quantity and value of money actually holds, attributing the deviations from these normal conditions to cyclical movements.

Marshall, by contrast, had brought up his pupils to the view that, although the quantity theory had originally been created as a simple relation connecting the exchange value of money to its quantity, the search for the conditions in which this direct relation does not hold was more fruitful than definition of the special cases in which it does. But it does not seem that even this difference constituted an insurmountable barrier. A mutual understanding existed in the form of a common preoccupation as to the consequences of the trade cycle and the need to eliminate, or at least reduce, its monetary causes.[10] In the wake of the publication of *PPM*, the main difference was perhaps more psychological than analytical, or pre-analytical (in the Schumpeterian sense). By this time, Fisher's mania for reform had no match in Cambridge, not even in such an active promoter of the gold exchange standard as Keynes. But at the earlier stage upon which the remaining part of this introduction is mainly focused, this psychological gap was yet to come.

In Search of a Common Ground

The dialogue at a distance between Fisher and the Cambridge economists began in 1896 with the publication of *Appreciation and Interest*. This short book by Fisher gained a special place in the history of economics as it contains the first presentation of the so-called "Fisher relation," connecting nominal and real rates of interest with expected inflation.[11] Published by Macmillan for the American Economic Association in August 1896, it provided ample empirical evidence that some measure of "foresight in regard to the appreciation or depreciation of money actually exists" (Fisher, 1896, p. 35). In the context in which it saw the light, *Appreciation and Interest* was a response to the typically bimetallist claims that an appreciating standard represented an injustice to debtors and a burden on business activity. By demonstrating that there was a positive correlation between price-movements and variations in the nominal rates of interests, Fisher was able to affirm that money appreciation was at least in part anticipated by borrowers and, therefore, that the additional burden imposed on them during a period of falling prices was lower than the bimetallists supposed. Moreover, the same evidence that expectations regarding inflation were incorporated in the market rates of interest also led Fisher to the conclusion that high rates did not necessarily create an obstacle to business activity, nor a low rate a stimulus to it, as they in fact reflected inflation expectations rather than the relative scarcity or abundance of loanable funds. In turn, this had implications for business cycles theory, which Fisher considered in the concluding parts of the 1896 book. In 1907, the same argument was reproduced in chapter XIV of *The Rate of Interest*, upon which Keynes based a large part of his lecture notes of 1909.

The main conclusions Fisher arrived at were that rising and falling prices (and wages) were directly correlated with high and low rates of interest, but also that the adjustment of interest to inflation was inadequate, the inadequacy of this adjustment being particularly evident in the short run.[12] The theory of the trade cycle that Fisher derived from these empirical observations was that, while the inadequacy of interest rates adjustment may be explained in terms of "*imperfection* of foresight," cyclical movements were to be attributed to "*inequality* of foresight."[13] In 1896, Fisher made explicit use of Marshall's supply and demand schedules in order to show how this result came about, and in both the 1896 and 1907 versions he presented his own explanation as a further advance in Marshall's treatment of the same subject as set out in *Principles of Economics*.

In 1896 and 1907, Fisher's cycles theory was based on the assumption that a restricted class of economic agents, the members of the "borrowing class ... who become 'captains of industry'," is endowed with "superior foresight" (1896, p. 77, 1907, p. 286). Thanks to their superior foresight, professional borrowers are capable of seeing that prices will be rising some time in advance of the lenders. During this period in which the borrowers' expectations have the advantage, the "demand schedule" for loanable funds moves upward, while the "supply schedule" remains "comparatively unchanged," thus producing a rise in the interest rate as well as an increased volume of loans and investments. The opposite holds when prices are falling. Borrowers now see that they cannot make a profit out of loaned funds unless they can finance themselves at a lower rate of interest. The rate of interest falls as a consequence of a lower demand for funds but does not fall enough to keep the level of investments at a stable level (Fisher, 1896, pp. 77–78, 1907, p. 286). The "maladjustment of interest" due to "inequality of foresight," therefore, is the crucial factor. Apparently, Fisher presented this part of the explanation as the element that was missing in Marshall's cycles theory in *Principles*. This is particularly evident at the end of chapter X of *Appreciation and Interest*, where Fisher concluded his treatment of cycles theory with a brief discussion of Marshall's position:

> Professor Marshall, who recognizes fully the distinction between money and commodity interest, says: "When we come to discuss the causes of alternative periods of inflation and depression of commercial activity, we shall find that they are intimately connected with those variations in the real rate of interest which are caused by changes

in the purchasing power of money. For when prices are likely to rise, business is inflated, and is managed recklessly and wastefully; those working on borrowed capital pay back less real value than they borrowed, and enrich themselves at the expense of the community. When afterwards credit is shaken and prices begin to fall, everyone wants to get rid of commodities and get hold of money, which is rapidly rising in value; this makes prices fall all the faster, and the further fall makes credit shrink even more, and thus for a long time prices fall because prices have fallen."

We would add that these effects of credit could not follow if the interest rates were perfectly adjusted. Interest, rather than credit, appears as the chief independent variable, objectively speaking, though behind it all is imperfection of foresight. (Fisher, 1896, p. 79; quotation from Marshall, *Principles of Economics*, 3rd ed., 1895, p. 674; the same quotation can be found in Fisher, 1907, p. 287 fn.)[14]

At this stage, the distinction between imperfection of foresight and inequality of foresight, with a stronger emphasis on the latter element as the source of maladjusted interest rates, seems to be a distinguishing feature of Fisher's theory.

In the subsequent chapter of the 1896 book, a few words were spent on some of the proposed remedies to the problem of price fluctuations that circulated at the time. At this stage of his career, the zeal for monetary reform that would later characterize the works of Fisher was still far off, and this was probably reflected in the limited range of his readings. As Laidler (2013, p. 179 fn. 8) pointed out, it is not clear whether Fisher was already acquainted, in 1896 and in 1907, with Marshall's article on "Remedies for fluctuations in general prices," originally published in the *Contemporary Review* of 1887.[15] On the basis of chapter XI, this seems to be excluded. Some considerations on Marshall's (1887) proposal for contracts in terms of unit of purchasing power would certainly have been very appropriate, but no mention of it was made.[16]

On the other hand, Marshall's references to Fisher (1896) were also rather selective. Speaking before the Committee on Indian Currency in 1898, Marshall made an explicit and very favorable reference to Fisher (1896), but only for the statistical evidence it could offer of the relationship between changes in the purchasing power of money and the rate of interest.[17] The point made by Marshall was that, although the long-run rate of interest is governed by the demand and supply of capital, the specific circumstances of India called for some further qualification. More specifically, a prolonged period of rising prices had had the effect of pushing nominal rates of interest at a higher level. It was at this point of his exposition that Marshall quoted Fisher (1896), which was cited for its empirical evidence that "the high rates do go with high prices" (Marshall, 1979 [1926], p. 271).

On the same day, Marshall was questioned about the rate of discount, that is, on the short-term rate of interest. Like Fisher, he noticed that the short-term rates tend to be more variable than the long-run rates, but no reference to the work of the American economist was made on this subject. Indeed, in this part of his testimony, Marshall developed a description of the business cycles that is in partial contrast with that of Fisher (1897, 1907), because he emphasized lender availability rather than borrowers' expectations as the crucial factor. In other words, while Fisher insisted on the misaligned expectations of borrowers and lenders, Marshall described the cycle on the basis of the transmission mechanism which was supposed to provide the link connecting the supply of money to prices via the banking system. Following this logic, once the cycle has been started elements of expectations (confidence) do in fact enter into play that are compatible with Fisher's theory, but there is no suggestion that either borrowers or lenders enjoy any form of superior foresight:

> Looking at the special case of the effect of an increase in currency on the rate of discount, the cycle in the West seems to be this. The new currency or the increase of currency goes, not to private persons, but to the banking centres; and, therefore, it increases the willingness of lenders to lend in the first instance, and lowers discount; but it afterwards rises prices, and, therefore, tends to increase discount. This latter movement is cumulative. The loans to one man make him a good customer for others at good prices, and make them therefore eager to borrow, and that makes them good customers; and so the movement grows. Thus, a fall in the purchasing power of money tends, after a while, to raise the rate of discount as well as the rate of interest on long investments. And, though the matter may be regarded by some as open to question, I myself go with those who hold that statistics bear out the *a priori* probability that, first, the rates of discount would generally be higher when prices are rising than when they are falling, because the borrowers would be eager for loans; and secondly, that they would generally be higher in periods of high prices, than in periods of low prices; not because one is the cause of the other, but because both are the result of the same cause – the prevalence of a confident spirit in the business world. (Evidence before the Committee on Indian Currency, 11 January 1899, in Marshall, 1979 [1926], p. 274)

In the last page of his 1909 lecture notes, Keynes reproduced an excerpt from this passage, which he must have considered as one of the most representative of Marshall's thought on the subject. As confirmed in Keynes (1911), the evidence before the Committee on Indian Currency contained the typical Marshallian explanation of the transmission mechanism, and precisely the one that would be missing in *PPM*. Along with Marshall's evidence before the Indian Currency Committee of 1898–1899 (reprinted in Marshall (1979/1926), Keynes mentioned the other evidence by Marshall on the same subject, before the Gold and Silver Commission in 1887:

"Professor Fisher's book contains no reference to this evidence, which constitutes the most important contribution to monetary theory published in England since the times of Ricardo, and there seems good reason to suppose that he is not acquainted with it" (Keynes, 1911, p. 377 fn.).

Whether Fisher was actually unacquainted with Marshall's testimony of 1887 it is hard to say. The references given in *Appreciation and Interest* indirectly suggest that he may plausibly have read it. Fisher cited Marshall's evidence to, and the report of, the 1886 Royal Commission on the Depression of Trade (1896, p. 78 fn., 86 fn., 90 fn.), and he cited the Report of the Gold and Silver Commission of 1888 (1896, 79 fn.), although without mentioning Marshall's evidence to this Commission.[18] For sure, Marshall's (1898) evidence contributed to the spread of Fisher's ideas in England. It was only in 1926 that Keynes edited Marshall's *Official Papers*, but Marshall's testimonies circulated freely at Cambridge, and from 1907 onward a footnote in Marshall's *Principles* suggested selected parts of Fisher's works as further reading on the topic of "Appreciation and Interest." In its definitive version the footnote reads as follows: "Compare Fisher's *Appreciation and Interest* 1896; and *The Rate of Interest* 1907, especially Chapters V, XIV and their respective appendices" (Marshall, 1997 [1961] I, p. 594n.).[19] In all probability, therefore, it is in this footnote that the origin of Keynes's lecture is to be found, because it was exactly on these parts of Fisher's works that Keynes based his notes of 1909. What is less easy to explain is why Keynes's (1909) lecture on Fisher has passed altogether unnoticed. And this is not the only question related to Keynes's early reception of Fisher waiting for an answer.

Keynes and Fisher in Light of the 1909 Lecture

Other unsettled questions that have emerged in the literature revolve around Keynes's review of *PPM* in 1911. For Laidler (1991, p. 64), it is "something of a mystery" that Keynes (1911) chose the transmission mechanism through which a variation in the quantity of money alters prices, rather than the theory of the demand for money, as the distinguishing feature of the Cambridge "oral tradition" – a view which finds indirect support in Pigou (1917).[20] This may be explained by observing that what Keynes avowedly aimed at in reviewing *PPM* was neither a comprehensive account of the book nor of the Cambridge "oral tradition," but rather to focus on those parts of Fisher's work that he found less convincing. Moreover, Keynes's concern for the transmission mechanism may be explained on the basis of the work on applied economics, and especially on banking, which he was engaged on during the same period. Probably, the fact that the young Keynes took more interest in the ongoing debates on policy issues than in the development of pure theory in some respects prejudiced his interpretation of *PPM* as well as his own perception of the Cambridge oral tradition.[21] For Dimand (1995, p. 250), however, Keynes (1911) did not pay enough attention to "Fisher's chapter 4 on transition periods during which monetary changes have real effects, the source of Fisher's monetary theory of economic fluctuations." Moreover, on the basis of Dimand's reconstruction, it is quite curious that Keynes (1911) criticized Fisher for the lack of any explanation of the transmission mechanism in chapter 4 of *PPM* and that, two years later, he presented a paper at the Political Economy Club in which Fisher's account of the transmission mechanism is presented as the standard view on the subject.[22]

On the basis of the lectures of 1909, a further question may be added. In his review, Keynes *did* spend some words on Fisher's account of the cycle in Chapter 4 of *PPM*, but he did not notice an element that, in light of the 1909 notes, could certainly have captured his attention. Keynes wrote that Fisher's theory "can be accepted," even though it was "possibly expounded too emphatically from the standpoint of interest" (Keynes, 1911, p. 377). But he did not take any notice of the fact that the part played by the interest rate had changed since 1896 and 1907, and that any explanation of interest rate maladjustment had been removed.

Likewise, in his books of 1896 and 1907 (chapter XIV), Fisher argued that the rate of interest was the main cause of fluctuations in business activity because it lagged behind prices. However, unlike his approach in his previous books, here he assumed this disturbance rather than explaining it.[23] The critical point was now found in the consequences, rather than in the causes, of interest rate maladjustment. The "borrowing class" and its "superior foresight" had no place in *PPM*. What remained of Fisher's theory as Keynes received it in 1909 was that the "profits" accruing to the "enterpriser-borrower" during the upward movement of prices, and the commercial "failures" in the descending phase of the cycle, were the signals that determined borrowers' decisions, which were no longer taken on the basis of some superior foresight but rather as a sort of continuous adaptation to changing (and apparently unexpected) circumstances. But all these changes passed unnoticed in Keynes's review of *PPM* in 1911. When the lectures on Fisher of 1909 are taken into account, therefore, it is even more difficult to find a satisfactory interpretation of this review.

At least two interpretations may be suggested. On the one hand, the focus on the transmission mechanism as the missing part of Fisher's cycles theory, rather than on the evolution of the theory itself, seems to be a symptom of a momentary lack of concern for the theme of expectations as possible explanation of trade cycles. While the lectures on Fisher bear witness that in 1909 Keynes was at least taking into consideration that the theory of the trade cycle could be based on an analysis of business expectations, the 1913 paper on the role of bankers in relation to the trade cycle provides an explanation of cycles which is based on institutional factors rather than expectations. If Keynes was, in 1911, already oriented toward a theory of business cycles like the one presented in 1913, this would account for his lack of interest in the theme of expectations in his review of *PPM*. On the other hand, a contrasting interpretation might be that, deprived of its most original part on expectations, Fisher's account of the cycle looked very much like that of Marshall, but with a lacuna, which would be precisely the one pointed out by Keynes. Moreover, once this view is accepted, one further inference could be made. Possibly, what Keynes really meant when he said that no account of the transmission mechanism was given in *PPM* was not that Fisher had ignored the problem. Rather, the problem for Keynes might have been that what Fisher presented as an explanation of the transmission mechanism was for Keynes no more than a description.

That the mechanics of the cycle described in *PPM* had become more similar to Marshall's is indirectly suggested by Fisher's quotation from *Principles* in the text of chapter 4, which is the same as can be found in his books of 1896 and 1907 but purged of any negative qualification.[24] An obvious difference there is, and it is that, coherently with his monetary analysis, Fisher reasoned in terms of velocity of circulation. But, on the whole, the following passage from *PPM* (although "possibly expounded too emphatically from the standpoint of interest") closely resembles Marshall's exposition:

> It has been seen that rising prices tend towards a higher nominal interest, and falling prices tend towards a lower, but that in general the adjustment is incomplete. With any initial rise of prices comes an expansion of loans, owing to the fact that interest does not at once adjust itself. This produces profits for the entrepreneur-borrower, and his demand for loans further extends deposit currency. This extension still further raises prices, a result accentuated by a rise in velocities though somewhat mitigated by an increase in trade. When interest has become adjusted to rising prices, and loans and deposits have reached the limit set for them by bank reserves and other conditions, the fact that prices no longer are rising necessitates a new adjustment. Those whose business has been unduly extended now find the high rates of interest oppressive. Failures

result, constituting a commercial crisis. A reaction sets in; a reverse movement is initiated. (*PPM*, pp. 72–73)

It must be noticed, however, that although the *descriptions* of the cycle given by Fisher and Marshall now looked similar, the *explanations* behind them were different. However, as it probably occurred to Keynes while he was drafting his review of *PPM*, this difference is not at all evident from the text of *Principles*. It is in comparison with Marshall's testimony before the Gold and Silver Commission, to which Keynes (1911) gave so much emphasis, that the difference becomes apparent. It is quite likely that among the passages of the *Official Papers* that Keynes had in mind were the two quoted below. Together with the one quoted above from the evidence before the Indian commission (see above and Marshall, 1979 [1926], p. 274), these quotations show that expectations were crucial in Marshall's explanations of both the transmission mechanism and the cycle:

> ... equilibrium being established, we set ourselves to enquire what will be the result of a new disturbance, viz. the influx of a good deal of bullion into the City. This does not increase the amount of capital, in the strictest sense of the word ... but it does increase the amount of command over capital which is in the hands of those whose business it is to lend to speculative enterprise. Having the extra supply, lenders lower still more the rate which they charge for loans, and they keep on lowering it till a point is reached at which the demand will carry off the larger supply. When this has been done there is more capital in the hands of speculative investors, who come on the markets for goods as buyers, and so raise prices. Further, it must be remembered that the influx of bullion would have caused people meanwhile to expect a rise of prices, and, therefore, to be more inclined to borrow for speculative investments. Thus it might not be necessary to lower the rate of discount very much. The increased demand would meet the increased supply half-way, and, after a time, might outrun it, causing a rise in the rate of discount. But as this rise would be merely an incident in a series of changes which put more command over capital in the hands of speculative investors, it would go with an increased demand for goods and a continued rise of prices (Marshall, 1979 [1926], pp. 51–52);

> when the gold comes to the country it is known and people expect that prices will rise. Now if a person doubting whether to borrow for speculative purposes has reason to believe that prices will rise, he is willing to take a loan at 3 per cent., which before he would not have taken at 2 ½ per cent, and consequently the influx of gold into the country by making the people believe that price will rise increases the demand for capital and raises therefore, in my opinion, the rate of discount. (Marshall, 1979/1926, p. 131)

By contrast, at this stage, Fisher's account of the cycle was independent of any reference to expectations. With regard to the relation between the trend of prices and the rate of interest this is quite evident from the text of chapter IV of *PPM*. With regard to the issue that was more directly raised by Keynes (1911), that is, the transmission mechanism, a similar conclusion is supported by the brief reply to Keynes in the preface to the second edition of *PPM*, in which Fisher referred to his *Elementary Principles of Economics* (1912, pp. 242–247).[25] Here, an account of the transmission mechanism based on the equation of exchange is in fact given – but, once again, pursuing a line of reasoning that is altogether independent of expectations and speculative behavior. As in Marshall's example quoted above, one of the hypotheses considered by Fisher was of an equilibrium which is momentarily disturbed by an increase in the amount of gold, in this case coming into the pockets of miners and from there into circulation. The gist of Fisher's transmission mechanism is that people tend to get rid of any amount of money in excess of what they customarily consider to be appropriate. As a consequence of this behavior, when there is an increase in the amount of money at the disposal of some individuals (e.g., the miners) prices tend to rise because these individuals will purchase goods in order to get rid of the money that they consider in excess. Afterward, this momentary increase in the velocity of circulation continues until the rise of prices leads to a new equilibrium in which the velocity of circulation is the same as before and in which the level of prices has adjusted to the new level of the quantity of money.[26]

In light of the 1909, lecture it is hardly surprising that Keynes could find the analyses of business cycles and the transmission mechanism in *PPM* rather disappointing. After all, and apart from any issue about priority of publication, the contents of Fisher (1896, 1907) could be seen as interesting and original developments of a line of research with which the Cambridge Marshallians were familiar. Otherwise, *PPM* represented a deviation from this research program, and offered a version of cycles theory that, compared to that of Marshall, was neither original nor satisfactory, and therefore open to legitimate criticism. But for precisely the same reasons, and regardless of the trajectory actually followed in Keynes mind between 1909 and 1913, it is quite curious that, as Dimand observed, the only economist mentioned in Keynes's paper on business cycles of December 1913 is Fisher, and precisely as the authority on the transmission mechanism.

The year before, Keynes had met Fisher in London. All we know of the meeting is that it was the beginning of life-long friendly relations between two economists, and two men, who did not have very much in common.[27] It is possible, as Dimand (1995, p. 253) pointed out, that the mention of Fisher that Keynes made in 1913 came as a consequence of this friendly relationship, or, maybe, simply as the result of further reflection. Another possibility could be that Fisher's account of the cycle was good for reference as it was included in such a widely known book as *PPM*, a source certainly more readily accessible than Marshall's still quite esoteric *Official Papers*. Finally, a less benevolent hypothesis could be that Keynes preferred to associate the name of Fisher, rather than that of Marshall, with a theory which he was now overtly criticizing as scarcely satisfactory. Be that as it might be may, what can be said is that, compared to the 1909 manuscript, Keynes was now considering the problem of business fluctuations along lines more directly influenced by D. H. Robertson,[28] and owing much less to Fisher (1896, 1907). It is in fact on the role of bankers (i.e., of the lenders), rather than of the "borrowing class," that Keynes insisted in his paper, and not for their expectations or degree of foresight but rather for the institutional elements that made it impossible for bankers to maintain real investments in equilibrium with real savings. Nonetheless, in this case, and indeed in the review of *PPM*, a few words on Fisher (1896, 1907) would not have been out of place. But, as usual, Keynes avoided any reference to the books he had read just a few years before.

As a matter of fact, the main responsibility for the complete oblivion into which the 1909 notes rapidly fell seems to be attributable to Keynes himself. On at least two occasions he could have mentioned that he had read another Fisher, and not only the 1911 text. But he did not.

Along with the very tentative hypotheses presented above on the basis of circumstantial evidence, other reasons for Keynes's lack of references to his earlier encounter with the "Fisher relation" can certainly be found. It may be noticed, for instance, that the theme of expectations was obviously not new to him. The parallel work he was doing on the theory of probability had already provided him with a personal approach to the subject that he was now beginning to apply in his lecturing, and in particular in his lectures on speculation, as Carabelli (1998) has clearly shown. On the specific topic of speculation, Fisher (1896, 1907) could have left a mark on Keynes, for these books provided interesting and innovative statistical evidence as to the relations between actual and expected trends of commodity prices. This is a kind of knowledge that Keynes may certainly have tacitly employed, in some form, in his almost life-long activity as a speculator, as well as in his writings on the subject.[29] But it is equally possible that Fisher's *theory* of cycles, as distinguished from their mere description by means of statistics, left no significant trace of itself in the development of Keynes's own thought on the subject. For sure, the 1909 notes show that Keynes dedicated considerable attention to Fisher's (1896, 1907) theory, but it is very difficult to say, on the basis of this new evidence, if he ever accepted this theory as valid. In 1909, he took into serious consideration

Fisher's distinction between inequality and imperfection of foresight, as well as the prominent place that Fisher (1896, 1907) attributed to the former element in his theory. But, in the concluding part of the document reproduced here, Keynes seems to rely on Marshall's explanation of the short-term non neutrality of money, which he must have considered more in tune with his own idea of human foresight. As he wrote in the 1909 notes, "the course of remote changes is totally unknown and is almost completely neglected in anticipations." As in the quintessentially Keynesian definition of radical uncertainty, of the remote future "we simply do not know" (CWK XIV, p. 114). This does not rule out the possibility that some – the borrowers, perhaps – may be at an advantage with regard to the *near* future. However, in 1909, Keynes did not develop this idea. Moreover, Fisher's silent abandonment of the original ideas on expectations introduced in 1896 in the text of *PPM* gave Keynes further reason to pass over his earlier encounter with Fisher.

Furthermore, we should bear in mind the broader context in which Keynes read Fisher, at a time when opinions on business cycle were fluid and no single theory prevailed over any other. Taking a much wider perspective, Schumpeter described this period as one of transition, the "hunt for the conditions in which money is neutral" (Schumpeter, 1986, p. 1054), that led many economists, and especially Keynes, to the conclusion that money simply cannot be neutral.

Along this common path, economists could meet with the same ease with which they parted company. Sometimes there was a mix between common concern over economic fluctuations viewed as an economic disease and differences of opinion on the diagnosis and cure, and sometimes there was a gap in terms of degree of commitment. In the case of Fisher and his Cambridge colleagues, probably there were both, and even though this did not prevent the establishment of relations of mutual respect, the common ground was not large enough to support any form of concrete collaboration.

Traces of the beginning of a dialogue on currency reform remained, but they were of no practical consequence. As far as Marshall was concerned, Fisher simply arrived too late. While Marshall had been relatively active at the time of the bimetallist controversy in England, there is no evidence that Fisher ever thought seriously of doing something in this field before 1911. The correspondence between them in 1911 and 1912 shows that it was too late to gain Marshall's support.[30] In 1911, Marshall's response showed some note of skepticism, but was on the whole supportive and sympathetic. One year later, the tone had changed. Whitaker's reconstruction of the events is that, this time, Fisher had probably sent a copy of his "Memorandum on a More Stable Gold Standard: A Proposal for a 'Compensated Dollar' as Partial Remedy for the Rising Cost of Living" (1912).[31] In his reply, Marshall expressed some reservations on the feasibility of the project, and concluded with an explicit request to receive no more letters on the subject.[32]

Fisher's scheme for a compensated dollar received some attention, but no more than halfhearted support, in Pigou's *Wealth and Welfare*. Making more explicit an attitude which seems also to emerge from Marshall's letters, Pigou was more sympathetic with the ends Fisher was pursuing than the proposed means.[33] By contrast, Keynes was rather enthusiastic about Fisher's plan, probably because, at the international level, it was based on the gold exchange standard, the emerging monetary system that Keynes was then actively promoting.[34] So much can be gleaned from the few lines that Keynes dedicated to the compensated dollar plan at the end of his review of *PPM* in 1911, and more evidently in a lesser known letter to Fisher of 14 July 1911. Only an incomplete draft of this correspondence has remained in the KP, but the letter was eventually sent, and then forwarded to Kemmerer. It is now available in the Kemmerer papers and in volume IV of the Works of Fisher (pp. 10–11).[35] But even on the part of Keynes, support on monetary reform did not last very long.[36]

Meanwhile, it was as if Keynes had completely forgotten his earlier work on the relation between "appreciation and prices" based on Fisher (1896, 1907), with the consequence that, when Keynes began to cite these works by Fisher in his writings, the impression was that he had only come across them at a much later stage in his career.

It was only during the 1920s that the Fisher of *Appreciation and Interest* resurfaced in the writings of Keynes. An almost resentful reference to Fisher (1896) can be found in the obituary of Marshall, written in 1924, when Keynes placed "the distinction between the 'real' and the 'money' rate of interest, and the relevance of this to the credit cycle" (CWK X, p. 192) in the list of Marshall's (and therefore not Fisher's) most original contributions to economic theory. In the *Treatise on Money*, the only significant reference to Fisher's Appreciation and Interest was made in the context of discussion of the "Gibson Paradox," and merely to say that Fisher's theory could not explain the paradox and was rather contradicted by it.[37] Subsequently, Fisher's analysis of the relationship between "appreciation and interest" was explicitly criticized and rejected by Keynes during the drafting of the *General Theory*, and again in the 1936 book, where Keynes finally rejected Fisher's (1896) treatment of expectations:

> it is not clear [in Fisher, 1896] whether the change in the value of money is or is not assumed to be foreseen. There is no escape from the dilemma that, if it is not foreseen, there will be no effect on current affairs; whilst, if it is foreseen, the prices of existing goods will be forthwith so adjusted that the advantages of holding goods are again equalised, and it will be too late for holders of money to gain or to suffer a change in the rate of interest which will offset the prospective change during the period of the loan in the value of the money lent. (1936, p. 142)

On the basis of the notes of 1909, such a line of attack on Fisher is puzzling. While for Fisher (1896), as reported also by Keynes in 1909, the crucial factor is that price-movements are only imperfectly foreseen, in 1936 Keynes saw no alternative between the two horns of a "dilemma" in which price-movements are either perfectly foreseen or altogether unanticipated. Moreover, on the same page of the *General Theory*, the possibility of different degrees of foresight is also explicitly ruled out. In 1936, this latter hypothesis was attributed to Pigou, but it is clear from a document of 1933 reproduced in vol. XXIX of the CWK that Keynes also had Fisher in mind when he discussed the possibility.[38]

This sequel of disparaging remarks was interrupted in 1937, with the inclusion of Fisher in the imaginary family tree that Keynes described in a footnote to his "Alternative Theories the Rate of Interest" in the *Economic Journal* of June 1937. Here Keynes mentioned Hawtrey as his "grandparent" and Robertson as his "parent" for having preceded him in the departure from "classical economics. In reply to Ohlin, who had insisted on the importance of the Swedish school, in the remaining part of the footnote Keynes excluded Wicksell, including Fisher instead as his great-grandparent: "I might also meet Professor Ohlin's complaint by adopting Wicksell as my great-grandparent, if I had known his works in more detail at an earlier stage in my own thought and also if I did not have the feeling that Wicksell was *trying* to be 'classical.' As it is, so far as I am concerned, I find, looking back, that it was Professor Irving Fisher who was the great-grandparent who first introduced me strongly towards regarding money as a 'real' factor" (CWK XIV, pp. 202–203).

The lectures notes reproduced below constitute evidence that this actually happened "at a much earlier stage" in Keynes's own thought. The same notes also show that there must have been some genuine feeling in the words of a letter that Keynes sent to Fisher from Bretton Woods on 7 July 1944: "Your letter has given me the greatest possible pleasure. You were one of my earliest teachers on these matters and nothing is more satisfactory to any of us than to satisfy one of those from whom we have learned" (Keynes to Fisher, 7 July 1944, quoted in Fisher, 1956; see also

Dimand, 1995, p. 248). Even though these few lines were part of a letter in which Keynes rejected Fisher's proposal for 100 percent reserve banking, and even though this may come as something of a surprise, it is true that Fisher had been one of Keynes's "earliest teachers."

"Appreciation and interest. The relation between Money, the Rate of Interest, and the Rate of Discount," by J.M. Keynes (1909)

[Additions to the original text are in square brackets. All other editorial comments are in the footnotes. The file can be subdivided in three parts. The first, indicated below as Part 1, is on "Appreciation and Interest" and corresponds to pages 1–10 of the original page numeration by Keynes (KP UA/6/1/5/2-11); Part 2, corresponds to 6 pages (not numbered by Keynes) of notes from reading Fisher (1907), plus a cover page (KP UA/6/1/5/12-18); Part 3, on "The relation between Money, the Rate of Interest, and the Rate of Discount," corresponds to pp. 11–14 in Keynes's original numeration plus three pages that were not numbered by Keynes (KP UA/6/1/5/19-25].

[Cover page (KP UA/6/5/1):]

Appreciation and interest. The relation between Money, the Rate of Interest, and the Rate of Discount

25.2.09 30 min. pp. 1–5
1.3.09 45 min. pp. 6–14

[Part 1]

Appreciation and Interest [corresponding to pp. 1–11 of Keynes's numeration]

The subject of this lecture is the relation between the rate of interest and changes in the level of prices.

I am not sure that Prof. I.F[isher] *first* called attention to the relations in question, but he was certainly the first to emphasise it in a monograph published some years ago now [Fisher, 1896]. He has recently restated and amplified his argument in his volume on the "Rate of Interest" [Fisher, 1907] and this lecture is chiefly based on chap[ters] V and XIV of that book.

The relation, which arises out of the use of money as a standard of deferred payments, can simply be stated. When we incur a loan, we do so in order to make certain purchases. What we bargain to repay at the end of a stated period is not the equivalent of these purchase, but a sum of money equal to the sum lent us plus another sum by way of interest.

If, therefore, the sum of money representing the capital has a lower purchasing power at the end of the period than at the beginning, the debtor has evidently gained at the expense of the creditor, unless it is made up to the latter by an exceptionally high rate of interest.

This fact is probably well known to all of you. That a depreciating currency benefits debtors and that an appreciating currency damages them is one of the best know facts in monetary science.

The point of Prof. I. F[isher]'s theory arises out of the circumstance that this is only the result of *unforeseen* changes in the value of money. If depreciation is for any reason to be anticipated, the lender will protect himself by charging by way of interest an amount beyond normal interest which will compensate him for the lessened value of the capital sum which he anticipates. He will do this, so long as other people agree with him in his anticipation, whether or not this anticipations are correct or not. There is, therefore, a direct relation between the rate of interest and the market anticipations with regard to future changes in the exchange value of the standard for deferred payment.

The theoretical considerations are, therefore, extremely simple. The inductive verification leads to some points leaving a good deal of interest.

We had better distinguished money-interest and commodity-interest. In the second we make allowance for changes in the value of the standard in which the capital is measured.

If the money interest is 5 on capital 100, we may find at the end of the period that the amount of representative composite commodity which 105 will buy at the end of the period is 103 where 100 is the amount of commodity which £100 buys at the beginning of the period.

In this case money interest at 5% is equal to commodity interest at 3%.

The commodity interest is the real interest. It is this which measures the benefit to be obtained by lending over buying goods and stocking them.

"The fact that interest *in money* is high, say 15%, may merely indicate that general prices are expected to rise at the rate of 10%, and that the rate of interest in terms of *goods* is not high, but only 4 ½ %" (I.F.) [Fisher, 1907, p. 84].

This is not less so because the trader looks at it from a somewhat different point of view. He borrows at a high rate, perhaps, because, even allowing for the high rate, he thinks it will be advantageous for him to make his purchases, whether of raw materials or of stocks and shares, now rather than at a later date.

Or he borrows at a high rate because he requires money and cannot raise it more profitably at the moment by selling his belongings. In both cases he acquiesces in the temporary high rate because he expects the prices of the things with which he is concerned to be higher later on than they are now. In the first case he has to buy eventually and prefers to buy now when things are cheap; in the second he desires to realise eventually but prefers *not* to realise now when prices are low.

This point of view is not always the clearest from which to survey the phenomenon of "dear money," but it brings out clearly its relation to more general theory.

"The business man takes account of a change in the purchasing power of money, under guise of a change in the prices of other things" (I.F.) [Cf. Fisher, 1907, p. 257].

"Appreciation of money is in effect taken account of in the practical man's forecast of all the economic elements which concern him, the prices of his product, the cost of his living, the wages of his workmen, and so forth" [Fisher, 1907, pp. 257–8).

"Moreover he takes account of the relative importance of these factors as affecting himself, not as they are in the [elaborate] averages of the statistician." [Fisher, 1907, p. 258].

We may now turn to the inductive verification.

During a period of progressive paper inflation the rate of interest in contracts drawn on a paper basis is high. [cf. Fisher, 1907, p. 257].

An excellent test is supplied by two kinds of U.S. bonds, one payable in coin and the other in currency. [cf. Fisher, 1907, pp. 259–60].

In 1870 the investor received a *higher* interest in gold. This is to be explained by the hope of resumption. Paper was so depreciated that there was a prospect of a great rise in its value. From 1894 to 1896 the higher rate of interest in the paper standard was due to the free-silver proposals of the Democrats.

See IF for details. [cf. Fisher, 1907, pp. 260–61).

Another example is the rates of interest on the sterling and rupee loans of the Gov.t of India. These were sold on the same market and were absolutely comparable in the degree of their security. When silver was fast depreciating (1888 to 1992) and before the rupee was fixed, the rate in the rupee loan was 4 and in sterling 3. Since belief has been firmly established in the steadiness of the rupee, there has been no appreciable difference between these yields.

Turning now to the comparison of successive periods:

Fisher has examined where a rise of prices is accompanied by a rise of interest, and his results are summarised in this table[39]:

	England	Germany	France	U.S.	India	Japan	China	Total
Favourable	23	15	8	8	3	6	1	64
Unfavourable	7	5	2	2	1	4	1	22

This justify him in saying that on the whole the rate of interest tends to be relatively high when prices are rising and relatively low when prices are falling.

But the rate of interest does not fully adjust itself to price movements. (See over)

Prof. I. F.'s tables show that when money interest has proved low, commodity interest is generally high, and vice versa.

For instance, [in] 1853–1857 money interest was 5.3% [and] commodity interest 2.9%, [while in] 1874–1879 [money interest was] 2.7/ [and commodity interest] 7%. [cf. Fisher, 1907, p. 277].

The probable reason is that price-movements are very imperfectly foreseen. Exceptionally high and low rate of commodity interest are tricks played by money on those who have placed too much faith in its stability. There was nothing to justify a commodity-rate of 1.8% in the U.S.A. during the period 1898–1905. This low rate must have been due to inadvertence. The inrushing streams of gold caught merchants napping. They put up interest, it is true, to 4.6%; they should have put it 2 or 3% higher.[40]

A table shows that the virtual interest in commodities is from 4 to 8 times as variable as the market interest in money.[41] Evidently those who are in doubt as to whether prices will rise or fall prefer to act on the hypothesis that money will remain stable, rather than on the hypothesis that representative commodity will remain stable.

For 1871–1873 commodity interest in London was *minus* 2.5%. This shows that lenders would have been better off had they simply bought commodities in 1871 and held them until 1873. [cf. Fisher, 1907, p. 280].

It is evident that a comparatively small variation in the purchasing power of the principal will sweep away the whole of the interest. In N[ew] Y[ork] during the inflation period 1861–1865 commodity interest sank to *minus* 13.4%.

Three general facts are inductively established by Fisher:

(1) Rising and falling prices and wages are directly correlated with high and low rates of interest.
(2) The adjustment of interest to price movements is inadequate.
(3) This adjustment is more nearly adequate for long than for short periods.

[cf. Fisher, 1907, p. 284]

We can now understand why a high rate of interest need not retard trade nor a low stimulate it [Cf. Fisher, 1907, p. 280] (See over)

281 Jevons wrote: "During 1854–1857 the rate of interest was only for a few months below 5%, but for many months above it ... In 1861 interest rose to 6 and 8%, and all this, to the surprise of the older generation, without the general stoppage of trade, the breach of credit, and the flood of bankruptcy, which has hitherto attended such rates of interest" [...]

But were these rates high? ... The average market rate for 1853–1857 does appear to be the highest in the London table[42]; but unmasking it of the money element, we find it is equivalent to a commodity interest of 2.9%. This is a very low rate. Merchants with increasing prices and money profits would find it easy to pay loans on such a basis.

Prof Bonamy Price in 1874–1879 was surprised of commercial depression with a low rate of interest; but the commodity-rate of interest, so far from being low, was 7% [Cf. Fisher, 1907, pp. 281–2].

282 When long periods of price-movements are taken, the influence of appreciation on interest is more certain ... [Fisher, 1907, p. 282].

283 In every case interest is high when prices are rising and low when they are falling [Fisher, 1907, p. 283]

284 The actual course of events is as follows: – Suppose an upward movement of prices begins. Business profits (measured in *money*) will rise; ... Borrowers can now afford to pay higher money-rates. If, however, only a few persons at first see this, the interest will not be fully adjusted, and borrowers will realize an extra margin of profit. This raises an expectation of a similar profit in the future and this expectation, acting on the demand for loans, will raise the rate of interest ... . When a fall of prices begins, the reverse effects appear .... The delay in the adjustment leaves a relatively low interest at the beginning of an ascent of prices, and a relatively high interest at the beginning of a descent [Fisher, 1907, pp. 284–5]

[**Part 2**, cover page:]
I. Fisher the Rate of Interest

[**Part 2**, text:]
Inductive verification – monetary Chap XIV

This is a very good chapter, especially pp. 277–88.

p. 277 It will be seen from the tables that the virtual rate of interest reckoned in commodities usually varies inversely with the rate reckoned in money for 1853–1857, money interest was 5.3% and for 1874–1879 2.7%; but commodity interest was 2.9% in the first period and 7% in the second. One possible explanation is that when prices are rising the cause may not be monetary but may lie in a progressive scarcity of commodities produced and exchanged; and, reversely, when prices are falling.

The second possible reason is that the price movements are often imperfectly foreseen. The high or low rate in commodities is then an abnormal phenomenon. It is, as it were, a trick played by money on those who put too much faith in its stability. Thus, during 1898–1905 the increase of prices in U.S.A. is known to have been due largely to the increase of gold production. There is no evidence that commodities were getting scarce and incomes decreasing, but reather the reverse. There seems, therefore, no reason which would justify the low commodity-rate of interest of 1.8%, which we found to have been virtually paid during that period. This low rate must, in all probability, have been due to inadvertence. The increasing streams of golds caught the merchants napping. They should have stemmed the tide by putting up interest, not only to 4.6%, as they did, but 2 or 3% higher [Cf. Fisher, 1907, pp. 277–8].

279 It is impossible to decide what part these two factors – foreseen changes in real income and unforeseen changes in their monetary measure – may play in each individual case. Probably the latter is the more important.

A table[43] shows that the virtual interest in commodities is from four to eight times as variable as the market interest in money [Cf. Fisher, 1907, p. 279].

280 For 1871–1873 commodity interest in London was *minus* 2.5%. This shows that money lenders would have been better off had they simply bought commodities in 1871 and held them until 1873.

In New York during the inflation period 1861–1865, commodity interest sank to minus 13.4% [Cf. Fisher, 1907, p. 280].

[the following quotation from Fisher (1907, p. 285) is the beginning of a new page (KP UA/6/1/5/15). On top of this page Keynes wrote "Cf Marshall p. 674." Maybe *Principles of Economics*, 3rd ed., 1895, p. 674, as quoted in Fisher, 1896, p. 79 (see above):]

285 What has been said bears directly on the theory of "credit cycles." Periods of speculation and depression are due to *inequality* of foresight. [cf. Fisher, 1907, p. 285]

286 When prices are rising, borrowers are more apt to see it then lenders. Hence, while the borrower is willing to pay a higher interest than before for the same loan, lenders are willing to loan for the same interest as before. This causes an increase of loans and investments, and constitutes part of the stimulus to business which takes place in times of rising prices.

When prices fall, on the other hand, borrowers see that they cannot employ money productively except on easier terms, but lenders do not see why terms should be easier.

While *imperfection* of foresight transfer wealth from creditor to debtor or the reverse, *inequality* of foresight produces overinvestment during rising prices and relative stagnation during falling prices. In the former case society is trapped into devoting too much investment of productive energies for future return, while in the contrary case underinvestment is the rule [Cf. Fisher, 1907, p. 286–7].

288 The typical debtor to-day is the stockholder, and the typical creditor, the bondholder. What is actually going on to-day in

consequence of a steadily cheapening dollar is a vast transfer of advantage from bondholders to stockholders. It is this transfer which has produced many of our latest millionaires. Their millions have been silently abstracted from the pockets of the unsuspecting "safe" investors in bonds, depositors in saving banks, and the salaried class. […]

What is called "prosperity" is often not general prosperity, but prosperity of the debtor or stockholding or entrepreneur classes, who are always much in evidence, at the expense of the creditor, bondholding, salaried classes, who bear their losses silently behind the scenes [Cf. Fisher, 1907, p. 288].

[The following four quotations are from chapters XV and XVI of Fisher, 1907].

292 Among communities and peoples noted for lack of foresight and for negligence with respect to the future – China, India, Java, negroes in Southern States, peasant communities of Russia, American Indians – interest is high, there is a tendency to run into debt and to dissipate rather than accumulate capital, and their dwellings and other instruments are of a very flimsy and perishable character" [Cf. Fisher, 1907, p. 292].

322 The facts quoted must convince any one that the rate is not inversely correlated to the quantity of money … It is the established policy of large banks, like the B[ank] of E[ngland]., to protect their reserves by raising the rate of interest. From this the conclusion is drawn that the scarcity of bank reserves produces a high rate of interest [Cf. Fisher, 1907, p. 322].

323 But a low reserve is merely a symptom of a general ebb tide in the income of the community. A bank of discount and deposit stands between those who have surplus income to deposit and those who wish to eke out a lean income by borrowing. […] Bank deposits grow, as compared with loans, when men's income are temporarily flush, that is, when their income curves are descending; loans grows as compared with deposits when their incomes are temporarily scant. […] The banker must keep in equilibrium between his two classes of customers. He regulates his reserves by adjusting the rate of discount. To him, his action appears in the light of protecting and utilizing his reserve; but the state of the incomes of his customers, not the banker, is the prime factor. A rise of the discount rate is therefore due, in the

last analysis, to the predominance of ascending incomes – and vice versa." [Fisher, 1907, p. 323].

325 It is true, however, that money, as money, is more vitally related to panic loans. In ordinary loans, money enters merely as a *convenient* medium for securing something else – capital; in a panic loan, however, the money enters as a *necessary* medium for the legal discharge of a debt. In an ordinary loan the borrower is free to adjust the amount borrowed according to the rate of interest; in a panic loan, on the other hand, there is no such elastic choice.

In such a case it may be truly said that the scarcity of money had made interest high.

It is therefore important, in order not to have violent changes in the rate of interest, that the currency should be *elastic*. [Cf. Fisher, 1907, p. 325].

[**Part 3**:]

The relation between Money, the Rate of Discount, and the Rate of Interest

Strictly speaking there is a direct algebraic connexion between the rate of interest and the rate of discount.

In the language of the money market the connexion is not so quite close.

The rate of interest refers to permanent investments. It gives a right to future income – sometimes of an amount fixed in money –, but it gives no right to receive back the money value for the capital – unless at the end of some long period.

e.g. Consols.

Thus if I can purchase with £100 the right to a future annual income of £3, the rate of interest is said to be 3%.

The rate of discount, on the other hand, refers to short loans. It is the charge for the use of money for a short period, and involves the right, not to a future annual income over a long series of years, but to receive a capital sum of money at the end of a short period.

e.g. Treasury Bills.

Thus if by paying £98 now I can purchase the right to receive £100 in money at the end of a year, the rate of discount is said to be 2%.

A little reflection will show how it follows from this that the rate of discount is more closely connected with anticipated changes in the demand for money – i.e. with anticipated changes of prices – than the rate of interest is.

The course of remote changes is totally unknown and is almost completely neglected in anticipations; and a change of 5% say in the value of money during the next year, even if it is taken into account, has an almost negligible effect upon the rate of interest.

A similar anticipated change, however, would turn a rate of discount of 2% into one of 7%.

We may put this in a somewhat different way by saying that the rate of discount – as that term is commonly used – takes account of anticipated changes in the future rate of interest, which the rate of interest does not.

This goes far to explain the great discrepancy which is occasionally apparent between the two.

Let us take a case, which is imaginary in detail, but which is not far removed from the facts of the last year.

Let us suppose that in Feb.y 1908	the price of Consols was 81 and the yield 3
	the rate of discount 7
Feb.y 1909	[the price of Consols was] 85 [and the yield] 3-
	[the rate of discount] 3

We might have said prima facie why is anyone so foolish as to buy Consols yielding only 3% when he can invest lend it with equal security for 7%. We see in the event that the former would have proved slightly the more profitable investment.

The rate of interest on permanent investments shows small absolute variations, but there may be large variations in the money value of the principal. The rate of discount shows large variations, but there is *no* variation in the money value of the principal.

The probable net yield being equal taking everything into account, Consols will prove the more attractive alternative investment to some classes of investors, Treasury bills to others.

Consols to those who desire a fixed and certain future income.

Treasury Bills to those who have capital liabilities to discharge in money at no distant date e.g. Banks, Foreign Gov.ts.

Whether or not the probable net yield of the first exceeds that of the second depends:

(1) upon the amount of investment which each class desires to make
(2) upon the amount offered to them. e.g. the volume of Treasury Bills has been somewhat reduced lately.

Interest being word with reference to long periods, discount is used with reference to intermediate periods – 3, 6 or 12 months.

The corresponding charge for lending money from day to day is the charge for money "at call and short notice."

It is now clear why the rate of discount fluctuates very much more than the rate of interest.

Both are determined in the long run by the average profitableness of business and enterprise. In the case of the rate of discount this is the equilibrium about which it oscillates. But at any moment the deviation may be great and the rate is determined partly by the present and anticipated "demand for money or cash down," partly by anticipated changes in the rate of interest, which it has been explained cause a much greater *absolute* change in the rate of discount. This is why money is said to be "dear" when the rate of discount is high. On such occasions it is necessary to pay a high price to receive money down in return for a promise to return money down six months hence, – high that is to say compared with the rate of interest. This means that the market anticipates a lower demand for money at the end of six months than at the present time – i.e. rising prices -, or that it anticipates a lower rate of interest (independent of monetary changes) then than now. The effect of this second influence will, however, be relatively small.

[At the top of the last page Keynes wrote "omit this page," and then continued with the following notes based on two quotations from Marshall's *Official Papers*:]

We may now push hour analysis somewhat further.

No interpretation can be given of a rise in discount, unless it is known to what cause the change is due. Speaking generally, discount will rise in consequence of a great willingness of borrowers to borrow, or of a greater unwillingness of lenders to lend: the first generally indicates increased confidence and perhaps increased prosperity; the latter generally indicates the opposite (M) [Marshall, 1979 [1926], p. 273].

Let us then examine and classify the causes which affect the willingness of lenders to lend short loans.

(i) The first we have already discussed in connexion with Quantity Theory.

New currency goes to banking centres; and therefore, it increases the willingness of lenders to lend in the first instance, and lowers discount; but it afterwards rises prices, and therefore tends to increase discount. This latter movement is cumulative. The loans to one man make him a good customer for others at good prices, and make them therefore eager to borrow, and that makes them good customers; and the movement grows. (M.) [Cf. Marshall, 1979 [1926], p. 274].

This is interesting and at first confusing. The first effect of an influence which will ultimately make prices rise is to *lower* the rate of discount. This is due to the fact that any raising of the rate of discount due to anticipations of future rising prices will be for the moment small, and quite outweighed by the tendency to *lower* the rate on account of the temporary strengthening of the professional borrowers.

NOTES

1. See Moggridge (1992, Ch. 7), Skidelsky (1983, Ch. 7), and Cristiano (2014, pp. 113–123).
2. See KP/ UA/6. For a more detailed survey of these papers see Cristiano (2014, pp. 137–152).
3. See KP UA/6/1/5/1-25.
4. Although certainly not the first, as shown by Humphrey (1984). It may be mentioned here that Fisher first used the equation of exchange in an article on "The role of capital in economic theory," published in the *Economic Journal* in 1897. Keynes (1911) did not cite this article, hence his belief, as expressed in his review of *PPM*, that Fisher first used the equation of exchange in 1911.
5. Marshall's *Money Credit and Commerce* did not appear until 1923.
6. Similar remarks can be found in Keynes (1923, p. 63).
7. See the "Editorial introduction" in Barber et al. vol. IV. See also Dimand (2013, p. 292). Examples of naïve statistical confutation of the quantity theory can be found in some articles published in the *Journal of Political Economy* by a group of Laughlin's students: see McLean Hardy (1895), Mitchell (1896), and Parker Willis (1896).
8. This latter point in particular is emphasized by Laidler (1991, p. 71). Fisher's equation of exchange is $MV + M'V' = \sum pQ = PT$, where M and M' represent

money proper and chequable deposits, V and V' their velocities of circulation, p and Q are the price of any commodity and its quantity, P is the price level, and T is the volume of transactions. Fisher admitted that V, V', and T are not constant, but he also emphasized that they did not depend on the quantity of money. Thus, Fisher was able to state, on the one hand, that misaligned movements of M and P could be taken as a confutation of the quantity theory only by a misinterpretation of it in which movements of the other variables, which were carried along with the trade cycles, were not considered; and, on the other, he could positively affirm that as far as the Vs and T remained constant, the quantity theory provided a causal nexus connecting any change of M to a corresponding change of P.

9. It may be mentioned here that when Fisher entered the field of monetary theory he was already the author of a doctoral dissertation on general equilibrium analysis, *Mathematical investigations in the Theory of Value and Prices*, published in 1892.

10. Skidelsky (1995, p 81) has suggested that Fisher and the Cambridge economists were "monetary radicals because they were social conservatives," and that, for all of them, "[m]acroeconomic stabilization was the antidote to socialism." See also Laidler (1991, pp. 89–100, 1999, p. 86).

11. See Dimand and Gomez Betancourt (2012) for a reconstruction of the circumstances in which Fisher (1896) was published and for an accurate assessment of its relevance to the history of economic analysis.

12. See Fisher (1896, p. 75, 1907, p. 284).

13. See Fisher (1896, pp. 76–79, 1907, pp. 284–288).

14. In the Variorum edition, the same passage corresponds to the fourth paragraph of § 7 in chapter VI of Book VI. See Marshall (1997 [1961] I, pp. 594–595).

15. The article is reprinted in Pigou's *Memorials of Alfred Marshall* (1966 [1925]) and in vol. 1 of the *Collected Essays* of Alfred Marshall edited by Groenewegen in 1997. As Laidler also pointed out in the same paper, Fisher was certainly acquainted with the 1887 article in 1914, when he drafted his "Objections to a compensated dollar answered," published in *American Economic Review*, 14 supplement 2, pp. 819–839, and reprinted in Barber et al. Vol. 4.

16. The brief discussion takes Edgeworth (1895) as its starting point. At this stage of his career Fisher had already established a fruitful personal relationship with Edgeworth, but not with Marshall. Moreover, during his *wanderjahr* in 1893 and 1894 Fisher went to Oxford to meet Edgeworth but he did not go to Cambridge. See Barber et al. I, pp. 4–6.

17. "[O]ne of the ablest of the younger school of American economists, Mr. Fisher of Yale, has written a book on *Appreciation and Interest*, which bears very closely upon this matter" (Marshall, 1926, p. 271).

18. See Dimand (1995, pp. 250–251) for a more detailed discussion.

19. C.W. Guillebaud reports that the second clause was inserted in 1910 (Marshall, 1997 [1961] II, p. 636).

20. See Laidler (1991, p. 64).

21. This hypothesis is indirectly suggested by Moggridge (1992, p. 200) and finds some support in Cristiano (2014).

22. See Keynes (1913) and Dimand (1995, pp. 253–254).

23. See especially *PPM*, pp. 57–58, 72–73.

24. This time the quotation is from the 5th edn. of *Principles* (1907) London, Macmillan, p. 594. See *PPM*, pp. 71–72.

25. The Preface to the second edition of *PPM* is reproduced in Barber et al. (1997 IV, pp. 26–27). See also Dimand (1995, p. 251).

26. As Keynes apparently failed to notice, a much shorter but nonetheless similar account is given also in the text of *PPM*, pp. 153–154. On the other hand, a sentence of the review which Keynes italicized suggests that Keynes had in fact taken due notice of Fisher's explanation, but did not consider it satisfactory. Introducing his account of Fisher's theory Keynes wrote: "The following is an abbreviated account (in his [Fisher's] own words, though the italics are mine) of the theory which he presents in Chapter IV: – Let us begin by assuming a slight initial disturbance such as would be produced by an increase in the quantity of gold. *This, through the equation of exchange, will cause a rise of prices*" (Keynes, 1911, p. 376). That Fisher explained the transmission mechanism by means of the equation of exchange was therefore clear to Keynes. It is another matter to say that he considered this to be a satisfactory explanation and not just mere description. See also Laidler (1991, p. 77) on this point.

27. See Skidelsky (1992, p. 168) and Dimand (1995, p. 253).

28. See CWK XIII, p. 1.

29. On Keynes's thought on speculation and his activity as a speculator see Moggridge (1983), Carabelli (1998, 2002), Carabelli and Cedrini (2012), Fantacci, Marcuzzo, and Sanfilippo (2010), Fantacci, Marcuzzo, Rosselli, and Sanfilippo (2012), and Marcuzzo and Sanfilippo (2016).

30. The part of this correspondence which survived, now reproduced in Whitaker (1996 III, pp. 288–301), is one-sided. Only three letters have remained, all of them sent by Marshall, the first on 16 September 1911, the other two on 14 October (incomplete) and 15 October 1912. As the third letter was in fact an afterthought to the second, the whole correspondence can be reduced to two moments. The first was in 1911, when Fisher most likely took the initiative of writing to Marshall as part of his campaign for an International Commission. According to Whitaker, "Marshall had probably received a duplicated typescript of Fisher's 'Memorandum as to an International Commission on the Cost of Living' (1913 [1911])" (Whitaker III, p. 290). See also Gomez Betancourt and de Boyer des Roches (2013, pp. 268–269).

31. Whitaker based his reconstruction on a copy of the Memorandum that he found in the Library of Congress. As Whitaker noted, "The idea of varying the gold content of the dollar so as to stabilize the price level was to become something of an obsession to Fisher."

32. "I must adhere to my rule of not going into any complex matter that does not arise out of the particular writing which I have in hand at the time. May I therefore ask you to be so very good as to let these few weak words be my last on the subject?" (Marshall to Fisher, 14 October 1912, in Whitaker, 1996 III, p. 300). The way in which Marshall put an end to the correspondence ought not to be taken as proof that, in this period of his life, he had lost any interest in monetary issues. Quite possibly Marshall's letter was, rather, a consequence of the pressing need to carry out the long delayed project of providing a sequel to the *Principles of Economics* (Groenewegen, 1995, p. 637).

33. See Pigou (1912, pp. 437–438).
34. See Dimand (1995, p. 252).
35. Gomez Betancourt and de Boyer des Roches (2013, p. 267) have found traces of another correspondence between Keynes and Fisher in an exchange between Kemmerer and Fisher in 1913. In a letter of 6 January 1913 Kemmerer pointed out to Fisher an article by Aneurin Williams in the *Economic Journal* of 1892 in which a scheme very similar to the compensated dollar had been proposed. Fisher replied on 15 January saying that he was already acquainted with this article, which had been sent to him by "the editor of the Economic Journal, Mr. Keynes."
36. As Dimand (1995) has argued, Fisher's compensated dollar followed a method which was the opposite to the approach later proposed by Keynes in *A Tract on Monetary Reform*. While Fisher suggested an ex post remedy, in which the gold content of the currency was to be altered so to adjust it to variations in the purchasing power of the standard, Keynes's aim was to prevent these variations. Moreover, on the basis of the reconstruction made by Boianovsky (2013, p. 223), it seems that Keynes supported Fisher's plan only until 1916, when Wicksell presumably convinced him that the plan was ill-conceived.
37. See CWK VI, p. 181.
38. See CWK XXIX, pp. 83–84. See also CWK XIII, p. 518, where Keynes deals with Fisher's theory in a letter to D. H. Robertson of 25 February 1935.
39. The table is in Fisher (1907, p. 277), followed by this comment: "Summarizing the cases for the seven countries examined we find 64 favorable and 22 unfavorable to the theory … . The favorable cases are about three times as numerous as the unfavorable cases. This is a large preponderance, especially when we consider that there are so many causes affecting the rate of interest besides the mere appreciation or depreciation of the monetary standard. We therefore conclude with great confidence that, 'other things being equal,' *the rate of interest is relatively high when prices are rising and relatively low when prices are falling*."
40. This is an extrapolation based on Fisher's own words (Cf. Fisher, 1907, p. 278). It probably reflects Keynes's preference for one of the two explanations that Fisher took into consideration. The first of these hypotheses, introduced for the first time in the 1907 text, was connected with the theory of interest that Fisher was now proposing and that Keynes did not take into consideration. The other, which Keynes apparently found more to his taste, was based on expectations: "There are two possible explanations for this inverse relation. One is that when prices are rising the cause may not be monetary but may lie in a progressive scarcity of commodities produced and exchanged; and, reversely, when prices are falling, the cause may lie in progressive abundance. From the theory of interest maintained throughout this book it follows that a progressive scarcity of commodities, implying as it does a progressive descending income curve, tends to make the rate of interest low; and reversely, progressive abundance, implying an ascending income curve, tends to make interest high. When, therefore, general price-movements represent changes in the income-stream of enjoyable services, the rate of 'commodity interest' would naturally be high when prices were falling and low when prices were rising, whatever might be true of 'money interest.' The second possible reason that commodity-interest and money-interest vary inversely during price-movements is that these movements are often *imperfectly foreseen*. The high or low rate in

commodities is then an abnormal phenomenon. Thus, during 1898–1905 the increase of prices in the United States is known to have been due largely to the increase of gold production. There is no evidence that commodities were getting scarce and incomes decreasing, but rather the reverse. There seems, therefore, no reason which would justify the low commodity-rate of interest of 1.8 per cent. which we found to have been virtually paid during that period. This low rate must, in all probability, have been due to inadvertence. The inrushing streams of gold caught merchants napping. They should have stemmed the tide by putting up interest, not only to 4.6 per cent., as they did, but two o three per cent. higher" (Fisher, 1907, p. 278). Keynes's rendering of Fisher was therefore very selective, but was to some extent justified by Fisher himself (Fisher, 1907, p. 279). Moreover, in the notes from reading Fisher here set our as "Part 2," both explanations were cited.

41. See Fisher (1907, p. 279).
42. See table in Fisher (1907, p. 272).
43. See table in Fisher (1907, p. 279).

ACKNOWLEDGMENT

I am grateful to two anonymous referees for their constructive comments.

REFERENCES

Anderson, B. M. (1917). *The value of money*. New York, NY: The Macmillan Company.

Barber, W. J., assisted by Dimand, R., & Foster, K. (Eds.). (1997). The works of Irving Fisher (Vols. 1–14). London: Pickering and Chatto.

Boianovsky, M. (2013). Fisher and Wicksell on money: A reconstructed conversation. European Journal of the History of Economic Thought *(EJHET)*, *20*(2), 206–237.

Carabelli, A. (1998). Le lezioni di Keynes del 1910 sulla speculazione: alcune osservazioni sulla loro attualità. In S. Vercelli (Ed.), *Incertezza, razionalità e decisioni economiche*. Bologna: Il Mulino.

Carabelli, A. (2002). Speculation and reasonableness: A non-Bayesian theory of rationality. In S. Dow & J. Hillard (Eds.), *Keynes, uncertainty and the global economy. Beyond Keynes* (Vol. II, pp. 165–185). Aldershot: Edward Elgar.

Carabelli, A., & Cedrini, M. (2012). *On the new appeal of chapter 12 of the general theory. Complicating remarks on the Keynes-Hume connection and the presumed novelty of the analysis of financial markets in the general theory*. CESMEP Working Paper No. 02/2012.

Cristiano, C. (2014). *The political and economic thought of the young Keynes. Liberalism, markets and empire*. London: Routledge.

Dimand, R. W. (1995). Irving Fisher, J. M. Keynes, and the transition to modern macroeconomics. In A. Cottrell & M. S. Lawlor (Eds.), New perspectives on Keynes, *supplement to* History of Political Economy Review (Vol. 27, pp. 247–266).

Dimand, R. W. (2013). David Hume and Irving Fisher on the quantity theory of money in the long run and the short run. *EJHET, 20*(2), 284–304.

Dimand, R. W., & Gomez Betancourt, R. (2012). Irving Fisher's appreciation and interest (1896) and the Fisher relation. *Journal of Economic Perspectives, 26*(4), 185–196.

Edgeworth, F. Y. (1895). Thoughts on monetary reform. *Economic Journal, 5*(19), 434–451.

Fantacci, L., Marcuzzo, M. C., Rosselli, A., & Sanfilippo, E. (2012). Speculation and buffer stocks: The legacy of Keynes and Kahn. *EJHET, 19*(3), 453–473.

Fantacci, L., Marcuzzo, M. C., & Sanfilippo, E. (2010). Speculation in commodities: Keynes's "practical acquaintance" with futures markets. *Journal of the History of Economic Thought, 32*(3), 397–418.

Fisher, I. (1896). Appreciation and interest. New York: The Macmillan Company. In W. J. Barber, J. Tobin, R.W. Dimand, & K. Foster (Eds.), (1997), *The works of Irving Fisher* (Vol. 1, pp. 189–298). London: Pickering & Chatto.

Fisher, I. (1907). The rate of interest. Its nature, determination and relation to economic phenomena. New York: The Macmillan Company, in *The works of Irving Fisher*. In W. J. Barber, J. Tobin, R.W. Dimand, & K. Foster (Eds.), (1997), *The works of Irving Fisher* (Vol. 3, pp. 9–472). London: Pickering & Chatto.

Fisher, I. (1912). Elementary principles of economics. New York: The Macmillan Company. In W. J. Barber, J. Tobin, R.W. Dimand, & K. Foster (Eds.), (1997), *The works of Irving Fisher* (Vol. 5, pp. 7–581). London: Pickering & Chatto.

Fisher, I. (1913 [1911]). The purchasing power of money. Its determination and relation to credit and crisis. In W. J. Barber, J. Tobin, R.W. Dimand, & K. Foster (Eds.), (1997), *The works of Irving Fisher* (Vol. 4, pp. 15–559). London: Pickering & Chatto.

Fisher, I. N. (1956). *My father Irving Fisher*. New York, NY: Comet Press Books.

Gomez Betancourt, R., & de Boyer des Roches, J. (2013). Origins and development of Irving Fisher's compensated dollar plan. *EJHET, 20*(2), 261–283.

Groenewegen, P. D. (Ed.). (1997). *Collected essays 1872–1917. Alfred Marshall*. Bristol: Overstone Press.

Groenewegen, P. D. (1995). A soaring eagle. Alfred Marshall 1842–1924. Aldershot: Elgar.

Humphrey, T. M. (1984). Algebraic quantity equations before Fisher and Pigou. *Federal Reserve Bank of Richmond Economic Review, 70*(5), 13–22.

Keynes. (1909). *Appreciation and interest. The relation between money, the rate of interest, and the rate of discount*. John Maynard Keynes's Papers. Cambridge: King's College Archive Centre, UA/6/1/5/1-25.

Keynes, J. M. (1911). Fisher, Irving assisted by Harry G. Brown, *The purchasing power of money*. *Economic Journal*, (In CWK Vol. X) (September), 375–381.

Keynes, J. M. (1913). How far bankers are responsible for the alternations of crisis and depression? *CWK vol. XIII*, 2–14.

Keynes, J. M. (1923). *A tract on monetary reform* (CWK Vol. IV). London: Macmillan.

Keynes, J. M. (1936). *The general theory of employment interest and money* (CWK Vol. VII). London: Macmillan.

Keynes, J. M. (1971–1989). The collected writings of John Maynard Keynes (CWK). In Managing (Ed.), *Sir Austin Robinson and Donald Moggridge*. London: Macmillan.

Laidler, D. (1991). *The golden age of the quantity theory: The development of neoclassical monetary economics*. New York, NY: Harvester Weahtsheaf.

Laidler, D. (1999). *Fabricating the Keynesian revolution*. Cambridge: Cambridge University Press.

Laidler, D. (2013). Professor Fisher and the quantity theory – A significant encounter. *EJHET, 20*(2), 174–205.

Marcuzzo, M. C., & Sanfilippo, E. (2016). Keynes and the interwar commodity option markets. *Cambridge Journal of Economics*, *40*(1), 327–348

Marshall, A. (1979 [1926]). In J. M. Keynes (Ed.), *Official papers by Alfred Marshall*. London: Macmillan, Greenwood Press.

Marshall, A. (1997 [1961]). *Principles of economics* (Vol. 2). Ninth (Variorum) Edition with annotations by C.W. Guillebaud. Bristol: Overston Press.

Marshall. (1887). Remedies for fluctuations of general prices. *Contemporary Review*, *51*, 355–375.

McLean Hardy, S. (1895). The quantity theory of money and prices, 1860–1891. *Journal of Political Economy*, *3*(2), 145–168.

Mitchell, W. C. (1896). The quantity theory of the value of money. *Journal of Political Economy*, *4*(2), 139–165.

Moggridge, D. E. (1983). Keynes as an investor. Editorial introduction to the Vol. XII, economic articles and correspondence, investment and editorial. In *The collected writings of John Maynard Keynes* (pp. 1–113). London: Macmillan.

Moggridge, D. E. (1992). *Maynard Keynes. An economist biography*. London: Routledge.

Parker Willis, H. (1896). Credit devices and the quantity theory. *Journal of Political Economy*, *4*(3), 281–308.

Pigou, A. C. (1912). *Wealth and welfare*. London: MacMillan & Co.

Pigou, A. C. (1917). The value of money. *Quarterly Journal of Economics*, *32*(1), 38–65.

Pigou, A. C. (Ed.). (1966 [1925]). *Memorials of Alfred Marshal*. New York, NY: Kelley.

Schumpeter, J. A. (1986 [1954]). *History of economic analysis*. London: Routledge.

Skidelsky, R. (1983). *John Maynard Keynes: A biography* (Vol. 1). Hopes betrayed, 1883-1920, London: Macmillan.

Skidelsky, R. (1992). *John Maynard Keynes. The economist as saviour, 1920–1937*. London: Macmillan.

Skidelsky, R. (1995). J.M. Keynes and the quantity theory of money. In M. Blaug (Ed.), *The quantity theory of money. From lock to Keynes and Friedman* (pp. 80–96). Cheltenham: Edward Elgar.

Whitaker, J. K. (Ed.). (1996). *The correspondence of Alfred Marshall, economist* (Vol. 3). Cambridge: Cambridge University Press.

Printed in the United States
By Bookmasters